Global Economic Prospects

A World Bank Group Flagship Report

JANUARY 2026

Global Economic Prospects

WORLD BANK GROUP

1818 H Street NW, Washington, DC 20433
Telephone: 202-473-1000; Internet: www.worldbank.org

1 2 3 4   29 28 27 26

ISSN: 1014-8906

ISBN (paper): 978-1-4648-2267-4

ISBN (electronic): 978-1-4648-2268-1

DOI: 10.1596/978-1-4648-2267-4

Cover design: Bill Pragluski, Critical Stages LLC.

The Library of Congress Control Number has been requested.

The cutoff date for the data used in the report was December 16, 2025.

Summary of Contents

Contents

Boxes

Figures

Figures

Acknowledgments

This World Bank Group Flagship Report is a product of the Prospects Group in the Development Economics (DEC) Vice Presidency. The project was managed by M. Ayhan Kose and Carlos Arteta, under the general guidance of Indermit Gill.

The preparation of the analytical chapters was overseen by Dana Vorisek. The report was prepared by a team that included Marie Albert, Francisco Arroyo Marioli, Tommy Chrimes, Bram Gootjes, Phil Kenworthy, Gitanjali Kumar, Jiwon Lee, Emiliano Luttini, Joseph Mawejje, Kate McKinnon, Edoardo Palombo, Nikita Perevalov, Peter Selcuk, Shijie Shi, Naotaka Sugawara, Takuma Tanaka, Garima Vasishtha, Collette Wheeler, and Hamza Zahid. Additional contributions were provided by Mirco Balatti, Dawit Mekonnen, Alen Mulabdic, Kersten Stamm, and Neha Varma.

Main research assistance was provided by Sergiu Dinu, Jiayue Fan, Mario Guillen Salvatore, Maria Hazel Macadangdang, Rafaela Martinho Henriques, Shiqing Hua, Vasiliki Papagianni, Juan Felipe Serrano Ariza, Kaltrina Temaj, Chao Wang, and Canran Zheng. Additional research assistance was provided by Giovanni Biasiucci, Nikita Makarenko, and Sadhna Naik. Modeling and data work was provided by Shijie Shi.

Adriana Maximiliano handled design and production. Graeme Littler produced the online products, with assistance from the Open Knowledge Repository, and provided editorial support, with contributions from Adriana Maximiliano and Michael Harrup. Joe Rebello managed communications and media outreach with a team that included Kristen Milhollin, Mariana Lozzi Teixeira, and Leslie Yun, with extensive support from the World Bank's media and digital communications teams.

Regional projections and write-ups were produced in coordination with country teams, country directors, and the offices of the regional chief economists.

Many reviewers provided extensive advice and comments. The analysis also benefited from comments and suggestions by staff members from World Bank Group country teams and other World Bank Group Vice Presidencies as well as Executive Directors in their discussion of the report on December 11, 2025. However, both forecasts and analysis are those of the World Bank Group staff and should not be attributed to Executive Directors or their national authorities.

Foreword

First, the good news: in the face of one shock after another, the global economy has proved to be surprisingly shock-proof since the pandemic.

Despite steep tariff increases and historically high policy uncertainty during the last 12 months, global GDP growth in 2025 is set to come in at 2.7 percent—the pace that was predicted in this report in January 2025. That rate should hold roughly steady through 2027. Inflation is abating. Interest rates are coming down. Investors are again showing signs of exuberance. At least by one measure, the global recovery from the coronavirus recession will go down as the strongest in six decades: global GDP per person in 2025 was 10 percent higher than it was on the eve of the pandemic. Subsequent shocks—wars, inflation, and tariffs—did less damage than most economists feared.

Yet a grimmer picture emerges if we take stock of the world economy after the first 25 years of this century. That is what this report does. It shows that global growth has unmistakably downshifted to a slower gear since the pandemic. It is now at a pace insufficient to reduce extreme poverty and create jobs where they're needed most. If the forecasts in this edition of *Global Economic Prospects* materialize, the average growth rate of this decade will be the lowest since the 1960s.

That depressing statistic hides an even more disconcerting detail. While nearly all advanced economies will be richer in per capita income than they were before the pandemic, one out of four developing countries—and more than a third of all low-income economies—will be *poorer than they were five years ago.*

In short, growth in the 2020s has hardly been the rising tide that lifts all boats—certainly not the kind that freed more than a billion people from extreme poverty in the 1990s and 2000s. It has been, instead, a source of divergence in the living standards of low- and high-income economies. More than half of the 10 percent rise in global GDP per person since 2019 has been attributable to the performance of the wealthiest economies. By the end of this year, developing economies will have an average GDP per person of around \$6,500—barely 12 percent of the average of advanced economies. The gap for low-income countries is even more striking: their GDP per person is less than \$700, about 1 percent of the level in high-income economies.

These trends cannot be explained by misfortune alone. In far too many developing countries, they reflect avoidable policy mistakes. As this report makes clear, these economies were better prepared to cope with the 2009 global financial crisis than they were with the COVID-19 recession—in fact, they were better prepared than most high-income economies. That's because developing economies went on a reform spree in the 1990s and 2000s: they cut public debt, adopted more flexible exchange rates, adopted inflation-targeting systems, and built up their rainy-day funds.

When the 2009 recession arrived, developing economies were able to ramp up government spending to support their economies instead of cutting back—something they had never done before. The reform momentum in developing economies, however, did not last: by the time the COVID-19 crisis came, debt in developing economies had skyrocketed to all-time highs. Budget deficits were more than four times the average before 2009. The result was unsurprising: developing economies had little to spare. The fiscal stimulus they were able to deliver to their economies, accordingly, was much smaller than the dose administered by high-income economies. No surprise, then, that their recovery has been feebler.

The main lesson of the last 25 years is that when developing economies have the right policies, they control their own destiny. This is especially so for middle-income economies. When they do that, they bring immense benefits to their own citizens—as well as the two billion people living in low- and high-income economies around the globe. They must now do so again. In the next decade, a job-creation challenge of historic proportions will confront many of them. It will need to be tackled when global economic conditions are hardly conducive—when trade relationships are rapidly being reconfigured, when the debt of developing economies is at a half-century high, and when foreign-aid budgets of high-income economies are shrinking.

An important step will be to re-establish policy discipline, starting with a return to fiscal orthodoxy. In normal economic times, government ought to set and live by rules on how much they can spend and borrow. Fiscal rules can help ensure that government spending is kept on a tight leash when the private economy is doing well, so that public funds are available when times are tough. This report offers the first comprehensive analysis of the use of fiscal rules in developing economies. It finds that such rules, which have become increasingly common over the last 25 years, are effective in improving fiscal balances in developing economies.

Timing is crucial for determining whether fiscal rules are effective. Governments tend to adopt fiscal rules under duress, when economic conditions are weak, rather than in good times. Bad timing can lead to bad rule design. Weak governance and insufficient enforcement capacity—more prevalent in developing economies than in high-income countries—also hinders the effectiveness of fiscal rules. These deficiencies, however, are correctable. Governments can choose to adopt fiscal rules when the economy is healthy; they can choose to strengthen governance capacity.

It is proper to find comfort in the fact that the global economy has defied expectations—that it did not crack under the extraordinary strains of the 2020s. Yet it would be dangerous to assume that the danger has passed. The resilience displayed in 2025 did not stem from economic strength. It was mainly the result of hard-to-repeat maneuvers: beleaguered firms scrambling to import before higher tariffs took effect, and debt-laden governments keeping the fiscal spigots open. But it will take more than business agility and fiscal laxity to steer the global economy back on track: there is no substitute for good economic policy.

The remedy is no secret: governments that live within their means while adopting policies that encourage investors to push the limits of enterprise outward. It has worked before, and it will work again.

Indermit Gill
Senior Vice President and Chief Economist
The World Bank Group

Executive Summary

The global economy has shown notable resilience to heightened trade tensions and policy uncertainty. Last year, stockpiling of traded goods, strong risk appetite, and a surge in artificial intelligence (AI) spending supported activity, while supply chains adapted to rising trade barriers. The faster-than-expected pace of growth capped a five-year global recovery from the 2020 recession unmatched in more than six decades, but this masks a sharp divergence. While advanced economies have recovered robustly, with nearly 90 percent now above pre-pandemic per capita income levels, more than one-quarter of emerging market and developing economies (EMDEs)—particularly low-income countries and those affected by fragility and conflict—still have per capita incomes below 2019 levels.

Looking forward, global growth is projected to edge down to 2.6 percent this year as several supportive factors fade. In particular, trade growth is set to weaken as firms scale back inventory accumulation and tariff effects intensify. Although EMDEs also proved more resilient to last year's trade headwinds than previously anticipated, prospects across regions remain uneven.

Near-term risks to the global outlook are tilted to the downside. Growth could falter if trade tensions escalate, barriers rise further, or financial market sentiment deteriorates amid asset price declines, fiscal concerns, or inflation surprises. On the upside, AI-related activity could broaden, and firms' adaptability to new trade conditions could support growth.

Global efforts are needed to improve the trade environment, ease financing constraints, and mitigate climate risks. To catalyze investment and support long-term growth, policy makers in EMDEs should advance domestic reforms to diversify trade, strengthen macroeconomic frameworks, and remove structural bottlenecks. Without stronger economic dynamism, many EMDEs will struggle to create enough jobs for expanding working-age populations. Key pillars to address this jobs challenge include policies that promote physical, digital, and human capital infrastructure; that secure a better business environment; and that mobilize private capital to help meet substantial investment needs.

In addition to the global and regional outlooks, this edition of *Global Economic Prospects* features two analytical chapters. One chapter provides a comprehensive analysis of the use of fiscal rules, which set clear limits on government budgetary aggregates or debt to help manage public finances. Another chapter explores the promise, performance, and prospects of frontier market economies, a diverse group of EMDEs with limited but growing integration into global financial markets.

Rebuilding Fiscal Space: The Case for Fiscal Rules: At a time when global shocks have become more frequent and government debt among EMDEs has climbed to a 55-year high, fiscal rules are an important policy tool for promoting fiscal discipline. As a component of fiscal policy, fiscal rules can shape economic activity, investment dynamics, and jobs. More than half of EMDEs have at least one fiscal rule, up from about 15 percent in 2000. Fiscal rules are associated with improvements in budget balances that extend to the medium and long term. Among EMDEs, improvements in the cyclically adjusted primary balance (CAPB) peak five years after fiscal rules are adopted, reaching a cumulative 1.4 percentage points of trend GDP. The gains are more pronounced when domestic institutions are strong and economic conditions are favorable at the time of adoption.

Fiscal rules are also associated with a greater likelihood of consolidation episodes—multi-year periods of improvement in the CAPB as a percent of trend GDP. During a fiscal consolidation episode, the CAPB in the typical EMDE improves by 1.6 percentage points of trend GDP per year. Fiscal rules with credible enforcement provisions are associated with a higher likelihood of expenditure-based consolidation, while rule frameworks with simple design features are associated with a higher likelihood of revenue-based consolidation.

Policy makers should focus on three priorities to enhance the effectiveness of fiscal rules in promoting fiscal discipline. First, fiscal rules should be designed so that they manage trade-offs between enforceability, flexibility, and simplicity. Building and sustaining the credibility of fiscal rules is also essential to their success. Finally, policy makers must recognize that fiscal rules are unlikely to be effective in isolation. A supportive complementary policy environment is important, including measures to strengthen institutions, enhance spending efficiency, and pursue responsible debt management.

Frontier Market Economies: Promise, Performance, and Prospects: Frontier markets—a subset of EMDEs characterized by meaningful but limited access to international financial markets—have considerable promise. Already home to one-fifth of the world's population, but only 5 percent of its output, frontier markets are projected to account for most of the global population increase to 2050. Many frontier markets have large natural resource endowments. Relative to other developing economies, they also have more physical capital, healthier and better-educated workforces, and stronger institutions. Outcomes in frontier markets will be pivotal for global job creation and development progress.

Frontier markets' economic outcomes since 2000 have not fully delivered on this promise, however. Per capita output and investment growth in the median frontier market halved between the 2000s and the early 2020s. Poverty reduction progress has slowed. Financial openness has increased, and frontier markets' share of global capital flows has risen, but financial integration remains partial. Surges in capital inflows support growth but are often followed by disruptive stops. Although sovereign debt maturities have increased, the composition of debt implies vulnerabilities. Around 40 percent of frontier markets have defaulted since 2000. In the five years from 2020, frontier markets experienced more defaults than all other economies combined.

To capitalize on frontier markets' potential, a multifaceted policy approach is required. Some frontier markets have fared better than others, and faster-growing frontier markets since 2000 share some key features: stronger investment growth, more improved institutions, and better-contained government debt. Advancing financial integration while improving oversight capacity, developing local financial markets, and enhancing policy buffers can help harness investment. Expanding and diversifying exports can support resilience and development. Bolstering macroeconomic stability and enhancing policy credibility can provide a platform for effective financial integration. Catalyzing investment and productivity growth, including via strong foundational infrastructure, is essential to helping frontier markets capitalize on their market access, demographic potential, and resource endowments.

Abbreviations

AE	advanced economy
AGOA	African Growth and Opportunity Act
AI	artificial intelligence
AIPI	Artificial Intelligence Preparedness Index
CAPB	cyclically adjusted primary balance
CGFS	Committee on the Global Financial System
CPI	consumer price index
EAP	East Asia and Pacific
ECA	Europe and Central Asia
EM7	Brazil, China, India, Indonesia, Mexico, the Russian Federation, and Türkiye
EMBI	Emerging Markets Bond Index
EMDEs	emerging market and developing economies
EMs	emerging markets
EU	European Union
FCS	fragile and conflict-affected situations
FDI	foreign direct investment
FM	frontier markets
FTSE	Financial Times Stock Exchange
FY	fiscal year
GCC	Gulf Cooperation Council
GDP	gross domestic product
GFC	global financial crisis
GNI	gross national income
HIPC	heavily indebted poor countries
IDA	International Development Association
IEA	International Energy Agency
IMF	International Monetary Fund
LAC	Latin America and the Caribbean
LIC	low-income country
LNG	liquefied natural gas
LP	local projection
MNA	Middle East, North Africa, Afghanistan and Pakistan
MSCI	Morgan Stanley Capital International
NRI	non-resource-rich countries
ODA	official development assistance
ODE	other developing economies
OECD	Organisation for Economic Co-operation and Development
OPEC+	Organization of the Petroleum Exporting Countries and other affiliated oil producers
PMI	purchasing managers' index
PPP	purchasing power parity
PVAR	panel vector autoregression
R&D	research and development
RTA	regional trade agreement
SAR	South Asia

SSA	Sub-Saharan Africa
TFP	total factor productivity
UN	United Nations
USMCA	United States-Mexico-Canada Agreement
VIX	Chicago Board Options Exchange Volatility Index
WAEMU	West African Economic and Monetary Union
WDI	World Development Indicators
WTO	World Trade Organization

CHAPTER 1

GLOBAL OUTLOOK

The global economy has shown notable resilience to heightened trade tensions and policy uncertainty. Last year, stockpiling of traded goods, strong risk appetite, and a surge in artificial intelligence (AI) spending supported activity, while supply chains adapted to rising trade barriers. The faster-than-expected pace of growth capped a five-year global recovery from the 2020 recession unmatched in more than six decades, although vulnerable emerging market and developing economies (EMDEs) are lagging far behind. Looking forward, global growth is projected to edge down to 2.6 percent this year as several supportive factors fade. In particular, trade growth is set to weaken as firms scale back inventory accumulation and tariff effects intensify. With output growth subdued, vulnerable EMDEs—particularly low-income countries and economies facing fragile and conflict situations—confront significant challenges. More broadly, without stronger economic dynamism, many EMDEs will struggle to create enough jobs for expanding working-age populations. Near-term risks are tilted to the downside. Growth could falter if trade tensions escalate, barriers rise further, or financial market sentiment deteriorates amid asset price declines, fiscal concerns, or inflation surprises. On the upside, firms' adaptability to new trade conditions could support growth, and AI-related activity could broaden. Global efforts are needed to improve the trade environment, ease financing pressures in vulnerable EMDEs, and address climate risks. To catalyze private investment and support long-term growth and job creation, policy makers in EMDEs can advance reforms to diversify trade, strengthen fiscal and monetary frameworks, and address long-standing structural bottlenecks.

Summary

The global economy has been markedly more resilient than expected, despite last year's historic escalation in trade tensions and policy uncertainty. This resilience reflected significant front-loading of trade, supply-chain adjustments, limited tariff pass-through, easier global financial conditions, and a surge in AI-related investment. As these supports fade, global activity and job creation are set to ease (refer to figure 1.1.A). The modest slowdown comes on the heels of a post-pandemic rebound over 2021–25 that represented the strongest recovery from a global recession in more than six decades; however, this rebound was remarkably uneven and came at the expense of higher inflation and debt (refer to box 1.1).

The outlook for global trade continues to be dampened by elevated trade tensions and policy uncertainty associated with higher tariffs (refer to figure 1.1.B). After global trade growth was propped up last year by the front-loading of goods trade ahead of tariff increases, it is projected to decelerate markedly in 2026, as stockpiling fades and the impact of tariff measures builds. In 2027, trade growth is expected to firm, as trade flows more fully adjust to tariff hikes and policy uncertainty recedes.

The weakening of global trade and a slowdown in some major economies are also expected to weigh on demand for energy and industrial commodities. Crude oil prices are projected to fall as demand softens and the Organization of the Petroleum Exporting Countries and other affiliated oil producers (OPEC+) boost crude oil supply, with oil markets envisaged to face a substantial excess of supply (refer to figure 1.1.C). Meanwhile, the prices of industrial metals are set to be cushioned somewhat by green energy demand, partly offsetting muted growth of industrial and manufacturing activity.

Inflation has moderated in most countries, moving closer to central bank targets. While higher tariff rates contributed to a modest rise in U.S. goods inflation, the impact was attenuated by stockpiling of goods, among other mitigating factors. Going forward, global inflation is expected to edge down further, albeit with the continued effects of tariffs driving greater variation across major economies. Projected disinflation at the global level reflects various forces including the impact of softening labor markets in many economies, subdued demand for tradable goods, and falling energy prices.

Note: This chapter was prepared by Carlos Arteta, Nikita Perevalov, Peter Selcuk, Collette Wheeler, Garima Vasishtha, and Phil Kenworthy. Additional contributions were provided by Mirco Balatti, Gitanjali Kumar, Joseph Mawejje, Dawit Mekonnen, Alen Mulabdic, Shijie Shi, Kersten Stamm, Naotaka Sugawara, Takuma Tanaka, and Neha Varma.

TABLE 1.1 Real GDP[1]

(Percent change from previous year unless indicated otherwise)

	2023	2024	2025e	2026f	2027f	Percentage-point differences from June 2025 projections 2025e	2026f	2027f
World	**2.8**	**2.8**	**2.7**	**2.6**	**2.7**	**0.4**	**0.2**	**0.1**
Advanced economies	**1.6**	**1.7**	**1.7**	**1.6**	**1.6**	**0.5**	**0.2**	**0.0**
United States	2.9	2.8	2.1	2.2	1.9	0.7	0.6	0.0
Euro area	0.5	0.9	1.4	0.9	1.2	0.7	0.1	0.2
Japan	0.7	-0.2	1.3	0.8	0.8	0.6	0.0	0.0
Emerging market and developing economies	**4.4**	**4.3**	**4.2**	**4.0**	**4.1**	**0.3**	**0.2**	**0.2**
East Asia and Pacific	5.2	5.0	4.8	4.4	4.3	0.3	0.4	0.3
China	5.4	5.0	4.9	4.4	4.2	0.4	0.4	0.3
Indonesia	5.0	5.0	5.0	5.0	5.2	0.3	0.2	0.2
Thailand	2.0	2.5	2.0	1.8	2.5	0.2	0.1	0.2
Europe and Central Asia	3.6	3.6	2.4	2.4	2.7	0.0	-0.1	0.0
Russian Federation	4.1	4.3	0.9	0.8	1.0	-0.5	-0.4	-0.2
Türkiye	5.0	3.3	3.5	3.7	4.4	0.4	0.1	0.2
Poland	0.2	3.0	3.3	3.2	2.9	0.1	0.2	0.0
Latin America and the Caribbean	2.4	2.4	2.2	2.3	2.6	-0.1	-0.1	0.0
Brazil	3.2	3.4	2.3	2.0	2.3	-0.1	-0.2	0.0
Mexico	3.4	1.4	0.2	1.3	1.8	0.0	0.2	0.0
Argentina	-1.9	-1.3	4.6	4.0	4.0	-0.9	-0.5	0.0
Middle East, North Africa, Afghanistan and Pakistan	2.1	2.6	3.1	3.6	3.9	0.4	-0.1	-0.1
Saudi Arabia	0.5	2.7	3.8	4.3	4.4	1.0	-0.2	-0.2
Iran, Islamic Rep.[2]	5.3	3.7	-1.1	-1.5	0.6	-0.6	-1.8	-1.2
Egypt, Arab Rep.[2]	3.8	2.4	4.4	4.3	4.8	0.6	0.1	0.2
South Asia	8.0	6.3	7.1	6.2	6.5	1.0	-0.2	0.0
India[2]	9.2	6.5	7.2	6.5	6.6	0.9	0.0	-0.1
Bangladesh[2]	5.8	4.2	3.7	4.6	6.1	0.4	-0.3	0.4
Sri Lanka	-2.3	5.0	4.6	3.5	3.1	1.1	0.4	0.0
Sub-Saharan Africa	3.0	3.7	4.0	4.3	4.5	0.3	0.2	0.2
Nigeria	3.3	4.1	4.2	4.4	4.4	0.6	0.7	0.6
South Africa	0.7	0.6	1.3	1.4	1.5	0.6	0.3	0.2
Ethiopia[2]	7.2	8.1	7.2	7.1	7.7	0.8	0.6	0.5
Memorandum items:								
Real GDP[1]								
High-income countries	1.7	1.9	1.7	1.7	1.8	0.4	0.2	0.1
Middle-income countries	4.9	4.4	4.4	4.1	4.2	0.3	0.1	0.2
Low-income countries	1.0	3.6	5.0	5.7	5.6	0.2	-0.1	0.0
EMDEs excluding China	3.8	3.8	3.7	3.7	4.0	0.3	-0.1	0.0
Commodity-exporting EMDEs	2.9	3.3	3.0	3.1	3.3	0.1	-0.1	-0.1
Commodity-importing EMDEs	5.2	4.7	4.7	4.4	4.4	0.4	0.3	0.2
Commodity-importing EMDEs excluding China	4.9	4.3	4.4	4.3	4.7	0.4	-0.1	0.1
EM7	5.4	4.8	4.5	4.1	4.1	0.4	0.2	0.2
World (PPP weights)[3]	3.4	3.3	3.3	3.1	3.2	0.4	0.1	0.1
World trade volume[4]	**0.6**	**3.4**	**3.4**	**2.2**	**2.7**	**1.6**	**-0.2**	**0.0**
						Level differences from June 2025 projections		
Commodity prices[5]								
WBG commodity price index	108.0	105.1	98.2	90.9	94.1	4.0	1.9	2.2
Energy index	106.9	101.5	90.0	79.9	84.9	3.8	-0.3	0.5
Oil (US$ per barrel)	82.6	80.7	69.0	60.0	65.0	3.0	-1.0	0.0
Non-energy index	110.2	112.5	114.6	113.1	112.7	4.3	6.3	5.6

Source: World Bank.

Note: e = estimate; f = forecast. EM7 = Brazil, China, India, Indonesia, Mexico, the Russian Federation, and Türkiye; WBG = World Bank Group. World Bank forecasts are frequently updated based on new information. Consequently, projections presented here may differ from those contained in other World Bank documents, even if basic assessments of countries' prospects do not differ at any given date. For the definition of EMDEs, developing countries, commodity exporters, and commodity importers, please refer to table 1.2. The World Bank is currently not publishing economic output, income, or growth data for Turkmenistan and República Bolivariana de Venezuela owing to lack of reliable data of adequate quality. Turkmenistan and República Bolivariana de Venezuela are excluded from cross-country macroeconomic aggregates. The region name "Middle East and North Africa" has been revised to "Middle East, North Africa, Afghanistan and Pakistan," reflecting the inclusion of Afghanistan and Pakistan in the region starting July 1, 2025.

1. Headline aggregate growth rates are calculated using GDP weights at average 2010-19 prices and market exchange rates.

2. GDP growth rates are on a fiscal year (FY) basis. Aggregates that include these countries are calculated using data compiled on a calendar year basis. For India and the Islamic Republic of Iran, the column for 2023 refers to FY2023/24. For Bangladesh, the Arab Republic of Egypt, and Ethiopia, the column for 2023 refers to FY2022/23.

3. World growth rates are calculated using average 2010-19 purchasing power parity (PPP) weights, which attribute a greater share of global GDP to emerging market and developing economies (EMDEs) than market exchange rates.

4. World trade volume of goods and nonfactor services.

5. Indexes are expressed in nominal U.S. dollars (2010=100). Oil refers to the Brent crude oil benchmark. For weights and composition of indexes, refer to https://worldbank.org/commodities.

Along with continued global disinflation, global financial conditions eased in the second half of last year (refer to figure 1.1.D). This was fueled by strong risk appetite and U.S. monetary policy easing amid softness in the U.S. labor market. Globally, equity indexes have seen substantial gains since June. The positive risk sentiment spilled over to EMDEs, which experienced strong debt-related inflows. EMDEs also benefited from the depreciation of the U.S. dollar, which boosted local currency bond returns. In addition, sovereign and non-financial corporate bond issuance by EMDEs in foreign currencies picked up and bond spreads narrowed further, despite steepening yield curves in advanced economies.

In all, global growth is estimated to have averaged 2.7 percent in 2025, 0.4 percentage point above June projections, in part as a result of stronger-than-expected growth in major economies (refer to figure 1.1.E and table 1.1). As supportive factors fade, growth is forecast to edge down to 2.6 percent in 2026, driven by a notable slowdown in demand for traded goods and softening domestic demand in many major economies. It is then set to pick up slightly to 2.7 percent in 2027, as domestic demand benefits from earlier monetary policy easing and trade improves amid declining uncertainty. This baseline projection assumes no major new trade-related shocks materialize.

After remaining at 1.7 percent in 2025, growth in advanced economies is expected to edge down to 1.6 percent this year, as the effects of higher trade barriers weigh on activity, and remain at that pace in 2027. These projections reflect the offsetting effects of trade policy-related headwinds on the one hand, and the gradually waning boost from monetary policy easing, additional fiscal support, and tech-related investments on the other. Relative to previous projections, this outlook envisions a somewhat smaller and more delayed impact of trade policy shifts and uncertainty in major advanced economies, in line with the resilience seen in the global economy so far.

Growth in EMDEs was stronger than expected in 2025, at an estimated 4.2 percent. Activity in China proved more robust than anticipated, mostly on account of fiscal stimulus and increased shipments to non-U.S. markets. Many other

FIGURE 1.1 Global economic prospects

After exceeding expectations last year, global growth is forecast to edge down in 2026, with the slowdown partly reflecting the rise in trade barriers and elevated policy uncertainty. Oil prices are projected to soften alongside decelerating demand and increasing oil supply from the Organization of the Petroleum Exporting Countries and other affiliated oil producers (OPEC+). The drag on global growth from trade tensions is being partly offset by easier global financial conditions due to strong risk appetite. As a result, global growth this year is expected to be stronger relative to previous projections. Following the pandemic, an uneven and incomplete global economic recovery has left per capita incomes in many vulnerable EMDEs, particularly low-income countries and economies facing fragile and conflict situations, below pre-pandemic levels.

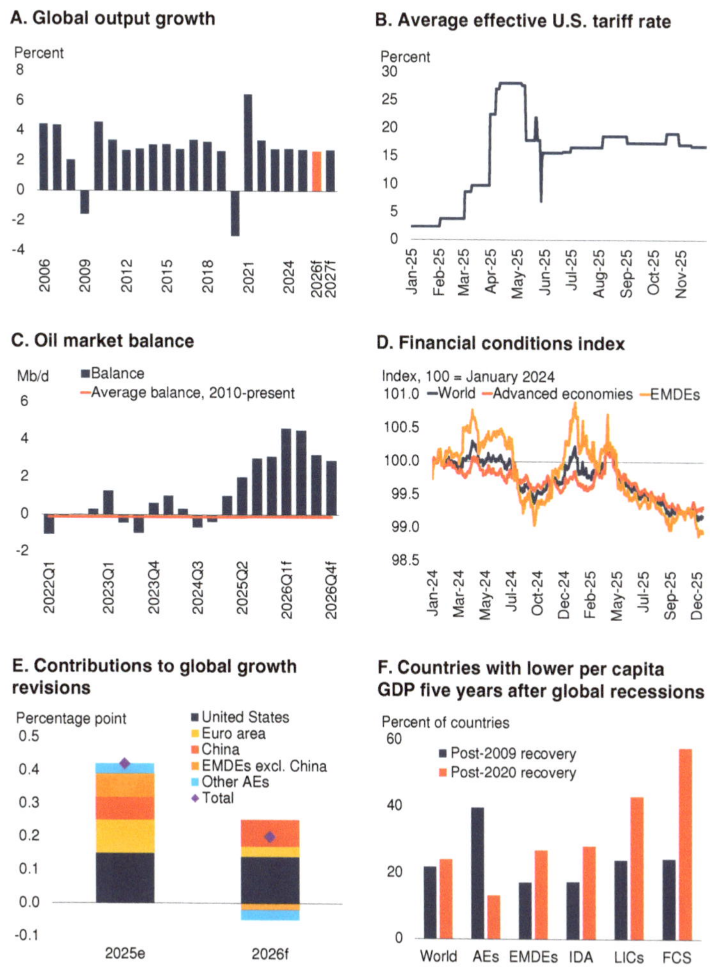

Sources: Bloomberg; International Energy Agency (IEA); The Budget Lab; UN World Population Prospects (database); World Bank.

Note: e = estimate; f = forecast. AEs = advanced economies; EMDEs = emerging market and developing economies; excl. = excluding; FCS = fragile and conflict-affected situations; IDA = countries eligible for International Development Association support; LICs = low-income countries; Mb/d = million barrels a day. FCS country group based on current World Bank FCS classification.

A.E. GDP aggregates calculated using real U.S. dollar GDP weights at average 2010-19 prices and market exchange rates.

B. Estimated U.S. average effective tariff rate, with the last observation (November 30, 2025) assuming the published policy stance as of November 17, 2025.

C. Data from IEA's December 2025 edition of *Oil Market Report*. Data from 2025Q4 to 2026Q4 are IEA forecasts.

D. Lines show financial conditions indexes for world, advanced economies, and EMDEs, computed as weighted averages using nominal GDP in U.S. dollars as weights. Higher index values represent tighter financial conditions. Index base is the average for January 2024. Last observation is December 16, 2025.

E. Panel shows contributions to global growth forecast revisions from the June 2025 edition of *the Global Economic Prospects* report.

F. Each bar represents the share of economies whose per capita GDP remains below its pre-recession level five years after the recession. For the 2009 recession, the comparison is between 2008 and 2014; for the 2020 recession, it is between 2019 and 2025.

EMDEs also benefited from stronger net exports, in addition to more solid investment. Growth in EMDEs is forecast to decelerate to an average of 4 percent in 2026–27, as the projected slowdown in China is partly offset by a gradual pickup in other EMDEs next year. Growth in China is expected to decelerate across the forecast horizon, as the effects of continued fiscal stimulus and other policy support measures are outweighed by lackluster confidence amid a structural slowdown.

In 2026, growth in EMDEs excluding China is projected to remain steady at 3.7 percent. More supportive financial conditions are set to boost investment, but this tailwind is expected to be offset by slightly softer consumption growth amid generally restrained confidence, and by the payback from earlier front-loading of EMDE exports as trade restrictions remain elevated. In 2027, growth in these economies is forecast to gain momentum, edging up to 4 percent. The projected pickup reflects an acceleration in domestic demand, driven by stronger investment and firmer consumption, in addition to a recovery in trade and manufacturing, with commodity exporters also supported by a modest rise in industrial commodity prices.

With an uneven and incomplete global economic recovery following the pandemic-related recession of 2020, per capita incomes in many vulnerable EMDEs—particularly low-income countries (LICs) and countries facing fragile and conflict situations (FCS)—remain below their pre-pandemic levels (refer to figure 1.1.F). Without stronger growth, many EMDEs will struggle to create sufficient jobs to productively employ growing working-age populations, especially as many economies and sectors undergo structural changes. This challenge is set to be amplified by the anticipated surge in young people entering the labor market in EMDEs over the next decade, requiring focus on key industries that are relatively labor-intensive, tradable, technologically upgradeable, and less susceptible to automation.

The global economic outlook is clouded by a high degree of uncertainty, and risks remain tilted to the downside (refer to figure 1.2.A). Heightened trade policy uncertainty amid a further proliferation of trade restrictions could weigh on trade prospects, business confidence, and investment. Furthermore, a substantial tightening in financial conditions could result from a correction in equity prices, more restrictive monetary policy due to stronger inflationary pressures, or higher government bond yields driven by concerns about elevated debt in major advanced economies. In a scenario where equity valuations decline sharply, leading to a plunge in risk appetite and consumer and business confidence, global growth could be up to 0.3 percentage point below baseline projections this year (refer to figure 1.2.B).

In addition, escalating conflict and geopolitical tensions could disrupt global trade and commodity markets. More frequent weather-related disasters with worsening impacts could hurt economic activity. These developments could also exacerbate risks to public health systems in vulnerable EMDEs, arising in part from declines in health-related official development assistance (ODA) as well as shortfalls in financing for pandemic preparedness.

On the upside, firms could continue to display considerable flexibility in adapting to rising trade barriers and policy uncertainty—for instance, through supply-chain reconfiguration—thus limiting trade disruptions and easing inflationary pressures. Optimism over AI and related technologies could continue to boost associated investment, raising near-term growth and potentially strengthening labor productivity over the longer term.

Effective policy action is essential to confront continued economic challenges facing the global economy, even if the nature and urgency of these challenges vary across countries. Global cooperation is critical to foster a predictable multilateral trade system and address emerging challenges. Both advanced economies and EMDEs can also deepen integration with willing partners and expand the scope of existing trade agreements or strengthen regional trading relationships, which could help insulate goods trade growth from adverse policy shifts elsewhere (refer to figure 1.2.C). The poorest and most vulnerable EMDEs, including LICs and FCS, face acute constraints in mobilizing resources, often exacerbated by elevated debt burdens. In this context, the international community needs to boost efforts to support comprehensive debt relief, particularly in a context of declining ODA and increasing climate-related disruptions, which affect EMDEs disproportionately.

In terms of domestic policy action, EMDEs would benefit from bolstering fiscal sustainability, particularly in the context of large fiscal deficits in major economies. To help ease tight fiscal constraints, boosting domestic revenue mobilization is critical. These efforts can be complemented by measures to improve spending efficiency and strengthen fiscal frameworks—including the appropriate use of fiscal rules, which tend to support needed fiscal adjustment (refer to figure 1.2.D). Meanwhile, EMDE central banks may need to slow the pace of monetary easing if inflationary pressures re-emerge, carefully weighing risks and trade-offs to growth. At the same time, safeguarding monetary policy independence is key, as it can help anchor inflation expectations and reinforce credibility.

To improve longer-term growth and jobs prospects, EMDEs need to pursue reforms that reflect their diverse circumstances and capitalize on unmet economic potential. This involves addressing long-standing structural bottlenecks, enacting reforms that boost investment and productivity, and fostering stability. Generating sufficient job opportunities will be critical given that 1.2 billion young people are expected to reach working age in EMDEs by 2035 (refer to figure 1.2.E). Key pillars to address this jobs challenge include policies that ensure the foundational physical, digital, and human capital infrastructure is in place to allow people—including women and youth—to thrive; that secure a better business environment, with policy and regulatory certainty so that firms can grow; and that mobilize private capital to help meet substantial investment needs. Some key sectors—infrastructure (including energy), agribusiness, health care, tourism, and value-added manufacturing—have particular potential for local job creation at scale in EMDEs.

Following a period of broadly stagnant investment growth over the past 15 years, most EMDEs have made little ground in lifting investment per worker levels to those observed in advanced

FIGURE 1.2 Global risks and policy challenges

Risks remain tilted to the downside. In a downside scenario, a sharp decline in equity valuations, plunging risk appetite and tighter financial conditions would reduce global growth this year by up to 0.3 percentage point. Countries can deepen their integration with willing partners and strengthen regional trading relationships. Fiscal rules can be used as a tool for aligning spending with revenues and charting the course for fiscal sustainability. EMDEs need to enact structural reforms to provide job opportunities for the 1.2 billion young people expected to reach working age by 2035. Stronger investment growth could, in turn supporting employment.

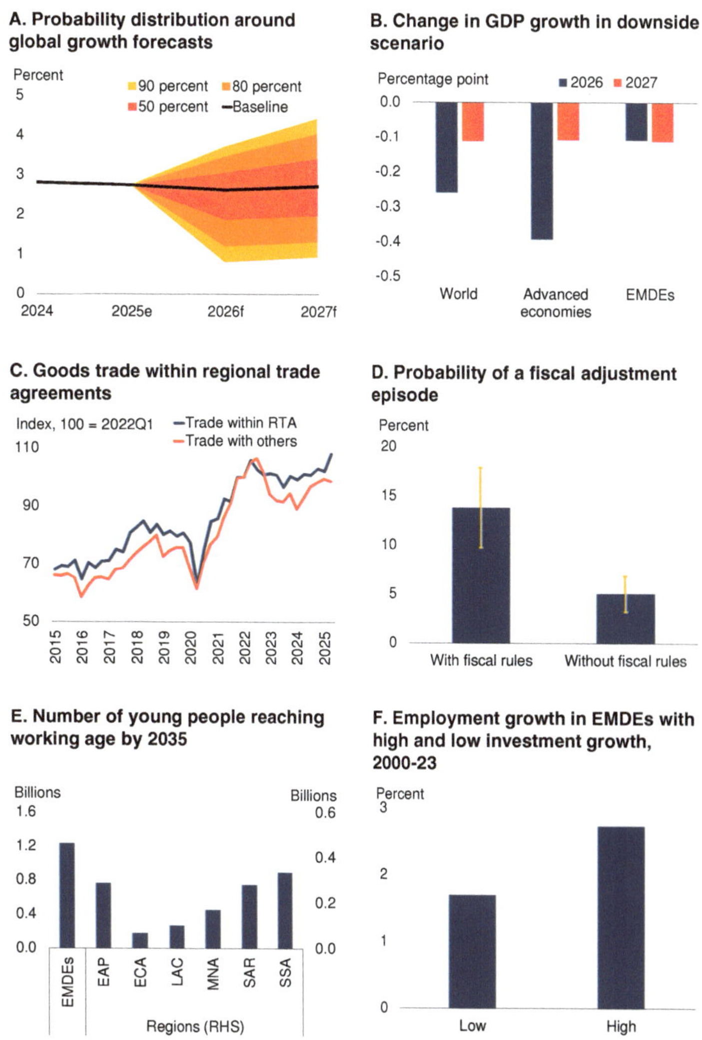

Sources: Bloomberg; Consensus Economics; Egger and Larch (2008); Haver Analytics; ILOSTAT (database); IMF; Ohnsorge, Stocker, and Some (2016); Oxford Economics; UN Comtrade; UN World Population Prospects (database); WDI (database); World Bank.

Note: e = estimate; f = forecast. EAP = East Asia and Pacific; ECA = Europe and Central Asia; EMDEs = emerging market and developing economies; LAC = Latin America and Caribbean; MNA = Middle East, North Africa, Afghanistan, and Pakistan; RHS = right-hand scale; RTA = regional trade agreement; SAR = South Asia; SSA = Sub-Saharan Africa.

A. Probabilities use the range and skewness implied by oil and equity price derivatives, and term spread forecasts. Values for 2026-27 use 12-month- and 24-month-ahead forecast distributions, employing data up to December 18, 2025.

B. Panel shows the deviation of growth from the baseline.

C. Blue shows nominal trade among countries with RTAs in force as of 2023; red shows other trade. RTAs data from Egger and Larch (2008). Sample of 70 reporting countries trading with 241 partner economies. Last observation is 2025Q2.

D. Results from probit regressions (details in annex 3.4). Panel shows the likelihood of starting a fiscal adjustment episode associated with the presence of fiscal rules. The vertical lines show 90 percent confidence intervals. Sample consists of 122 economies, including 89 EMDEs and 33 advanced economies.

E. Bars show the number of young people (aged 15-24) in regions by 2035.

F. Bars show group medians. "Low" and "high" indicate annual growth in the top and bottom third of the distribution of investment growth. Sample of 69 EMDEs from 2000-23.

BOX 1.1 Global recovery: Surprisingly strong, disappointingly uneven

The post-pandemic rebound marks the strongest recovery from a global recession in more than six decades. Five years after the pandemic's onset, global GDP per capita in 2025 was roughly 10 percent higher than in 2019—an increase exceeding that of previous global recoveries. Yet this strength masks a sharp divergence. Advanced economies have recovered robustly, with nearly 90 percent now above pre-pandemic per capita income levels. In contrast, more than one-quarter of emerging market and developing economies (EMDEs)—particularly low-income countries and those affected by fragility and conflict—still have per capita incomes below pre-pandemic levels. Differences in the scale and duration of policy responses have partly contributed to this divergence. Weak growth in many EMDEs has intensified an already-formidable jobs challenge posed by the rapid expansion of young populations. Amid a more difficult external environment, EMDEs need to accelerate reforms, rebuild policy space, and foster stronger job creation.

Two global recessions occurred in the first quarter of the twenty-first century. The 2020 recession, induced by the COVID-19 pandemic, was the deepest of the post-World War II period, with global per capita GDP contracting by nearly 4 percent (refer to figure B1.1.1.A). It was also the most synchronized recession of recent decades, with close to 90 percent of economies experiencing declines in GDP per capita (refer to figure B1.1.1.B). The 2009 recession, triggered by the global financial crisis (GFC), also involved a sharp contraction—of nearly 3 percent in global per capita GDP—but the proportion of countries where per capita GDP fell was much smaller, at 60 percent.

This box examines three questions: (i) How does the post-pandemic recovery differ from the post-GFC recovery? (ii) How have the recoveries of advanced economies and EMDEs differed? and (iii) How have policy responses differed across the two episodes?

Methodology

With a global recession defined as a decline in global real GDP per capita on annual data, there have been five global recessions since 1960: in 1975, 1982, 1991, 2009, and 2020. For the purposes of this box, a post-recession recovery period is defined as the first five years following the trough of each recession (2010–14 for the 2009 episode; 2021–25 for the 2020 episode).[a] The analysis uses annual data for 1960–2025 for 38 advanced economies and 146 EMDEs.

Post-pandemic recovery: Surprisingly strong and resilient

The 2009 and 2020 global recessions had different origins. The 2020 episode was associated with public health shutdowns and policy responses that drove simultaneous demand and supply contractions. The 2009 recession, by contrast, reflected years of financial sector excesses and rising private debt that eroded confidence and created severe balance sheet strains (Guénette, Kose, and Sugawara 2022; World Bank 2020).

The recoveries following these episodes were shaped by these differing origins but also influenced by a wide range of developments, including post-recession shocks and policy responses. The recovery from the 2020 recession unfolded amidst a series of interlinked shocks: severe supply chain disruptions in 2021, a sharp surge in energy prices after Russia's invasion of Ukraine in early 2022, and the historic inflation spike of 2021–23, which prompted one of the most synchronized global monetary tightening phases in decades (World Bank 2024a). The recovery was further threatened by elevated geopolitical tensions—including the conflict in the Middle East—alongside escalating trade restrictions and associated policy uncertainty (World Bank 2022, 2025a).

The post-2009 environment was characterized by adverse developments of a different kind: the lingering effects of the financial crisis, including private sector debt overhangs, renewed banking sector stress, and the euro-area sovereign debt crisis in 2011–12. Commodity prices—first metals and agricultural goods, then oil—fell sharply from their 2011 peaks as a result of slowing demand growth and ample supplies (World Bank 2015).

Despite multiple shocks, the post-pandemic recovery has been the strongest after any global recession since 1960, substantially exceeding the post-2009 recovery (refer to figure B1.1.1.C). Five years into the recovery, global GDP per capita exceeds its 2019 level by 10 percent, a pace stronger than in previous post-

Note: This box was prepared by M. Ayhan Kose, Jiwon Lee, and Naotaka Sugawara.

a. Kose, Sugawara, and Terrones (2020) provide a detailed analysis of global recessions and recoveries.

BOX 1.1 Global recovery: Surprisingly strong, disappointingly uneven (*continued*)

FIGURE B1.1.1 Growth during global recessions and recoveries

The 2020 global recession was the deepest and most synchronized of the five global recessions since 1960. Despite subsequent adverse shocks, the global recovery since 2020 has been the strongest, with its strength driven largely by the robust rebound in advanced economies. EMDEs have experienced a weaker pickup in GDP per capita since 2020 than after the 2009 global recession.

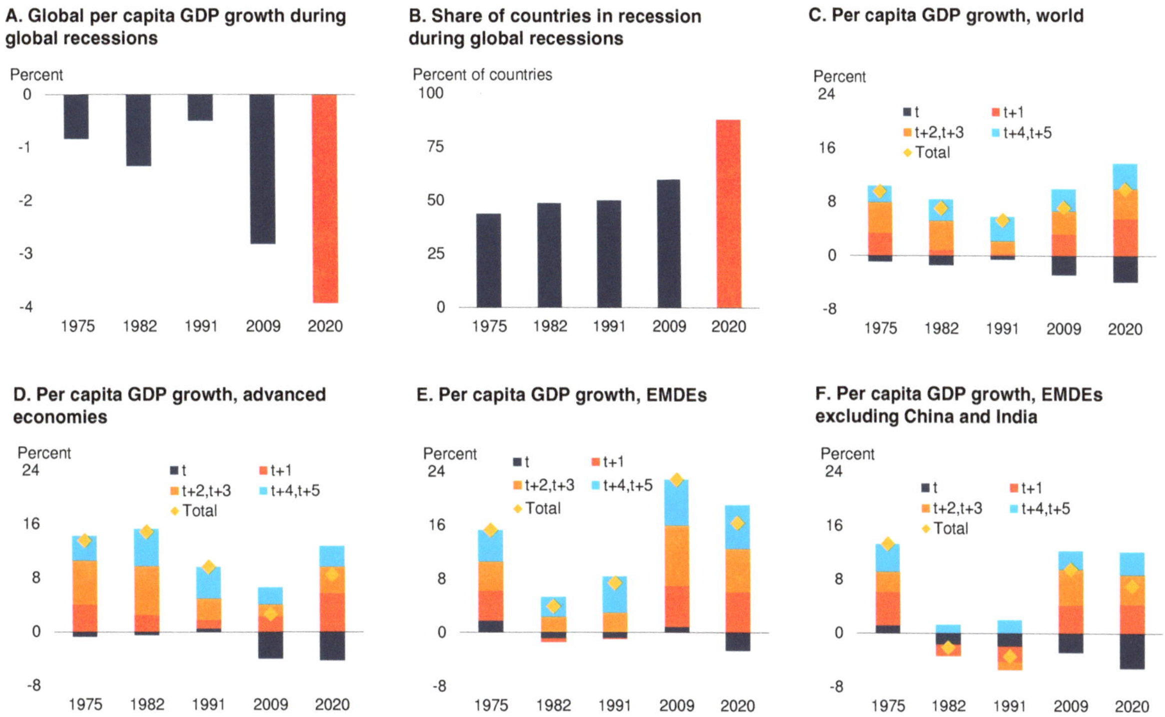

Source: World Bank.
Note: EMDEs = emerging market and developing economies.
A. Global per capita GDP growth in the years of global recessions since 1960.
B. Panel shows the proportion of countries in recession, defined as an annual contraction in per capita GDP.
C.-F. Year *t* refers to the year of global recessions, as denoted on the horizontal axis. Panels show changes in real per capita GDP from a year earlier during global recessions and the subsequent cumulative recoveries. Diamonds for "Total" present cumulative changes in real per capita GDP up to five years after the respective global recessions, including the years of the global recessions.

recession episodes. The first year of the rebound delivered the largest annual increase in global per capita GDP across the five episodes examined here.[b] Overall, the post-pandemic recovery has demonstrated exceptional resilience in an extremely challenging global environment.

b. This finding is consistent with earlier results, which suggest that deeper recessions tend to be followed by stronger recoveries in the first year (Claessens, Kose, and Terrones 2012; Wynne and Balke 1992; Zarnowitz 1992).

Disappointingly uneven between advanced economies and EMDEs

The strength of the global recovery since 2020 masks a striking divergence between advanced economies and EMDEs (refer to figures B1.1.1.D and B1.1.1.E). In advanced economies, per capita GDP increased by about 13 percent over 2021–25, compared with an increase of less than 7 percent over 2010–14. In contrast, in EMDEs, the cumulative growth of per capita GDP over 2021–25 was 3 percentage points smaller than over 2010–14, when EMDEs registered

BOX 1.1 Global recovery: Surprisingly strong, disappointingly uneven (*continued*)

their strongest post-recession expansion since the 1960s. Accounting for the deep 2020 contraction, cumulative per capita income growth in these economies remains more than 6 percentage points below that following the 2009 recession. In EMDEs excluding China and India, gains in per capita GDP in both the post-pandemic recovery and the post-GFC recovery have been relatively modest (refer to figure B1.1.1.F).

In terms of performance relative to the pre-recession GDP trend, a similar divergence emerges. Although the global economy as a whole fared much better following the pandemic than after the GFC, this aggregate outcome masks sharply different experiences across country groups. Five years into the post-pandemic recovery, global per capita GDP was about 1 percent below its pre-pandemic trend in 2025—nearly one-sixth of the shortfall observed five years after the GFC (refer to figure B1.1.2.A). This improvement was driven almost entirely by advanced economies, where per capita GDP had mostly returned to trend. In contrast, per capita GDP in EMDEs remained about 4 percent below trend, underscoring the persistence of weaker post-pandemic recoveries. By comparison, during the post-GFC recovery, per capita GDP in advanced economies remained well below trend five years after the recession.

Relative to pre-recession levels, per capita GDP remained lower in roughly one-quarter of all economies five years into the post-pandemic recovery, a share similar to that observed five years after the 2009 recession (refer to figure B1.1.2.B). Beneath this similarity, however, there again lies a divergence between advanced economies and EMDEs. While in 2025, per capita GDP in nearly 90 percent of advanced economies exceeded its 2019 level, it remained below 2019 levels in more than one-quarter of EMDEs. This is also a larger share than after the GFC, when only one in six EMDEs had lower per capita GDP in 2014 than in 2008.

These sustained declines in per capita GDP are heavily concentrated among the poorest EMDEs (Chrimes et al. 2024; World Bank 2025a, 2025b). In about 30 percent of countries eligible for support from the International Development Association (IDA), over 40 percent of low-income countries (LICs), and nearly 60 percent of economies in fragile and conflict-affected situations (FCS), per capita GDP is estimated to have been lower in 2025 than in 2019. These shares are substantially higher than in the post-GFC recovery: per capita GDP in 2014 was lower than in 2008 in about 17 percent of IDA-eligible countries and about 25 percent of LICs and FCS countries.

Using GDP per capita as a proxy for income, weak per capita GDP growth in these economies points to a reversal of income convergence with advanced economies since the eve of the pandemic. Thus, since 2019, these vulnerable developing economies—and even all EMDEs excluding China and India—have become relatively poorer compared with advanced economies (refer to figure B1.1.2.C). The per capita income differential between LICs and advanced economies has widened by 10 percent in 2025, relative to the gap in 2019. In FCS, the widening of the per capita income gap has been larger, by almost 15 percent in 2025, compared with the pre-pandemic level. This contrasts sharply with the experience following the 2009 episode. Compared with the level in 2008, the per capita income gap with advanced economies narrowed by about 3 percent, 7 percent, and 18 percent in LICs, FCS, and IDA-eligible countries, respectively, five years after the 2009 recession.

Similar patterns also emerge across EMDE regions. All regions saw slower income convergence with advanced economies during the post-pandemic recovery than after the GFC. Sub-Saharan Africa, the Middle East, North Africa, Afghanistan and Pakistan, and Latin America and the Caribbean have fallen further behind as they have become relatively poorer compared with advanced economies (refer to figure B1.1.2.D).

The weak post-pandemic recovery has significant implications for both poverty reduction and job creation, particularly in the most vulnerable EMDEs. While poverty rates declined during the post-GFC recovery, they increased during the post-pandemic recovery in the most vulnerable EMDEs (refer to figure B1.1.2.E). Over the next decade, hundreds of millions of young people are expected to enter labor markets in developing economies. Yet as generating growth has become more difficult in the post-pandemic period, the jobs challenge—creating sufficient employment opportunities for this rapidly expanding cohort—has grown even more daunting, especially in the most

BOX 1.1 Global recovery: Surprisingly strong, disappointingly uneven (*continued*)

FIGURE B1.1.2 Divergence of recoveries, poverty, and jobs

The strength of the post-2020 recovery has differed sharply across country groups. In advanced economies, per capita GDP has returned to its pre-recession trend, while in EMDEs it remains below trend. By 2025, per capita GDP in nearly 90 percent of advanced economies had surpassed its 2019 level; in contrast, it remained lower in more than one-quarter of EMDEs. Outcomes are even weaker among the poorest EMDEs, including IDA-eligible countries, LICs, and FCS. Persistently weak growth in these economies since 2019 has stalled income convergence with advanced economies. Poverty rates have risen during the post-pandemic recovery in the most vulnerable EMDEs, which also face a more acute jobs challenge as young people account for a much larger share of the population than in other EMDEs.

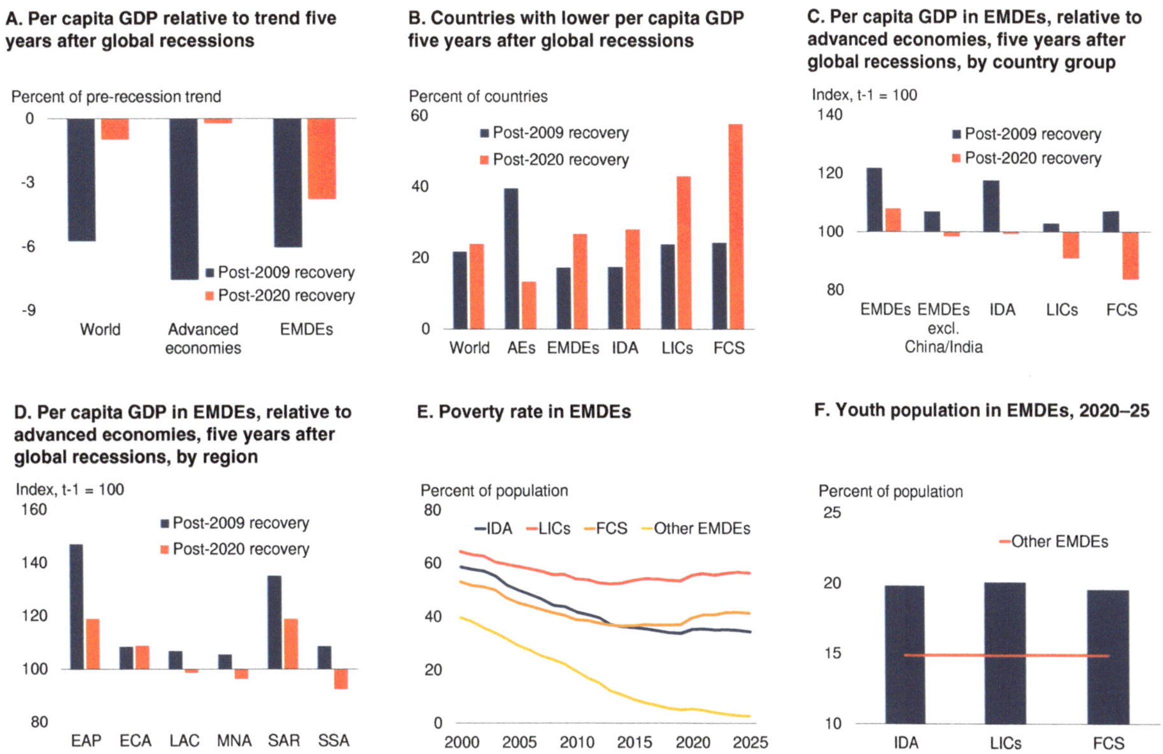

Sources: UN World Population Prospects (database); World Bank.

Note: AEs = advanced economies; EAP = East Asia and Pacific; ECA = Europe and Central Asia; EMDEs = emerging market and developing economies; FCS = fragile and conflict-affected situations; IDA = countries eligible for support from the International Development Association; LAC = Latin America and the Caribbean; LICs = low-income countries; MNA = Middle East, North Africa, Afghanistan and Pakistan; SAR = South Asia; SSA = Sub-Saharan Africa.

A. Each bar shows the percent difference in per capita GDP from the trend level five years after the global recession. For the post-2009 recovery, it refers to 2014; for the post-2020 recovery, it is for 2025. The trend level is computed by assuming to grow at the regression-estimated trend growth rate over the 10 years prior to the global recession, that is, 1999–2008 for the post-2009 recovery and 2010–19 for the post-2020 recovery.

B. Each bar represents the share of economies whose per capita GDP remains below its pre-recession level five years after the recession. For the post-2009 recovery, the comparison is between 2008 and 2014; for the post-2020 recovery, it is between 2019 and 2025.

C.D. Each bar shows per capita GDP five years after the global recession—denoted as year *t*—relative to the level in advanced economies, which is presented as an index with the relative share one year prior to the respective global recessions equal to 100.

E. Poverty rate is defined as the share of the population living on less than $3 per day in 2021 purchasing power parity. Aggregates are computed as weighted averages using the total population as weights. Data for 2025 are the estimates. Other EMDEs refer to EMDEs excluding IDA-eligible countries, LICs, and FCS.

F. Each bar shows the share of the youth population, defined as those aged 15–24, averaged over 2020–25, based on the 2024 Revision of World Population Prospects. Aggregates are computed as weighted averages using the total population as weights. Other EMDEs refer to EMDEs excluding IDA-eligible countries, LICs, and FCS.

BOX 1.1 Global recovery: Surprisingly strong, disappointingly uneven (*continued*)

FIGURE B1.1.3 Fiscal policies and trade

Divergent fiscal policy responses after the 2009 and 2020 recessions have contributed to the differing recovery paths. The post-pandemic external environment has further constrained EMDEs, with subdued global trade growth.

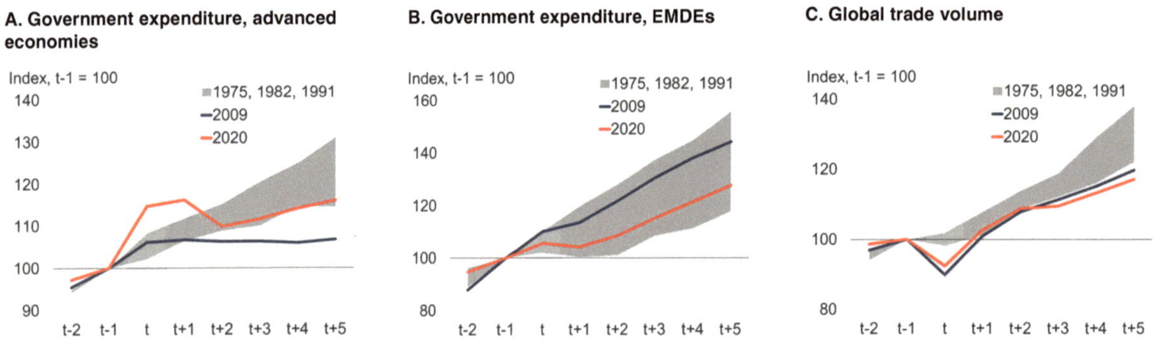

Sources: Kose et al. (2022); World Bank.

Note: EMDEs = emerging market and developing economies.

A.-C. Year *t* denotes a global recession year (shaded in light gray). The darker shaded area indicates the range of the three global recessions—in 1975, 1982, and 1991—for which data are available. In panels A and B, government expenditure is adjusted by the GDP deflator and expressed as an index number equal to 100 one year prior to year *t* (that is, *t*-1 = 100). In panel C, trade is likewise expressed as an index based on the average of exports and imports of goods and services.

vulnerable EMDEs. The share of the youth population (ages 15–24) is considerably higher in IDA-eligible countries, LICs, and FCS than in other EMDEs (refer to figure B1.1.2.F). Moreover, in IDA-eligible countries, the number of young people not in employment, education, or training is estimated to have risen by nearly 15 percent between 2016 and 2025. The increase was even larger in LICs and FCS, at almost 20 percent over the same period.

Policy responses: A role reversal

Policy responses across the two recoveries differed sharply (refer to figures B1.1.3.A and B1.1.3.B). Following 2009, advanced economies rapidly scaled back fiscal support while leaning heavily on extended monetary accommodation. By contrast, many EMDEs, following sustained reforms and the accumulation of policy buffers in the pre-GFC years, were able, for the first time, to implement countercyclical policies to support demand and activity (Koh and Yu 2020).

In the post-pandemic recovery, this pattern reversed. Advanced economies deployed far larger—and longer sustained—fiscal expansions while, beginning in late 2021, monetary policies were tightened rapidly in response to surging inflation. EMDEs entered the pandemic with much larger fiscal deficits and public debt burdens than before the GFC, leaving them with limited fiscal space; the support they provided in 2020 further increased debt levels (Mawejje 2025; World Bank 2021). On the eve of the pandemic, at end-2019, government debt in EMDEs averaged about 54 percent of GDP. However, five years after the global recession, it exceeded 70 percent of GDP. During the post-GFC recovery, in contrast, the increase in the government debt-to-GDP ratio was only 6.2 percentage points over 2008–14. Some EMDEs tightened monetary policy earlier than advanced economies to contain inflationary pressures. These differing policy mixes and constraints partly explain the divergence between the recovery paths of advanced economies and EMDEs.

External environment: More challenging

The external environment during the post-pandemic recovery has been considerably more difficult than during the post-GFC recovery. Global trade growth has been weaker than in any post-global recession recovery since 1960, reflecting post-pandemic supply chain disruptions, rising geopolitical fragmentation, and a surge in trade restrictions that has driven policy uncertainty to unprecedented levels (refer to figure B1.1.3.C; World Bank 2025a).

BOX 1.1 Global recovery: Surprisingly strong, disappointingly uneven (*continued*)

A difficult task ahead

Three major messages emerge from this comparison of the post-pandemic global recovery with the post-GFC recovery. First, the post-pandemic global recovery has been the strongest since 1960, despite a series of contemporaneous overlapping adverse shocks. Second, the recovery has been highly uneven, with advanced economies pulling ahead while many vulnerable EMDEs—especially IDA-eligible countries, LICs, and FCS—have fallen further behind, accompanied by higher poverty rates. These economies also face an acute jobs challenge, as young people account for a much larger share of the population than in other EMDEs. Third, starkly different policy responses across the two episodes, related partly to the more limited fiscal space in EMDEs, help explain these divergent outcomes.

Burdened by higher debt, weaker growth prospects, a larger jobs challenge, and a more difficult external environment, many EMDEs now face a demanding set of tasks (World Bank 2025a). A key lesson from their successful response to the 2009 global recession stands out: robust policy responses and relatively strong growth performance were made possible by earlier advances in structural reforms, the strengthening of macroeconomic policy frameworks, and the rebuilding of policy buffers. Reestablishing these foundations will be essential for EMDEs to promote growth, create jobs, and deliver broad-based gains in living standards.

economies. This lack of investment is closely associated with lackluster productivity growth, given that investment embodies technological upgrades and can catalyze the infusion of new approaches to production. To this end, EMDEs will need to strengthen macroeconomic stability, improve the investment climate, and promote cross-border trade and finance flows. Policies that lift investment growth could help support stronger employment growth (refer to figure 1.2.F). In frontier markets, a diverse group of economies with some financial market access, the full benefits of financial integration have proven elusive amid relatively limited financial development, macroeconomic buffers, and institutional depth. These limitations can also exacerbate the impact of adverse global market shocks.

Global context

The global economy has shown greater-than-expected resilience to major shifts in the trading system, heightened policy uncertainty, and geopolitical tensions. In part, this reflects short-term support for activity last year that stemmed from the stockpiling of traded goods, as well as easier financial conditions amid expectations of further monetary easing. Nonetheless, global growth faces ongoing headwinds as earlier front-loading of trade unwinds and tariff costs are increasingly passed on to consumers, weighing on major economies and demand for traded goods. Softer activity in major economies is also set to reduce global demand for energy and industrial commodities. With moderating energy prices, global headline inflation is expected to ease further toward central bank targets, though with wide differences across countries.

Global trade

After a 90-day pause, the U.S. administration reinstated broad reciprocal tariff increases in August 2025 and introduced additional country- and sector-specific tariffs, exempting countries with finalized trade agreements. As a result, the average effective U.S. tariff rate rose to about 17 percent by late 2025—the highest level since the 1930s and near the rate assumed in June, but well below the mid-April peak of about 28 percent (refer to figure 1.3.A). Since then, trade policy uncertainty has subsided somewhat from historical highs as the conclusion of new bilateral trade agreements has helped clarify future tariff trajectories.

Anticipation of rising U.S. tariffs, driven by earlier policy announcements, led to a sizable front-loading of imports ahead of tariff increases,

FIGURE 1.3 Global trade

Recent trade policy changes raised the average effective U.S. tariff rate to about 17 percent, the highest since the 1930s and close to June assumptions but well below the estimated mid-April peak. After an initial surge in trade driven by front-loading ahead of tariff increases, U.S. goods imports slowed in the second half of 2025, driven by a contraction among those from countries facing relatively higher tariffs. Export-diversified countries saw improvements in their new export orders PMIs and are expected to experience less volatile and stronger trade growth, on average, over the forecast horizon.

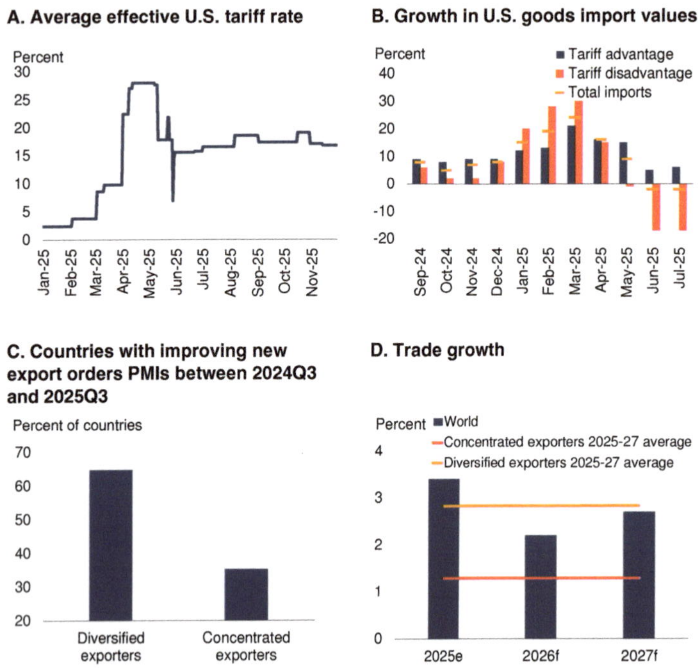

Sources: Global Trade Alert; Haver Analytics; The Budget Lab; UN Comtrade; World Bank.

Note: e = estimate; f = forecast. PMI = purchasing managers' index.

A. Estimated U.S. average effective tariff rate, with the last observation (November 30, 2025) assuming the published policy stance as of November 17, 2025.

B. Panel shows U.S. goods import value growth (year-on-year, three-month average) from countries with a "tariff advantage (disadvantage)," defined as having trade-weighted tariffs lower (higher) than those faced by competitors. Relative tariff advantage data are from Global Trade Alert as of September 6, 2025. Last observation is July 2025.

C. Panel shows the share of countries where manufacturing new export order PMIs improved between 2024Q3 and 2025Q3. The sample includes 34 countries with available PMI data. "Diversified exporters" refers to countries with a 2023 destination-based HHI below the median, and "Concentrated exporters" refers to those with an HHI above the median. Last observation is September 2025.

D. Trade in goods and services is measured as the average of export and import volumes. Panel shows global trade volume growth in goods and services. "Diversified exporters" refers to countries with a 2023 destination-based Herfindahl-Hirschman Index (HHI) below 0.25; "Concentrated exporters" refers to countries with an HHI above 0.25 in 2023.

particularly from countries facing higher tariffs compared with their competitors in the U.S. market (refer to figure 1.3.B). Subsequently, U.S. imports slowed markedly, with imports from countries subject to higher tariffs contracting in the second half of last year, and imports from other countries generally rising. The full impact from higher tariffs is expected to unfold gradually, partly because at imposition they did not apply to goods already in transit to the United States—a process that can take up to two months (CBO 2025b). This lag is reflected in the large gap observed in mid-2025 between implied tariffs, as measured by customs duty revenues, and the higher average effective tariff rate—a gap that has narrowed rapidly in recent months (Azzimonti 2025).

Economies with relatively diversified export destinations have generally seen improvements in their manufacturing PMI readings for new export orders, whereas those with more concentrated export markets have tended to experience declines (refer to figure 1.3.C). Meanwhile, services trade growth has slowed markedly, reflecting a pronounced deceleration in travel services following the post-pandemic recovery in global tourist arrivals. Transport services, which are closely tied to both travel and goods trade, have also decelerated notably.

Growth in global goods and services trade is expected to slow further this year, from 3.4 percent in 2025 to 2.2 percent in 2026, as the front-loading that supported trade in 2025 fades. Global trade growth in 2025 is 1.6 percentage points higher than June expectations, reflecting stronger stockpiling than anticipated. In turn, the unwinding of this temporary boost, along with delayed tariff effects, has resulted in a 0.2 percentage point downgrade to the trade growth projection in 2026. In 2027, trade growth is expected to firm to 2.7 percent, broadly in line with global output growth, as the impact of tariff hikes diminishes and policy uncertainty recedes. Countries with more diversified export destinations are expected to experience stronger trade growth over the forecast horizon (refer to figure 1.3.D). Tariff rates in effect as of late 2025 are assumed to prevail throughout the forecast period.

The trade outlook remains subject to substantial downside risks. While progress in trade negotiations and limited retaliation have helped ease tensions since mid-2025, uncertainty persists, particularly over the implementation of recent agreements and the trajectory of trade relations among major economies. There is a significant risk that trade tensions could re-escalate, especially as higher tariffs could redirect exports to third countries, leading domestic producers in those countries to seek protection from increased import competition. In addition, a rise in geopolitical tensions and broader use of secondary sanctions could further dampen global trade (Mulabdic and Yotov 2025).

Commodity markets

Subdued economic activity—including slowing growth in China—and fading front-loading of commodities trade are expected to weigh on demand for energy and industrial commodities in 2026. Commodity prices are projected to decline by 7 percent in 2026, matching the decline in 2025, yet remain about 20 percent above their 2015–19 nominal average (refer to figure 1.4.A). In 2027, commodity prices are expected to edge up 4 percent, reflecting supply rebalancing in the oil market as the decline in prices in 2026 curtails production in the following year. Relative to the June forecast, commodity prices are slightly higher owing to a less pronounced impact of tariffs on economic activity than initially envisaged.

The price of Brent crude oil averaged $69 per barrel in 2025 and is projected to fall to $60 per barrel in 2026, with prices facing downward pressure as growth of supply is envisaged to outpace demand next year. Global oil consumption is expected to grow by about 0.7 million barrels per day (year-on-year) in 2026—roughly the same pace as last year and about half of the pre-pandemic average (IEA 2025). Taken together with increased OPEC+ oil production in 2025, oil markets are anticipated to experience growing imbalances over 2026, with substantial excess supply (refer to figure 1.4.B).

Oil price risks are tilted to the downside, in part reflecting potential for oversupply from OPEC+ and U.S. shale, and for a sharper-than-expected slowdown in demand if downside risks to global growth materialize. In contrast, higher global oil prices could be triggered if OPEC+ reverses oil production increases. In addition, there is potential for further sanctions and other disruptions to oil exports related to geopolitical tensions in the Middle East, Russia's invasion of Ukraine and, in the near-term, developments in the República Bolivariana de Venezuela.

FIGURE 1.4 Commodity markets

Commodity prices are forecast to decline by 7 percent in 2026 as lower oil prices related to sluggish oil demand growth and increasing oversupply are partly offset by a slight firming in base metal prices. After rising 42 percent in 2025, gold prices are expected to remain elevated over the forecast horizon. Food prices are projected to be broadly stable in 2026–27 as grain and edible oil supply growth return to long-term trends.

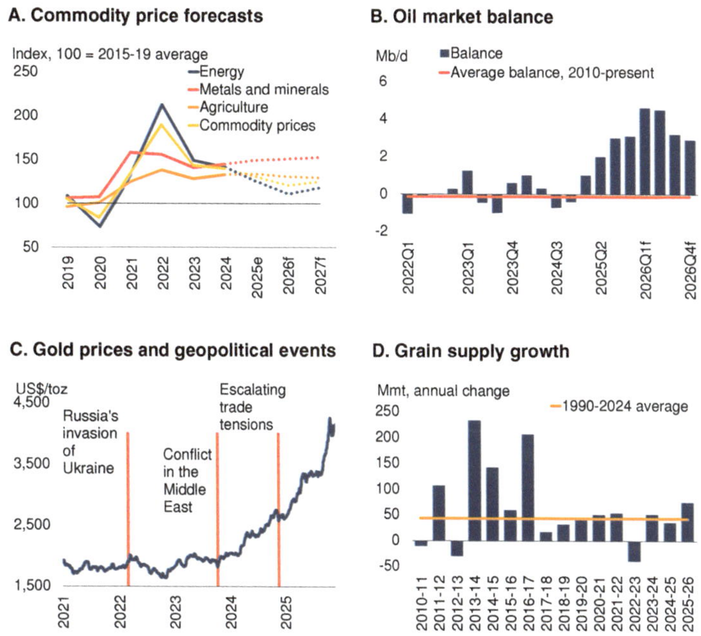

Sources: Bloomberg; International Energy Agency (IEA); U.S. Department of Agriculture; World Bank.

Note: e = estimate; f = forecast. Mb/d = million barrels a day; Mmt = million metric tons; toz = troy ounce.

A. Commodity prices line refers to the World Bank commodity price index, excluding precious metals. Dashed lines indicate forecasts.

B. Data from IEA's December 2025 edition of *Oil Market Report*. Data from 2025Q4 to 2026Q4 are IEA forecasts.

C. Panel shows seven-day moving average of daily gold prices. Last observation is December 17, 2025.

D. Year spans indicate crop seasons. Data updated as of December 17, 2025. Supply is the sum of beginning stocks and production and excludes imports. Grains include barley, maize, rice, oats, rye, sorghum, and wheat.

Continuing a trend from 2025, benchmark European and U.S. natural gas prices are projected to diverge over 2026 and 2027, with U.S. prices increasing by 11 percent and European prices falling by a similar magnitude. These trends reflect structural shifts in the global gas market: more U.S. natural gas is being exported as LNG, lifting demand and domestic prices, while Europe is benefiting from the greater global availability of LNG as it shifts away from piped gas from the Russian Federation. In addition, a sharp fall in China's LNG imports last year freed up supplies for other buyers.

Metal prices are projected to remain broadly stable in 2026–27, with growing demand for materials to support the green energy transition offsetting weak industrial activity, especially in China, which accounts for about half of global metal consumption. Recent trade measures have had a limited impact on metals prices so far but could gradually affect investment flows and add to price volatility, particularly for metals related to the shift toward low-carbon energy production. Gold prices surged by 42 percent in 2025 on strong investor demand, continued central bank purchases, and safe-haven inflows amid elevated geopolitical tensions and policy uncertainty (refer to figure 1.4.C). These same factors are expected to sustain markedly high gold prices over the next two years, albeit with central bank purchases likely to moderate.

After remaining broadly stable in 2025, agricultural prices are expected to decline modestly in 2026, then ease further in 2027. Food prices are forecast to stay largely stable in 2026–27 as supply growth converges toward long-term trends (refer to figure 1.4.D). Beverage prices—particularly cocoa and coffee—are projected to ease in 2026–27, from their weather-driven record highs in 2025, but remain at historically elevated levels.

Global inflation

Despite remaining above pre-pandemic norms, global inflation has continued to trend closer to central bank targets, albeit with notable heterogeneity across and within country groups. Global headline inflation edged up last year, to an estimated 3.2 percent, reflecting a pickup in some advanced economies, while it generally moderated in EMDEs. Global core inflation eased gradually, reflecting slowing wage growth as labor demand softened, though differences across economies remained significant, particularly in the evolution of goods prices. Goods price inflation rose modestly in advanced economies in 2025, and more so in the United States where higher tariffs came into effect. In contrast, goods inflation declined in many EMDEs as demand for tradables eased following intensive stock-building earlier in the year.

Overall, the impact of tariffs on goods price inflation, particularly in the United States, has so far been more limited than initially anticipated (Cavallo, Llamas, and Vazquez 2025). Delays in tariff increases allowed firms to build inventories at lower tariff levels, postponing the pass-through to inflation. Moreover, U.S. firms partly absorbed costs through lower profit margins and, in some cases, reoriented supply chains toward countries with preferential trade agreements. Nevertheless, U.S. goods prices have broken away from the previously subdued inflationary trend, picking up since mid-2025. Both imported and domestically produced U.S. consumer goods prices have risen, the latter likely reflecting downstream price spillovers in supply chains and reduced competition from imports (refer to figure 1.5.A). In contrast, foreign suppliers likely have not absorbed a meaningful share of tariff costs, as indicated by the overall stability of U.S. manufacturing import prices, which would otherwise have had to decline substantially to offset the sharp rise in tariffs (refer to figure 1.5.B).

Services price inflation continued to outpace goods inflation last year, though it has eased alongside weakening labor markets. The adoption of new AI-related technologies in some service companies appears to have boosted productivity, suggesting the potential for further reduction in price pressures, particularly in advanced economies (Brynjolfsson, Li, and Raymond 2023; Gibson 2024; Noy and Zhang 2023).

Going forward, model-based inflation projections show global inflation in 2026 edging down to 2.6 percent, 0.3 percentage point lower than previously expected (refer to figure 1.5.C). However, the outlook remains uncertain because of the magnitude and scope of trade policy shifts. In the United States, the inflationary impact of tariffs is projected to peak in early 2026, as the pass-through of tariff increases reaches completion, while inflation in other advanced economies is anticipated to soften amid slowing activity and moderating external demand. Similarly, surveys of professional forecasters point to a moderation in advanced economy inflation this year amid subdued growth and weakening labor markets (refer to figure 1.5.D). In EMDEs, inflation is expected to edge down further in 2026, as labor markets move closer into balance and wage growth gradually cools, particularly in many export-oriented industries.

Global financial developments

Global financial conditions eased over the second half of 2025, fueled by solid risk appetite, expectations of policy easing by the Federal Reserve, and the depreciation of the U.S. dollar. Equity markets have been buoyant globally (refer to figure 1.6.A). The S&P 500 index reached elevated valuations, reflecting expectations of future gains from AI investments and adoption. The optimism spilled over to equity markets in EMDEs, especially in China. Corporate bond spreads in advanced economies have remained compressed, accompanied by robust issuance in both the investment-grade and high-yield categories. Despite elevated policy uncertainty, financial market volatility has remained contained, except for short-lived spikes around tariff announcements in the second half of 2025. These developments have raised concerns of stretched valuations in equity and corporate bond markets, increasing their vulnerability to sudden price corrections.

Sovereign bond yield curves in advanced economies steepened, as the rise in term premia pushed long-term yields higher (refer to figure 1.6.B). Market participants remain concerned about the ability of these economies to rein in their public finances, and higher borrowing costs have put further pressure on government debt levels. In the United States, policy rate cuts due to the softening labor market added to the easing of financial conditions and pushed the yield curve lower, impacting short-term yields and, to a lesser extent, longer-term yields.

Easier financial conditions in global markets, underpinned by expectations of looser monetary policy in the United States, have allowed many central banks in EMDEs to leave policy rates unchanged. The depreciation of the U.S. dollar in 2025 and the resulting appreciation of EMDE currencies contributed to the moderation in inflation, which has provided room for EMDEs to respond to trade headwinds without being constrained by exchange rate pressures (refer to figure 1.6.C).

While advanced economy term premia have risen, EMDE sovereign bond spreads have generally narrowed. Taking advantage of this, higher-rated sovereigns expanded their issuance of foreign-currency debt (refer to figure 1.6.D). The depreciation of the U.S. dollar also delivered strong returns for investors in local-currency bonds of EMDEs. Robust demand for EMDE assets has resulted in strong portfolio inflows in recent months, concentrated in purchases of debt securities. The recipients of these flows have mainly been larger EMDEs with solid fundamen-

FIGURE 1.5 Global inflation

U.S. goods prices, including those for both imported and domestically produced consumer goods, began to rise following the introduction of tariffs. U.S. import prices have remained stable since April 2025, suggesting that foreign suppliers likely have not absorbed a meaningful share of tariff costs. Model-based projections show global inflation edging down to 2.6 percent in 2026, 0.3 percentage point lower than previously expected. Surveys of forecasters also indicate that inflation is expected to ease this year.

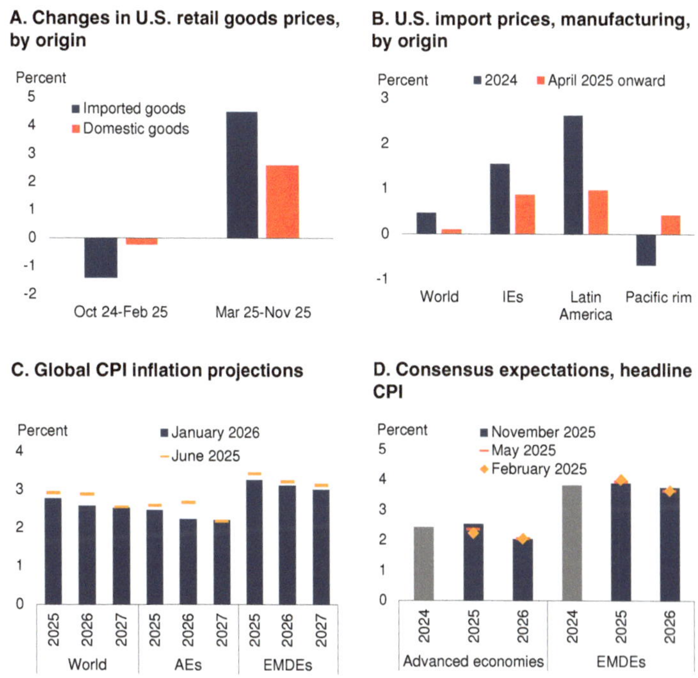

Sources: Cavallo, Llamas, and Vazquez (2025); Consensus Economics; Oxford Economics; U.S. Bureau of Labor Statistics; World Bank.

Note: AEs = advanced economies; CPI = consumer price index; EMDEs = emerging market and developing economies; IEs = industrial economies.

A. Panel shows the price changes of imported and domestic U.S. goods between October 2024 and February 2025 and between March 2025 and November 2025. Product-level retail price data collected from online stores of large U.S. retailers (Cavallo, Llamas, and Vazquez 2025). Last observation is November 1, 2025.

B. Panel shows the average monthly year-over-year percent change for the manufacturing sector, or manufacturing North American Industry Classification System (NAICS) indexes (31-33), over indicated periods for regions indicated. Refer to the U.S. Bureau of Labor Statistics for the regional composition. Import prices exclude tariffs.

C. Model-based GDP-weighted projections of consumer price inflation using Oxford Economics' Global Economic Model. Sample includes 69 countries, out of which 35 are EMDEs, and excludes Argentina and República Bolivariana de Venezuela.

D. Panel shows median headline CPI inflation expectations for 33 advanced economies and up to 50 EMDEs derived from Consensus Economics surveys in respective months of 2025.

FIGURE 1.6 Global financial developments

Financial conditions have eased globally, owing to strong risk appetite, as reflected in buoyant equity markets and low volatility. However, yield curves have steepened in advanced economies owing to higher term premia amid investor concerns about fiscal trajectories. The depreciation of the U.S. dollar in 2025 contributed to easier financial conditions in EMDEs. Higher-rated EMDE sovereigns responded to narrower bond spreads by increasing their issuance of foreign-currency-denominated debt.

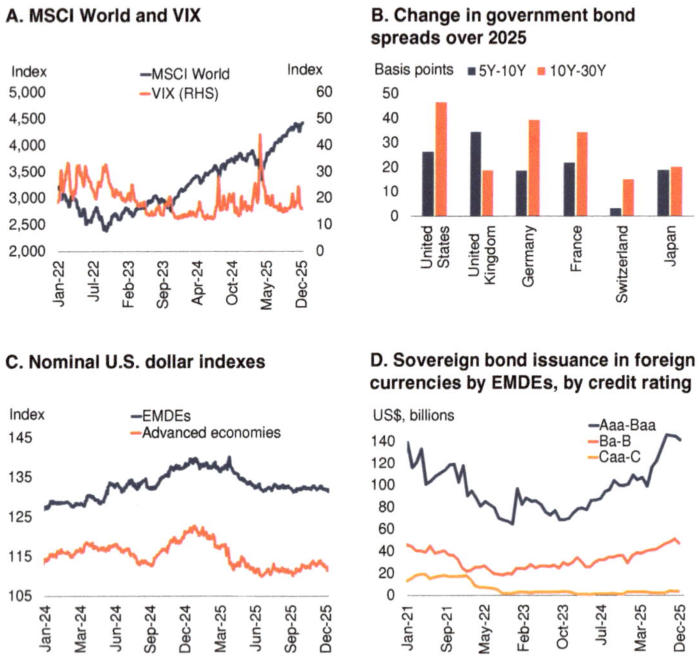

Sources: Bloomberg; Dealogic; Federal Reserve Economic Data (FRED) (database); Moody's Analytics; World Bank.

Note: EMDEs = emerging market and developing economies; MSCI World = Morgan Stanley Capital International World Index; RHS = right-hand scale; VIX = Chicago Board Options Exchange (CBOE) Volatility Index. Credit ratings are from Moody's Analytics.

A. Panel shows 5-day moving averages. The blue line represents the value of the MSCI World equity index. The red line represents the value of the VIX, which measures market expectations of near-term volatility implied by S&P 500 index options. Last observation is December 2025.

B. Changes in spreads between different maturities of sovereign bonds reflecting the slope of yield curves using 5-year, 10-year, and 30-year yields, calculated between January 1, 2025 and December 12, 2025.

C. Lines represent a trade-weighted average of the foreign exchange value of the U.S. dollar against 7 advanced economies (red) and 19 emerging market (blue) economies, as defined by the Federal Reserve Board. A higher value indicates an appreciation of the U.S. dollar. Last observation is December 12, 2025.

D. Sovereign bond issuance in U.S. dollars, euros, pounds sterling, Japanese yen, or Swiss francs by 58 EMDEs shown as 12-month rolling sums. Last observation is December 2025.

tals and sound policy frameworks, suggesting that investors have been selective in taking on risk. While the accumulation of debt by large EMDEs and the associated expansion in output can lead to positive growth spillovers for other EMDEs, it can also exacerbate existing debt vulnerabilities, especially since borrowing costs remain elevated (World Bank 2025a).

Major economies: Recent developments and outlook

Advanced economies

Growth in advanced economies in 2025 remained resilient to the escalation in trade tensions and rise in policy uncertainty, with the immediate drag of these factors proving less pronounced than anticipated in June. Trade policy changes were less disruptive than expected owing to front-loading of traded goods ahead of tariff increases; delayed tariff implementation; successful efforts by businesses to pivot their trade to jurisdictions covered by existing lower-tariff agreements; expanded use of tariff mitigation techniques such as bonded warehouses; and limited and delayed pass-through of tariff costs to consumers. In addition, sharply higher investment in AI-related equipment and structures helped support growth last year in the United States.

Going forward, the outlook for advanced economies is expected to be increasingly dampened by the impact of earlier tariff hikes and is susceptible to further shifts in trade and fiscal policies and increases in policy uncertainty. Growth is forecast to average 1.6 percent this year, with a slight firming in U.S. activity accompanied by deceleration in other major advanced economies. Growth is projected to remain stable in 2027, as a slight deceleration in the United States is countered by a pickup in the euro area, aided by additional defense spending in some large European economies.

The aggregate advanced economy forecast reflects offsetting forces. On the one hand, a marked trade slowdown this year is expected to weigh on net exports outside of the United States as front-loading fades and trade restrictions and uncertainty curb domestic demand. On the other, more accommodative monetary and fiscal policies are set to support activity over the forecast horizon. In particular, tax cut extensions (in the United States) and increases in public investment (in some large euro area economies) are expected to help offset trade-related headwinds, albeit to varying degrees.

In the **United States**, activity slowed in 2025 to an estimated 2.1 percent amid a surge in spending on imported goods early in the year due to front-loading, and a slowdown in consumer spending. In addition, growth was further dampened by the federal government shutdown in the last quarter. Consumer sentiment weakened amid persistent inflation, partly on account of modest but growing tariff pass-through. Confidence was further dampened by a sudden stall in net hiring in the second and third quarters of 2025 (refer to figure 1.7.A). This was partly driven by the reduced supply of labor, including the availability of immigrant workers, which is likely to have a prolonged effect on labor force dynamics (CBO 2025a). In contrast, business investment surged in 2025, significantly boosting growth, mostly as new technologies led to scaling up of investment in technology equipment and intellectual property, such as software, and as firms front-loaded imports of machinery and equipment in anticipation of tariffs (refer to figure 1.7.B).

U.S. growth is projected to average 2.2 percent in 2026. On the one hand, the impact of elevated tariffs is set to increasingly weigh on consumption and investment. On the other, the extension of tax breaks and other measures adopted in the U.S. budget in mid-2025, incorporated in the current projection, and the reopening of the federal government at the end of last year are anticipated to support growth in 2026 (CBO 2025b; 2025c). In 2027, U.S. growth is expected to ease to 1.9 percent, slightly below estimates of potential growth, as the drag from tariffs and policy uncertainty persists, along with the waning boost from past monetary easing and budget measures.

Following two years of anemic activity, growth in the **euro area** picked up to an estimated 1.4 percent in 2025, surprising to the upside. The upward revision to growth last year reflects the front-loading of exports, especially from Ireland to the United States, and postponement of U.S. tariffs, in addition to stronger-than-expected growth in domestic demand.

With the boost from front-loading unwinding, and the adverse impact from higher U.S. tariffs on the demand for European exports intensifying, growth is projected to slow in 2026, to 0.9 percent (refer to figure 1.7.C). Exports are expected to be further dampened by losses in price competitiveness due to higher energy prices following Russia's invasion of Ukraine and, to some degree, the recent appreciation of the euro. Sluggish export growth is anticipated to be partly offset by steady private consumption and investment, aided by less restrictive financial conditions and past monetary policy easing. Private consumption is also expected to be supported by stable real wage growth amid moderating inflation.

Growth in the euro area is forecast to firm to 1.2 percent in 2027, underpinned by an improvement in exports and investment as uncertainty fades and confidence rises. Investment is also expected to benefit from additional public capital expenditure and private sector incentive schemes related to defense and infrastructure investments in some large economies.[1] However, in many euro area member countries, fiscal policy is constrained by the expiration of grant financing under NextGenerationEU and the need for adjustment to meet EU fiscal sustainability rules, with some economies cutting spending to non-defense categories and increasing social security contributions and taxes.

In **Japan**, growth is estimated to have firmed to 1.3 percent in 2025 reflecting a rebound in consumption and capital spending, along with the front-loading of exports. Growth is forecast to decelerate to 0.8 percent in 2026 as the effects of front-loading fade and external demand slows, and then remain at the same pace in 2027 as consumption and investment maintain momentum despite tighter monetary policy.

China

Growth in China edged down to an estimated 4.9 percent in 2025, 0.4 percentage point above June forecasts. This upward revision reflects additional fiscal support and stronger-than-expected exports.

[1] Germany's fiscal package includes infrastructure projects and defense spending, but its growth impact will likely be muted by structural bottlenecks and the mix of expenditures, which also covers current budget items. Defense multipliers are uncertain and are typically lower in EU countries as a result of small domestic defense industries and high import leakage (Olejnik and Kuna 2025).

FIGURE 1.7 Major economies: Recent developments and outlook

In the United States, net hiring stalled in the second and third quarters of 2025 alongside escalating trade tensions and reduced immigration. In contrast, U.S. business investment remained robust, providing a significant boost to U.S. growth in 2025. This partly reflected the ongoing adoption of new technologies, which led to a scaling up of investment in AI-related intellectual property, such as software, and in equipment and infrastructure. In the euro area, growth is set to slow this year due to the drag from trade tensions and then gradually firm as investment and exports recover. Export growth in China remained resilient despite higher tariffs, partly on account of increased shipments to non-U.S. destinations and lower exposure to the United States.

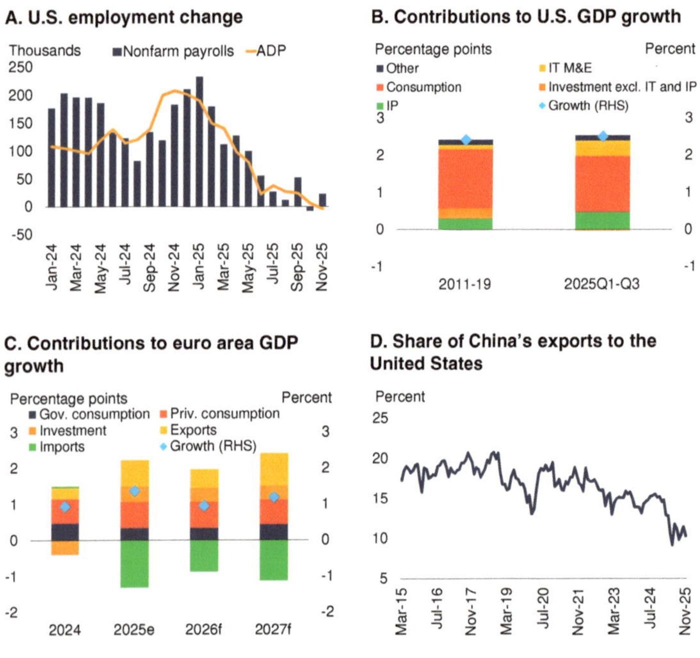

Sources: ADP, Inc.; Federal Reserve Economic Data (FRED; database); Haver Analytics; U.S. Bureau of Economic Analysis; U.S. Bureau of Labor Statistics; World Bank.

Note: e = estimate; f = forecast. excl. = excluding; Gov. = government; IP = intellectual property investment; IT = information technology (part of M&E); M&E = machinery and equipment; Priv. = private; RHS = right-hand scale.

A. Panel shows 3-month moving average changes in nonfarm payrolls and ADP, Inc. private employment.

B. Panel shows average contributions to seasonally adjusted annualized rate of quarterly growth in GDP from selected components. Investment refers to private non-residential fixed investment.

C. Panel shows the annual real GDP growth contribution for each expenditure-side component. Discrepancies between GDP growth and the sum of its components reflect inventories and residuals.

D. Last observation is November 2025.

Consumption was buoyed by fiscal stimulus through the goods trade-in program and other consumer subsidies. Investment growth slowed, however, largely driven by a contraction in real estate investment as the property sector softened further. Export growth was resilient as a result of front-loading earlier in the year and increased shipments to non-U.S. markets along with lower exposure to the United States (refer to figure 1.7.D). Monetary policy continued to be accommodative as inflation remained low, reflecting soft domestic demand.

Growth in 2026 is expected to slow to 4.4 percent as subdued consumer confidence, the prolonged property sector downturn, and a softer labor market are envisaged to weigh on consumption and investment. Accommodative monetary and fiscal policies are expected to provide a partial offset but are likely to be constrained by rising debt levels. However, relative to the June projections, the forecast for this year is 0.4 percentage point higher, owing to further fiscal stimulus, continued resilience of exports, and improved investor sentiment due to relatively more stable trade policy and partial tariff relief. In 2027, growth is projected to ease further to 4.2 percent as structural challenges such as declining productivity growth, high debt levels, and demographic headwinds are expected to continue to weigh on potential growth.

Emerging market and developing economies

After stronger-than-expected activity last year driven by trade front-loading, EMDE growth is set to slow in 2026 as the payback from front-loading, trade restrictions, and subdued confidence outweigh the benefits of more supportive financial conditions. Excluding China, growth is projected to hold at 3.7 percent. Next year, growth in EMDEs is forecast to edge up as an ongoing deceleration in China, mainly reflecting structural challenges, is more than offset by an upswing in other EMDEs, where growth is projected to rise to 4 percent. This strengthening in EMDEs excluding China is anticipated to be broad based across investment, consumption, and trade, with some economies lifted by firmer industrial commodity prices. Nevertheless, to sustainably lift living standards, EMDEs will need to mobilize new drivers of investment and job creation while rebuilding policy space.

Recent developments

Growth across EMDEs in 2025 was stronger than expected. Trade, especially exports, performed better than anticipated despite higher tariffs and

FIGURE 1.8 Recent developments in emerging market and developing economies

Growth in EMDEs in 2025 was generally resilient despite various global headwinds, with activity sustained by solid service sector momentum. EMDE exports benefited from the front-loading of trade ahead of U.S. tariffs and the surge in investment in digital and AI-related equipment, particularly in the United States. Manufacturing output growth slowed alongside goods trade growth in the second half of 2025, with forward-looking indicators of goods exports pointing to weaker trade activity in 2026, especially as the boost from front-loading fades.

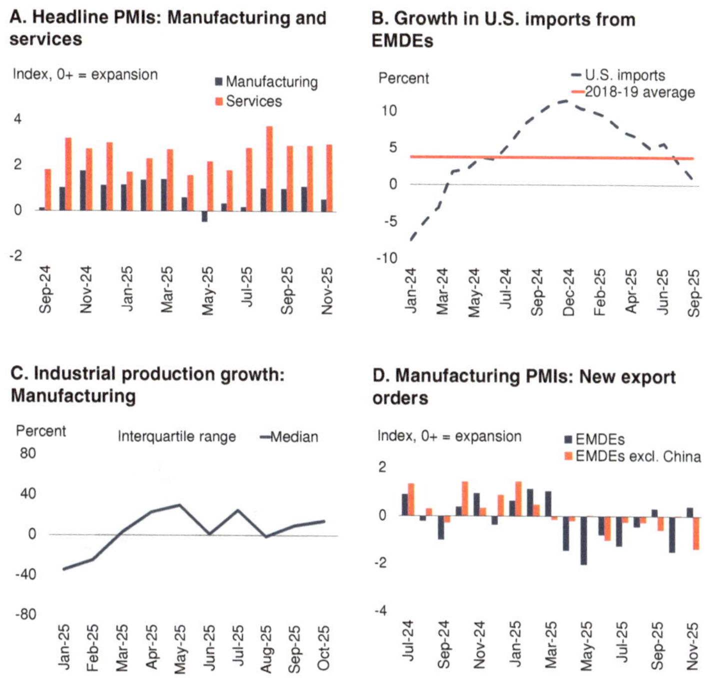

Sources: Haver Analytics; United States International Trade Commission (USITC); World Bank.
Note: EMDEs = emerging market and developing economies; excl. = excluding; PMI = purchasing managers' index.
A.D. Panel shows the 2024 GDP-weighted average of PMI for up to 17 EMDEs. PMI scores above (below) zero indicate expansion (contraction). Monthly scores are centered on 50, the expansionary threshold. Last observation is November 2025.
B. Year-over-year growth of import values of physical arrivals of merchandise from foreign countries in U.S. dollars for up to 153 EMDEs. Dashed line shows 3-month moving average of the median, and red line shows the average of the 2018-19 median for up to 152 EMDEs. Last observation is September 2025.
C. Panel shows the median of the 3-month annualized rate of growth of manufacturing industrial production, non-seasonally adjusted, for 34 EMDEs. Shaded area shows the interquartile range. Last observation is October 2025.

elevated uncertainty, while services activity remained resilient (refer to figure 1.8.A). Overall, in 2025, EMDEs grew at an estimated pace of 4.2 percent, compared with June forecasts of 3.9 percent (refer to box 1.2 and chapter 2 for regional outlooks).

In the first half of 2025, activity surprised to the upside amid solid external demand related to the front-loading of trade ahead of the implementation of tariffs, with robust export activity persisting in the second half of 2025 in some regions, particularly in East Asia and Pacific (EAP; refer to figure 1.8.B). The strength in export growth also reflected robust demand for semiconductor exports from several EMDEs in EAP, driven by surging investment in digital and AI-related equipment, especially in the United States.

Despite strength in exports in some regions, manufacturing output growth slowed in the second half of last year across many EMDEs, including in several economies with sizable manufacturing sectors (refer to figure 1.8.C). Outside of electronics, forward-looking indicators of goods trade and manufacturing activity, such as new export orders PMIs, have remained in contractionary territory in recent months, pointing to weaker goods trade growth ahead (refer to figure 1.8.D).

In contrast, service sector activity remained resilient across EMDEs throughout 2025, aided by easing global financial conditions, in part related to a depreciation of the U.S. dollar, which supported steady credit growth and consumer confidence. At the same time, lower energy prices provided a tailwind for activity in some energy-importing EMDEs. In the last quarter of 2025, indicators of new services sector activity remained robust, following an upswing in some large EMDEs mid-year, while both wage and retail sales growth continued at a broadly solid pace.

Reliance on primary commodity exports remained a source of divergence across EMDEs in 2025, with slower growth in some commodity exporters, and generally more solid conditions across commodity importers. Nevertheless, in the second half of 2025, activity firmed in oil-exporting EMDEs after OPEC+ agreed to increase oil output volumes. Across LICs, growth increased to an estimated 5 percent in 2025, driven by better-than-expected outturns in major LICs facing fragile and conflict-affected situations.

EMDE outlook

The outlook for EMDEs continues to be shaped in part by global trade policy developments, as external demand slows following the front-loading

BOX 1.2 Regional perspectives: Outlook and risks

Emerging market and developing economy (EMDE) regions proved more resilient to last year's trade tensions than expected, with trade supported by the temporary front-loading of exports and with domestic demand underpinned by easier global financial conditions. Nevertheless, prospects over 2026–27 are uneven across regions and remain generally subdued amid a less favorable global trade environment. The challenge of generating sufficient job opportunities for the 1.2 billion young people who will reach working age in EMDE regions by 2035 is set to intensify, particularly in regions where working-age populations continue to rise rapidly. Risks to the outlook remain tilted to the downside, including those from renewed trade frictions and policy uncertainty, tighter global financial conditions, elevated fiscal vulnerabilities, rising geopolitical tensions and conflict, and climate- and public-health-related shocks.

Introduction

Global economic conditions remain challenging amid ongoing trade tensions, but trade agreements between major economies, together with easier global financial conditions, have brought some relief in recent months. In 2026–27, growth is projected to diverge across EMDE regions. In EAP, growth is set to moderate over the forecast horizon, whereas in SAR it is expected to decelerate this year before picking up in 2027 as trade flows improve. Growth in ECA and LAC is forecast to remain the weakest among the regions this year, with activity relatively steady before improving in 2027. In contrast, growth is anticipated to firm in MNA and SSA over the forecast horizon. Yet, in most regions, projected growth remains slower than during 2000–19 and insufficient to support adequate job creation or sustained convergence in real per capita incomes with advanced economies. Risks to the growth outlook remain tilted to the downside.

Against this background, this box considers two questions:

- What are the cross-regional differences in the outlook for growth?
- What are the key risks to the outlook for EMDE regions?

Outlook

Growth trends in 2026–27 are set to diverge across EMDE regions. Growth over the forecast horizon is expected to slow in EAP, in tandem with China's growth trajectory; it is projected to decelerate in 2026 in SAR, largely owing to the increase in tariffs, and then rebound in 2027 as exports recover. In ECA and LAC, growth is expected to remain relatively steady this year before rising in 2027, as headwinds from elevated trade tensions and subdued external demand ease. Growth in both regions is anticipated to remain the lowest among the six regions, partly because of persistent structural constraints. In MNA and SSA, growth in 2026–27 is forecast to rise amid oil production increases, ongoing reforms in some large economies, solid domestic investment growth, a continued easing of inflation, and security improvements in several countries affected by fragility and conflict (refer to chapter 2). In most regions, growth is set to stay below 2000–19 averages, even as growth expectations have improved since June due partly to lower U.S. tariffs assumptions in some regions (refer to figures B1.2.1.A, B1.2.1.B, and B1.2.2.A; refer to chapter 1).

In EAP, the moderation in growth over 2026–27 partly reflects increased trade barriers, but it is also driven by the slowdown in China. In China, subdued consumer confidence, a prolonged property sector downturn, and a softer labor market are compounding the structural deceleration resulting from slowing productivity growth, high debt, and population aging. Excluding China, growth in the region is projected to moderate this year before picking up in 2027, reflecting the unwinding of front-loading, followed by a recovery in global trade, along with stronger investment growth in some countries owing to domestic policy support. In SAR, the projected slowdown in 2026 mainly reflects the impact of increased U.S. tariffs on India's goods exports. Growth in SAR is then set to rebound in 2027, as exports improve and domestic demand firms, aided by strong services activity as the effects of political uncertainty dissipate in several economies.

In ECA and LAC, growth is expected to stabilize somewhat in 2026 before improving in 2027, with both regions exposed to elevated trade tensions and uncertainty, albeit to differing degrees. In ECA, growth this year is set to be dampened by weak external

Note: This box was prepared by Shijie Shi and Collette Wheeler.

BOX 1.2 Regional perspectives: Outlook and risks (*continued*)

FIGURE B1.2.1 Regional outlooks

Growth prospects for 2026–27 differ across EMDE regions. Growth in East Asia and Pacific (EAP) is projected to slow further, mainly reflecting the outlook for China. In South Asia (SAR), growth is expected to moderate this year amid higher U.S. tariffs and then rebound in 2027 as exports recover. Growth in Europe and Central Asia (ECA) and Latin America and the Caribbean (LAC) is forecast to edge up, but only modestly, amid weak external demand and structural constraints. Growth in the Middle East, North Africa, Afghanistan and Pakistan (MNA) and Sub-Saharan Africa (SSA) is expected to strengthen, with these regions benefiting from rising oil production and improved security conditions, respectively. In many regions, growth is likely to remain slower than 2000–19 averages, even as growth expectations have increased since June. Whereas EAP and SAR are expected to make further meaningful progress in per capita income catch-up with advanced economies, other regions are expected to experience more limited progress—particularly SSA, where rates of extreme poverty are the highest.

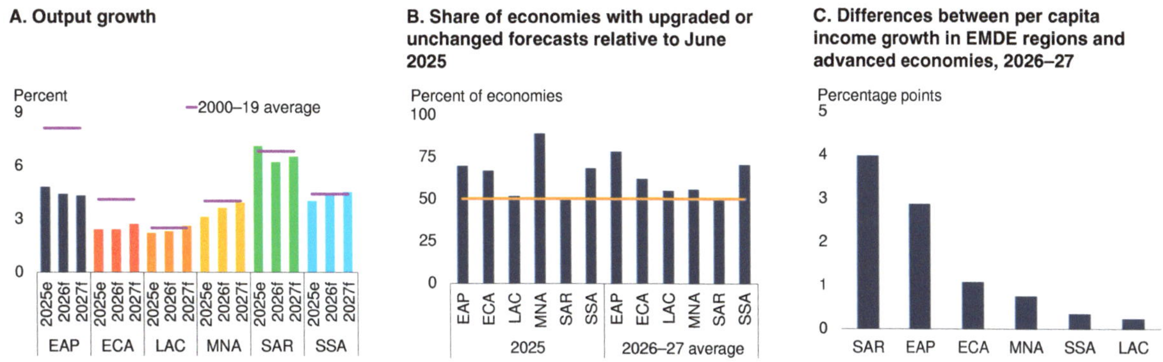

Sources: UN World Population Prospects; World Bank.

Note: e = estimate; f = forecast. EAP = East Asia and Pacific; ECA = Europe and Central Asia; EMDE = emerging market and developing economy; LAC = Latin America and the Caribbean; MNA = Middle East, North Africa, Afghanistan and Pakistan; SAR = South Asia; SSA = Sub-Saharan Africa.

A. Aggregated growth rates are calculated using GDP weights at average 2010–19 prices and market exchange rates. The purple lines refer to period averages of regional growth rates.

B. Share of countries within each country group with forecast upgrades or no forecast changes for 2025 and 2026–27, compared with the June 2025 edition of the *Global Economic Prospects* report. Orange line indicates 50 percent.

C. Bars represent the annual average GDP per capita growth in EMDE regions minus the annual average GDP per capita growth in advanced economies, expressed in percentage points.

demand from the euro area and elevated trade policy uncertainty. These drags are expected to be partly offset by solid domestic demand, underpinned by easing inflationary pressures, improving financial conditions, and increased defense spending and funding from the European Union. In contrast, domestic demand is projected to remain sluggish in 2026 in LAC, somewhat countering the positive effect of easing financing conditions. Growth is anticipated to firm in LAC in 2027, as trade flows recover and domestic demand improves, with the latter aided by declines in monetary policy rates in some large economies.

Growth is expected to rise over the forecast horizon in MNA and SSA, owing to commodity-driven developments and idiosyncratic factors. In MNA, the acceleration is largely accounted for by oil exporters, with increasing oil production set to outweigh the impact of lower oil prices this year, alongside a steady expansion in non-oil activity. Growth in MNA is also expected to benefit from recovering export growth and strengthening investment growth. In SSA, the projected pick-up over 2026–27 assumes that security improves in several fragile and conflict-affected situations (FCS) and that ongoing reforms in some large economies, solid domestic investment growth, and continued easing of inflation support activity. Ongoing reforms should also help support growth in SSA, contributing to solid private investment and FDI inflows.

Relative to June projections, growth in 2026 is revised up for EAP and SSA, slightly revised down for LAC, ECA and MNA, and a bit more notably for SAR. The upgrade for EAP reflects a smaller-than-expected impact of higher trade barriers, as well as domestic policy support in some economies (refer to chapter 2). The

BOX 1.2 Regional perspectives: Outlook and risks (*continued*)

upward revision for SSA is largely due to upgrades in its largest economies—particularly Nigeria, where continued steady expansion in services and a rebound in agricultural output are set to support activity, and South Africa, where activity is expected to be underpinned by private consumption and investment. In both countries, ongoing reforms in the business environment and the public sector are expected to continue supporting growth.

The downward revision to growth in ECA in 2026 is accounted for mainly by the Russian Federation. This reflects weaker-than-expected activity in late 2025 and its negative carry-over effect on 2026, more restrictive credit conditions, and a tighter labor market. For MNA, the downgrade for 2026 largely reflects a larger-than-expected increase in oil production by member countries of the Organization of the Petroleum Exporting Countries and other affiliated oil producers (OPEC+) in 2025, suggesting less room for expansion in 2026–27. The downward revision for SAR is primarily due to higher U.S. tariffs than previously assumed.

Trade prospects across EMDE regions continue to be shaped by shifts in trade policy, with export growth constrained by higher tariffs, elevated uncertainty, and subdued global growth. In EAP, export growth is projected to slow in 2026, as earlier front-loading unwinds and as uncertainty continues around rules-of-origin and tariff exemptions. In ECA, export growth is expected to remain constrained by weak euro area growth. In LAC, increased tariffs are likely to weigh on export growth, while stronger export growth to other trading partners and elevated metal and food prices are expected to partially offset this effect.

In MNA, oil exports are projected to rise in member countries of the Gulf Cooperation Council (GCC) as OPEC+ production cuts are phased out, with activity further supported by resilient non-oil goods and services exports. However, oil exports are anticipated to remain subdued in non-GCC oil exporters. In SAR, strong growth of services exports is expected to continue, but high U.S. tariffs are set to dampen India's goods exports and weigh on overall growth. In SSA, limited exposure to U.S. markets is likely to limit the adverse impact of higher tariffs. However, unless extended, the expiration of United States' African Growth and Opportunity Act (AGOA) in late 2025 will significantly affect countries reliant on textiles and vehicles, even as continued African Continental Free Trade Area (AfCFTA) implementation deepens regional trade integration.

While inflation has moderated in some EMDE regions, it has been more persistent in others. In EAP and SAR, headline and core inflation have generally eased to within or below central bank targets, supported by moderating food and energy prices. By contrast, inflation in ECA has proved more persistent, with firm wage growth, rising utility costs, and food price pressures keeping inflation above official targets in several economies. Inflation is more mixed in LAC, MNA, and SSA. In LAC, inflation has eased across much of the region but is anticipated to remain near the upper end of central bank target bands in some countries. In MNA, core inflation remains high in oil-importing economies but moderate in oil exporters. In SSA, headline inflation has generally eased with food prices falling on the back of strong harvests, but disinflation has recently slowed and core inflation has picked up for the first time in two years.

Monetary policy prospects diverge across EMDE regions, reflecting differences in the inflation outlook. In EAP and SAR, moderating inflation has allowed central banks to either maintain accommodative stances (EAP) or begin gradual easing (SAR). In contrast, in ECA, above-target inflation in many economies limits the scope for monetary easing. In LAC, shifts in the stance of monetary policy are likely to be mixed, with modest monetary easing expected in the largest economies, but some increases in real policy rates elsewhere. In MNA, inflation remains contained in GCC economies, where monetary policies are generally tied to U.S. policy through the peg to the U.S. dollar. By contrast, rising inflationary pressures in some MNA non-GCC oil exporters point to continued tightening, while in oil importers monetary policies are set to ease as inflation moderates. In SSA, the recent slowing of disinflation, with core inflation remaining firm, has led most central banks to pause easing.

Fiscal positions differ across EMDE regions. In MNA, GCC countries' fiscal deficits—which are already small—are expected to narrow further as higher oil

BOX 1.2 Regional perspectives: Outlook and risks (*continued*)

output offsets lower prices, while non-GCC oil exporters and oil importers are anticipated to continue to face large deficits and spending pressures. In SAR, India's fiscal deficit is expected to be gradually reduced through consolidation policies, while Bangladesh is undertaking reforms to strengthen revenues amid tight fiscal constraints. In ECA, fiscal consolidation is expected to be modest, partly driven by higher defense expenditures in some countries. In LAC, fiscal policies are generally constrained by rising debt burdens and high borrowing costs, with broadly contractionary policy stances anticipated through 2026–27. Many countries in SSA are undergoing fiscal consolidation too, with public finances under pressure from high interest burdens, weakening commodity prices, and declining aid flows. The fiscal stance is broadly neutral in EAP, but expansionary in China.

Convergence of real per capita incomes toward advanced economy levels is projected for 2026–27 in all regions but at widely differing paces (refer to figure B1.2.1.C). In SAR, still-rapid growth led by India is expected to allow further significant convergence, accompanied by a notable drop in poverty rates. Despite China's growth slowdown, rapid convergence is expected to continue in EAP. In ECA and LAC, more modest economic growth implies little progress in convergence with advanced economies, leaving many countries at risk of stagnation in real per capita incomes. In MNA, stronger growth in oil exporters indicates some prospective improvement, while fragile recoveries elsewhere will limit convergence for the region as a whole. In SSA, the region with the lowest per capita incomes, convergence with advanced-economy living standards is expected to stagnate.

Job creation remains a critical priority in the six regions. With 1.2 billion young people reaching working age (ages 15–64) in the six EMDE regions by 2035, economies have an opportunity to seize a demographic dividend and reduce extreme poverty. The challenge of creating sufficient jobs differs among the regions, however. In SSA, young people entering the labor market are driving the region's largest increase in its working-age population, which will require strong economic growth to ensure solid job creation. In SAR, most jobs are in low-skill agriculture and manual work, leaving the workforce only moderately exposed to artificial intelligence (AI). Highly skilled workers are likely to benefit, while moderately educated younger workers are more vulnerable to automation. Yet, the share of working-age individuals in employment is among the lowest across the six regions. In MNA, youth unemployment remains high, and female participation in the labor force remains the lowest globally, largely because of restrictive barriers.

Elsewhere, EAP faces the largest cohort of youth entering labor markets among the six regions. Yet many economies are facing high youth unemployment. This reflects the region's attempts to transition from its historically successful model of export- and investment-led growth—facilitated by a large-scale shift of labor from agriculture into industry—to a new model of more consumption-led growth. In ECA, population aging, sluggish productivity growth, and stalled reforms are limiting competition and resource reallocation. Across the region, many young people do not participate in labor markets, discouraged by limited job opportunities and skill mismatches between education and labor market demand. Meanwhile, in LAC, entrepreneurship and job creation are constrained by barriers to the growth of firms, including from shallow financial markets and shortages of skilled workers (World Bank 2025c).

Overall, job creation remains an urgent priority across EMDE regions, with challenges including structural bottlenecks in labor markets, weak private sector dynamism, and demographic pressures stemming from both rapidly growing working-age populations and aging and declining populations. Creating a sufficient number of jobs will require policies to strengthen infrastructure—particularly in energy and digital projects—improve the business environment, foster private investment, enhance human capital, and promote inclusion, especially for women and youth.

Risks

Risks to the growth outlook remain tilted to the downside across all EMDE regions. Although measures of uncertainty have receded somewhat from the record-high levels reached in 2025, further increases in U.S. tariffs or other trade restrictions, or a re-escalation of trade tensions, could lower growth prospects across

BOX 1.2 Regional perspectives: Outlook and risks (*continued*)

FIGURE B1.2.2 Regional risks

Although U.S. tariff rates are currently lower, on average, for some regions than assumed in the June 2025 baseline, renewed increases in tariffs, other trade restrictions, trade tensions, or policy uncertainty could weigh substantially on growth. The ratio of net interest payments to government revenues has risen markedly, with the EMDE average reaching its highest share since 2003 and every region facing higher shares than in the 2010s, highlighting fiscal vulnerabilities and the risk that tighter global financial conditions could further constrain already-limited fiscal space. Moreover, uneven AI preparedness across regions could concentrate productivity gains in a handful of economies, exacerbating productivity and income disparities between advanced economies and EMDEs, and among EMDEs themselves.

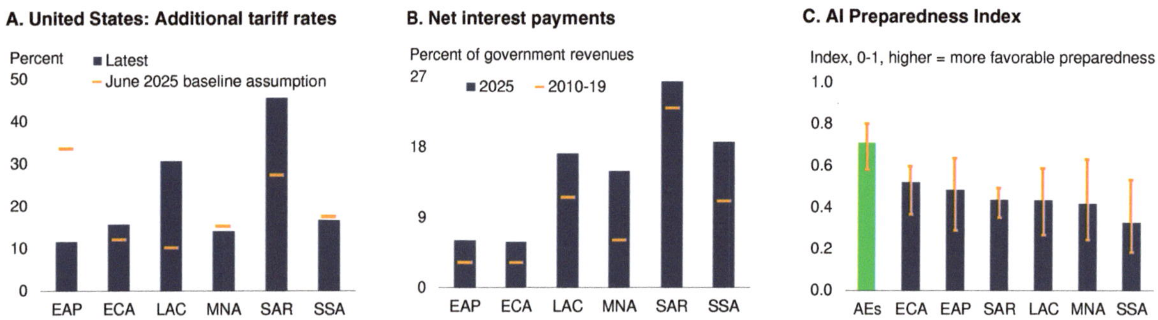

Sources: Cazzaniga et al. (2024); Kose et al. (2022); White House; World Economic Outlook (database); World Bank.

Note: AEs = advanced economies; AI = artificial intelligence; EAP = East Asia and Pacific; ECA = Europe and Central Asia; LAC = Latin America and the Caribbean; MNA = Middle East, North Africa, Afghanistan and Pakistan; SAR = South Asia; SSA = Sub-Saharan Africa.

A. Horizontal lines show the GDP-weighted averages of additional tariff rates specified in Annex I of Executive Order 14257 (issued April 2, 2025) and updated with subsequent modifications by the White House as of June 3, 2025. Bars show the GDP-weighted averages of additional tariff rates specified in Executive Order 14326 (issued July 31, 2025) and updated with subsequent modifications by the White House as of December 16, 2025.

B. Aggregates are computed as weighted averages, using government revenues in U.S. dollars as weights. Net interest payments are computed as differences between primary balances and overall fiscal balances. Data for 2025 are estimates.

C. Bars represent regional medians; whiskers show the minimum and maximum values within each country group. The index assesses the level of AI preparedness as of 2023 across 174 countries, covering four dimensions: digital infrastructure, human capital, technological innovation, and legal frameworks. Scores on the index range from 0 to 1, with higher values representing more favorable AI preparedness.

regions. The risk of financial stress also remains significant despite last year's easing in global financial conditions. Adverse shifts in risk appetite could trigger sharp market movements and lead to capital outflows and currency depreciations. Higher borrowing costs could add to fiscal pressures, especially given elevated debt levels. In several regions, the growth outlook hinges on assumed improvements in security conditions and reductions in violence and conflict; if such improvements do not materialize, growth could disappoint, especially in regions with a sizable number of fragile countries. All regions remain vulnerable to climate change-related extreme weather events and public health emergencies, especially in economies with limited buffers to respond.

A renewed escalation of trade tensions and policy uncertainty could weigh markedly on exports and investment. Recent increases in U.S. tariffs on imports from some large EMDEs have somewhat exceeded June expectations (refer to figure B1.2.2.A). A further escalation—for example, through the 2026 review of the United States–Mexico–Canada Agreement (USMCA)—could especially hit Mexico and Central America. Slower-than-expected growth in the United States would dampen exports in LAC, while weaker demand from China would reduce commodity revenues in regions with large commodity exporters, including ECA, LAC, MNA, and SSA.

Elevated government debt burdens and widening fiscal deficits increase the risk of upward pressure on borrowing costs, which have risen in recent years and remain high in regions such as LAC, SAR, and SSA (refer to figure B1.2.2.B). If financial conditions deteriorate, the combination of higher long-term interest rates, declining development aid, and already-narrow fiscal space could worsen debt sustainability

BOX 1.2 Regional perspectives: Outlook and risks (*continued*)

dynamics and amplify the risk of fiscal crises. Countries with high external financing needs are particularly vulnerable to tighter-than-expected global financial conditions. Economies heavily reliant on remittances face added risks from tighter financial conditions, reduced migration, or softer growth in host countries, which could reduce these inflows. The resulting pressures could weaken current account positions, strain exchange rates, slow consumption growth, and heighten fiscal and debt vulnerabilities.

Last year's appreciations of EMDE currencies against the U.S. dollar have helped support investor appetite, reduce existing dollar-denominated debt burdens, and dampen imported inflation. At the same time, however, these appreciations, if sustained, could weigh on the international competitiveness of the countries concerned. If they reverse sharply, several economies could experience renewed inflationary pressures and heightened concerns about debt sustainability.

An abrupt decline in risk appetite could lead to a tightening of global financial conditions relative to baseline assumptions. This could result in disorderly market shifts, capital outflows from EMDEs, and currency depreciations. Particularly in economies with inadequate macroprudential oversight, such shifts could destabilize financial systems. More-persistent-than-expected inflation could prompt major central banks to tighten monetary policies, dampening growth.

Several regions continue to experience varying degrees of violence, marked by high insecurity and conflict. A key downside risk to the growth outlook—given the baseline assumption that conflicts in several regions, especially MNA and SSA, de-escalate—is the possibility that they persist, intensify, or broaden. Given the large human and economic losses caused by armed conflict, this could substantially set back growth and the convergence of real per capita incomes with advanced economies. Regions where major armed conflicts persist, including ECA, MNA, and SSA, are particularly vulnerable to this risk. In EAP, recent political turmoil and social unrest in some economies illustrate how such instability can also put growth at risk, including by eroding investor and consumer confidence and discouraging tourism.

The rising trend in global temperatures and associated increase in the frequency of extreme weather events—such as droughts (ECA, MNA, SAR, SSA) and flooding (EAP, ECA, LAC, MNA, SAR, SSA)—pose risks to agricultural output, food security, external balances, and fiscal sustainability. The potential emergence of new public health crises remains another vulnerability, particularly for EMDEs with limited capacity to respond, including those in SSA. These constraints stem from weak health care systems, reduced foreign aid flows, limited fiscal resources, elevated conflict and violence, and often weak governance.

An upside risk to the growth outlook in all EMDE regions is greater-than-assumed benefits from the development and deployment of AI. This could raise productivity growth globally, presenting opportunities for EMDEs (refer to figure B1.2.2.C). Faster AI adoption—especially in some economies in EAP, ECA, and SAR with supportive regulatory frameworks, a well-equipped and skilled workforce, and strong investment in digital infrastructure—could boost productivity growth, spur innovation, and enable firms to scale up high-value activities (IMF 2025a).

However, the benefits from AI deployment are likely to be uneven: most EMDEs, including those in SSA, lag advanced economies in digital infrastructure, human capital, education and training, and legal frameworks, limiting their capacity to capture the productivity gains from AI. At the same time, accelerated automation could displace workers in labor-intensive sectors and exacerbate inequality in the absence of policies to facilitate reskilling and labor market transitions (World Bank 2025d). Overall, while AI offers significant long-term potential to boost growth, it also poses structural risks that could widen productivity and income gaps between advanced economies and EMDEs, and among EMDEs themselves, if adoption remains substantially uneven.

FIGURE 1.9 Outlook for emerging market and developing economies

Growth in EMDEs excluding China is forecast to remain steady at 3.7 percent in 2026 as the effects of increased trade restrictions are offset by easing financial conditions. In 2027, activity is expected to accelerate to 4 percent amid a recovery in trade and manufacturing, as well as slightly firmer prices for some commodities. Benign financial conditions are envisaged to bolster domestic demand over 2026-27 across investment-grade-rated EMDEs, and rising oil production is also expected to support activity in some commodity-exporting EMDEs. In contrast, the payback from the front-loading of trade in 2025 will dampen both activity and net exports in commodity-importing EMDEs in 2026.

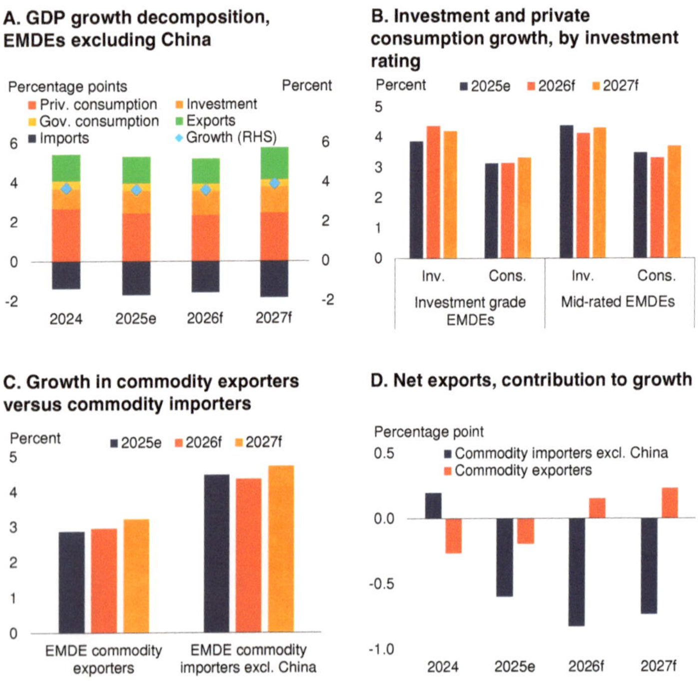

Sources: Moody's Analytics; World Bank.

Note: e = estimate; f = forecast. Cons. = consumption; EMDEs = emerging market and developing economies; excl. = excluding; Gov. = government; Inv. = investment; Priv. = private; RHS = right-hand scale.

A. Panel shows the contribution to annual real GDP growth by component. Discrepancies between GDP growth and the sum of its components reflect inventories and residuals, as well as a smaller sample size for component data due to availability. Headline GDP growth reflects table 1.1 data.

B. Panel shows the annual growth of investment (Inv.) and consumption (Cons.). "Investment grade" refers to Aaa-Baa and "Mid-rated" refers to Ba-B noninvestment grades according to Moody's.

C. Panel shows annual forecast growth in EMDE commodity exporters and EMDE commodity importers excluding China.

D. Panel shows yearly contributions to GDP growth in percentage points for EMDE commodity exporters and EMDE commodity importers excluding China.

of trade in 2025. Nevertheless, improving confidence and easier financial conditions are expected to underpin domestic activity by lifting investment growth and supporting a gradual pickup in private consumption growth over the forecast horizon.

Growth in EMDEs is projected to decelerate to 4 percent in 2026—driven in part by the projected slowdown in China—and then to firm slightly to 4.1 percent in 2027 as the recovery in global trade gathers momentum. Growth in EMDEs excluding China is forecast to remain steady at 3.7 percent in 2026, with the effects of increased U.S. trade restrictions, restrained confidence, and the payback from export front-loading in 2025 expected to offset the boost from easier global financial conditions on domestic demand (refer to figure 1.9.A). In 2027, growth is anticipated to accelerate to 4 percent, as the drag from trade tensions gradually wanes, lifting export growth, and as industrial commodity prices firm modestly.

Across EMDEs excluding China, domestic demand is anticipated to anchor growth over 2026–27. Investment is projected to progressively gain momentum in 2026, in line with the continued effects of a decline in financing costs, including from the compression of EMDE sovereign bond spreads with advanced economies, and last year's U.S. dollar depreciation. Over 2027, receding uncertainty, benign financial conditions, and firming global growth momentum are envisaged to support a further acceleration in investment growth among investment-grade and mid-rated EMDEs (refer to figure 1.9.B). In addition, firming trade activity, rising metals prices, and improving oil production are also anticipated to progressively reinforce a broader pickup in industrial activity across many EMDEs over the forecast horizon.

Private consumption growth is anticipated to edge down in 2026, before a modest recovery takes hold in 2027. This year, sharp decelerations in private consumption in a few large EMDEs are expected to weigh on already-muted activity in many other EMDEs where weak confidence and subdued manufacturing sector activity, related to the global trade slowdown, are anticipated to dampen employment and wage growth. In 2027, a recovery in global manufacturing and supportive financial conditions are envisaged to support rising confidence and improve labor market activity, contributing to a pickup in private consumption growth across many EMDEs. Fiscal policy and government consumption among EMDEs are expected to have a limited effect on aggregate EMDE activity over 2026–27, as policy becomes modestly restrictive. Excluding China, however, the EMDE fiscal stance is anticipated to remain contractionary this year and then assumed to adopt a more neutral stance in 2027.

Growth in commodity-exporting EMDEs is expected to accelerate modestly over 2026–27, to an average of 3.2 percent, up from 3 percent in 2025 (refer to figure 1.9.C). The expected pickup reflects rising net exports among energy exporters in 2026 as oil production rises alongside the unwinding of OPEC+ production cuts. In 2027, investment and consumption is anticipated to firm across energy exporters as oil prices and confidence rise, in parallel to continued solid performance among metal exporters related to supportive metals prices and improving global industrial activity.

Growth in commodity-importing EMDEs excluding China is expected to soften slightly from 4.4 percent in 2025 to 4.3 percent in 2026, then rebound to 4.7 percent in 2027. In 2026, the effects of increased trade restrictions and the unwinding from earlier front-loading are expected to put negative pressure on net exports (refer to figure 1.9.D). In parallel, still-restrained confidence over 2026 is also anticipated to dampen domestic demand, particularly private consumption. However, by 2027, the slowdown in exports is expected to reverse, and both investment and consumption are envisioned to grow at a solid rate as consumer and business confidence improve and financial conditions remain benign.

The more challenging global trade environment expected in the near term is likely to weigh on job creation, particularly in some export-oriented sectors in EMDEs. Tariff burdens and the attendant dampening of demand may be particularly harmful to the lower-value, labor-intensive goods-producing sectors in many economies where margins are already thin, reducing the demand for workers. At the same time, strain on global value chains may hamper longer-term productivity gains, while limited fiscal space in many EMDEs could hinder countries' ability to support the sectors and workers that are the worst affected by tariffs. This is especially true in regions where many economies have large manufacturing sectors or face growing pressure to create jobs, especially as 1.2 billion young people are set to reach working age across EMDEs over the next decade (World Bank 2025e).

LICs outlook

Following a prolonged period of below trend growth during 2020–24, activity in LICs is projected to rise from 5 percent in 2025 to an average of 5.6 percent over 2026–27. Improving momentum is anticipated to be supported by firming domestic demand, a recovery in export growth, a moderation in inflation, and continued reform momentum in some countries (refer to box 1.3). Growth in LICs facing fragile and conflict-affected situations (FCS LICs) is forecast to increase to an average of 4.8 percent in 2026–27, predicated on a de-escalation of conflict. Having picked up to 5.6 percent last year, growth in non-FCS LICs is anticipated to strengthen further, to 6.7 percent in 2026 and 7 percent in 2027, supported by investment in infrastructure and extractive sectors.

The outlook for LICs remains highly uncertain, however. Fragility and conflict remain key differentiators of growth performance. Although the incidence of violence declined in 2025, the number of violent events reported remains significantly above the 2010–19 average. Despite the anticipated acceleration in growth, many LICs will continue to face daunting challenges, including ubiquitous poverty, violent conflict, food insecurity, slow progress in debt restructuring, and severely limited fiscal space. The projected decline in commodity prices over the next few years and reduced official development assistance (ODA) will increase pressure on growth and fiscal balances for LICs.

Per capita income growth

Many EMDEs are on a trajectory that implies a very slow pace of convergence with advanced economy living standards. Per capita income growth in EMDEs over 2026–27 is projected to be 3.1 percent—about 1 percentage point below its 2000–19 average. For EMDEs excluding China and India, the pace of per capita income growth is expected to be even slower—at 2 percent over

FIGURE 1.10 Per capita income growth

Annual per capita income growth is set to remain tepid across many EMDEs, while falling short of the pace needed to stem projected increases in extreme poverty and make up for the ground lost since 2020, especially in FCS economies. Funding cuts to ODA are expected to amount to nearly 2 percent of gross national income in LICs facing fragility and conflict in 2026 and could exacerbate the ongoing rise in extreme poverty in these countries. These headwinds come as many LICs and FCS economies are set to experience growth in their young populations, deepening the pressure to generate jobs in these economies.

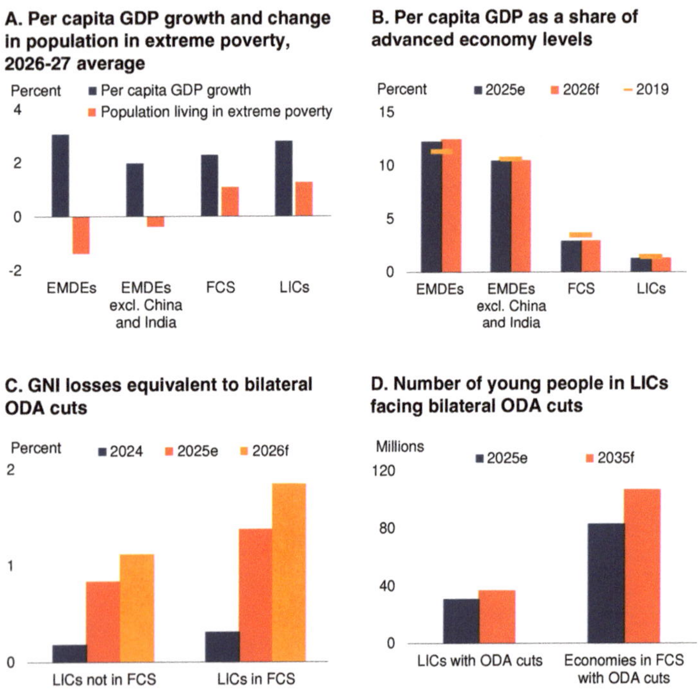

Sources: Center for Global Development; Donor Tracker; Mahler, Yonzan, and Lakner (2022); UN World Population Prospects (database); World Bank.

Note: e = estimate; f = forecast. EMDEs = emerging market and developing economies; excl. = excluding; FCS = fragile and conflict-affected situations; GNI = gross national income; LICs = low-income countries; ODA = official development assistance. FCS country group is based on current World Bank FCS classification. GDP per capita for aggregates are calculated as aggregated GDP divided by the aggregate population. GDP aggregates are calculated using real U.S. dollar GDP weights at average 2010-19 prices and market exchange rates.

A.C. "Extreme poverty" is defined as living on less than $3 per day in 2021 dollars at purchasing power parity.

A. Panel shows annual average growth in per capita GDP and population living in extreme poverty over 2026-27.

B. Bars and horizontal lines are calculated as per capita GDP by country group as a share of advanced economy per capita GDP.

C. Projections of 2024-26 ODA levels are from the Center for Global Development's Donor Tracker (May 14, 2025). Values are relative to the 2023 GNI of countries affected. Sample includes 72 EMDEs, of which 24 are LICs.

D. Panel shows the population of individuals aged 15-24 by country group based on economies facing ODA cuts as determined by the Center for Global Development's Donor Tracker as of May 14, 2025. Sample includes 72 EMDEs, of which 24 are LICs.

2026–27, similarly below its long-term average, but by a narrower margin. While per capita growth is set to accelerate above the 2000–19 pace across LICs and FCS, it remains too slow to make up for the ground lost since 2020, and insufficient to stem the projected increase in the population living in extreme poverty in these economies (refer to figure 1.10.A).

Weaker growth is set to extend a period of stagnation in living standards across many EMDEs that started in the 2010s and was aggravated by the pandemic. Although just over half of EMDEs are expected to experience per capita GDP growth pick up in 2026, the aggregate level of per capita income in EMDEs excluding China and India relative to advanced economies is expected to remain slightly lower this year than in 2019, with essentially no gains made in catching up to advanced economies following the pandemic and a sizable shortfall for FCS economies (refer to figure 1.10.B).

Several other developments, including reduced development aid and a rise in violence among pockets of intense conflict, could further add to the expected increase in the number of people living in extreme poverty. Following announced cuts to bilateral ODA in 2024 and 2025, FCS LICs are estimated to experience a loss in aid of nearly 2 percent of gross national income (GNI) by 2026 compared to 2023 levels, with non-FCS LICs seeing a loss of about 1 percent (refer to figure 1.10.C; Center for Global Development 2025 and Donor Tracker 2025). ODA cuts are likely to have an outsized impact on some of the poorest and most fragile economies—LICs and FCS, where the number of people living in extreme poverty is expected to continue to grow. The reduction in funding will likely leave poor populations more vulnerable to the adverse impacts of extreme weather events, violent conflict, and especially health risks—as the funding reduction to ODA health initiatives is projected to be particularly deep (OECD 2025).

To the extent that it curbs educational access, health care availability, and broader poverty reduction, the decreases in ODA may weigh on human capital accumulation in vulnerable countries. This comes at a time when many FCS LICs and non-FCS LICs face a large jobs challenge, brought on by a steep rise in their youth populations. By 2035, the population aged 15 to 24 potentially facing ODA cuts is anticipated to exceed 110 million in FCS LICs economies and reach nearly 40 million in non-FCS LICs, representing about one in seven of the total global population of young people by 2035 (refer to figure 1.10.D). Without sufficient job creation, the surge in the youth population, coupled with the shifting global trade environment and the weakening of investment and FDI flows in recent decades, threatens to intensify extreme poverty, further adding to the challenges faced by these economies.

Global outlook and risks

Summary of global outlook

Global growth is forecast to edge down a notch in 2026, to 2.6 percent, with the softness in activity masked somewhat by the substantial positive carryover from last year (refer to figure 1.11.A). The slowdown this year is mainly driven by the delayed impact of high trade barriers, leading to weaker demand for traded goods. Slowing international trade growth and ongoing policy uncertainty are also anticipated to dampen manufacturing activity and weigh on consumer spending (refer to figure 1.11.B). The moderation in consumption growth this year also reflects softening labor markets in some advanced economies and slowing wage growth in EMDEs.

These headwinds to global growth are expected to be countered somewhat by continued support from the easing in global financial conditions and fiscal expansion in some large economies. Although the deceleration in 2026 is expected to be relatively broad-based, affecting about half of economies worldwide, it is anticipated to be largely centered on advanced economies, with 76 percent of them expected to experience slower growth compared with 44 percent of EMDEs.

Global growth is projected to edge up to 2.7 percent in 2027, as trade flows adjust and policy uncertainty wanes. Global activity is also expected to be supported by improving domestic demand, reflecting earlier easing in monetary policy. Nevertheless, the outlook for the global economy remains subdued and highly uncertain, hindering prospects for job creation (ILO 2025).

Risks to the outlook

Risks to the outlook continue to be tilted to the downside, although some upside risks are also present (refer to figure 1.12.A). Growth could underperform the forecasts if trade tensions escalate amid further increases in trade barriers, or if shocks lead to sizable declines in asset prices, resulting in substantially tighter financial conditions. On the upside, the flexibility of supply chains could further mitigate trade policy-related headwinds, and the surge in AI-related activity could continue and broaden.

FIGURE 1.11 Global outlook

Global growth is projected to slow in 2026 as drags from higher trade tariffs and softening labor markets offset easing global financial conditions and positive carryover from 2025. Slowing international trade growth and ongoing policy uncertainty are expected to also weigh on investment and consumer spending.

A. Contributions to forecast growth, 2026

B. Contributions to global growth

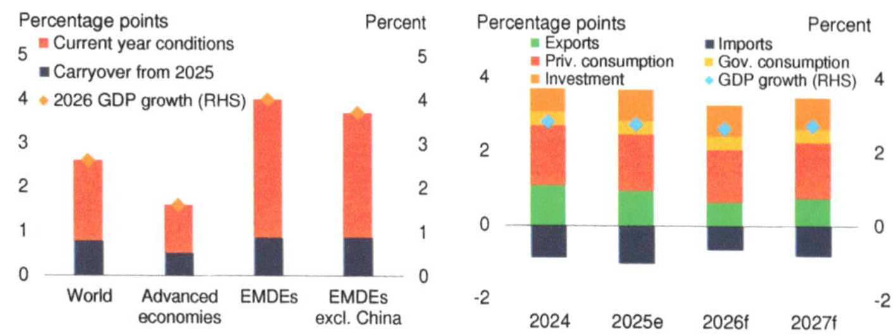

Source: World Bank.

Note: e = estimate; f = forecast. EMDEs = emerging market and developing economies; excl. = excluding; Gov. = government; Priv. = private; RHS = right-hand scale. Aggregates are calculated using U.S. dollar GDP weights at average 2010-19 prices and market exchange rates. Aggregates may differ from data in table 1.1 on account of sample size differences in quarterly and component data.

A. Panel shows contribution to annual growth. Carryover from 2025 to 2026 is estimated using a sample of 37 advanced economies and 44 EMDEs and assumes zero quarter-over-quarter growth in 2026.

B. Panel shows growth contribution for expenditure-side components. Discrepancies between GDP growth and components sum reflect inventories and residuals.

Downside risks

Resurgent trade tensions and trade policy uncertainty

Progress in negotiations with the United States and limited retaliation have eased trade tensions, though policy uncertainty remains high. The details of many recent trade agreements remain unclear, with considerable ambiguity surrounding their implementation. This raises the risk of renewed tensions if parties perceive that commitments are not being carried out. Moreover, the increased use of tariffs and other trade policy tools in response to a wide array of national security and strategic concerns implies that trade restrictions

FIGURE 1.12 Risks to the outlook

Risks to the outlook continue to be tilted to the downside. Amid compressed corporate bond spreads and subdued financial market volatility, asset prices may be vulnerable to an abrupt retrenchment in risk appetite. A sharp decline in equity valuations alongside plunging risk appetite and tighter financial conditions would reduce global growth by up to 0.3 percentage point relative to baseline projections this year. Proliferating or prolonged conflicts could inflict substantial losses in affected countries. In contrast, AI-related productivity gains could be stronger, particularly in economies with relatively high AI preparedness.

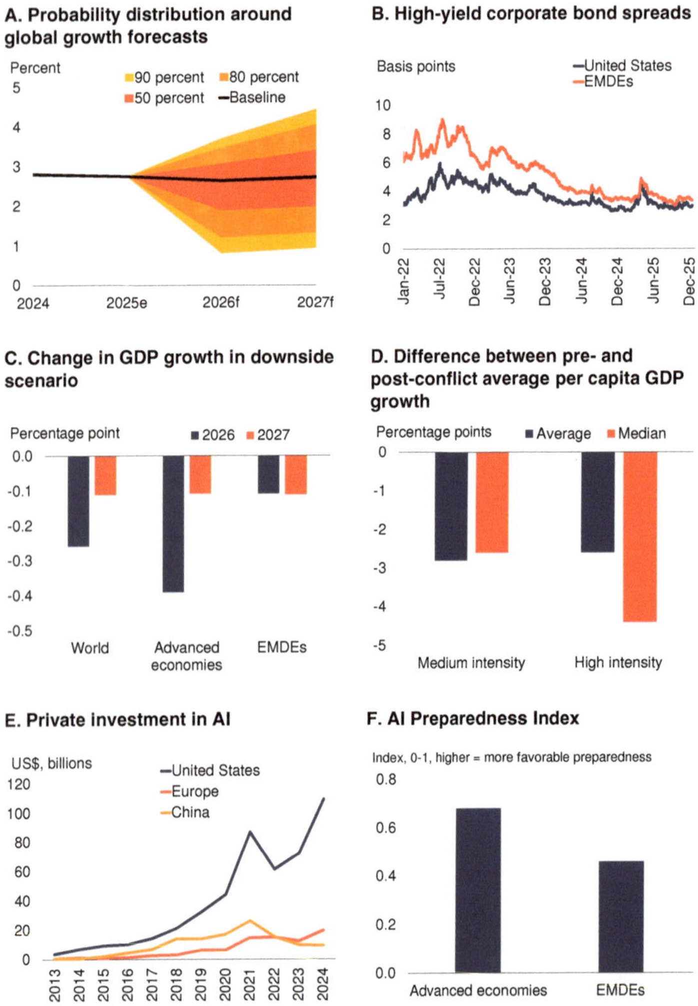

Sources: Bloomberg; Cazzaniga et al. (2024); Consensus Economics; Federal Reserve Economic Data (FRED) (database); IMF; Maslej et al. (2025); Ohnsorge, Stocker, and Some (2016); Oxford Economics; Uppsala Conflict Data Program; World Bank.

Note: e = estimate; f = forecast. AI = artificial intelligence; EMDEs = emerging market and developing economies.

A. Probabilities use the range and skewness implied by oil and equity price derivatives and term spread forecasts. Values for 2026-27 use 12-month- and 24-month-ahead forecast distributions, employing data up to December 18, 2025.

B. Lines indicate ICE BofA Option-Adjusted Spreads (OASs) for high-yield corporates in the United States and EMDEs. For U.S. corporates, the spread is calculated as the difference between a computed OAS index for bonds rated below Baa/BBB and the spot U.S. Treasury curve. For EMDEs, corporate debt rated BB1 or lower is used.

C. Panel shows the deviation of growth from the baseline.

D. Medium- (high-) intensity conflicts have at least 50 (150) fatalities per million at onset, with no exceedance of that threshold in the four prior years. Bars show average per capita GDP growth three years after a conflict versus three years before a conflict for up to 12 conflicts in 12 EMDEs for the period 2006-20.

E. Data include fundraisings for investment in AI-related technologies via private placements. For full definition refer to Maslej et al. (2025).

F. Panel shows scores on the AI Preparedness Index (AIPI) as of 2023 by Cazzaniga et al. (2024), covering 174 economies. Higher values represent more favorable AI preparedness. Country groups are as defined by the International Monetary Fund and aggregated using averages.

could escalate again on account of developments unrelated to international trade.

Additionally, there is a rising risk that tariff measures could broaden to third countries. When large economies increase tariffs, exporters redirect products to other markets, which could heighten competitive pressures on import-competing industries in those economies. This may lead to additional restrictive measures, including the use of safeguards or targeted tariff increases, which could further fragment trade flows and exacerbate global trade tensions.

A renewed increase in trade barriers, together with the associated uncertainty, could also depress business confidence and constrain investment, particularly in industries deeply integrated into global supply chains. This would dampen global trade further as investment goods have a higher import content than other goods. These developments could have an outsized impact on growth in jurisdictions that raise barriers and in export-oriented EMDEs. Over time, persistent high trade barriers and reduced trade may limit productivity growth by restricting cross-border diffusion of technology.

Tighter global financial conditions

Over the past year, buoyant investor sentiment has helped push some measures of U.S. equity valuations to about their highest levels since the dot-com bubble, with borrowing spreads on riskier assets at about record lows. Against this backdrop, the potential for a retrenchment in risk appetite to trigger large and sharp declines in asset prices has increased (refer to figure 1.12.B). The growing size and importance of nonbank financial intermediaries and their interconnections with the banking sector could amplify these price declines, leading to financial stress. A sharp tightening in financial conditions would weigh on global growth and could trigger capital flight from EMDEs, particularly in those with weaker credit ratings.

Several factors could trigger financial market disruptions. Weaker-than-expected earnings or disappointing productivity gains from AI-related sectors could prompt a sharp reassessment of AI-

BOX 1.3 Low-income countries: Recent developments and outlook

Growth in low-income countries (LICs) firmed in 2025, reaching 5 percent, and is projected to rise to 5.7 percent in 2026 before easing slightly to 5.6 percent in 2027. This forecast assumes a de-escalation of conflicts in several countries, stronger domestic demand growth, and continued easing of inflation. The projected gains in growth are concentrated among the largest LIC economies; growth in smaller LICs, especially those in fragile and conflict-affected situations, is expected to be insufficient to recover pandemic-related output losses. While real per capita income growth is projected to increase to 2.8 percent a year, on average, in 2026-27, this will not be enough to bring about significant reductions in extreme poverty, which will continue to be exacerbated in many cases by limited buffers to cushion the impacts of adverse shocks. Projected growth in LICs is also insufficient for job creation to keep pace with labor force growth. Risks to the outlook remain tilted to the downside. Persistent or escalating conflicts, as well as more severe or extreme weather events than assumed in the baseline, could further constrain activity, especially given limited policy space. Lower-than-expected commodity prices would also weigh on growth and further narrow fiscal space. These challenges are further compounded by heightened uncertainty, reflecting policy shifts in trade, reductions in official development assistance, intensifying geoeconomic tensions, and potential financial market deterioration.

Introduction

Growth in low-income countries (LICs) firmed last year, reaching an estimated 5 percent, as recovering private consumption more than offset slower investment and trade. Growth in LICs is expected to strengthen further to 5.7 percent in 2026, before edging down to 5.6 percent in 2027. These baseline projections are contingent on substantial improvements in security in several LICs in fragile and conflict-affected situations (FCS). Nevertheless, the pace of per capita income growth remains insufficient to fully recover pandemic-era losses or to support the rapid expansion of jobs needed to lift incomes and reduce extreme poverty.

Relative to the June forecasts, growth in 2025 has been revised up by 0.2 percentage point, reflecting stronger domestic demand, more favorable prices for some commodity exports, and stronger-than-expected economic activity in some FCS countries. However, the 2026 growth forecast has been revised down by 0.1 percentage point, reflecting the effects of planned fiscal consolidations, heightened policy uncertainty, and scarring in countries affected by, or emerging from, conflict. Nevertheless, growth in LICs tends to be volatile, reflecting structural vulnerabilities such as heavy reliance on primary sectors, exposure to conflict, volatile financial flows, and heightened susceptibility to climate change-related and other natural disasters (Dabla-Norris and Gündüz 2014).

Risks to the baseline growth projections are therefore high and tilted to the downside. If the assumed improvements in security situations in conflict-affected countries fail to materialize, growth, macroeconomic stability, and food security could deteriorate, undermining progress in job creation and poverty reduction. Growth in LICs could also be dampened by several external headwinds, including a flare-up in trade tensions, heightened policy uncertainty, and tighter global financing conditions. Lower commodity prices would worsen fiscal pressures, while intensifying climate change effects could further slow activity. For Sub-Saharan Africa LICs, unless extended, the expiration of the African Growth and Opportunity Act (AGOA) late last year is expected to affect duty-free access to the U.S. market. Further reductions to official development assistance (ODA) beyond those assumed in the baseline would exacerbate these challenges, leaving vulnerable economies with even weaker buffers against adverse shocks.

Against this backdrop, this box addresses three questions:

- What have been the main recent economic developments in LICs?
- What is the outlook for LICs?
- What are the risks to the outlook?

Recent developments

Growth in LICs firmed to 5 percent in 2025, up from 3.6 percent in 2024, supported by reduced conflict intensity in some FCS countries, higher government spending, and favorable commodity prices—particularly for exporters of coffee, gold, and other precious metals. Relative to last June's projections, estimated growth in

Note: This box was prepared by Joseph Mawejje and Edoardo Palombo.

BOX 1.3 Low-income countries: Recent developments and outlook (*continued*)

FIGURE B1.3.1 LICs: Recent developments

Favorable weather conditions supported higher agricultural output in LICs in 2025. Although the incidence of violence eased in some countries in 2025, the total number of reported violent events was still significantly higher than the 2010–19 average. Median consumer price inflation has declined in LICs, with the decrease supported by easing food prices, but relative food prices remain elevated.

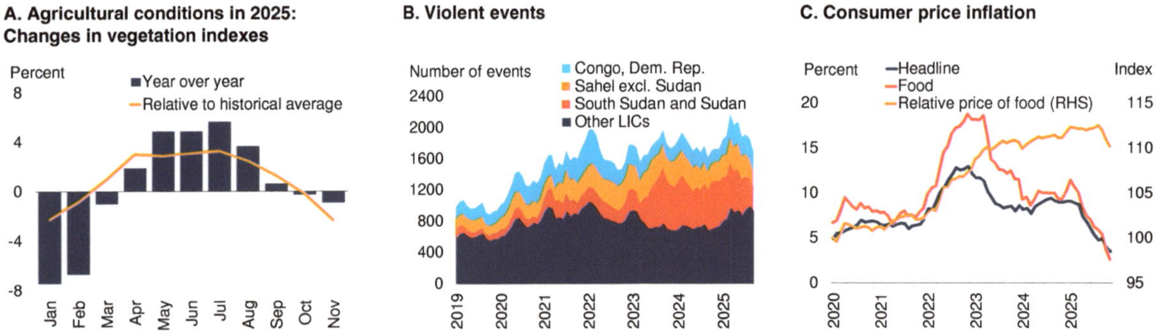

Sources: ACLED (database); FAO; Haver Analytics; Humanitarian Data Exchange; United States Department of Agriculture (USDA); World Bank.

Note: excl. = excluding; LICs = low-income countries; RHS = right-hand scale.

A. Panel shows average changes in normalized difference vegetation indexes (NDVIs) for countries in subregions where January to November overlaps with the main growing season. NDVIs are derived from remotely sensed data to assess vegetation health and density. NDVIs per country are weighted by province according to relative crop production, based on USDA weights. Sample includes Democratic Republic of Congo, Madagascar, Malawi, Mozambique, Rwanda, the Federal Republic of Somalia, and Uganda.

B. Three-month moving averages. "Violent events" include battles, explosions, violence against civilians, and riots. Last observation is September 2025. Sample includes 21 LICs, of which 6 are Sahel countries.

C. Median increases in consumer prices from 12 months earlier. Sample includes up to 21 LICs for headline inflation and up to 19 LICs for food inflation. Last observation is October 2025. Relative food price index is computed relative to headline inflation.

2025 has been revised up by 0.2 percentage point, reflecting stronger domestic demand and higher-than-expected commodity prices.

Growth has been upgraded for 14 of the 24 LICs, including the Democratic Republic of Congo, Afghanistan, and Uganda, the three largest LIC economies (refer to table B1.3.1). Growth in LICs in 2025 was driven by solid performance among agricultural commodity exporters (Gambia, Rwanda, Uganda) and a subset of industrial commodity exporters (Niger). In mid-2025, favorable weather and recovery from earlier drought conditions in eastern Africa helped raise agricultural output, supporting real incomes and stronger-than-expected consumption growth (refer to figure B1.3.1.A). The pickup in activity in 2025 was broad-based, with the pace of growth accelerating in over half of economies.

Fragility and conflict remain a key differentiator of growth performance, with growth in FCS countries generally weaker than elsewhere. The incidence of violence remains elevated, and the number of reported conflict events is still significantly higher than the 2010-19 average (refer to figure B1.3.1.B). In LICs in FCS nevertheless, growth strengthened to 4.5 percent in 2025, supported by improving security conditions in some countries and partial recoveries in agriculture and services, with growth exceeding expectations in several economies (Afghanistan, Burundi, Central African Republic). In the Democratic Republic of Congo, growth slowed for the third consecutive year, decelerating to 5.1 percent, reflecting weak investment growth, elevated conflict, and lower mining activity following a temporary ban on cobalt exports. In Afghanistan, an influx of returnees supported a recovery in activity, but conditions remain dire as the country has been buffeted by successive shocks, including droughts, earthquakes, and regional geopolitical tensions. In South Sudan, multiple shocks—including spillovers from the conflict in neighboring Sudan, persistent subnational violence, and disruptions to oil exports—weighed heavily on activity, with output contracting by 23.8 percent in fiscal year 2025.

BOX 1.3 Low-income countries: Recent developments and outlook (*continued*)

FIGURE B1.3.2 LICs: Outlook and risks

Growth in LICs is projected to pick up in 2026 and 2027. Fragility and conflict remain key differentiators of growth performance, with growth in LIC economies in FCS lagging growth in LICs not marred by conflict. Despite the projected rebound over 2026–27, LICs are not expected to fully recover to pre-pandemic levels of per capita income, with LICs in FCS making even slower progress. LICs in FCS are major recipients of ODA, and the retrenchment of international financial support will increase their vulnerability to various risks, including those related to health and climate change.

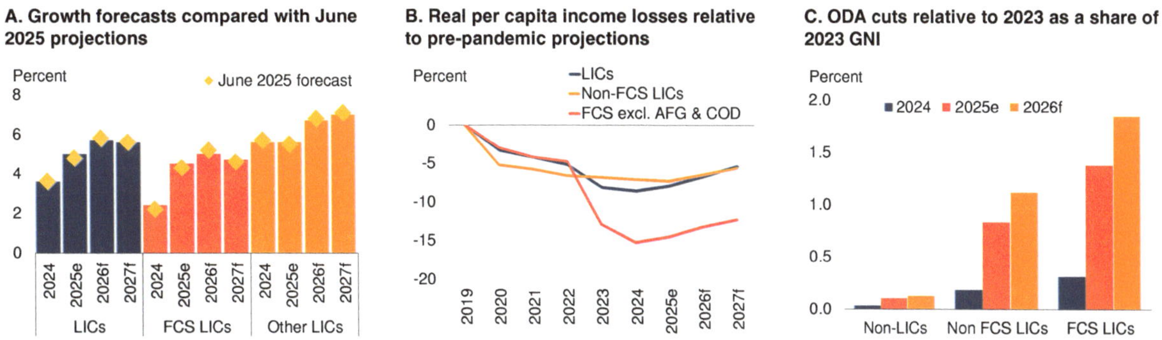

Sources: Centre for Global Development; World Bank.

Note: e = estimate; f = forecast. AFG = Afghanistan; COD = Democratic Republic of Congo; excl. = excluding; FCS = fragile and conflict-affected situations; GNI = gross national income; LICs = low-income countries; ODA = official development assistance.

A. Revisions relative to the forecasts published in the June 2025 edition of the *Global Economic Prospects* report. Sample includes 22 LICs.

B. Panel shows percentage deviation from the baseline projections for GDP per capita in January 2020 *Global Economic Prospects*.

C. Sample includes 72 EMDEs, of which 22 are LICs.

Among LICs not in FCS, growth was stable at 5.6 percent in 2025, supported by robust domestic demand growth, resilient export performance, and moderating inflation. In Uganda, growth edged up to 6.3 percent, bolstered by recovering household consumption, increased government spending, solid investment growth, and buoyant coffee exports. In Rwanda, growth moderated to a still-robust 7 percent, with solid investment growth and continued expansion in the services sector, but tempered by slower growth in agricultural output, reflecting the effects of climate shocks.

Median headline consumer price inflation in LICs has fallen in 2025, from 8 percent in January to about 5 percent in the second half, supported by easing food price inflation (refer to figure B1.3.1.C). The disinflation has been widespread, with inflation slowing in over 70 percent of LICs. In Sierra Leone, inflation stood at 4.6 percent in November 2025 from more than 14 percent at the start of the year, while Burkina Faso, Guinea-Bissau, and Niger experienced deflation in the second half of 2025, partly reflecting strong harvests that lowered food prices. The relative price of food in LICs, after rising sharply since 2020, stabilized in 2025 but remains elevated.

In the context of elevated global economic uncertainty, monetary policy in LICs remained cautious in 2025, with policy rates unchanged in many economies and adjusted only marginally in others. In the Democratic Republic of Congo, however, the central bank cut its policy rate by 750 basis points to 17.5 percent in October 2025, the first change in two years. Elsewhere, policy rates were lowered in Mozambique but remained unchanged in Uganda since October 2024 and in Rwanda since August 2025.

Food insecurity has intensified in LICs, exacerbated in many cases by conflict, climate change, natural disasters, and population displacement (FAO et al. 2025). In 2024, about 140 million people in LICs faced an acute food insecurity crisis or worse—an increase of 30 percent since 2020. Although the number of additional internally displaced persons each year in LICs has eased somewhat from its peak in 2019, it remains above historical levels (IDMC 2025). In 2024, LICs hosted an estimated 21 million refugees—more than half of the global total (UNHCR 2025).

BOX 1.3 Low-income countries: Recent developments and outlook (*continued*)

TABLE B1.3.1 Low-income country forecasts[a]

(Real GDP growth at market prices in percent, unless indicated otherwise)

	2023	2024	2025e	2026f	2027f	Percentage-point differences from June 2025 projections: 2025e	2026f	2027f
Low-Income Countries, GDP[b]	**1.0**	**3.6**	**5.0**	**5.7**	**5.6**	**0.2**	**-0.1**	**0.0**
GDP per capita (U.S. dollars)	-1.7	0.8	2.1	2.8	2.8	0.2	-0.1	0.0
Afghanistan[c d]	2.3	2.5	4.3	3.8	3.5	2.1	1.4	1.0
Burkina Faso	3.0	4.8	4.7	4.9	5.1	0.4	0.2	0.1
Burundi	2.7	3.9	4.6	4.9	5.5	1.1	1.2	1.5
Central African Republic	0.7	1.5	2.7	3.0	3.1	0.6	0.8	0.3
Chad	4.1	3.5	3.4	3.7	4.1	-0.1	-0.8	-0.3
Congo, Dem. Rep.	8.6	6.5	5.1	5.1	5.3	0.3	0.1	0.0
Eritrea	2.6	2.9	3.2	3.5	3.6	0.1	0.1	0.1
Gambia, The	5.0	5.3	5.7	5.5	5.3	0.1	0.2	-0.2
Guinea-Bissau	4.5	4.8	5.1	5.2	5.2	0.0	0.0	0.0
Liberia	4.7	4.0	4.6	5.4	5.6	-0.5	-0.1	-0.1
Madagascar	4.2	4.2	4.0	4.0	4.4	0.3	0.1	0.0
Malawi	1.9	1.7	1.9	2.6	3.1	-0.1	0.2	-0.1
Mali	3.5	4.0	4.9	5.0	5.0	0.1	0.2	0.3
Mozambique	5.5	2.1	1.1	2.8	3.5	-1.9	-0.7	0.0
Niger	2.0	10.3	6.5	6.7	6.6	-0.6	1.6	2.1
Rwanda	8.6	7.2	7.0	7.2	7.6	0.0	-0.1	0.3
Sierra Leone	5.7	4.3	4.3	4.4	4.6	0.2	0.2	0.4
Somalia, Fed. Rep.	4.2	4.1	3.0	3.5	3.5	0.0	0.0	0.0
South Sudan[d]	-1.3	-7.2	-23.8	48.8	0.8	10.9	7.7	-20.4
Sudan	-29.4	-14.0	6.1	5.1	3.7	1.1	-4.2	-0.4
Syrian Arab Republic[c]	-1.2	-1.5	1.0	..	..	0.0	..	..
Togo	6.4	5.3	5.0	5.4	5.6	0.0	0.0	0.1
Uganda[d]	5.3	6.1	6.3	6.4	9.8	0.1	0.2	-0.6
Yemen, Rep.[c]	-2.0	-1.5	-1.5	0.0	..	0.0	-0.5	..

Source: World Bank.

Note: e = estimate; f = forecast. World Bank forecasts are frequently updated based on new information and changing global circumstances. Consequently, projections presented here may differ from those contained in other Bank documents, even if basic assessments of countries' prospects do not significantly differ at any given moment in time.

a. The Democratic People's Republic of Korea is not projected on account of data limitations.

b. Aggregate growth rates are calculated using GDP weights at average 2010–19 prices and market exchange rates. Data for the Syrian Arab Republic and the Republic of Yemen are excluded.

c. Forecasts for the Syrian Arab Republic (beyond 2025) and the Republic of Yemen (beyond 2026) are excluded because of a high degree of uncertainty.

d. GDP growth rates are on a fiscal year basis. For example, the column for 2023 refers to FY2022/23.

Outlook

Growth in LICs is projected to strengthen to 5.7 percent in 2026 before stabilizing at 5.6 percent in 2027 (refer to figure B1.3.2.A). Compared with June projections, the forecast is 0.1 percentage point lower in 2026 but remains unchanged in 2027. The marginal downgrade to growth in 2026 masks improved growth forecasts for nearly 70 percent of LICs. These gains are offset by heightened policy uncertainty, subdued activity in FCS LICs (Mozambique, Sudan, the Republic of Yemen), and country-specific developments in a few cases (Chad, Liberia).

Growth in LICs will continue to face multiple domestic challenges, including high public debt and limited access to financing. In addition, LICs face external headwinds, including subdued global growth, increased trade barriers, fragmented global trade, and falling donor support. For the four-fifths of LICs in Sub-Saharan Africa, unless extended, the expiration of the United States' AGOA in late 2025 has eliminated duty-free access to the U.S. market. Against this backdrop, the outlook for LICs remains highly uncertain. The baseline projections are predicated on improved security in several LICs, the avoidance of debt crises, no further retrenchment in donor support, greater resilience in the

BOX 1.3 Low-income countries: Recent developments and outlook (*continued*)

face of extreme weather events and other natural disasters, and sustained institutional reform momentum across many LICs.

Government debt-to-GDP ratios in LICs are expected to decrease gradually from recent highs but to remain above 60 percent, on average, by the end of 2027. The projected decline in debt ratios reflects primary fiscal surpluses amid consolidation efforts, partly offset by interest payments that are expected to remain elevated. Despite progress in addressing fiscal imbalances and the narrowing of sovereign spreads, debt-servicing costs are expected to peak in 2026, reflecting higher borrowing costs, shifts to less concessional debt, and lagged effects of pandemic-related debt accumulation. The decline in ODA will further narrow fiscal space in LICs, limiting critical investment in growth-enhancing sectors such as health, education, infrastructure, and climate adaptation (Mawejje 2025).

Growth in FCS LICs is forecast to increase from 4.6 percent in 2025 to an annual average of 4.8 percent in 2026–27. This assumes that further improvements in security situations in some countries materialize, offsetting a projected slowing of activity in Afghanistan and Sudan. Growth in Sudan is forecast to slow in 2026 -27, reflecting the effects of protracted conflict and constrained post-rebound growth momentum amid a severely damaged industrial base. In South Sudan, a substantial recovery in 2026 following five years of contraction is expected to be supported by a normalization of activity and the resumption of oil exports.

Growth in non-FCS LICs is anticipated to pick up from 5.6 percent in 2025 to 6.7 percent in 2026 and 7.0 percent in 2027. This acceleration largely reflects strengthening growth in Uganda, driven by oil-related capital investment, robust domestic demand, solid export performance, and the anticipated start of oil production in the latter half of 2026. Excluding Uganda, growth in non-FCS LICs is expected to average 5.1 percent a year in 2026–27.

Real per capita income growth in LICs is expected to accelerate from 2.1 percent in 2025 to 2.8 percent in both 2026 and 2027. However, these gains are expected to be unevenly distributed, with much of the increase concentrated in the three largest LIC economies. In all LICs, real per capita incomes in 2027 are expected still to be about 5 percent below levels projected before the pandemic, with FCS LICs lagging even further behind (refer to figure B1.3.2.B). About 160 million youth—20 percent of the current LIC population—will reach working age in LICs over the next decade. This makes the creation of sufficient productive jobs an urgent challenge. With more than half of their population living in extreme poverty, only limited improvements in average living standards are expected in the next two years.

Risks

Risks to the growth outlook remain tilted to the downside, especially for FCS LICs, as the projections hinge partly on positive developments in security situations that may fail to materialize. The persistence or intensification of current conflicts—most notably in the Democratic Republic of Congo, South Sudan, and Sudan—poses a significant risk to growth, macroeconomic stability, and food security, and could precipitate prolonged humanitarian crises. Supply chain disruptions due to regional conflicts could further undermine both near-term growth and longer-term development prospects. Fiscal positions could also deteriorate if conflicts persist or intensify. Armed conflicts are associated with increases in defense expenditure and reductions in revenue capacity, and can significantly weaken countries' fiscal positions (Mawejje 2025).

The steep decline in ODA has increased risks to LICs' growth prospects. It has left these economies with thinner buffers to protect them from adverse shocks and heightened the risk of reversals in development. ODA flows from donor countries may be reduced by between 9 and 17 percent in the next couple of years, threatening critical investments in education, health care, and infrastructure, thereby undermining both actual and potential growth (OECD 2025). FCS LICs—notably Afghanistan, the Central African Republic, the Federal Republic of Somalia, and South Sudan—are especially vulnerable given their very high dependence on external donor support (refer to figure B1.3.2.C).

LICs' growth outlook also faces downside risks from weaker-than-expected global growth—particularly

BOX 1.3 Low-income countries: Recent developments and outlook (*continued*)

through its potential impacts on export demand and commodity prices. Further increases in trade restrictions represent another risk. While the direct impacts of higher tariffs by advanced economies may be limited for many LICs, given their relatively modest export exposure to these markets, indirect effects—operating through heightened trade policy uncertainty, weaker global growth, and lower commodity prices—could be substantially more damaging.

The possibility of a worsening of global financial market conditions is another risk. Such developments would also pose risks to the sustainability of LICs' fiscal positions. While many LICs have undertaken structural reforms to enhance resilience to external volatility—including reforms to deepen domestic debt markets and extend debt maturities—debt sustainability concerns linger, with 12 of the 24 LICs in, or at high risk of, debt distress, and none assessed at low risk in 2025. While government debt-to-GDP ratios in LICs are projected to decline in 2026–27, they remain elevated (IMF and World Bank 2025). For many LICs, inadequacy of official foreign reserves is another source of financial fragility.

Inflation in LICs could be driven higher than projected by several factors, including debt monetization, currency depreciations, conflict-related supply chain disruptions, and adverse weather conditions affecting food prices. This would push central banks in LICs to tighten monetary policy and financial conditions, thereby reducing growth. Alternatively, if central banks fail to respond effectively, higher inflation could threaten growth by eroding households' purchasing power.

Extreme weather events, such as droughts and floods, and other natural disasters have frequently had catastrophic consequences in LICs, more so than in other EMDEs, partly reflecting LICs' narrower buffers and weaker capacity (Mejia et al. 2019). If the adverse effects of climate change intensify, the pace of poverty reduction in LICs could become markedly slower (Jafino et al. 2020). Climate change-related and other natural disasters can exacerbate existing vulnerabilities, including by fueling conflict, displacement, and worsening food insecurity (FSIN and GNAFC 2025). This is exemplified by recent events such as landslides in Sudan, flooding in South Sudan, and drought in Malawi, which exacerbated already-dire situations. Climate change-related destruction of crops and livelihoods could push many LIC populations further into poverty, given their limited capacity and resources to adapt (Damania et al. 2025).

driven valuations. Risk appetite could also sour if policy stances from major central banks are tighter than anticipated in response to stronger inflation, whether due to renewed goods price pressures related to trade barriers or other unanticipated drivers. Stress may also emerge from sovereign bond markets: long-term yields in major advanced economies remain high, debt levels have increased, and fiscal deficits are set to remain large. Substantial shifts in expectations regarding deficits or concerns about monetary policy credibility could weaken demand for government debt, push up term premia, and lead to disorderly bond-market conditions.

To quantify the impact of tighter financial conditions, a global macroeconomic model is used to construct a scenario focused on a sharp correction in equity valuations as a potential trigger.[2] A correction to valuations such that the cyclically adjusted price-to-earnings ratio for the S&P 500 index returned to late-2019 levels would be associated with a decline in equity prices of about 20 percent, with negative consequences for business and consumer confidence. The effects of a retrenchment in risk appetite and a confidence shock in advanced economies could be substantial. A decline in household wealth would lead to weaker consumption. Financial institutions would likely amplify the downturn by tightening credit

[2] These simulations are conducted using the Oxford Economics Global Economic Model, a semi-structural macroeconomic projection model that includes 188 individual country blocks in its extended version, available at quarterly or annual frequencies (Oxford Economics 2019).

conditions, having suffered losses on tech-related exposures. Nonbank financial institutions could retrench and face redemptions, with adverse implications for banks with significant exposures to them (IMF 2025b). In turn, firms in advanced economies would reduce capital expenditure, both because of a rise in impaired assets in the tech sector, and because of general tighter credit availability and weaker demand. In such a scenario, growth in advanced economies would fall by 0.4 percentage point in 2026 relative to baseline projections.

Such a scenario would have a substantial adverse impact on EMDE equity and bond markets, with sovereign and corporate borrowing spreads rising. Drawdowns could be especially large in the equity markets of some EMDEs with large ICT exports. In addition, a sustained surge in sovereign spreads would weigh on government spending in heavily-indebted EMDEs. Furthermore, more limited credit availability and deteriorating business confidence would lead businesses to reduce investment and hiring. Consumers would react by cutting spending as confidence retreats and labor markets cool. Weaker domestic demand would be compounded by reduced exports to advanced economies, leaving growth in EMDEs 0.1 percentage point below baseline projections in 2026. Taken together, global growth in this scenario would be reduced by about 0.3 percentage point below baseline this year (refer to figure 1.12.C).

Increased conflict and geopolitical stress

The 2020s have been characterized by a marked increase in geopolitical tensions globally and increased violent conflict. Accumulating shocks—such as Russia's invasion of Ukraine and the conflict in the Middle East—have disrupted trading relationships and stoked geopolitical uncertainty. A re-intensification of ongoing major conflicts or prolonged uncertainty around their evolution will amplify headwinds to economic activity in affected countries, and potentially at the global level. In addition, developments in the República Bolivariana de Venezuela represent additional uncertainty, although it is too soon to ascertain the precise implications.

In EMDEs, conflicts can inflict substantial and long-lasting economic losses. Empirical estimates suggest that medium- to high-intensity conflicts have been associated with an average reduction in GDP per capita of about 13 percent after five years in the countries directly involved (World Bank 2025f). Moreover, median per capita GDP growth has fallen by an average of 2.7 percentage points relative to the three years preceding conflicts of medium-intensity, with an even sharper decline for high-intensity cases (refer to figure 1.12.D).

Conflicts can also have sizable cross-border effects, reducing growth in neighboring countries by discouraging private investment in the region and decreasing trade flows through disruptions to transportation networks and demand. Fiscal pressures in surrounding countries may also emerge owing to increased spending on defense, peace operations, and support for displaced persons. Beyond these regional effects, geopolitical tensions involving large, globally connected economies can have considerable cross-border spillovers, as illustrated by the large shocks to global commodity prices and concerns over food and energy security that followed Russia's invasion of Ukraine.

Weather-related natural disasters and public health crises

With changing climate patterns, the frequency and severity of weather-related disasters— such as heatwaves, extreme rainfall, droughts, and coastal flooding—are increasing. While natural disasters impact different countries to different extents, depending on their geographies and economic structures, EMDEs are generally more vulnerable to such events (World Bank 2025f). Natural disasters can inflict substantial macroeconomic damage through multiple channels, including infrastructure destruction, agricultural losses, and commodity price spikes. Such shocks can also pose challenges for monetary policy by impacting inflation and potentially monetary policy transmission, while possibly creating risks on balance sheets of financial institutions (Lagarde 2024). These effects come on top of considerable societal costs through loss of lives and livelihoods. Over the longer run, the adverse effects of extreme weather events may include increased uncertainty, reduced investment, and weaker trend productivity growth (Angeli et al. 2022).

In addition, changing climate patterns and attendant developments in the natural environment are altering burdens of disease—for instance by shifting the transmission patterns of infectious diseases, making deadly disease outbreaks and pandemics more likely, and worsening health outcomes (World Bank 2024b). Moreover, shifting weather trends also strain health systems, increasing demand for health services while simultaneously curtailing their ability to respond. Low- and middle-income countries are likely to be more susceptible to these impacts as a result of their higher levels of poverty and income inequality, and weaker health care systems (World Bank, forthcoming). In this context, the decline in health-related ODA raises the risks of new disease-related crises, and potentially pandemics, emerging. Net ODA for health services from Development Assistance Committee (DAC) countries is estimated to have declined by 14 to 29 percent, depending on the scenario considered, in 2025 compared with 2024, falling close to levels seen in the mid-2000s (OECD 2025).

The steep decline in health-related ODA heightens risks to ODA recipients' health systems, access to health care, global health security, and pandemic preparedness (Dzau et al. 2025; Penn et al. 2025). Acute disease outbreaks, especially serious and contagious pathogens, could interrupt activity in the near term and weigh on human capital in the long term. While vulnerable EMDEs are most susceptible, the COVID-19 pandemic illustrates that adverse global impacts could result.

Upside risks

Lower drag from higher trade barriers due to continued private sector adaptations

The baseline assumes that current levels of bilateral tariffs remain in place throughout the forecast horizon, resulting in a growing negative impact on activity that peaks in 2026. However, businesses and consumers may prove more adaptable than expected, limiting the drag on near-term growth. Recent developments in some regions indicate that businesses have made substantial progress in reconfiguring supply chains to take advantage of lower-tariff jurisdictions. Thus, tariff costs may be further reduced by a broader use of existing tariff exemptions and through trade agreements that are already in force or pending ratification. Businesses may also strengthen and diversify trading networks and build spare or alternate capacity, muting the impact on trade of additional policy shifts and associated uncertainty (Castro-Vincenzi 2024).

Private sector adaptations of this kind could ease upward price pressures in key economies and support growth despite high trade barriers and elevated uncertainty. These adaptations would also help boost business and consumer confidence globally, partly offsetting the negative effects on investment and consumption assumed in the baseline. Global economic activity could be further supported by an additional easing of financial conditions if private sector resilience leads tariff-induced inflation effects to dissipate faster than anticipated.

Technology-led investment and productivity gains

The growth in AI has heralded a boom in private investment in some economies, notably the United States (refer to figure 1.12.E). Increased investment in areas such as software and ICT equipment may broaden to more geographies, with the construction of data centers and further expansion of energy generation. Spillovers from technology-led investment could also lift exports in a wide range of economies, as demand for upstream commodities and components strengthens. The accelerating diffusion of AI may raise productivity in an increasing number of economies and trigger broader technological breakthroughs, supporting growth and productivity globally. Nascent evidence points to sizable task-level and firm-level productivity gains, suggesting that wider AI adoption could generate meaningful aggregate improvements.

While subject to a high degree of uncertainty, initial research suggests that the economy wide adoption of AI-related technology could boost

U.S. total factor productivity (TFP) growth by about 0.7 percentage point per year over the next decade.[3] The degree to which these estimates can be extrapolated to other economies depends on various factors including digital infrastructure, human capital, demographics, social acceptance, technological innovation, and legal frameworks, captured in the AI Preparedness Index (refer to figure 1.12.F; AIPI; Cazzaniga et al. 2024). The AIPI, a composite of select macrostructural indicators that are relevant for AI adoption, can be used to estimate the potential impact of AI on other economies using the U.S. productivity gain as a benchmark. Combining AIPI scores for various economies with TFP impact estimates from the literature suggest that AI could boost global TFP growth by about 0.5 percentage point, with the effects cumulating to a 2.7 percent increase on the level of TFP after 5 years.

Several factors could influence the pace and trajectory of AI-driven productivity growth impact. The diffusion of AI technology may occur faster than past technologies, given its use of existing digital infrastructure as means of application (Microsoft 2025). The extent to which the potential is realized will also depend on how quickly firms can integrate AI into production processes and restructure workflows. In the short term, productivity may soften as firms adjust to new technologies, with stronger gains emerging once these adjustments are complete (McElheran et al. 2025). While new digital technologies may create important growth opportunities in low- and middle-income countries and help address development challenges, gains could be limited by barriers to adoption, including weak investment in digital infrastructure, and research and development. These constraints risk further entrenching productivity differentials, with technological advances disproportionately benefiting higher-income economies with larger skilled workforces and greater digital adoption.

[3] Estimates suggest that AI-related technologies could raise U.S. TFP growth by between 0.1 and 2.6 percentage point annually, with a midpoint of about 0.7 percentage point (Acemoglu 2025; Aghion and Bunel 2024; Baily, Brynjolfsson, and Korinek 2023; Filippucci, Gal, and Schief 2024).

Policy challenges

Amid continued headwinds and elevated risks, policy makers face significant challenges at both global and national levels. Global action is needed to restore a cooperative, transparent approach to trade and support diversification of trade partnerships. Coordination is also essential to ease financing pressures in vulnerable EMDEs and address mounting climate-related risks. With fiscal space eroded and debt-servicing costs high, EMDEs need to reprioritize spending and strengthen fiscal frameworks, including through well-designed fiscal rules, while maintaining sound monetary and financial policies to safeguard macroeconomic stability. At the same time, rapid growth in working-age populations heightens the urgency of tackling the jobs challenge faced by EMDEs. Countries will need comprehensive strategies to boost job creation—improving infrastructure, attracting investment, enhancing workforce skills, and reducing labor market inefficiencies, which will also help raise productivity and support stronger long-term growth.

Key global challenges

Diversifying trade partnerships amid greater frictions

International trade has been a key driver of development over the past several decades, boosting output and productivity growth. However, the escalation of trade tensions in 2025, which has followed a pattern of fragmentation in recent years, has further shifted the global trade environment toward higher barriers and frictions. Elevated geopolitical tensions have made vulnerabilities in global supply chains more apparent and prompted countries to pursue reshoring policies or reduce dependence on certain import sources (Bown 2021).

To partly offset the adverse effects of frictions in some trade corridors, EMDEs can expand the scope of existing trade agreements and diversify their trade partnerships further, both within their regions and with other EMDEs. These trends are already underway. In recent years, trade among partners in regional trade agreements has been more resilient and expanding more rapidly than

FIGURE 1.13 Global policy challenges

Global trade headwinds could be countered by deepening regional trade ties. Indeed, trade within regional trade blocs has been more resilient in recent years and has grown faster than trade outside these blocs. Protecting natural resources and addressing climate risks are also critical for the global economy and sustaining jobs, with agriculture and fisheries employing almost a billion people worldwide.

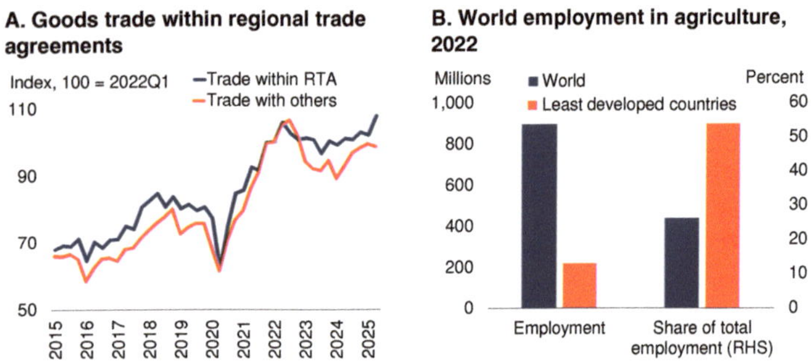

Sources: Egger and Larch (2008); Food and Agriculture Organization (FAO); UN Comtrade; World Bank.

Note: RHS = right-hand scale; RTA = regional trade agreement.

A. Panel shows nominal trade among countries with RTAs in force as of 2023 ("Trade within RTA") and among country pairs without trade agreements ("Trade with others"). Information on RTAs is updated from Egger and Larch (2008). The sample covers 70 reporting countries trading with 241 partner economies. Last observation is 2025Q2.

B. Total employment in the agrifood systems excluding nonagricultural employment is shown. "Agrifood systems" are defined as industries involved in growing, harvesting, processing, packaging, transporting, distributing, trading, buying, preparing, eating and disposing of food items. Income groupings are as defined by the FAO.

trade outside these blocs (refer to figure 1.13.A). There has also been renewed impetus for bilateral free trade agreements, such as the EU's commitment to reach trade deals with key Asian economies, as well as the revitalization of multilateral arrangements such as the Comprehensive and Progressive Trans-Pacific Partnership (CPTPP). Deeper trade integration with willing partners would help enhance exports from liberalizing countries, potentially resulting in higher global welfare (Rotunno and Ruta 2025).

The global policy community has an important role in reforming the multilateral trading system to address emerging challenges, including through efforts to restore a predictable and transparent approach to resolving trade tensions. Such a rules-based trade environment has historically supported convergence and poverty reduction in EMDEs (Helpman 2025; WTO 2024). This can be complemented by domestic policies to support spending adjustments that will help reduce macroeconomic imbalances—one of the key underlying sources of ongoing trade tensions.

Mobilizing resources for vulnerable EMDEs

Large EMDEs have so far proven resilient to the series of adverse shocks in recent years. However, economic outcomes have worsened in some vulnerable EMDEs. Many EMDEs are facing financing pressures amid limited fiscal space and elevated public debt. Notably, progress toward lifting tax revenues has been slow, leaving some poorer countries reliant on foreign aid, and on an unsustainable fiscal path (Choudhary, Ruch, and Skrok 2024). In some cases, these challenges are being exacerbated by declining flows of aid from advanced economies and limited progress on debt restructuring.

The global policy community can play a crucial role in supporting the most vulnerable EMDEs. For EMDEs in or near debt distress, debt restructuring is essential to mitigate the costs of debt crises. Recent debt restructuring episodes highlight the need for greater transparency, faster coordination, and enhanced information-sharing to secure sufficient and timely debt relief (Chen and Hart 2025). The global community can also facilitate donor coordination and seek to channel aid through country systems. This helps increase aid efficiency while also building local capacity and ensuring that aid aligns with countries' development priorities.

The global community also needs to prioritize efforts to mobilize private capital, including by sharing risks and pooling capital; setting up investment platforms; enhancing advisory services for development projects that can catalyze broader investment opportunities; and promoting coordination between investors, country governments, and development partners. Furthermore, strengthening cooperation between EMDEs and donor countries, and diversifying aid partners, could complement broader trade integration efforts and support shared development goals. The global community can bolster this by fostering a stable policy environment for cross-border knowledge, investment, and trade flows. Finally, these efforts need to be accompanied by technical assistance and capacity building to help vulnerable EMDEs mobilize their domestic resources more effectively.

Responding to changing climate patterns and extreme weather events

The growing effects of evolving climate trends amplify vulnerabilities in EMDEs. About 80 percent of people in LICs live with degraded land, polluted air, and water stress, which has serious implications for both labor productivity and health outcomes (Damania et al. 2025). The UN's annual assessment shows that the current trajectory of global emissions in 2030 still has a gap of between 3.5 percent and 5 percent relative to countries' commitments, which themselves fall short of the emissions reduction needed to align with 2°C and 1.5°C warming scenarios (UNEP 2024).

To curb emissions, economies need to shift toward decarbonizing energy generation and electrifying transport and heating. This, coupled with energy efficiency gains in production processes, can help decouple economic growth from further environmental degradation. Implementing policies such as carbon pricing—through taxes or cap-and-trade systems—can provide economic incentives for industries to reduce emissions, while also generating revenue that can be reinvested into other initiatives to support the transition (Black et al. 2024). Additionally, easing regulatory barriers for renewable energy projects and investing in upgrading power grid infrastructure will also promote energy reliability. Meanwhile, adaptation efforts can help reduce the damage from extreme weather events and build economic resilience (Carleton et al. 2025).

Successful implementation of these policies requires keeping transition costs manageable by leveraging falling renewable energy and storage costs, better targeting subsidies, and using carbon pricing revenues to ease the burden on poorer households (IEA 2024). Additional financing can come from phasing out costly fossil fuel subsidies, expanding green finance, and deploying debt instruments, such as debt-for-climate swaps and climate-resilient debt clauses. More efficient natural resource use can lower emissions and raise agricultural incomes with limited fiscal cost (Damania et al. 2023). These efforts not only mitigate climate risks and help preserve biodiversity, but can also create new economic opportunities, including generating jobs in renewable energy and green technology sectors. Resilient ecosystems are critical for protecting jobs: agriculture and fisheries employ almost a billion people worldwide (refer to figure 1.13.B; FAO 2024). Investing in less-polluting sectors often results in higher job creation per dollar spent compared with traditional industries providing a pathway to inclusive economic growth (Jaeger et al. 2021).

EMDE fiscal policy challenges

Overlapping shocks in recent years have eroded fiscal space in EMDEs. At the same time, spending pressures have been growing and sizable gaps persist in meeting multifaceted policy objectives, including environmental sustainability and inclusive development goals. Despite measures to strengthen fiscal positions, deficits and debt remain above pre-pandemic averages. Government debt in EMDEs reached nearly 70 percent of GDP in 2024—the highest level in the last 55 years. Spending on critical priorities, including public investment and social safety nets, has been constrained by the heightened cost of servicing debt (refer to figure 1.14.A; World Bank 2025g). In LICs, debt has continuously shifted toward less concessional sources of financing amid the decline in ODA in recent years. Consequently, these economies have experienced an increase in the cost of servicing debt. The combination of high borrowing costs and still-elevated debt levels will necessitate continued fiscal consolidation in LICs.

EMDEs, especially LICs, continue to substantially lag advanced economies in revenue collection. Building tax capacity is crucial to fostering sustainable debt dynamics while providing public services. It can also accelerate broader economic development, especially if complemented with reforms that deepen financial development and government effectiveness (Bellon and Warwick 2025). On the expenditure side, improvements to expenditure review, planning, and procurement processes can foster spending efficiency.

Fiscal sustainability can be enhanced by well-designed fiscal policy frameworks. Among EMDEs, there has been an increase in the use of fiscal rules, stabilization funds, and medium-term fiscal frameworks over time. Although more than half of EMDEs have adopted at least one type of

FIGURE 1.14 EMDE fiscal policy challenges

Fiscal space in EMDEs remains constrained amid high levels of government debt and elevated debt-servicing costs, highlighting the need to mobilize domestic revenues and use government spending effectively and efficiently. Historically, fiscal rules in EMDEs have tended to deliver improvements in fiscal balances, and they substantially increase the likelihood of a multiyear fiscal adjustment episode. Simple fiscal rules are more likely than complex rules to lead to a revenue-based adjustment episode.

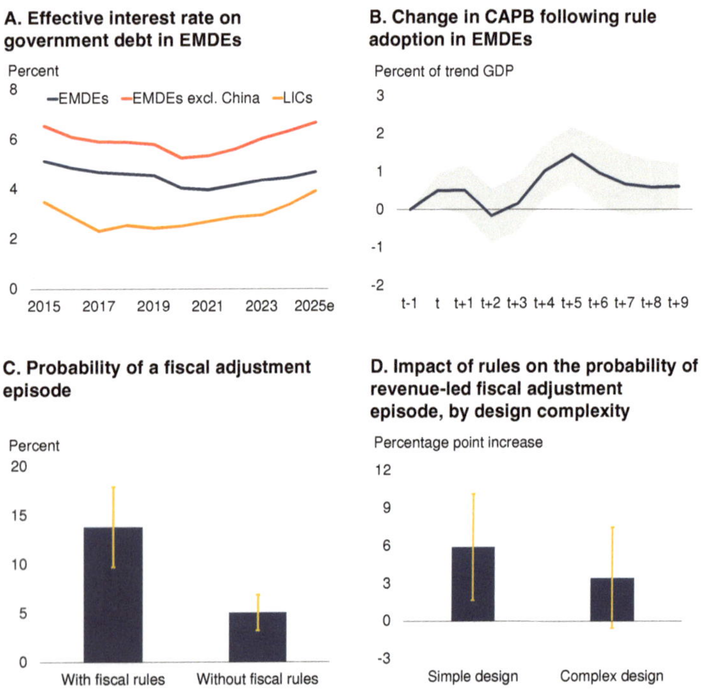

Sources: Fatás, Gootjes, and Mawejje (2026); International Monetary Fund; Organisation for Economic Co-operation and Development (OECD); World Bank.

Note: e = estimate. AEs = advanced economies; CAPB = cyclically-adjusted primary balance; EMDEs = emerging market and developing economies; excl. = excluding; LICs = low-income countries.

A. The effective interest rate is computed as interest payment divided by the average of government debt at the end of the current and previous years. Aggregates are computed as weighted averages, using nominal GDP in U.S. dollars as weights. Sample includes up to 143 EMDEs, including up to 23 LICs.

B. Results are from local projections (LP)–augmented inverse probability weighting (AIPW) regressions. Technical details are provided in annex 3.2. Panel shows the impulse response function of the CAPB (percent of trend GDP) to the adoption of a fiscal rule, with the rule(s) adopted at year t. Line shows the cumulative improvement in the CAPB in the years after fiscal rule adoption, compared with the counterfactual scenario of no rule adoption in year *t*. Shaded area shows 90 percent confidence intervals. Results are based on a sample of 116 countries (83 EMDEs and 33 AEs) with 58 cases of fiscal rule adoption (33 in EMDEs and 25 in AEs); the number of observations included in each regression ranges between 2,201 and 2,207.

C.D. Results are from probit regressions. Technical details are provided in annex 3.4. The vertical lines show 90 percent confidence intervals. Sample includes 122 economies, of which 89 are EMDEs and 33 are AEs.

C. Panel shows the likelihood of starting a fiscal adjustment episode associated with the presence of fiscal rules.

D. Rule design complexity is defined by the number of technical design features embedded in the rules, focusing specifically on elements related to enforceability (strict enforcement provision, correction mechanisms) and flexibility (escape clauses, stabilization features, golden rules). Rules with no more than two such features are classified as having simple design.

fiscal rule, the share remains far lower than in advanced economies, where roughly nine in ten economies have done so. A substantial body of evidence indicates that fiscal rules can help contain spending pressures, reduce fiscal deficits, and lower sovereign bond spreads (Heinemann, Moessinger, and Yeter 2018; Potrafke 2025). Beyond fiscal outcomes, an emerging strand of the literature has found fiscal rules to be associated with improved macroeconomic outcomes. Yet the literature also highlights potential unintended consequences of poorly designed fiscal rules, including the risk of inducing procyclical policies that may, in turn, dampen growth.

Historically, fiscal rules in EMDEs are associated with improvements in fiscal balances in the medium and long term (refer to figure 1.14.B and chapter 3). However, the gains of fiscal rule adoption are not automatically durable. The improvements tend to be more pronounced in economies with strong institutions, and when rules are adopted in favorable economic conditions.

In the last two decades, more EMDEs have adopted multiple fiscal rules, and the design features of rules have become increasingly complex, making the institutional burden of compliance more challenging (Alonso et al. 2025). At the same time, in the context of rapid accumulation of debt over a long period and a rising cost of servicing debt in recent years, it is useful to understand whether fiscal rules can act as a catalyst for sustained periods of fiscal consolidation. Evidence suggests they can: in a given year, economies with fiscal rules face a 14 percent probability of starting a fiscal adjustment episode—a multiyear period of improvement in the primary balance—compared with 5 percent in economies without rules (refer to figure 1.14.C). Rule design matters for the composition of adjustment. Strict enforcement mechanisms promote expenditure-based adjustment episodes, while simple design frameworks are associated with an increased probability of revenue-based adjustment (refer to figure 1.14.D).

EMDE monetary and financial policy challenges

Policy makers across EMDEs face ongoing risks to both growth and inflation in the context of a more challenging trade environment, as well as elevated wage growth and inflation expectations. While headline inflation rates have moderated in recent

FIGURE 1.15 EMDE monetary and financial policy challenges

EMDE policy makers face ongoing risks to both growth and inflation, requiring careful calibration. While headline inflation rates have moderated in recent years, they remain slightly but persistently above target in many EMDEs, prompting monetary authorities to slow the pace of policy easing. Independent monetary policy has been associated with lower inflation and inflation persistence and better-anchored inflation expectations. Against a backdrop of accelerating capital flows into EMDEs, financial regulators could enhance macroprudential buffers to contain potential financial stability risks.

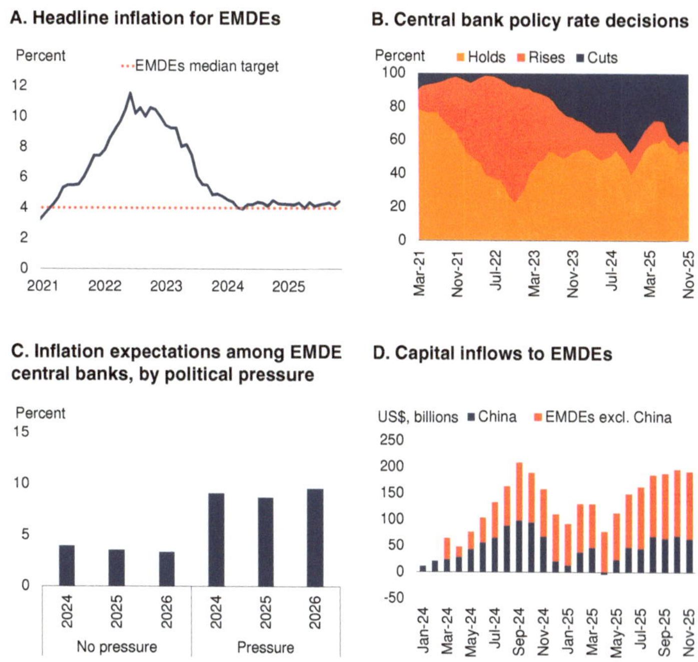

Sources: Binder (2021); Consensus Economics; Haver Analytics; IIF (database); World Bank.

Note: EMDEs = emerging market and developing economies; excl. = excluding.

A. Panel shows median headline inflation and median inflation target for a sample of 40 EMDEs. Last observation is November 2025.

B. Panel shows central bank policy rate decisions for a sample of 56 EMDEs. Last observation is November 2025.

C. Panel shows one-year-ahead expectation of headline inflation from Consensus Economics; for example, 2026 expectations are based on 2025 survey responses. Bars show the average, by year, of monthly median readings for each group. "No pressure" and "Pressure" classifications follow Binder (2021), using an updated data set on political pressure faced by central banks over 2010–22. Sample includes 51 EMDEs. Last observation is November 2025.

D. Panel shows cumulative net portfolio flows since January 2024. Sample includes 26 EMDEs. Last observation is November 2025.

years, they remain slightly but persistently above target in many EMDEs, prompting nearly 60 percent of central banks to hold policy rates last year, up from about 50 percent in the second half of 2024 (refer to figures 1.15.A and 1.15.B).

In an environment of heightened uncertainty and macroeconomic volatility, monetary policy needs to remain vigilant, carefully weighing risks and trade-offs between inflation and growth to ensure that the policy stance is appropriately calibrated. Such focused pursuit of monetary policy objectives requires a significant degree of central bank independence. In fact, independent monetary policy has been associated with lower inflation and inflation persistence, better anchoring of inflation expectations, and reduced regressive effects of inflationary shocks on poor households (Altissimo, Ehrmann, and Smets 2006; Binder 2021; Mishkin 2007; Tiberto 2025). Inflation expectations remain elevated in several EMDEs where central banks have faced political pressure over the past few years (refer to figure 1.15.C; Binder 2021). In these economies, high inflation expectations could become further entrenched in the event of additional volatility or unexpected shocks, further undermining monetary policy credibility.

In addition, clear communications, robust monetary frameworks, and a commitment to low and steady inflation through data-dependent decision-making can reinforce credibility. At the current juncture, policy makers need to also consider potential supply-side shifts including strains in supply chains, declines in productivity, and wage pressures, and their possible second-round effects on inflation (De Fiore, Sandri, and Yetman 2025; Greene 2025).

With cumulative net portfolio flows to EMDEs picking up in 2025, EMDE financial regulators could enhance macroprudential buffers to help contain potential financial stability risks (refer to figure 1.15.D). Precautionary steps can include comprehensive stress tests for financial institutions and the scrutiny of credit quality, liquidity levels, capital adequacy, foreign-currency-denominated liabilities, and their resilience to abrupt shifts in asset valuations and heightened volatility, including risks stemming from the sovereign–bank nexus (World Bank 2024c). These efforts can be complemented by reinforcing macroprudential frameworks, which can also incorporate climate-related assessments where physical and transition risks are material. In frontier markets, where portfolio flows tend to be more volatile and where institutional capacity may be more limited, ensuring effective oversight can help contain risks emanating from the financial sector.

EMDE structural policy challenges

Creating sufficient job opportunities

EMDEs face a major jobs challenge. By 2035, 1.2 billion young people will reach working age in EMDEs (refer to figure 1.16.A). Total working-age populations will continue to expand significantly in many countries beyond this horizon, particularly in Sub-Saharan Africa, the Middle East and North Africa, and South Asia, even as global population growth slows. Creating sufficient employment opportunities in places where the workforce is growing, especially for young people, is a critical priority to lift potential output growth and help contain migration pressures. In addition to job creation, policy makers should consider the quality of jobs—for example, the productivity of workers, their wages, employment-related benefits, and working conditions such as informal work arrangements. In most cases, policies that boost job creation can also enhance job quality. Related employment issues also include increasing social and labor protection, raising participation rates, and easing sectoral transitions for impacted workers.

Three pillars can help guide policy makers in tackling this jobs challenge: investing in foundational infrastructure, such as physical and digital infrastructure, as well as education and upskilling to build human capital; fostering an improved business environment with effective governance; and mobilizing private investment. Together these pillars can help invigorate growth by boosting investment and creating the necessary conditions for people and firms to thrive, including their ability to use emerging digital technologies effectively. EMDEs that have registered higher investment growth have also tended to experience stronger employment growth (refer to figure 1.16.B).

Some key sectors hold particular promise for local job creation at scale in EMDEs: infrastructure (including energy), health care, agribusiness, tourism, and value-added manufacturing (World Bank 2025e). These sectors have several characteristics in common: they contribute disproportionately to employment and value-added growth, and they tend to be relatively labor-intensive, tradable, and technologically upgradeable. These sectors can also offer some resilience to global headwinds and can contribute to the foundations of broader economic growth and job creation. For instance, some of these sectors are already supporting growth in Africa (Bhorat et al. 2025).

Mobilizing investment in EMDEs

Both public and private investment growth in EMDEs have significantly weakened since the global financial crisis as a result of a series of overlapping global shocks, waning economic integration, and continued structural challenges, such as institutional weakness. Average annual private investment growth dropped from 12 percent in 2000–09 to about 7 percent in 2010–23, while public investment growth fell from 10 percent to 5 percent over the same period. This has been compounded by a parallel softening in FDI inflows to EMDEs. Adopting policies to help mobilize private investment in EMDEs is critical given limited fiscal space to boost public investment and the need to counter the effects of ongoing global policy uncertainty.

Reigniting investment, particularly private investment, in EMDEs requires a coherent domestic agenda that lowers policy uncertainty, strengthens institutions, restores macro-fiscal credibility, and reconnects firms to global markets. In particular, high-quality institutions and a predictable, rules-based business environment are foundational for investment. Comprehensive policy packages raise the probability of generating an investment acceleration by about 9 percentage points (de Haan, Stamm, and Yu 2025). Scaling up public investment by 1 percent of GDP in EMDEs with high public investment efficiency and ample fiscal space can increase output by up to about 1.6 percent after five years (Adarov, Clements, and Jalles 2024).

A 10-percent increase in FDI inflows is associated with a 0.8 percent increase in GDP after three years across countries with stronger institutions, lower informality, better human capital, and greater trade openness (Adarov and Pallan 2025). There are also important synergies among public, private, and foreign direct investment, and they tend to rise together in response to stronger macroeconomic and structural conditions, jointly triggering virtuous cycles.

Fostering development in frontier market economies

Recent policy shifts threaten to impede global trade integration, hampering a historical driver of growth and income convergence in EMDEs. The challenge is acute in frontier market economies, a diverse group of countries characterized by partial integration with global financial markets—less than emerging markets, but more than other developing economies (refer to chapter 4, forthcoming). Since 2000, financial openness has increased markedly in frontier markets (refer to figure 1.16.C). Their share of global capital inflows has also risen. Yet the significant economic potential of this group of countries has not been realized over the last 25 years, with limited financial development and institutional progress impeding economies from realizing the full benefits of international financial integration and exacerbating the impact of global market shocks. Growth in output per capita has been mixed in frontier markets, progress on poverty reduction has slowed, and large gaps persist relative to emerging markets across a broad range of socioeconomic indicators. Capital deepening has also been modest (refer to figure 1.16.D).

Capitalizing on the economic potential of frontier market economies would drive improved development outcomes in these economies, which already account for over one-fifth of the global population. To achieve this, frontier markets need to advance financial integration while containing associated risks, building on their existing market access; bolster macroeconomic stability; and catalyze investment and productivity growth. Those frontier markets that have recorded the highest growth in income per capita over the last quarter-century have also tended to fare better than their peers in growing their capital stocks as well as in containing debt pressures, aided by improvements in institutional quality and broader structural reforms. The international community can help foster a more conducive environment for sustained frontier market development, which would benefit global job creation and growth.

FIGURE 1.16 EMDE structural policy challenges

EMDEs face a major jobs challenge, with 1.2 billion young people in these economies reaching working age over the next 10 years. As part of a broader policy package to durably improve growth and foster job creation, policy makers need to focus on measures that lift investment, as EMDEs with higher investment growth tend to record stronger employment growth. Progress is critical in frontier market economies: Despite the promise of market access, demographic potential, and increased financial openness, their per capita GDP growth since 2000 has been modest, and capital stocks remain low relative to those in emerging markets.

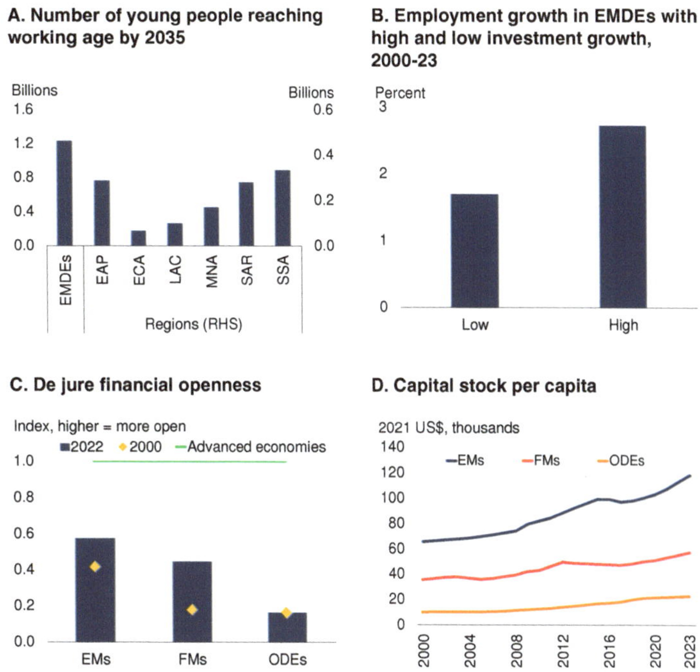

Sources: Chinn and Ito (2006); Feenstra, Inklaar, and Timmer (2015); Haver Analytics; ILOSTAT (database); UN World Population Prospects (database); WDI (database); World Bank.

Note: EAP = East Asia and Pacific; ECA = Europe and Central Asia; EMs = emerging markets; EMDEs = emerging market and developing economies; FMs = frontier markets; LAC = Latin America and the Caribbean; MNA = Middle East, North Africa, Afghanistan and Pakistan; ODEs = other developing economies, neither EMs nor FMs; RHS= right-hand scale; SAR = South Asia; SSA = Sub -Saharan Africa.

A. Bars show the number of young people (aged 15-24) in each region in 2035.

B. Bars show group medians. "Low" and "High" indicate annual investment growth in the top and bottom third of the distribution. Differences in median employment growth between "Low" and "High" in subsamples are statistically significant at the 1 percent level. Sample includes 69 EMDEs from 2000 to 2023.

C. Financial openness is proxied by the Chinn-Ito Index, which measures capital account openness using the first principal component of variables on regulatory controls over current or capital account transactions, with 1 (normalized) the most open (Chinn and Ito 2006). Values are medians. Balanced sample of 34 EMs, 37 FMs, and 69 ODEs.

D. Lines represent median value of capital stock per capita per country group. Sample includes 34 EMs, 39 FMs, and 62 ODEs. Last data available are 2023.

TABLE 1.2 Emerging market and developing economies[1]

Commodity exporters [2]		Commodity importers [3]	
Algeria*	Lao PDR	Afghanistan	Somalia, Fed. Rep.
Angola*	Liberia	Albania	Sri Lanka
Argentina	Libya*	Antigua and Barbuda	St. Kitts and Nevis
Armenia	Madagascar	Bahamas, The	St. Lucia
Azerbaijan*	Malawi	Bangladesh	St. Vincent and the Grenadines
Bahrain*	Mali	Barbados	Syrian Arab Republic
Belize	Mauritania	Belarus	Thailand
Benin	Mongolia	Bosnia and Herzegovina	Tonga
Bhutan*	Mozambique	Cambodia	Tunisia
Bolivia*	Myanmar*	China	Türkiye
Botswana	Namibia	Djibouti	Tuvalu
Brazil	Nicaragua	Dominica	Vanuatu
Burkina Faso	Niger	Dominican Republic	Viet Nam
Burundi	Nigeria*	Egypt, Arab Rep.	
Cabo Verde	Oman*	El Salvador	
Cameroon*	Papua New Guinea	Eswatini	
Central African Republic	Paraguay	Georgia	
Chad*	Peru	Grenada	
Chile	Qatar*	Haiti	
Colombia*	Russian Federation*	Hungary	
Comoros	Rwanda	India	
Congo, Dem. Rep.	São Tomé and Príncipe	Jamaica	
Congo, Rep.*	Saudi Arabia*	Jordan	
Costa Rica	Senegal	Kiribati	
Côte d'Ivoire	Seychelles	Lebanon	
Ecuador*	Sierra Leone	Lesotho	
Equatorial Guinea*	Solomon Islands	Malaysia	
Eritrea	South Africa	Maldives	
Ethiopia	South Sudan*	Marshall Islands	
Fiji	Sudan	Mauritius	
Gabon*	Suriname	Mexico	
Gambia, The	Tajikistan	Micronesia, Fed. Sts.	
Ghana*	Tanzania	Moldova	
Guatemala	Timor-Leste*	Montenegro	
Guinea	Togo	Morocco	
Guinea-Bissau	Trinidad and Tobago*	Nauru	
Guyana*	Uganda	Nepal	
Honduras	Ukraine	North Macedonia	
Indonesia*	United Arab Emirates*	Pakistan	
Iran, Islamic Rep.*	Uruguay	Palau	
Iraq*	Uzbekistan	Panama	
Kazakhstan*	West Bank and Gaza	Philippines	
Kenya	Yemen, Rep.*	Poland	
Kosovo	Zambia	Romania	
Kuwait*	Zimbabwe	Samoa	
Kyrgyz Republic		Serbia	

* Energy exporters.

1. Emerging market and developing economies (EMDEs) include all those that are not classified as advanced economies and for which a forecast is published for this report. Dependent territories are excluded. Advanced economies include Australia; Austria; Belgium; Canada; Croatia; Cyprus; Czechia; Denmark; Estonia; Finland; France; Germany; Greece; Hong Kong SAR, China; Iceland; Ireland; Israel; Italy; Japan; the Republic of Korea; Latvia; Lithuania; Luxembourg; Malta; the Netherlands; New Zealand; Norway; Portugal; Singapore; the Slovak Republic; Slovenia; Spain; Sweden; Switzerland; the United Kingdom; and the United States. Since Bulgaria became a member of the euro area on January 1, 2026, it has been removed from the list of EMDEs, and related growth aggregates, to avoid double counting.

2. An economy is defined as commodity exporter when, on average in 2017-19, either (1) total commodities exports accounted for 30 percent or more of total exports or (2) exports of any single commodity accounted for 20 percent or more of total exports. Economies for which these thresholds were met as a result of re-exports were excluded. When data were not available, judgment was used. This taxonomy results in the classification of some well-diversified economies as importers, even if they are exporters of certain commodities (for example, Mexico).

3. Commodity importers are EMDEs not classified as commodity exporters.

References

Acemoglu, D. 2025. "The Simple Macroeconomics of AI." *Economic Policy* 40 (121): 13–58.

ACLED (Armed Conflict Location & Event Data Project) database. Accessed on September 30, 2025. https://acleddata.com/data-export-tool.

Adarov, A., B. Clements, and J. T. Jalles. 2024. "Revisiting Public Investment Multipliers: Nonlinear Effects of the Business Cycle, Fiscal Space, Efficiency, and Capital Stock." Policy Research Working Paper 10954, World Bank, Washington, DC.

Adarov, A., and H. Pallan. 2025. "Foreign Direct Investment in Retreat: Policies to Turn the Tide." In *Accelerating Investment: Challenges and Policies*, edited by A. Adarov, Chapter 5. Washington, DC: World Bank.

Aghion, P., and S. Bunel. 2024. "AI and Growth: Where do we Stand?" Technical Report, London School of Economics.

Alonso-Albarran, V., C. Arroyo, O. Aydin, H. R. Davoodi, W. R. Lam, V. Balasundharam, G. Hegab, et al. 2025. "Fiscal Rules and Fiscal Councils: Recent Trends and Revisions since the Pandemic." IMF Working Paper 25/198, International Monetary Fund, Washington, DC.

Altissimo, F., M. Ehrmann, and F. Smets. 2006. "Inflation Persistence and Price-Setting Behaviour in the Euro Area—A Summary of the IPN Evidence." *ECB Occasional Paper,* No. 46. Frankfurt: European Central Bank.

Angeli M., C. Archer, S. Batten, A. Cesa-Bianchi, L. D'Aguanno, A. Haberis, T. Löber, et al. 2022. "Climate Change: Possible Macroeconomic Implications." *Quarterly Bulletin,* 2022 Q4. London: Bank of England.

Azzimonti, M. 2025. "Why Predicted and Actual Tariff Rates Diverged in May 2025." *Economic Brief,* No. 25-29. Richmond: Federal Reserve Bank of Richmond.

Baily, M., E. Brynjolfsson, and A. Korinek. 2023. "Machines of Mind: The Case for an AI-powered Productivity Boom." Brookings Institution, Washington, DC.

Bellon, M., R. Warwick. 2025. "State Capacity, Institutions and Growth: Taxing for Takeoff—Revisiting the Tax Tipping Point." IMF Working Paper 25/203, International Monetary Fund, Washington, DC.

Bhorat, H., B. Coulibaly, R. Newfarmer, and J. Page, eds. 2025. *New Pathways to Job Creation in Africa: The Promise of Industries without Smokestacks.* Washington, DC: Brookings Institution Press.

Binder, C. C. 2021. "Political Pressure on Central Banks." *Journal of Money, Credit and Banking* 53 (4): 715–44.

Black, S., R. de Mooij, V. Gaspar, I. W. H. Parry, and K. Zhunussova. 2024. "Fiscal Implications of Global Decarbonization." IMF Working Paper 24/045, International Monetary Fund, Washington, DC.

Bown, C. P. 2021. "How COVID-19 Medical Supply Shortages Led to Extraordinary Trade and Industrial Policy." *Asian Economic Policy Review* 17 (1): 114–35.

Brynjolfsson, E., D. Li, and L. R. Raymond. 2023. "Generative AI at Work." NBER Working Paper 31151, National Bureau of Economic Research, Cambridge, MA.

Carleton, T. D. Esther, K. Jack, and G. Zappala. 2025. "The Economics of Climate Adaptation: From Academic Insights to Effective Policy" *VoxEU* (blog). April 15, 2025. https://cepr.org/voxeu/columns/economics-climate-adaptation-academic-insights-effective-policy.

Castro-Vincenzi, J. 2024. "Climate Hazards and Resilience in the Global Car Industry." Harvard University, Cambridge, MA.

Cavallo, A., P. Llamas, and F. Vazquez. 2025. "Tracking the Short-Run Price Impact of U.S. Tariffs." NBER Working Paper 34496, National Bureau of Economic Research, Cambridge, MA.

Cazzaniga, M., F. Jaumotte, L. Li, G. Melina, A. J. Panton, C. Pizzinelli, E. J. Rockall, et al. 2024. "Gen-AI: Artificial Intelligence and the Future of Work." IMF Staff Discussion Note 24/001, International Monetary Fund, Washington, DC.

CBO (Congressional Budget Office). 2025a. *An Update to the Demographic Outlook.* Washington, DC: Congressional Budget Office.

CBO (Congressional Budget Office). 2025b. *H.R. 1, One Big Beautiful Bill Act (Dynamic Estimate).* Washington, DC: Congressional Budget Office.

CBO (Congressional Budget Office). 2025c. *A Quantitative Analysis of the Effects of the Government Shutdown on the Economy Under Three Scenarios, as of October 29, 2025.* Washington, DC: Congressional Budget Office.

Chen, Y., and T. Hart. 2025. "Common Framework, Uncommon Challenges: Lessons from the Post-COVID Debt Restructuring Architecture." *ODI Global Insight* (blog). February 21. 2025. https://odi.org/en/insights.

Chinn, M., and H. Ito. 2006. "What Matters for Financial Development? Capital Controls, Institutions, and Interactions." *Journal of Development Economics* 81 (1): 163–92.

Choudhary, R., F. U. Ruch, and E. Skrok. 2024. "Taxing for Growth: Revisiting the 15 Percent Threshold." Policy Research Working Paper 10943, World Bank, Washington, DC.

Chrimes, T., B. Gootjes, M. A. Kose, and C. Wheeler. 2024. *The Great Reversal: Prospects, Risks, and Policies in International Development Association (IDA) Countries.* Washington, DC: World Bank.

Claessens, S., M. A. Kose, and M. E. Terrones. 2012. "How do Business and Financial Cycles Interact?" *Journal of International Economics* 87 (1): 178–90.

Dabla-Norris, E., and Y. B. Gündüz. 2014. "Exogenous Shocks and Growth Crises in Low-Income Countries: A Vulnerability Index." *World Development* 59 (360): 360–78.

Damania, R., E. Ebadi, K. Mayr, J. Russ, and E. Zaveri. 2025. *Reboot Development: The Economics of a Livable Planet.* Washington, DC: World Bank.

Damania, R., S. Polasky, M. Ruckelshaus, J. Russ, M. Amann, R. Chaplin-Kramer, J. Gerber, et al. 2023. *Nature's Frontiers: Achieving Sustainability, Efficiency, and Prosperity with Natural Capital.* Washington, DC: World Bank.

De Fiore, F., D. Sandri, and J. Yetman. 2025. "Household Perceptions and Expectations in the Wake of the Inflation Surge: Survey Evidence." *BIS Bulletins* 114, Bank for International Settlements, Basel.

De Haan, J., K. Stamm, and S. Yu. 2025. "The Magic of Investment Accelerations." In *Accelerating Investment: Challenges and Policies,* edited by A. Adarov, Chapter 2. Washington, DC: World Bank.

Dzau, V. J., J. Halton, J. Kaseya, B. Oramah, J.-A. Røttingen, M. Lucera, and B. Camero. 2025. "Closing the Deal: A G20 Panel Report on Financing for Pandemic Threats." *The Lancet* 406 (10517): 22969–98.

Egger, P., and M. Larch. 2008. "Interdependent Preferential Trade Agreement Memberships: An Empirical Analysis." *Journal of International Economics* 76 (2): 384–99.

FAO (Food and Agriculture Organization of the United Nations). 2024. *The State of World Fisheries and Aquaculture. Blue Transformation in Action.* Rome: FAO.

Fatás, A., B. Gootjes, and J. Mawejje. 2026. "Dynamic Effects of Fiscal Rules: Do Initial Conditions Matter?" *Journal of International Money and Finance* 161 (February): *103499.*

Feenstra, R. C., R. Inklaar and M. P. Timmer. 2015. "The Next Generation of the Penn World Table." *American Economic Review* 105 (10): 3150–82.

Filippucci, F., P. Gal, and M. Schief. 2024. "Miracle or Myth? Assessing the Macroeconomic Productivity Gains from Artificial Intelligence." Technical Report, OECD Publishing, Paris.

FSIN (Food Security Information Network) and GNAFC (Global Network Against Food Crises). 2025. *Global Report on Food Crises 2025.* Rome: Food Security Information Network; Global Network Against Food Crises.

Gibson, K. 2024. "Leveraging AI in Business: 3 Real-World Examples." *Harvard Business School Online* (blog). September 4, 2024. https://online.hbs.edu/blog/post/ai-in-business.

Greene, M. 2025. "The Supply Side Demands More Attention." Speech at the University of Glasgow Business School, September 25, 2025.

Guénette, J. D., M. A. Kose, and N. Sugawara. 2022. "Is a Global Recession Imminent?" Equitable Growth, Finance, and Institutions Policy Note 4, World Bank, Washington, DC.

Heinemann, F., M. D. Moessinger, and M. Yeter. 2018. "Do Fiscal Rules Constrain Fiscal Policy? A Meta-Regression-Analysis." *European Journal of Political Economy* 51 (January): 69–92.

Helpman, E. 2025. "The Future of Global Trade." NBER Working Paper 34189, National Bureau of Economic Research, Cambridge, MA.

IDMC (Internal Displacement Monitoring Centre). 2025. *Global Report on Internal Displacement 2025.* Geneva: Internal Displacement Monitoring Centre.

IEA (International Energy Agency). 2024. *Strategies for Affordable and Fair Clean Energy Transitions.* May. Paris: IEA.

IEA (International Energy Agency). 2025. *Oil Market Report.* October. Paris: IEA.

ILO (International Labour Organization). 2025. *World Employment and Social Outlook: May 2025 Update.* Geneva: ILO.

IMF (International Monetary Fund). 2025a. *World Economic Outlook: Global Economy in Flux, Prospects Remain Dim.* Washington, DC: IMF.

IMF (International Monetary Fund). 2025b. *Global Financial Stability Report: Shifting Ground beneath the Calm.* October. Washington, DC: IMF.

IMF (International Monetary Fund) and World Bank. 2025. *Debt Vulnerabilities in Low-Income Countries: Recent Developments and Trends.* Washington, DC: International Monetary Fund; World Bank.

Jaeger, J., G. Walls, E. Clarke, and J. C. Altamirano. 2021. "The Green Jobs Advantage: How Climate-Friendly Investments Are Better Job Creators." Working Paper, World Resources Institute, Washington, DC.

Jafino, B. A., B. J. Walsh, J. Rozenberg, and S. Hallegatte. 2020. "Revised Estimates of the Impact of Climate Change on Extreme Poverty by 2030." Policy Research Working Paper 9417, World Bank, Washington, DC.

Koh, W. C., and S. Yu. 2020. "Macroeconomic and Financial Sector Policies." In *A Decade After the Global Recession: Lessons and Challenges for Emerging and Developing Economies,* edited by M. A. Kose and F. Ohnsorge, 209–53. Washington, DC: World Bank.

Kose, M. A., S. Kurlat, F. Ohnsorge, and N. Sugawara. 2022. "A Cross-Country Database of Fiscal Space." *Journal of International Money and Finance* 128 (November): 102682.

Kose, M. A., N. Sugawara, and M. E. Terrones. 2020. "Global Recessions." Policy Research Working Paper 9172, World Bank, Washington, DC.

Lagarde, C. 2024. "Central Banks in a Changing World: The Role of the ECB in the Face of Climate and Environmental Risks." Speech, European Central Bank, Frankfurt.

Mahler, D. G., N. Yonzan, and C. Lakner. 2022. "The Impact of COVID-19 on Global Inequality and Poverty." Policy Research Working Paper 10198, World Bank, Washington, DC.

Maslej, N., L. Fattorini, R. Perrault, Y. Gil, V. Parli, N. Kariuki, E. Capstick, et al. *Artificial Intelligence Index Report 2025.* AI Index Steering Committee, Institute for Human-Centered, Stanford University. https://doi.org/10.48550/arXiv.2504.07139.

Mawejje, J. 2025. *Fiscal Vulnerabilities in Low-Income Countries: Evolution, Drivers, and Policies.* Washington, DC: World Bank.

McElheran K., M.-J. Yang, Z. Kroff, and E. Brynjolfsson. 2025. "The Rise of Industrial AI in America: Microfoundations of the Productivity J-curve(s)." U.S. Census Bureau Working Paper 25–27, Center for Economic Studies, Washington, DC.

Mejia, S. A., C. Baccianti, M. Mrkaic, N Novta, E. Pugacheva, and P. Topalova. 2019. "Weather Shocks and Output in Low-Income Countries: Adaptation and the Role of Policies." IMF Working Paper 19/178, International Monetary Fund, Washington, DC.

Microsoft. 2025. *The Fastest Diffusion in Human History: A Report on Generative AI Adoption.* Redmond, WA: Microsoft Corporation.

Mishkin, F. S. 2007. "Inflation Dynamics." *International Finance* 10 (3): 317–34.

Mulabdic A., and Y. V. Yotov. 2025. "Geopolitical Risks and Trade." Policy Research Working Paper 11219, World Bank, Washington, DC.

ND-GAIN (Notre Dame Global Adaptation Initiative Country Index) database. Accessed on October 22, 2025. https://gain.nd.edu/our-work/country-index/download-data.

Noy, S., and W. Zhang. 2023. "Experimental Evidence on the Productivity Effects of Generative Artificial Intelligence." *Science* 381 (6654): 187–92.

OECD (Organisation for Economic Cooperation and Development). 2025. "Cuts in Official Development Assistance: OECD Projections for 2025 and the Near Term." *OECD Policy Brief* 26, OECD Publishing, Paris.

Ohnsorge, F., M. Stocker, and M. Y. Some. 2016. "Quantifying Uncertainties in Global Growth Forecasts." Policy Research Working Paper 7770, World Bank, Washington, DC.

Ohnsorge F., and S. Yu (eds). 2022. *The Long Shadow of Informality: Challenges and Policies.* Washington, DC: World Bank.

Olejnik, Ł. W., and J. Kuna. 2025. "Military Expenditures as a Part of Endogenous Fiscal Policy in 21 EU-NATO Countries: The Fiscal Consequences of Rising Defence Budgets." *Defence and Peace Economics*: 1–30.

Oxford Economics. 2019. "Global Economic Model." Oxford Economics, Oxford, U.K.

Penn, C., D. Morgan, Y. Ahmad, K. Elgar, and C. James. 2025. "Smart Spending to Combat Global Health Threats: Tracking Expenditure on Prevention, Preparedness, and Response, and Other Global Public Goods for Health." OECD Health Working Paper 175, OECD Publishing, Paris.

Potrafke, N. 2025. "The Economic Consequences of Fiscal Rules." *Journal of International Money and Finance* 153 (March): 103286.

Rotunno, L., and M. Ruta. 2025. "Trade Partners' Responses to US Tariffs." IMF Working Paper 25/147, International Monetary Fund, Washington, DC.

Tiberto, B. P. 2025. "How Does Central Bank Independence Influence the Relationship Between Inflation, Income Inequality and Poverty?" *Journal of International Money and Finance* 159 (December): 103423.

UNEP (United Nations Environment Programme). 2024. *Emissions Gap Report 2024: No More Hot Air … Please! With a Massive Gap between Rhetoric and Reality, Countries Draft New Climate Commitments.* United Nations Environment Programme, Nairobi.

United Nations. 2024. "World Population Prospects 2024." Department of Economic and Social Affairs, Population Division, United Nations, New York. https://population.un.org/dataportal.

UNHCR (United Nations High Commissioner for Refugees). 2025. *Global Trends: Forced Displacement in 2024.* Copenhagen: United Nations High Commissioner for Refugees.

World Bank. 2015. *Commodity Markets Outlook.* October. Washington, DC: World Bank.

World Bank. 2020. *Global Economic Prospects.* June. Washington, DC: World Bank.

World Bank. 2021. *Global Economic Prospects.* January. Washington, DC: World Bank.

World Bank. 2022. *Commodity Markets Outlook.* April. Washington, DC: World Bank.

World Bank. 2024a. *Global Economic Prospects.* January. Washington, DC: World Bank.

World Bank. 2024b. *The Cost of Inaction: Quantifying the Impact of Climate Change on Health in Low- and Middle-Income Countries.* Washington, DC: World Bank.

World Bank. 2024c. *Finance and Prosperity 2024.* Washington, DC: World Bank.

World Bank. 2025a. *Global Economic Prospects.* January. Washington, DC: World Bank.

World Bank. 2025b. *Global Economic Prospects.* June. Washington, DC: World Bank.

World Bank. 2025c. *Latin America and the Caribbean Economic Review, October 2025: Transformational Entrepreneurship for Jobs and Growth.* Washington, DC: World Bank.

World Bank. 2025d. *South Asia Development Update: Jobs, AI, and Trade.* Washington, DC: World Bank.

World Bank. 2025e. "Foundations for Growth and Jobs." Development Committee Meeting, World Bank, Washington, DC.

World Bank. 2025f. *Global Economic Prospects.* June. Washington, DC: World Bank.

World Bank. 2025g. *International Debt Report 2025.* Washington, DC: World Bank.

World Bank. Forthcoming. *At a Crossroads. Prospects for Government Health Financing Amidst Declining Aid.* Government Resources and Projections for Health Series. Washington, DC: World Bank.

WTO (World Trade Organization). 2024. *World Trade Report 2024: Trade and Inclusiveness. How to Make Trade Work for All.* September. Geneva: WTO.

Wynne, M. A., and N. S. Balke. 1992. "Are Deep Recessions Followed by Strong Recoveries?" *Economics Letters* 39 (2): 183–89.

Zarnowitz, V. 1992. *Business Cycles: Theory, History, Indicators, and Forecasting.* Chicago: University of Chicago.

CHAPTER 2

REGIONAL OUTLOOKS

EAST ASIA and PACIFIC

Growth in the East Asia and Pacific (EAP) region is projected to decelerate to 4.4 percent this year and 4.3 percent in 2027, as a slowdown in China outweighs a pickup in the rest of the region. In China, growth is expected to decline from an estimated 4.9 percent in 2025 to 4.4 percent in 2026 and 4.2 percent in 2027, owing to subdued demand amid an ongoing structural slowdown. Growth in the rest of the region is projected to edge down to 4.5 percent this year and then recover to 4.7 percent in 2027, reflecting the delayed impact of higher trade barriers, with some offset from domestic policy support. Risks to the outlook remain tilted to the downside, owing to the potential for a renewed rise in trade tensions and associated uncertainty. The challenging trade environment and sluggish global growth could weaken the pace of job growth in EAP. Other downside risks include tighter global financial conditions, slower-than-expected growth in China, social unrest and political uncertainty, and natural disasters. Conversely, on the upside, the impact of higher trade barriers may be limited by the ability of firms to adapt, and EAP economies could reap productivity gains from artificial intelligence-related investment and adoption, on account of their greater digital readiness.

Recent developments

Growth in the East Asia and Pacific (EAP) region moderated to an estimated 4.8 percent in 2025—stronger than envisaged in June—from 5 percent in 2024, reflecting a smaller and delayed impact of higher trade barriers and associated uncertainty. In China, the slowdown was moderated by fiscal stimulus in the form of consumer subsidies, which supported consumption growth (refer to figure 2.1.1.A). The strength in exports reflected front-loading ahead of the implementation of tariffs and increased shipments to non-U.S. markets (refer to figure 2.1.1.B). Investment growth slowed, owing to a continued contraction in real estate investment, as sales and prices in the property sector fell further (refer to figure 2.1.1.C).

Elsewhere in EAP, growth eased to an estimated 4.6 percent in 2025, reflecting a slowdown in exports. However, activity was stronger than previously projected in many economies, owing to front-loading and resilient private consumption. More recently, weather-related disruptions dampened growth in the Philippines and a contraction in public investment as well as slowing tourism revenues led to a deceleration in Thailand (refer to figure 2.1.1.D). Industrial production increased, especially in Malaysia, the Philippines, and Viet Nam, largely owing to artificial intelligence (AI)-driven demand for semiconductor exports (refer to figure 2.1.1.E). Growth of output in travel-related services was reflected in the recovery of tourist arrivals to pre-pandemic levels in some countries, while in others, the recovery stalled due to slower outbound tourism from China (refer to figure 2.1.1.F). Private investment remained subdued across the region due to elevated policy uncertainty and high debt—except in Indonesia and Malaysia, where it was underpinned by state-led initiatives and foreign direct investment, respectively. In the Pacific Island economies, growth is estimated to have picked up in 2025, fueled by tourism and strong mining activity.

Inflation has continued to moderate in most EAP economies to rates within or below central bank target ranges, and monetary policies were accommodative. In China, headline consumer price inflation remained low, with the decline in food and energy prices outweighing a rise in core

Note: This section was prepared by Gitanjali Kumar.

FIGURE 2.1.1 EAP: Recent developments

Growth in China was resilient in 2025, boosted by strong consumption growth that was supported by fiscal measures and robust exports due to front-loading in anticipation of higher U.S. tariffs. Export growth also benefited from an increase in shipments to non-U.S. markets. Real estate investment contracted as the property sector deteriorated further. In EAP excluding China, growth was strong in 2025, as export growth remained solid because of front-loading. Industrial production growth was robust in some economies on account of AI-driven demand for semiconductors. Tourist arrivals recovered to pre-pandemic levels in a few economies.

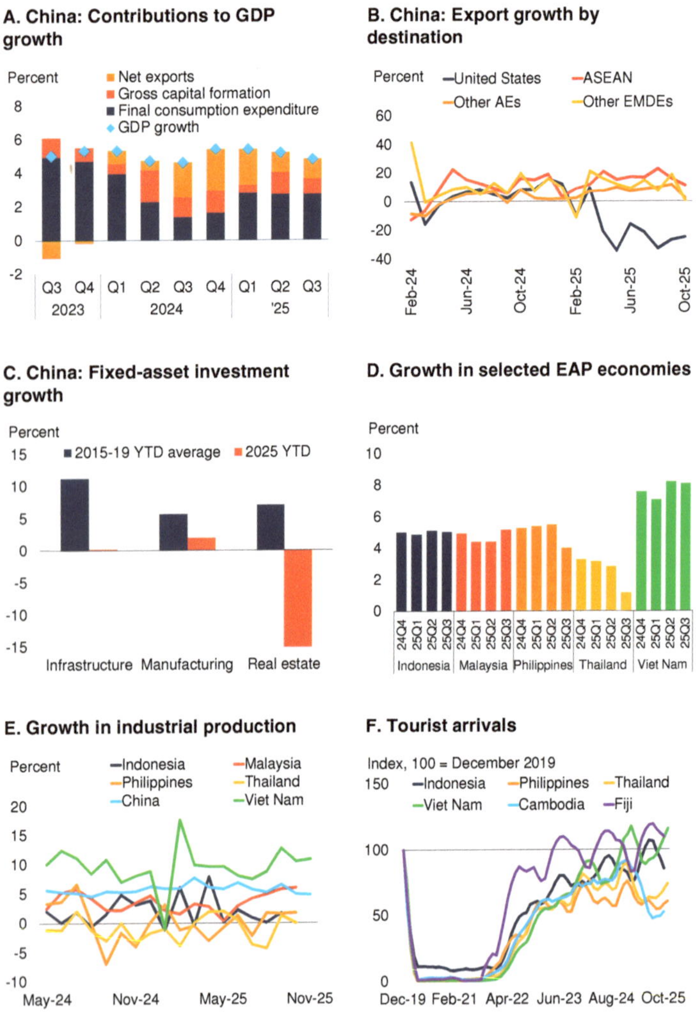

Sources: Haver Analytics; World Bank.

Note: AEs = advanced economies; AI = artificial intelligence; ASEAN = Association of Southeast Asian Nations (Brunei, Cambodia, Indonesia, Lao People's Democratic Republic, Malaysia, Myanmar, the Philippines, Singapore, Thailand, Timor-Leste, and Viet Nam); EAP = East Asia and Pacific; EMDEs = emerging market and developing economies.

A. Year-on-year real GDP growth and expenditure contributions. Last observation is 2025Q3.

B. Year-on-year export growth by destination. Last observation is October 2025.

C. Blue bars denote the simple average of year-on-year growth of year-to-date (YTD) nominal fixed asset investment subcomponents from January to November from 2015 to 2019. Red bars denote year-on-year growth of YTD nominal fixed-asset investment subcomponents from January to November 2025.

D. Year-on-year real GDP growth. Last observation is 2025Q3.

E. Year-on-year growth in industrial production. Last observation is November 2025 for China and Viet Nam. Last observation is October 2025 for Malaysia, the Philippines, and Thailand. Last observation is September 2025 for Indonesia.

F. Index of three-month moving average of tourist arrivals. Last observation is November 2025 for the Philippines, Thailand, and Viet Nam. Last observation is October 2025 for Cambodia, Fiji, and Indonesia.

inflation, which was mostly led by an increase in the prices of goods supported by fiscal stimulus.

After financial conditions tightened sharply upon the announcement of tariffs in April, they eased across the region in the second half of last year, aided by the depreciation of the U.S. dollar. Enthusiasm over AI fueled large gains in equity markets. Amid robust debt issuance, the region saw large capital inflows, dominated by debt flows. In Indonesia, however, brief political turmoil and accelerated monetary policy easing led to capital outflows and a depreciation of the rupiah, requiring central bank intervention.

Outlook

Growth in EAP is projected to moderate to 4.4 percent in 2026 and 4.3 percent in 2027, mainly owing to a deceleration in China (refer to figure 2.1.2.A and table 2.1.1). In contrast, growth in EAP excluding China is projected to edge down to 4.5 percent this year and then rise to 4.7 percent next year, as investment growth helps to offset the waning contribution of net exports (refer to figure 2.1.2.B). Compared with the June projections, the growth forecast for EAP has been revised up by 0.4 percentage point for 2026 and 0.3 percentage point for 2027, reflecting a smaller impact of higher trade barriers than previously anticipated, as well as domestic policy support in some economies.

In China, growth is expected to slow to 4.4 percent in 2026, 0.4 percentage point higher than the June forecast. The higher projection reflects additional fiscal stimulus, resilient exports, and improved investor sentiment due to relatively more stable trade policy and partial tariff relief. However, subdued consumer confidence, the property sector slump, and a softer labor market are expected to restrict growth. Manufacturing investment is anticipated to slow, owing to uncertainty regarding policies aimed at addressing supply-demand imbalances in some sectors, which is putting pressure on profitability. Subdued domestic demand is also expected to maintain downward pressure on consumer and producer prices. Growth is projected to soften further to 4.2 percent in 2027, as structural challenges—including slowing productivity growth, high debt, and population aging—weigh on potential growth.

Elsewhere in EAP, activity is expected to moderate this year before picking up next year. This reflects the unwinding of front-loading, along with stronger investment growth in some countries, owing to domestic policy support. Growth in Indonesia is expected to be sustained by fiscal stimulus and state-led investment. In the Philippines, planned structural reforms are likely to boost investment and productivity, but concerns around governance remain. In Thailand and Viet Nam, the delayed impact of higher tariffs is expected to dampen activity and exports this year, but the recovery in global trade and investment growth will lead to a rebound in 2027 (refer to table 2.1.2). Growth in the Pacific Island economies is forecast to slow to 3.4 percent in 2026 and 3.0 percent in 2027, largely accounted for by Papua New Guinea, where mining production is projected to normalize, and Fiji, where tourism activity is slowing down to its pre-pandemic trend. Growth in the other Pacific economies is expected to be underpinned by tourism, remittances, public investment, and grants.

Higher trade barriers and the unwinding of earlier front-loading are expected to slow export growth across the region over the forecast horizon (refer to figure 2.1.2.C). However, the impact will be smaller than previously expected, on account of the increase in Chinese shipments to non-U.S. markets and AI-driven demand for semiconductors, which should support exports in many EAP economies. Even so, the outlook for trade hinges on future developments related to tariffs and market access. Bilateral trade agreements with the United States are likely to induce changes to the pattern of trade in the region, depending on the relative tariff rates across countries and sectors. Trade diversion and the relocation of production, as observed after the 2018 increases in U.S. tariffs, could lead to a reconfiguration of supply chains and allow some countries to benefit from export-led development, including through job creation (Rotunno et al. 2024). Indeed, announcements and completed transactions of FDI from China to other major economies in the region have increased in recent years (refer to figure 2.1.2.D).

FIGURE 2.1.2 EAP: Outlook

Growth in EAP is projected to decelerate to 4.4 percent in 2026 and 4.3 percent in 2027, as a slowdown in China outweighs a pickup in the rest of the region. In the Pacific Island economies, growth is expected to ease owing to the normalization of mining activity in Papua New Guinea and slowing tourism in Fiji. Higher trade barriers and the unwinding of the front-loading of exports are expected to slow export growth in the region. FDI from China to other major economies in the region has grown in recent years.

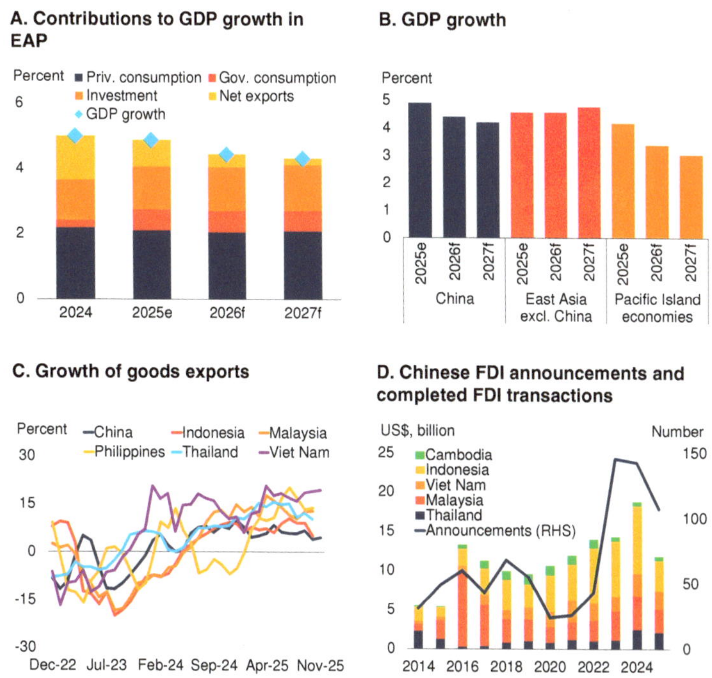

Sources: fDI Markets; Haver Analytics; Macro Poverty Outlook (database); Rhodium Group China Cross-Border Monitor (database); World Bank.

Note: e = estimate; f = forecast. EAP = East Asia and Pacific; FDI = foreign direct investment; Gov. = government; Priv. = private.

A. Annual real GDP growth and contributions of expenditure components. Projections for 2026 and 2027 are by the World Bank. Discrepancies between GDP growth and the sum of its components reflect inventories and residuals.

B. Annual real GDP growth. Projections for 2026 and 2027 are by the World Bank. Aggregate growth rates are calculated using average 2010-19 GDP weights and market exchange rates.

C. Three-month moving average of year-on-year growth in goods exports. Last observation is November 2025 for China and Viet Nam. Last observation is October 2025 for Indonesia, Malaysia, the Philippines, and Thailand.

D. Bars show the value of completed major Chinese FDI transactions (both greenfield and acquisitions) by destination, in all industries. Line shows the number of FDI announcements. Last observation is 2025Q3.

The impact of higher trade barriers on inflation is also ambiguous. Tariff-induced supply chain disruptions can lead to inefficiencies in production and costlier inputs, thereby raising prices and contributing to inflation. On the other hand, trade rerouting and diversion of exports to countries with lower tariffs can generate deflationary pressures in those markets. Major EAP central banks are well placed to respond to their respective domestic conditions, as recent declines in infla-

FIGURE 2.1.3 EAP: Risks

EAP is vulnerable to a rise in trade tensions, as economies have high exposure to U.S. markets. Tighter financial conditions globally could lead to financial strains in economies with elevated debt levels. Further slowing of domestic demand in China would dampen growth elsewhere in the region. On the upside, high levels of AI preparedness of major economies in the region bode well for potential productivity gains in these economies from AI adoption.

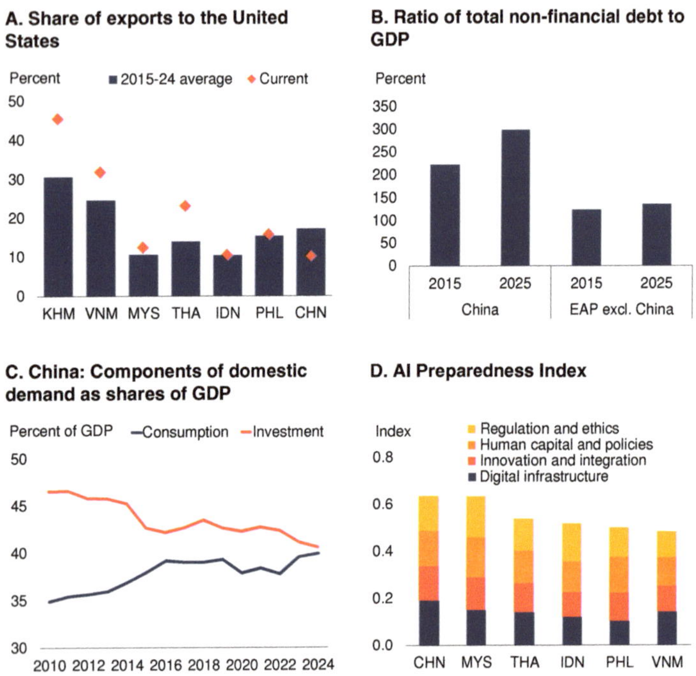

Sources: Cazzaniga et al. (2024); Haver Analytics; Institute of International Finance; World Bank.

Note: AI = artificial intelligence; CHN = China; EAP = East Asia and Pacific; EMDEs = emerging market and developing economies; IDN = Indonesia; KHM = Cambodia; MYS = Malaysia; PHL = the Philippines; THA = Thailand; VNM = Viet Nam.

A. Blue bars show the average share of exports to the United States from 2015 to 2024; diamonds show the current share of exports to the United States. Last observation is November 2025 for Cambodia, China and Viet Nam. Last observation is October 2025 for Indonesia, Malaysia, the Philippines, and Thailand.

B. Total non-financial debt includes household, government, and non-financial corporation debt. EAP excluding China includes Indonesia, Malaysia, the Philippines, Thailand, and Viet Nam. The aggregate is calculated as a GDP-weighted average. 2015 refers to 2015Q3 and 2025 refers to 2025Q3.

C. Panel shows consumption and investment shares of GDP. Last observation is 2024.

D. Bars show the contribution of the components of the AI Preparedness Index to the overall score. The score ranges from 0 to 1 and a higher score indicates more favorable preparedness. Last observation is 2023.

tion, the easing of financial conditions globally, and portfolio inflows have provided room for them to respond appropriately to the effects of trade headwinds.

Risks

Risks to the regional outlook remain tilted to the downside. The possibility of a further increase in trade restrictions and policy uncertainty poses a significant risk to EAP growth. Other downside risks include tighter global financial conditions, slower-than-expected growth in China, political uncertainty and social unrest in some economies, and natural disasters. On the upside, a lower drag from higher trade barriers due to private-sector adaptability and AI-led expansion of investment and exports could lead to higher growth prospects in the region.

A renewed rise in global trade tensions could further depress demand for EAP exports. Although many economies in the region have entered into trade agreements with the United States, trade policy uncertainty continues to be high, as details related to rules-of-origin and transshipments remain unclear (World Bank 2025a). Tariff exemptions for sectors such as electronics and semiconductors could also prove temporary. Persistently elevated or rising policy uncertainty would dampen private investment and growth, as firms delay capital expenditures and hiring decisions. Economies with large manufacturing sectors and high exposure to U.S. markets are particularly vulnerable (refer to figure 2.1.3.A). The challenging trade environment and consequent changes to the structure of job markets, combined with divergent demographics across EAP economies, could negatively impact job growth. Vulnerable groups such as women and the youth are likely to be affected the most.

Tighter financial conditions globally would have adverse implications for growth. A correction in equity markets, an unexpected increase in inflation, or concerns about weakening fiscal positions in key advanced economies could curtail risk appetite and increase risk premia. Strains in global financial markets could spill over to the region through financial channels, including capital outflows, declines in equity markets, and higher borrowing costs. These effects would negatively impact growth, especially in economies with elevated debt levels (refer to figure 2.1.3.B). A decline in global growth associated with tighter financial conditions would further slow activity in the region, particularly through lower exports.

Domestic demand in China could soften by more than expected, owing to a more persistent downturn in the property sector, with rising debt constraining fiscal space at the local government level (refer to figure 2.1.3.C). Slower growth in

China would spill over to other economies in the region, particularly through trade and tourism. In addition, political uncertainty and social unrest in key economies could also dampen regional growth by depressing investor and consumer sentiment, as well as deterring tourism flows.

Across EAP, more frequent natural disasters have cost lives and caused substantial economic losses in recent years. The earthquake in Myanmar last March resulted in about 3,800 fatalities, with over 5,000 injuries, and led to disruptions in production and supply chains, labor shortages, and factory closures (World Bank 2025b). The Philippines suffered powerful earthquakes late last year. In Mongolia, extreme cold weather last winter, for the second consecutive year, led to a sharp contraction in the agricultural sector (World Bank 2025c). More recently, unusually strong typhoons and flooding have affected many economies.

On the upside, the ability of the private sector to adapt to higher trade barriers would boost growth in the region and reduce the drag from slower export growth. In addition, increased technology-led investment and the adoption of AI could lift growth by more than expected and underpin stronger-than-expected demand for EAP exports. There is some evidence that automation in both low-tech and high-tech manufacturing in some EAP economies has boosted employment and labor earnings (Arias et al. 2025). In addition, many EAP economies rank high in terms of AI preparedness, which suggests that they could benefit more from AI-induced productivity gains (refer to figure 2.1.3.D).

TABLE 2.1.1 East Asia and Pacific forecast summary

(Real GDP growth at market prices in percent, unless indicated otherwise)

	2023	2024	2025e	2026f	2027f	Percentage-point differences from June 2025 projections: 2025e	2026f	2027f
EMDE EAP, GDP[1]	**5.2**	**5.0**	**4.8**	**4.4**	**4.3**	**0.3**	**0.4**	**0.3**
GDP per capita (U.S. dollars)	5.1	4.9	4.8	4.3	4.2	0.4	0.3	0.3
(Average including countries that report expenditure components in national accounts)[2]								
EMDE EAP, GDP[2]	5.3	5.0	4.9	4.4	4.3	0.4	0.4	0.3
PPP GDP	5.2	5.0	4.9	4.5	4.4	0.4	0.4	0.3
Private consumption	8.1	5.2	5.0	4.9	4.8	0.1	0.1	0.0
Public consumption	6.6	1.5	4.3	4.4	4.1	-1.1	-0.6	0.4
Fixed investment	4.4	3.3	3.6	3.7	3.8	-1.1	-0.3	0.0
Exports, GNFS[3]	0.4	10.8	6.0	3.7	3.2	3.7	1.0	0.3
Imports, GNFS[3]	2.6	5.9	3.2	2.7	3.1	-0.9	-1.7	-0.5
Net exports, contribution to growth	-0.5	1.4	0.8	0.4	0.2	1.1	0.6	0.2
Memo items: GDP								
China	5.4	5.0	4.9	4.4	4.2	0.4	0.4	0.3
East Asia and Pacific excluding China	4.3	4.8	4.6	4.5	4.7	0.4	0.0	0.0
Indonesia	5.0	5.0	5.0	5.0	5.2	0.3	0.2	0.2
Thailand	2.0	2.5	2.0	1.8	2.5	0.2	0.1	0.2
Commodity exporters	4.8	4.7	4.7	4.9	4.9	0.4	0.2	0.2
Commodity importers excluding China	3.9	5.0	4.5	4.3	4.6	0.4	0.0	0.0
Pacific Island Economies[4]	4.6	3.6	4.2	3.4	3.0	0.1	0.1	0.0

Source: World Bank.

Note: e = estimate; f = forecast. EMDE = emerging market and developing economy; PPP = purchasing power parity. World Bank forecasts are frequently updated based on new information and changing global circumstances. Consequently, projections presented here may differ from those contained in other World Bank documents, even if basic assessments of countries' prospects do not differ at any given moment in time.

1. GDP and expenditure components are measured in average 2010–19 prices and market exchange rates. Excludes the Democratic People's Republic of Korea and dependent territories.

2. Subregion aggregate excludes the Democratic People's Republic of Korea, dependent territories, Fiji, Kiribati, the Marshall Islands, the Federated States of Micronesia, Myanmar, Palau, Papua New Guinea, Samoa, Timor-Leste, Tonga, Tuvalu, and Vanuatu, for which data limitations prevent the forecasting of GDP components.

3. Exports and imports of goods and nonfactor services (GNFS).

4. Includes Fiji, Kiribati, the Marshall Islands, the Federated States of Micronesia, Nauru, Palau, Papua New Guinea, Samoa, the Solomon Islands, Tonga, Tuvalu, and Vanuatu.

TABLE 2.1.2 East Asia and Pacific country forecasts [1]

(Real GDP growth at market prices in percent, unless indicated otherwise)

	2023	2024	2025e	2026f	2027f	Percentage-point differences from June 2025 projections: 2025e	2026f	2027f
Cambodia	5.0	6.0	4.8	4.3	5.1	0.8	-0.2	0.0
China	5.4	5.0	4.9	4.4	4.2	0.4	0.4	0.3
Fiji	9.4	3.5	2.8	3.0	3.1	0.2	0.1	-0.1
Indonesia	5.0	5.0	5.0	5.0	5.2	0.3	0.2	0.2
Kiribati	2.7	5.3	3.9	3.2	2.5	0.0	0.2	0.3
Lao PDR	3.7	4.1	4.2	4.0	3.9	0.7	0.6	0.5
Malaysia	3.5	5.1	4.1	4.1	4.0	0.2	-0.2	-0.3
Marshall Islands [2]	-4.0	3.0	2.5	4.1	2.4	-0.8	1.4	0.1
Micronesia, Fed. Sts. [2]	0.8	0.7	1.0	1.5	0.8	-0.3	0.1	0.1
Mongolia	7.2	5.1	5.9	5.6	5.5	-0.4	0.4	0.3
Myanmar [2 3]	1.0	-1.0	-1.8	3.0	..	0.7	0.0	..
Nauru [2]	0.6	1.6	2.1	1.9	1.9	0.7	0.6	0.6
Palau [2]	2.2	12.8	6.7	3.5	2.7	-1.9	0.0	0.3
Papua New Guinea	3.8	3.8	4.7	3.5	3.1	0.0	0.0	0.0
Philippines	5.5	5.7	5.1	5.3	5.4	-0.2	-0.1	-0.1
Samoa [2]	15.2	4.8	4.2	4.4	3.3	-1.1	1.8	1.2
Solomon Islands	2.7	2.5	2.5	2.6	2.8	-0.1	-0.1	-0.1
Thailand	2.0	2.5	2.0	1.8	2.5	0.2	0.1	0.2
Timor-Leste	2.4	4.1	4.0	3.4	3.8	0.5	0.0	0.3
Tonga [2]	2.8	1.7	2.7	2.3	1.8	0.5	0.5	0.2
Tuvalu	4.0	3.1	3.0	2.6	2.7	0.2	0.3	0.5
Vanuatu	2.1	0.9	1.7	2.8	2.7	3.5	0.5	0.1
Viet Nam	5.1	7.1	7.2	6.3	6.7	1.4	0.2	0.3

Source: World Bank.

Note: e = estimate; f = forecast. World Bank forecasts are frequently updated based on new information and changing global circumstances. Consequently, projections presented here may differ from those contained in other World Bank documents, even if basic assessments of countries' prospects do not significantly differ at any given moment in time.

1. Data are based on GDP measured in average 2010–19 prices and market exchange rates.

2. Values for Timor-Leste represent non-oil GDP. For the following countries, values correspond to the fiscal year: the Marshall Islands, the Federated States of Micronesia, and Palau (October 1–September 30); Myanmar (April 1–March 31); and Nauru, Samoa, and Tonga (July 1–June 30).

3. Data for Myanmar beyond 2026 (which corresponds to the year ending March 2027) are excluded because of a high degree of uncertainty.

EUROPE and CENTRAL ASIA

Growth in Europe and Central Asia (ECA) is expected to hold steady at 2.4 percent in 2026, as solid domestic demand counters the drags from weak euro area growth and heightened trade tensions. Growth is then projected to firm to 2.7 percent in 2027, driven primarily by accelerating activity in Türkiye. More broadly, the pickup in regional growth next year reflects rebounding exports and rising private consumption amid easing inflation. However, growth remains restrained by structural bottlenecks and population aging, and limited job creation is likely to constrain youth entry into the labor market. Downside risks to the outlook include a prolonged extension or intensification of Russia's invasion of Ukraine, a further escalation of trade tensions and policy uncertainty, more persistent inflationary pressures, and tighter financial conditions. On the upside, growth could be supported by an earlier-than-expected end of active hostilities associated with the invasion, faster productivity gains from artificial intelligence, or stronger trade supported by deeper regional integration or export diversification.

Recent developments

Growth in Europe and Central Asia (ECA) is estimated to have slowed to 2.4 percent in 2025, reflecting softer private consumption—especially in the Russian Federation—in part due to the lagged effects of tight monetary policy. Trade modestly expanded in the first half of last year, partly reflecting the front-loading of goods trade ahead of tariff increases. Excluding Russia, Türkiye, and Ukraine, regional growth held steady at 3.2 percent, with Central Asia remaining the fastest-growing subregion.

High-frequency indicators point to subdued activity in the second half of 2025: manufacturing PMIs remained in contractionary territory in Russia, Türkiye, Poland, and Kazakhstan, and new export orders rebounded only partially after declining following the April tariff announcements (refer to figures 2.2.1.A and 2.2.1.B). In contrast, services activity continued to be resilient. Growth also benefited from easing global financing conditions, with sovereign spreads narrowing and equities rising (refer to figure 2.2.1.C).

External headwinds have persisted amid elevated trade policy uncertainty and subdued euro area growth, constraining exports—particularly in Central Europe and the Western Balkans' automotive sectors. While the region has limited direct exposure to the U.S. market, it remains vulnerable through supply chain integration and spillovers from further softening in euro area growth.

Tourism and remittances continued to be important drivers of economic activity in 2025, although their contributions to regional growth moderated. Tourist arrivals remained above pre-pandemic levels but increased more slowly than during the post-pandemic rebound. Remittance inflows, which had surged in previous years alongside strong growth in Russia, have normalized.

In Russia, growth is estimated to have slowed markedly to 0.9 percent in 2025, reflecting tight monetary policy and elevated inflation. The 0.5 percentage point downward revision from June forecasts reflects weaker-than-expected household and corporate borrowing amid tight credit conditions. Estimated oil production was revised down to 9.2 mb/d in late 2025 following attacks

---

Note: This section was prepared by Marie Albert.

FIGURE 2.2.1 ECA: Recent developments

Manufacturing PMIs remained in contractionary territory in the largest economies—the Russian Federation, Türkiye, Poland, and Kazakhstan—through the second half of 2025, pointing to softness in the sector. New export orders rebounded only partially following declines after the April tariff announcements. Financial conditions eased, with spreads narrowing and equities rising. Headline inflation remained elevated in 2025, above pre-pandemic levels, driven by sharp increases in food prices.

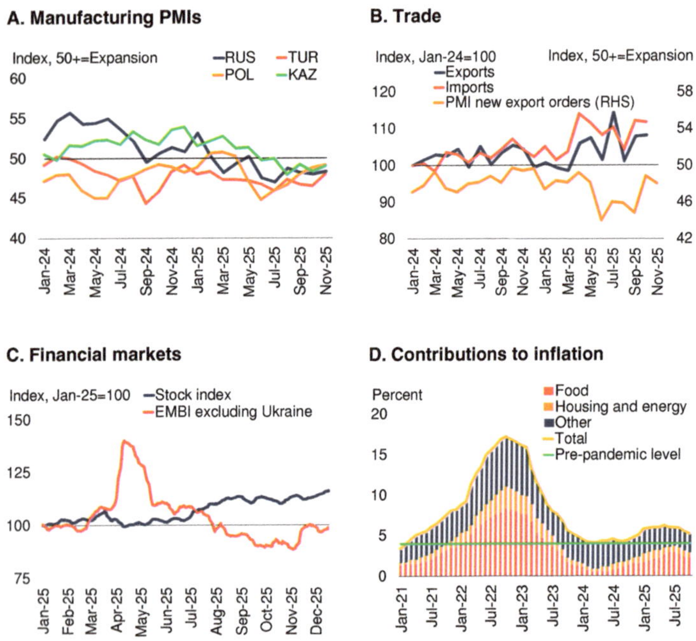

Sources: Haver Analytics; International Monetary Fund; J.P. Morgan; World Bank.

Note: EMBI = Emerging Market Bond Index; KAZ = Kazakhstan; PMI = purchasing managers' index; POL = Poland; RHS = right-hand scale; RUS = Russian Federation; TUR = Türkiye.

A. Lines show PMI manufacturing indexes for Kazakhstan, Poland, the Russian Federation, and Türkiye. Last observation is November 2025.

B. Blue and red lines show indices of total ECA goods export and import values. Sample includes 14 ECA countries. Orange line represents the average PMI new export orders index. Sample includes Poland, the Russian Federation, and Türkiye. Last observation is October 2025 for imports and exports and November 2025 for new export orders.

C. Lines denote the average ECA stock index and EMBI spread (excluding Ukraine). The stock index is the average of national benchmark stock indexes. Sample includes 13 economies for stock index and 6 economies for EMBI spread. Last observation is December 16, 2025.

D. Bars show the contributions of subcomponents to average headline inflation. Yellow and green lines represent the historical average year-on-year headline ECA inflation (excluding Türkiye) and the pre-pandemic level (2019 average), respectively. Sample includes 17 ECA economies. Last observation is October 2025.

on refineries, while lower oil prices, new sanctions, and a stronger ruble further constrained export and fiscal revenues (IEA 2025).

In Türkiye, growth is estimated to have edged up to 3.5 percent in 2025—0.4 percentage point higher-than-expected in June. Activity was supported by solid domestic demand, particularly robust construction investment, and monetary easing throughout the year. International reserves and equity markets recovered following financial market volatility earlier in 2025, reflecting some easing of political tensions.

Ukraine continued to face significant challenges from Russia's invasion. Growth is estimated to have slowed to 2 percent in 2025, with attacks on energy infrastructure weighing on activity. Weak agricultural output growth in early 2025 was partly offset by a modest recovery in industrial production and rising real wages in the second half of the year.

In the second half of 2025, median inflation in ECA picked up again after moderating in the first half. Average headline and core rates remained elevated and above pre-pandemic levels, with most countries exceeding central bank targets (refer to figure 2.2.1.D). Price pressures were largely driven by rising food and utility costs, notably in Central Asia and Romania, while wage growth remained robust. A few Central Asian countries raised monetary policy rates; however, most economies kept stances unchanged, while some—including the three largest economies—cut rates as inflation moderated.

Outlook

Growth in ECA is forecast to hold steady at 2.4 percent in 2026 and then firm to 2.7 percent in 2027, with the pickup driven largely by Türkiye (refer to figure 2.2.2.A; table 2.2.1). This year, solid domestic demand—driven by easing inflation, improving financial conditions, and increasing absorption of European Union funds and defense spending—is expected to help offset slower trade stemming from weak euro area growth and elevated trade tensions. These external drags are expected to ease in 2027, supporting a moderate rebound in exports. Excluding Russia, Türkiye, and Ukraine, regional growth is forecast to average 3.1 percent in 2026–27, but with mixed country trends. Growth is projected to strengthen in about 33 percent of ECA countries in 2026 and just over 60 percent in 2027, as uncertainty recedes. Forecasts for about 60 percent of the economies for 2026–27 have been revised upward since June, reflecting stronger-than-expected private demand.

ECA headline inflation is anticipated to decline gradually in 2026 across most countries, supported by moderating commodity prices (refer to figure 2.2.2.B; World Bank 2025d). Yet, inflation is expected to remain above central bank targets in many economies, suggesting a cautious approach to monetary easing. Though many economies are set to undertake fiscal consolidations in 2026–27, deficit reductions are expected to be modest, exerting only a limited drag on growth (refer to figure 2.2.2.C). Nevertheless, fiscal deficits are likely to remain large—driven by high public investment, interest costs, social transfers, and defense spending—and government debt is projected to continue rising across the region.

In Russia, growth is projected to stabilize, averaging 0.9 percent in 2026–27 (refer to table 2.2.2). Private consumption and investment are set to moderate due to tight financial conditions and reduced fiscal support. The current account surplus is expected to remain modest, dampened by lower oil prices and constrained production under OPEC+ quotas, while the fiscal deficit is anticipated to remain elevated because of lower export revenues.

In Türkiye, growth is forecast to pick up to 3.7 percent in 2026 and 4.4 percent in 2027. Private consumption growth is expected to strengthen, supported by rising real wages amid continued gradual disinflation. The current account deficit is expected to widen, while the fiscal deficit is projected to narrow, mainly reflecting reduced earthquake-related reconstruction spending.

Ukraine's growth is projected to stabilize at 2 percent in 2026, under a baseline assuming Russia's invasion continues through the end of the year, alongside EU accession reforms, a new IMF program, and continued high military expenditures. Assuming a ceasefire is in place by 2027, growth is projected to pick up to 4 percent in 2027—0.5 percentage point below the June forecast, reflecting continued high defense-related resource allocation amid persistent uncertainty. Reconstruction investment is foreseen as a major growth driver. The impact on human capital will continue to dampen potential growth.

FIGURE 2.2.2 ECA: Outlook

Growth in the region is projected to hold steady in 2026 and then firm in 2027, led by Türkiye. Some countries cut their policy rate in 2025 and are expected to continue gradual easing in 2026 as inflation moderates. However, many ECA central banks are likely to maintain a cautious stance, with inflation projected to remain elevated in most economies. Fiscal policy is projected to shift gradually toward slight consolidation in 2026–27. ECA's labor market faces demographic pressures, with a shrinking workforce and rising dependency in most subregions, except in Central Asia.

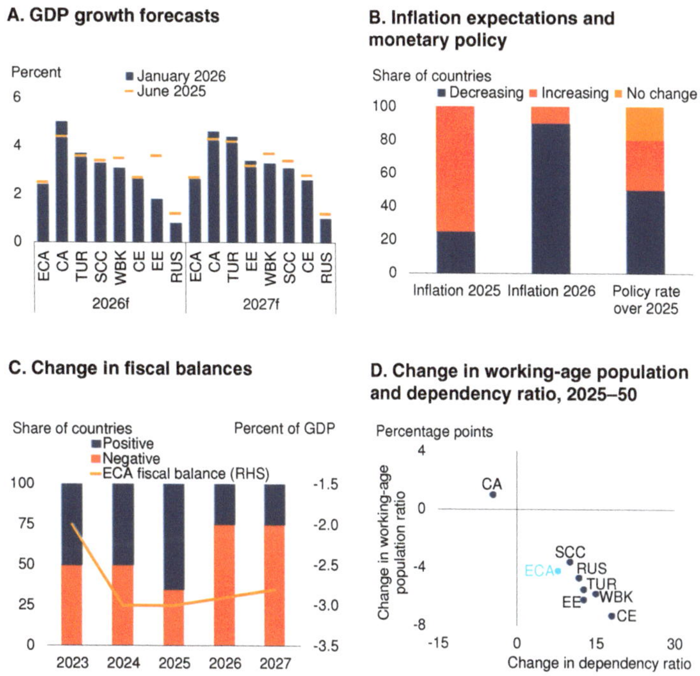

Sources: Consensus Economics; Haver Analytics; International Labour Organization; Macro Poverty Outlook (database); United Nations; World Bank.

Note: f = forecast. CA = Central Asia; CE = Central Europe; ECA = Europe and Central Asia; EE = Eastern Europe; RHS = right-hand scale; RUS = Russian Federation; SCC = South Caucasus; TUR = Türkiye; WBK = Western Balkans.

A. Bars and dashes represent GDP growth forecasts as reported in the January 2026 and June 2025 editions of the *Global Economic Prospects* report, respectively.

B. Blue and red bars show the share of countries with decreasing and increasing year-on-year expected inflation in 2025 and 2026, based on the November 2025 Consensus Economics survey, and monetary policy rate between November and January 2025. Orange bar represents the share of countries with no change in the monetary policy rate between November and January 2025. Sample includes 20 ECA economies.

C. Bars show the percentage of ECA economies (sample of 20 countries) with either a positive or negative change in fiscal balance compared with the previous year. A positive value indicates fiscal expansion, whereas a negative value indicates fiscal consolidation. Line indicates the median fiscal balance across ECA economies, expressed as a share of GDP.

D. Scatter plot shows the percentage-point change in working-age population as share of total population and in dependency ratio between 2025 and 2050 by ECA subregion. Dependency ratio is defined as the number of people aged 0–14 or 65 and over divided by the number of people aged 15–64.

Growth in Central Europe is set to increase to 2.6 percent in 2026–27, supported by stronger investment—particularly in Poland and Romania—underpinned by higher EU funding. Subdued euro area demand and elevated trade policy uncertainty are expected to weigh on trade, but Germany's fiscal support package will partly offset these headwinds and contribute to a rebound in exports in 2027 (refer to chapter 1). Fiscal challenges persist, particularly in Romania, where fiscal consolidation is expected to weigh on growth.

Growth in the Western Balkans is anticipated to pick up to 3.1 percent in 2026, driven by a modest rise in investment, partly reflecting anticipated EU Reform and Growth Facility financing. Growth is projected to increase further in 2027, to 3.3 percent, as exports rebound, aided by Germany's fiscal package—which will strengthen public investment and stimulate external demand—and a broader euro area recovery.

In the South Caucasus, growth is envisaged to slow to 3.3 percent in 2026 and 3.1 percent in 2027. In Azerbaijan, activity is expected to be constrained by weaker hydrocarbon output, lower global oil prices, and a tighter fiscal stance. In Armenia and Georgia, private consumption is anticipated to moderate as activity normalizes from a high base, while weaker remittances and lower export earnings are projected to weigh on current accounts. The preliminary August 2025 peace agreement between Armenia and Azerbaijan is expected to strengthen stability and deepen integration.

In Central Asia, growth is forecast to weaken to 5 percent in 2026, falling further to 4.6 percent in 2027. Private consumption is projected to soften amid high inflation, while Russia's slowdown is likely to curb exports and remittances, which will be further pressured by tighter migration policies. As frontier markets, Kazakhstan and Uzbekistan have sustained robust per capita growth over 2000–25 (refer to chapter 4). However, Kazakhstan's growth is projected to slow in 2026 as oil production stabilizes, and lower oil prices dampen export earnings and fiscal revenues. Although growth in 2026 is anticipated to slow in the Kyrgyz Republic, Tajikistan, and Uzbekistan, higher gold prices should help support activity.

ECA faces unique labor and demographic challenges, with population aging set to weigh on growth. Slower labor force expansion—except in Central Asia—is projected to raise the region's dependency ratio to 63 percent in 2050 (refer to figure 2.2.2.D). At the same time, over the next decade, about 63 million young people are expected to enter the workforce, but limited job creation and persistent skill mismatches may constrain their absorption (World Bank 2025e). In the Western Balkans, the labor force could fall short by 2.5 percent over five years unless participation rises or emigration slows (World Bank 2025f).

Risks

Risks to the outlook are tilted to the downside, especially given persistent geopolitical tensions related to Russia's invasion of Ukraine and elevated policy uncertainty. Additional risks include an escalation of trade tensions, more-persistent-than-expected inflation, and the emergence of financial stress.

Geopolitical tensions remain a significant downside risk for ECA, with risk and uncertainty remaining elevated and exceeding pre-invasion levels (refer to figure 2.2.3.A). A prolonged extension or intensification of Russia's invasion could further weaken Ukraine's economy and sustain high geopolitical uncertainty. Potential setbacks in the Armenia-Azerbaijan peace process also add to downside risks. Conversely, an earlier-than-expected end of hostilities associated with Russia's invasion could accelerate reconstruction-driven investment in Ukraine and boost regional investor confidence. Progress in the Armenia-Azerbaijan peace process could strengthen South Caucasus integration.

Policy and trade uncertainty in the region remains high, posing a downside risk. Tariffs have risen significantly since January 2025, and further increases may occur (refer to figure 2.2.3.B). Persistent trade policy uncertainty and additional restrictions could further dampen exports, investment, and confidence, particularly through euro area demand. Elevated geopolitical risks could reduce international trade—by about 30–40 percent (Mulabdic and Yotov 2025). Central Europe and the Western Balkans are particularly exposed to a broad slowdown given their high trade openness and integration into European value chains. Stronger competition from China may also pressure manufacturing exporters such as Poland and Türkiye (EBRD 2025).

On the upside, deeper regional integration—bolstered by new agreements—could support trade and growth. Recent momentum includes the establishment of the EU–Central Asia Strategic Partnership, the signing of both the EU–Uzbekistan Enhanced Partnership and Cooperation Agreement, and the U.S.–Central Asia Economic Cooperation Statement of Intent. Deeper Central European Free Trade Agreement–EU ties could have boosted members' exports by 4–27 percent (Mulabdic and Ruta 2018), with further gains possible from improved trade facilitation, payments integration, and lower non-tariff barriers. Combined with export diversification, lower tariffs, and reduced trade uncertainty, these developments could ease inflationary pressures and boost confidence.

Inflation is expected to remain above target in most ECA economies in 2026 (refer to figure 2.2.3.C). However, inflation could prove higher or more persistent than anticipated, owing to tighter labor market conditions, faster wage growth, higher import tariffs, and supply chain disruptions—particularly in Central Europe—which could push up domestic prices. This may require tighter monetary policy.

More restrictive global monetary and fiscal policies, renewed trade tensions, or a sharp repricing of risk amid global asset price corrections could trigger capital outflows, lead to exchange rate pressures, and raise corporate and sovereign borrowing costs. Economies with large external financing needs, particularly in the Western Balkans and parts of Central Europe, remain most exposed to sudden tightening in global financial conditions.

More frequent and severe extreme weather events—heatwaves, droughts, and floods—pose another downside risk to ECA growth, as they continue to threaten agricultural productivity, water resources, and infrastructure, particularly in Central Asia and parts of Central and Eastern Europe. Extreme heat could potentially reduce GDP by up to 2.5 percent by midcentury in parts of the region, with urban areas expected to face rising temperatures (World Bank 2025g). Without strengthened adaptation and more resilient infrastructure, these risks will increasingly weigh on growth, fiscal stability, and health.

FIGURE 2.2.3 ECA: Risks

Risks to the outlook remain tilted to the downside. Geopolitical risks and uncertainty are elevated, exceeding levels observed before Russia's invasion of Ukraine. A further escalation of trade tensions, including the possibility of additional tariffs on ECA exports, would dampen growth. Inflation, which is projected to remain above target in most ECA countries in 2026, could become more persistent than expected if it rises further owing to factors such as tighter labor markets, faster wage growth, or trade-related disruptions. Strong AI-driven productivity gains, notably in Central Europe, could support growth, provided labor market adjustments are effectively managed.

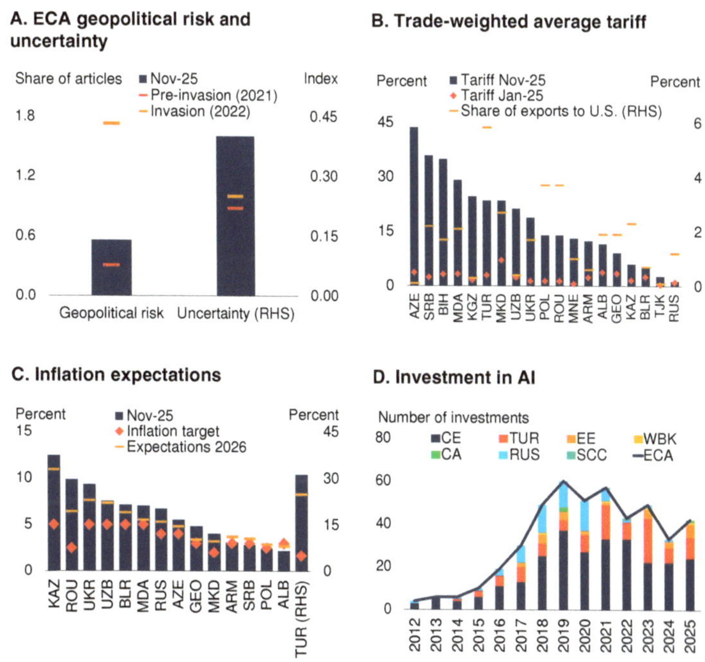

Sources: Ahir, Bloom, and Furceri (2022); Caldara and Iacoviello (2022); Centre d'Études Prospectives et d'Informations Internationales; Consensus Economics; Haver Analytics; International Monetary Fund; Organisation for Economic Co-operation and Development; World Bank; World Trade Organization.

Note: AI = artificial intelligence; ALB = Albania; ARM = Armenia; AZE = Azerbaijan; BIH = Bosnia and Herzegovina; BLR = Belarus; CA = Central Asia; CE = Central Europe; ECA = Europe and Central Asia; EE = Eastern Europe; GEO = Georgia; KAZ = Kazakhstan; KGZ = the Kyrgyz Republic; MDA = Moldova; MNE = Montenegro; MKD = North Macedonia; POL = Poland; RHS = right-hand scale; ROU = Romania; RUS = Russian Federation; SCC = South Caucasus; SRB = Serbia; TJK = Tajikistan; TUR = Türkiye; UKR = Ukraine; UZB = Uzbekistan; WBK = Western Balkans.

A. Bars show the average ECA geopolitical risk (GPR) index based on Caldara and Iacoviello and the uncertainty index (UI) in November 2025. Red and orange dashes represent average ECA values in 2021 and 2022, respectively. GPR measures the share of articles mentioning adverse geopolitical events in leading newspapers. UI is computed by counting the frequency of the word "uncertainty" (or its variant) in EIU country reports. The index is normalized by total number of words and rescaled by multiplying by 1,000. A higher value means higher uncertainty and vice versa. Sample includes 5 ECA economies for GPR and 8 ECA economies for UI. "Invasion" refers to Russia's invasion of Ukraine.

B. Bars and diamonds show trade-weighted average tariff rates in November 2025 and January 2025, respectively. Dashes represent the share of total exports to the United States in 2023.

C. Dashes show year-on-year inflation expectations for 2026 from the November 2025 Consensus Economics survey for 15 ECA economies. Bars and diamonds represent November 2025 headline inflation and inflation targets, respectively.

D. Bars represent number of venture capital investments in AI by subregion. The value for 2025 shows cumulative data last updated on October 1, 2025.

Artificial intelligence (AI) could present an upside risk for ECA. Venture capital investment in AI firms has grown sharply, notably in Central Europe (refer to figure 2.2.3.D). Rising productivity gains from faster AI adoption could expand tradable services and entrepreneurship, particularly in digitally advanced economies, and could boost global GDP by up to 4 percent over the next decade (Cerutti et al. 2025). About 30 percent of ECA jobs are exposed to generative AI—especially in Central Europe and the Western Balkans—underscoring the importance of reskilling, on-the-job training, and innovation that complements human skills (World Bank 2025e).

TABLE 2.2.1 Europe and Central Asia forecast summary

(Real GDP growth at market prices in percent, unless indicated otherwise)

	2023	2024	2025e	2026f	2027f	Percentage-point differences from June 2025 projections 2025e	2026f	2027f
EMDE ECA, GDP[1]	**3.6**	**3.6**	**2.4**	**2.4**	**2.7**	**0.0**	**-0.1**	**0.0**
GDP per capita (U.S. dollars)	4.0	3.5	2.1	2.2	2.6	-0.1	-0.2	0.0
EMDE ECA excluding Russian Federation, Türkiye, and Ukraine, GDP	2.0	3.2	3.2	3.2	3.0	0.1	0.1	-0.1
EMDE ECA excluding Russian Federation and Ukraine, GDP	3.2	3.2	3.3	3.4	3.6	0.2	0.1	0.0
EMDE ECA excluding Türkiye, GDP	3.1	3.7	2.0	1.9	2.1	-0.2	-0.3	-0.1
EMDE ECA plus Bulgaria and Croatia	3.6	3.6	2.4	2.4	2.7	0.0	-0.1	0.0
(Average including countries that report expenditure components in national accounts)[2]								
EMDE ECA, GDP[2]	3.5	3.5	2.1	2.2	2.5	-0.1	-0.2	-0.1
PPP GDP	3.6	3.5	2.1	2.2	2.6	-0.1	-0.2	0.0
Private consumption	5.7	5.0	2.5	2.5	2.8	-0.5	-0.5	-0.2
Public consumption	3.6	3.1	2.0	2.1	1.7	0.4	0.5	0.2
Fixed investment	11.1	1.2	2.8	3.5	3.3	0.5	0.4	0.1
Exports, GNFS[3]	-1.1	0.5	1.3	1.2	2.6	-0.2	-1.0	-0.1
Imports, GNFS[3]	6.5	1.0	3.0	2.7	3.6	0.1	-0.5	0.4
Net exports, contribution to growth	-2.6	-0.2	-0.6	-0.5	-0.4	-0.1	-0.1	-0.2
Memo items: GDP								
Commodity exporters[4]	4.3	4.4	1.8	1.5	1.8	-0.2	-0.4	-0.1
Commodity exporters excl. Russian Federation and Ukraine	5.1	5.4	5.5	4.6	4.2	0.9	0.5	0.2
Commodity importers[5]	2.9	2.9	2.9	3.2	3.5	0.1	0.0	0.0
Central Europe[6]	0.5	2.2	2.3	2.7	2.6	-0.2	0.0	-0.2
Central Europe plus Bulgaria and Croatia	0.7	2.3	2.4	2.7	2.7	-0.1	0.0	-0.1
Western Balkans[7]	3.4	3.6	2.7	3.1	3.3	-0.5	-0.4	-0.4
Eastern Europe[8]	4.7	3.1	2.0	1.8	3.4	0.0	-1.8	0.2
South Caucasus[9]	4.0	5.8	3.7	3.3	3.1	0.1	-0.1	-0.3
Central Asia[10]	5.6	5.7	6.2	5.0	4.6	1.2	0.6	0.3
Russian Federation	4.1	4.3	0.9	0.8	1.0	-0.5	-0.4	-0.2
Türkiye	5.0	3.3	3.5	3.7	4.4	0.4	0.1	0.2
Poland	0.2	3.0	3.3	3.2	2.9	0.1	0.2	0.0

Source: World Bank.

Note: e = estimate; f = forecast. EMDE = emerging market and developing economy; PPP = purchasing power parity. World Bank forecasts are frequently updated based on new information and changing global circumstances. Consequently, projections presented here may differ from those in other World Bank documents, even if basic assessments of countries' prospects do not differ at any given moment in time. The World Bank is currently not publishing economic output, income, or growth data for Turkmenistan owing to a lack of reliable data of adequate quality. Turkmenistan is excluded from cross-country macroeconomic aggregates. Since joining the euro area—Croatia on January 1, 2023, and Bulgaria on January 1, 2026—both countries have been added to the euro area aggregate and removed from the ECA aggregate in all tables to avoid double counting.

1. GDP and expenditure components are measured in average 2010-19 prices and market exchange rates, thus aggregates presented here may differ from other World Bank documents.
2. Aggregates presented here exclude Azerbaijan, Bosnia and Herzegovina, Kazakhstan, Kosovo, the Kyrgyz Republic, Montenegro, Serbia, Tajikistan, and Uzbekistan.
3. Exports and imports of goods and nonfactor services (GNFS).
4. Includes Armenia, Azerbaijan, Kazakhstan, the Kyrgyz Republic, Kosovo, the Russian Federation, Tajikistan, Ukraine, and Uzbekistan.
5. Includes Albania, Belarus, Bosnia and Herzegovina, Georgia, Hungary, Moldova, Montenegro, North Macedonia, Poland, Romania, Serbia, and Türkiye.
6. Includes Hungary, Poland, and Romania.
7. Includes Albania, Bosnia and Herzegovina, Kosovo, Montenegro, North Macedonia, and Serbia.
8. Includes Belarus, Moldova, and Ukraine.
9. Includes Armenia, Azerbaijan, and Georgia.
10. Includes Kazakhstan, the Kyrgyz Republic, Tajikistan, and Uzbekistan.

TABLE 2.2.2 Europe and Central Asia country forecasts [1]

(Real GDP growth at market prices in percent, unless indicated otherwise)

	2023	2024	2025e	2026f	2027f	Percentage-point differences from June 2025 projections: 2025e	2026f	2027f
Albania	4.0	4.0	3.7	3.5	3.5	0.5	0.4	0.4
Armenia	8.3	5.9	5.2	4.9	4.7	1.2	0.7	0.2
Azerbaijan	1.4	4.1	1.9	1.8	1.7	-0.7	-0.6	-0.6
Belarus	4.1	4.0	1.9	1.3	0.8	-0.3	0.1	0.0
Bosnia and Herzegovina [2]	2.0	3.0	2.6	3.0	3.2	-0.1	-0.1	-0.3
Bulgaria	1.7	3.4	3.0	2.9	3.1	1.0	0.7	0.7
Croatia	3.8	3.8	3.1	2.9	2.7	0.0	-0.1	-0.1
Georgia	7.8	9.7	7.0	5.5	5.0	1.5	0.5	0.0
Kazakhstan	5.1	5.0	6.0	4.5	3.9	1.5	0.9	0.4
Kosovo	4.1	4.6	3.8	3.8	3.9	0.0	0.0	0.1
Kyrgyz Republic	9.0	9.0	9.2	6.5	6.8	2.4	1.0	1.0
Moldova	1.2	0.1	2.9	2.7	3.8	2.0	0.3	-0.6
Montenegro	6.5	3.2	3.3	3.2	3.2	0.3	0.3	0.2
North Macedonia	2.6	3.0	3.2	3.0	3.0	0.6	0.3	0.2
Poland	0.2	3.0	3.3	3.2	2.9	0.1	0.2	0.0
Romania	2.3	0.9	0.8	1.3	1.9	-0.5	-0.6	-0.6
Russian Federation	4.1	4.3	0.9	0.8	1.0	-0.5	-0.4	-0.2
Serbia	3.7	3.9	2.1	3.0	3.2	-1.4	-0.9	-1.0
Tajikistan	8.3	8.4	8.0	6.2	4.7	1.0	1.3	0.0
Türkiye	5.0	3.3	3.5	3.7	4.4	0.4	0.1	0.2
Ukraine	5.5	2.9	2.0	2.0	4.0	0.0	-3.2	-0.5
Uzbekistan	6.3	6.6	6.2	6.0	5.9	0.3	0.1	0.1

Source: World Bank.

Note: e = estimate; f = forecast. World Bank forecasts are frequently updated based on new information and changing global circumstances. Consequently, projections presented here may differ from those contained in other World Bank documents, even if basic assessments of countries' prospects do not significantly differ at any given moment in time. The World Bank is not currently publishing economic output, income, or growth data for Turkmenistan owing to a lack of reliable data of adequate quality. Turkmenistan is excluded from cross-country macroeconomic aggregates.

1. Data are based on GDP measured in average 2010–19 prices and market exchange rates, unless indicated otherwise.

2. GDP growth rate at constant prices is based on production approach.

LATIN AMERICA and THE CARIBBEAN

After moderating to an estimated 2.2 percent last year, growth in Latin America and the Caribbean is projected to edge up to 2.3 percent in 2026 and 2.6 percent in 2027. The positive impact of easier financing conditions and high metal and food commodity prices on regional growth this year is expected to be tempered by elevated trade tensions and uncertainty—despite some signs of resilience—as well as constrained fiscal space and sluggish consumption and investment in several countries. Restoring strong output growth is critical for sustaining wage employment creation and improving job quality. Risks to the outlook are tilted to the downside. Additional increases in trade barriers and associated uncertainty, or a softening of commodity prices, could dampen exports, investment, and fiscal revenues. Given elevated debt burdens, an unexpected tightening of financial conditions could result in capital outflows, and climate-related shocks pose a risk to vulnerable sectors such as agriculture, fisheries, and energy.

Recent developments

Economic activity in Latin America and the Caribbean (LAC) slowed in the second half of 2025, amid elevated global uncertainty, marginally below the June forecast (refer to figure 2.3.1.A and table 2.3.1). Despite some resilience in LAC's goods trade in 2025, several indicators—including industrial production and manufacturing and services PMIs—point to subdued activity going forward. For 2025 as a whole, growth rates of private and public consumption, as well as investment, were estimated to be higher than anticipated in the June forecast, although still relatively subdued. Stronger domestic demand was supported by import growth that exceeded expectations. Despite elevated trade tensions, exports also remained solid during the year, as commodity exporters weathered trade tensions relatively well (refer to figure 2.3.1.B and to chapter 1).

In most LAC countries in 2025, inflation rates remained within central bank target ranges (refer to figure 2.3.1.C). In Argentina, the marked tightening of fiscal and monetary policy has substantially dampened inflation. Monetary policy easing resumed in several economies, with Chile and Mexico cutting interest rates, while Brazil maintained its policy rate at 15 percent amid sticky inflation expectations.

Capital flows to the region have picked up, supporting financing needs. However, this was accompanied by widening current account deficits in some countries, as LAC experienced real appreciation that was more pronounced than in other regions (refer to figure 2.3.1.D). Sovereign issuance increased last year, as spreads narrowed from early-year peaks and equity prices surged during the second half of 2025 amid easing global financial conditions.

Outlook

Regional growth is projected to firm gradually over the next two years (refer to figure 2.3.2.A and table 2.3.1). In 2026, growth in LAC is expected to edge up slightly, to 2.3 percent, as trade tensions and related uncertainty remain elevated and domestic demand continues to be sluggish in some countries, partly offsetting the positive effect of easing financing conditions. Regional growth is then anticipated to firm to 2.6 percent in 2027, as trade flows recover and domestic demand improves, with the latter assuming that monetary policy rates in several large economies decline

---

Note: This section was prepared by Francisco Arroyo Marioli and Emiliano Luttini.

FIGURE 2.3.1 LAC: Recent developments

Growth decelerated in the second half of 2025 across LAC, amid elevated global uncertainty and subdued domestic demand. Exports remained resilient during 2025 despite elevated global trade tensions. Inflation has remained stable in much of the region, though it is still above central bank targets in some countries. Real exchange rates have appreciated in the region amid widening current account deficits.

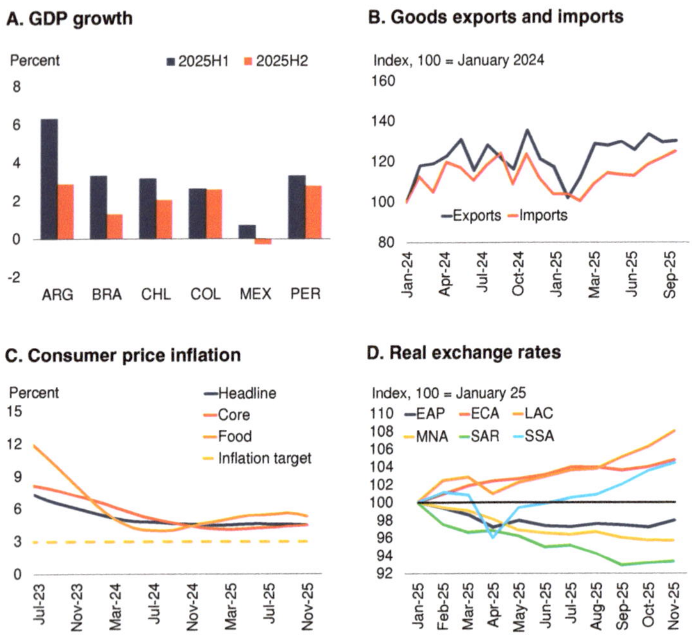

Sources: Bank for International Settlements (BIS) (database); Haver Analytics; UN Comtrade (database); White House; World Bank.

Note: ARG = Argentina; BRA = Brazil; CHL = Chile; COL = Colombia; EAP = East Asia and Pacific; ECA = Europe and Central Asia; LAC = Latin America and the Caribbean; MEX = Mexico; MNA = Middle East and North Africa; PER = Peru; SAR = South Asia; SSA = Sub-Saharan Africa.

A. Bars show year-over-year seasonally adjusted annual growth rates.

B. Value-weighted average exports and imports for Argentina, Brazil, Chile, Colombia, Mexico, and Peru. Last observation is September 2025.

C. Year-over-year consumer price inflation. Aggregate is a 12-month moving weighted average for Brazil, Chile, Colombia, Mexico, and Peru. Last observation is November 2025.

D. Panel shows broad indexes of the multilateral real effective exchange rate as calculated by the BIS. An increase indicates an appreciation of the economy's currency against a broad basket of currencies. Country aggregates are formed as follows: EAP = China, Indonesia, Malaysia, the Philippines, Thailand; ECA = Bosnia and Herzegovina, Hungary, North Macedonia, Poland, Romania, the Russian Federation, Serbia, Türkiye; LAC = Brazil, Chile, Colombia, Mexico, Peru; MNA = Algeria, Morocco, Saudi Arabia, United Arab Emirates; SAR = India; SSA = South Africa.

toward neutral ranges. Given the high prevalence of self-employment in LAC, restoring strong output growth is essential to sustain wage employment creation and support improvements in job quality by increasing participation in wage employment relative to self-employment (Loungani, Luttini, and Pallan 2025). Relative to June 2025 projections, forecasts for 2026 are downgraded for thirteen countries, upgraded for eight countries, and unchanged for eight countries (refer to table 2.3.2). It is too early to assess the macroeconomic implications of recent events involving the República Bolivariana de Venezuela.

Trade tensions and elevated uncertainty continue to dampen the near-term growth outlook. Average tariff rates on exports to the United States have remained broadly stable since June, and tariffs imposed in 2025 are assumed to remain in place over the forecast horizon, posing headwinds to exports. Commodity exporters are likely to remain comparatively insulated from the increase in trade barriers, as the redirection of their basic-materials exports is likely to occur more readily than for non-commodity exporters, whose differentiated products typically require a more involved process of customer acquisition (Fitzgerald and Haller 2024; Kohn et al. 2024). For metal and food commodity exporters, export prices are expected to remain elevated, providing continued support to their terms of trade, which have trended up in recent years (refer to figure 2.3.2.B).

Macroeconomic policy space is expected to remain limited, which may affect the region's ability to respond to further adverse shocks. Inflation has eased across much of the region but is anticipated to remain near the upper end of target bands in some countries. Accordingly, shifts in the stance of monetary policy are likely to be mixed, with modest monetary easing expected in the largest economies, but some increases in real policy rates elsewhere (refer to figure 2.3.2.C). Fiscal positions are also anticipated to remain constrained: high borrowing costs and fragile debt dynamics limit the scope for fiscal support, with most governments expected to maintain broadly contractionary stances in 2026 and 2027 (refer to figure 2.3.2.D).

Growth in Brazil is projected to moderate to 2 percent in 2026 before inching up to 2.3 percent in 2027. With gross government debt on an upward trajectory and expected to continue rising, fiscal sustainability remains a concern. Near-term fiscal prospects are constrained by mandatory expenditure commitments, elevated real rates, and modest external demand. Although monetary policy is envisaged to ease somewhat after interest rates reached 15 percent in 2025, still-high real interest rates, trade-related headwinds, and elevated global uncertainty are anticipated to weigh on investment and exports.

Mexico's economy is anticipated to expand 1.3 percent in 2026 and 1.8 percent in 2027, as it recovers from a spike in trade policy-uncertainty and as firms adapt to the new trade environment. Ongoing tariff disputes and the pending United States–Mexico–Canada Agreement (USMCA) review are nonetheless expected to continue weighing on investment and trade, as roughly 80 percent of the country's exports are destined for the United States. The central bank is expected to continue easing policy through 2026; even so, aggregate demand is projected to remain subdued. Fiscal consolidation efforts are expected to reduce the share of government spending in GDP in the short term; however, more ambitious consolidation efforts may be required to stabilize the public debt and create fiscal space (IMF 2025b).

Argentina's growth is projected to moderate to 4 percent in 2026—0.5 percentage point lower than projected in June—and remain at 4 percent in 2027. Domestic policy uncertainty late last year led to bouts of exchange rate pressure, prompting increases in market interest rates that are expected to weigh on domestic demand and growth this year. Support from the United States, including the provision of swap lines, helped stabilize financial conditions (IMF 2025c). The transition to an exchange rate band in April 2025 is projected to increase exchange rate flexibility, strengthening the exchange rate's role as a shock absorber.

Colombia's economy is projected to expand by 2.6 percent in 2026 and 2.8 percent in 2027, supported by resilient consumption and a gradual recovery in private investment as inflation falls within target and monetary easing continues. Nonetheless, policy uncertainty continues to cloud the outlook, tempering investment growth. The current account deficit widened in 2025 amid strong import demand but is expected to stabilize at levels somewhat above those of the pre-pandemic period. Fiscal deficits are anticipated to remain sizable but gradually narrow, conditional on the implementation of consolidation efforts (IMF 2025a).

FIGURE 2.3.2 LAC: Outlook

Growth in LAC is expected to edge up to only 2.3 percent in 2026 amid elevated trade tensions and uncertainty and sluggish domestic demand. However, growth projections are mixed across the region. Terms of trade in commodity exporters are expected to remain steady but at higher levels than before the pandemic, contributing to exports' stable purchasing power, especially for metal and food commodity exporters. Real policy rates are expected to decline slowly in the largest regional economies. Fiscal stances are projected to remain broadly contractionary in 2026–27.

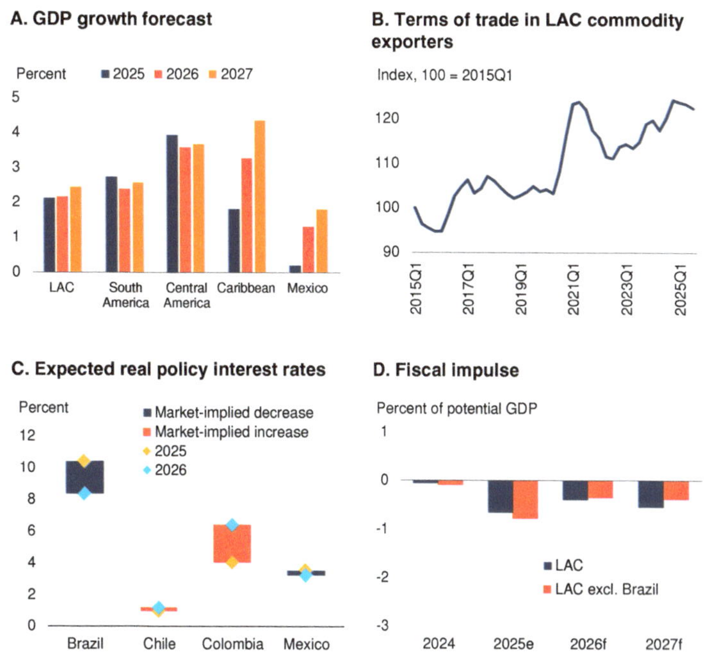

Sources: Bloomberg; Consensus Economics; Haver Analytics; International Monetary Fund (IMF) World Economic Outlook (database); World Bank.

Note: e = estimate; f = forecast. excl. = excluding; LAC = Latin America and the Caribbean.

A. Bars show year-over-year real annual growth rates. GDP weights are based on average real U.S. dollar GDP (at average 2010–19 prices and market exchange rates) for the period 2000–24. Data for 2026–27 are forecasts.

B. Value-weighted terms-of-trade indexes for total trade for Argentina, Brazil, Chile, and Peru. Last observation is 2025Q3.

C. Yellow diamonds denote the end-of-November-2025 policy rate minus the 2025 inflation expectation from Consensus Economics. Blue diamonds denote the one-year-ahead market-implied policy rate, using a 30-day average of data up to December 12, 2025, minus the 2026 inflation expectation from Consensus Economics. Bars show the expected change in real interest rates from 2025 to 2026.

D. Fiscal impulse is the negative annual change in the structural primary balance for 18 LAC economies, using data from the October 2025 International Monetary Fund (IMF) World Economic Outlook database. A positive value indicates fiscal expansion, and a negative value indicates contraction.

Chile's growth is forecast to slow to 2.2 percent in 2026 and 2.1 percent in 2027. Domestic demand is expected to recover gradually as the monetary policy rate converges to the neutral range and inflation returns to target. Investment in copper and lithium mining is anticipated to bolster growth, benefiting from strong demand from the renewable energy sector globally and especially in China. At the same time, weaker commodity demand from China's real estate sector is expected to partly offset these gains by curbing export growth.

Peru's activity is projected to expand by 2.5 percent in 2026 and 2027. Growth is expected to be underpinned by copper and infrastructure investment, even as domestic consumption softens under tighter fiscal policy and lingering political uncertainty. Inflation has eased to levels close to the central bank's target, allowing policy rates to remain near neutral levels (BCRP 2025).

In the Caribbean, subregional growth is set to increase to 5.2 percent in 2026 and 6.6 percent in 2027, driven by Guyana's ongoing oil boom. Excluding Guyana, the subregion is projected to grow by about 2.9 percent and 3.7 percent, supported by tourism and related services. The Dominican Republic is expected to expand by an average of 4.5 percent over the forecast horizon, benefiting from reforms aimed at attracting foreign investment and progress on export diversification. Jamaica's growth is projected at -2.3 percent in 2026 and 3.7 percent in 2027, remaining constrained by structural bottlenecks and the extent and speed of reconstruction following Hurricane Melissa. Haiti's growth is forecast to rebound to 2 percent in 2026 after seven consecutive years of contraction, conditional on modest gains in stability and security.

In Central America, growth is projected to remain broadly stable at 3.6 percent in 2026 and 3.7 percent in 2027. Remittance flows are set to decline, adversely affecting economic activity (Estevão et al. 2025). On the upside, despite trade-related uncertainty, the subregion is expected to continue benefiting from U.S. growth and resilient exports. Panama's activity is forecast to expand by 4.1 percent in 2026, driven by finance, business, and logistics services, with FDI expected to continue financing current account deficits. Costa Rica's economy is expected to grow by 3.6 percent in 2026, supported by solid consumption. Service exports, which account for a large share of total exports in Costa Rica and Panama, are envisaged to remain insulated from tariffs.

Risks

Risks to the regional outlook remain tilted to the downside. Rising trade barriers, weaker external demand, and an unexpected decline in global commodity markets could further constrain growth and policy space. Elevated debt levels and current account deficits increase exposure to financial market stress and limit the ability of macroeconomic policies to respond to shocks. The growing incidence of climate-related events poses a significant threat to key sectors and could exacerbate existing vulnerabilities. On the upside, rapid advances in artificial intelligence could support growth by spurring investment in digital infrastructure and by raising productivity through broad technology adoption.

A key downside risk is an escalation of trade barriers. Further tariff increases or a trade-restrictive outcome to the USMCA review in 2026 would weigh on regional activity. Given its tight economic linkages to the United States, Mexico is particularly vulnerable, while related supply-chain disruptions could have broader negative spillovers to other economies (refer to figure 2.3.3.A). More generally, higher-than-anticipated trade barriers and persistently heightened global uncertainty could weigh on external demand by curbing growth in major trading partners, further dampening regional investment and exports.

Weaker-than-expected global growth could also lead to a pronounced slump in commodity prices. Lower prices for key regional exports would then weigh on fiscal revenues and external balances. This, in turn, could compound existing vulnerabilities in economies with narrow fiscal space or large current account deficits (Arroyo Marioli and Vegh 2023). An additional regional risk stems from immigration policies. Tightening immigration policies could constrain remittance inflows in the Caribbean, Central America, and elsewhere, weighing on consumption growth and current account balances (refer to figure 2.3.3.B; Combes and Ebeke 2011; Hassan and Holmes 2016).

Financial market volatility could amplify existing vulnerabilities, even if they are, on average, less acute than a decade ago. Elevated public debt levels in several economies leave the region exposed to sudden changes in global financial conditions (refer to figure 2.3.3.C). Ongoing current account deficits underscore the region's reliance on external financing, which could lead to currency volatility and significant asset price adjustments should a souring risk sentiment prompt capital outflows (refer to figure 2.3.3.D). Such dynamics would complicate efforts to stabilize public finances and could require more pronounced adjustments than currently envisaged.

Climate change remains a significant source of risk for the region. Agriculture, fisheries, and energy sectors are vulnerable to extreme weather events. Natural disasters, including floods and storms, could place heavy strain on less-developed economies and exacerbate pre-existing weaknesses in infrastructure (World Bank 2014). A shift toward La Niña conditions, for example, would heighten the likelihood of droughts in southern South America, with potentially severe consequences for agricultural output and rural livelihoods.

The adoption of artificial intelligence could potentially boost productivity within the region, especially in countries with more educated labor forces, which are better positioned to harness the benefits of this emerging technology. Those economies capable of hosting critical digital infrastructure, such as data centers, could also experience strengthening in investment growth as the build-out of enabling computing capacity continues. Yet, countries exhibiting deficient infrastructure, unsupportive regulatory environments, and limited human capital are less likely to benefit (Bakker et al. 2024). The emergence of artificial intelligence may also cause disruptions in the region's labor markets: employment complemented by the technology is likely to expand, while in fields subject to substitution may shrink.

FIGURE 2.3.3 LAC: Risks

Risks to the regional outlook remain tilted to the downside. The region is highly exposed to trade shocks, with several economies dependent on exports to China and the United States. Remittances constitute a large share of income in parts of Central America and the Caribbean, leaving economies in these areas vulnerable to slowdowns in host countries and shifts in immigration policies. Elevated debt burdens limit fiscal space, and some countries are particularly exposed to external financing shocks given sizable current account deficits.

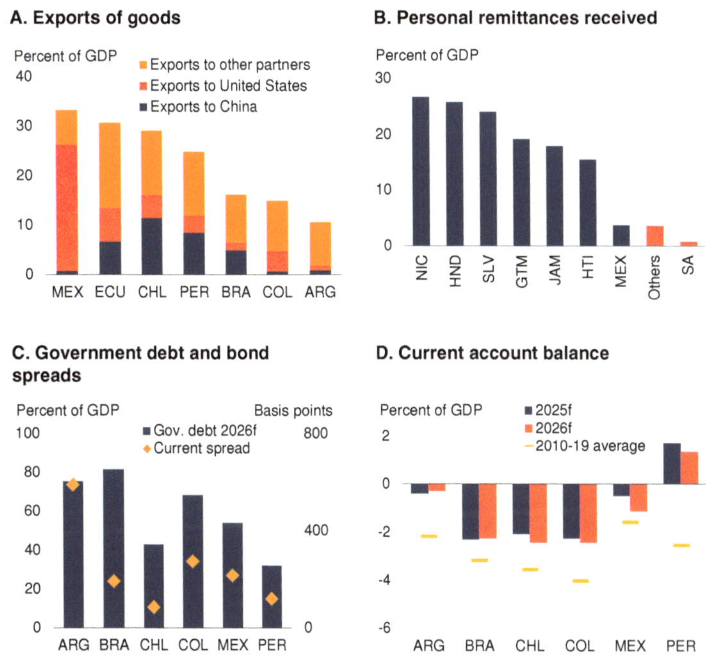

Sources: BACI (database); Haver Analytics; IMF, World Economic Outlook database; J.P. Morgan; World Bank.

Note: e = estimate; f = forecast. ARG = Argentina; BRA = Brazil; CHL = Chile; COL = Colombia; ECU = Ecuador; EMBI = JPMorgan Emerging Markets Bond Index; Gov. = government; GTM = Guatemala; HND = Honduras; HTI = Haiti; JAM = Jamaica; MEX = Mexico; NIC = Nicaragua; PER = Peru; SA = South America; SLV = El Salvador.

A. Goods exports to China and the U.S. as a share of GDP. Last observation is 2023.

B. Bars show personal remittances received as a percentage of GDP in 2024. "Others" refers to Central American and Caribbean countries not displayed individually in the panel.

C. General government gross debt as a percentage of GDP and EMBI bond spread as of December 15, 2025. Data for 2026 are projections.

D. Bars show current account balance as percent of GDP from October 2025 International Monetary Fund (IMF) World Economic Outlook database.

TABLE 2.3.1 Latin America and the Caribbean forecast summary

(Real GDP growth at market prices in percent, unless indicated otherwise)

	2023	2024	2025e	2026f	2027f	Percentage-point differences from June 2025 projections: 2025e	2026f	2027f
EMDE LAC, GDP[1]	**2.4**	**2.4**	**2.2**	**2.3**	**2.6**	**-0.1**	**-0.1**	**0.0**
GDP per capita (U.S. dollars)	1.6	1.6	1.5	1.6	1.9	0.0	-0.1	-0.1
(Average including countries that report expenditure components in national accounts)[2]								
EMDE LAC, GDP[2]	2.3	2.2	2.2	2.2	2.5	0.0	-0.1	0.0
PPP GDP	2.3	2.1	2.2	2.2	2.5	0.0	-0.1	0.0
Private consumption	2.6	2.9	2.9	2.3	2.5	0.3	-0.2	-0.2
Public consumption	3.0	1.2	1.9	1.7	1.2	0.2	0.2	0.0
Fixed investment	2.5	2.7	3.2	2.8	2.9	1.1	0.8	0.6
Exports, GNFS[3]	-0.5	4.2	1.9	2.7	3.3	1.7	0.5	0.6
Imports, GNFS[3]	0.4	4.5	4.1	2.8	3.1	2.2	0.6	0.5
Net exports, contribution to growth	-0.2	-0.2	-0.6	-0.1	0.0	-0.2	0.0	0.0
Memo items: GDP								
South America[4]	1.8	2.4	2.7	2.4	2.5	-0.1	-0.2	-0.1
Central America[5]	4.9	3.5	3.9	3.6	3.7	0.6	0.0	-0.1
Caribbean[6]	4.3	7.0	3.3	5.2	6.6	-0.6	-0.6	-0.1
Caribbean excluding Guyana	2.0	3.2	1.7	2.9	3.7	-1.3	-0.2	0.2
Brazil	3.2	3.4	2.3	2.0	2.3	-0.1	-0.2	0.0
Mexico	3.4	1.4	0.2	1.3	1.8	0.0	0.2	0.0
Argentina	-1.9	-1.3	4.6	4.0	4.0	-0.9	-0.5	0.0

Source: World Bank.

Note: e = estimate; f = forecast. EMDE = emerging market and developing economy; PPP = purchasing power parity. World Bank forecasts are frequently updated based on new information and changing global circumstances. Consequently, projections presented here may differ from those in other World Bank documents, even if basic assessments of countries' prospects do not differ at any given moment in time. The World Bank is currently not publishing economic output, income, or growth data for República Bolivariana de Venezuela owing to a lack of reliable data of adequate quality. República Bolivariana de Venezuela is excluded from cross-country macroeconomic aggregates.

1. GDP and expenditure components are measured in average 2010–19 prices and market exchange rates.

2. Aggregate includes all countries in notes 4, 5, and 6, plus Mexico, but excludes Antigua and Barbuda, Barbados, Dominica, Grenada, Guyana, Haiti, St. Kitts and Nevis, St. Lucia, St. Vincent and the Grenadines, and Suriname.

3. Exports and imports of goods and nonfactor services (GNFS).

4. Includes Argentina, Bolivia, Brazil, Chile, Colombia, Ecuador, Paraguay, Peru, and Uruguay.

5. Includes Costa Rica, El Salvador, Guatemala, Honduras, Nicaragua, and Panama.

6. Includes Antigua and Barbuda, The Bahamas, Barbados, Belize, Dominica, the Dominican Republic, Grenada, Guyana, Haiti, Jamaica, St. Kitts and Nevis, St. Lucia, St. Vincent and the Grenadines, Suriname, and Trinidad and Tobago.

TABLE 2.3.2 Latin America and the Caribbean country forecasts[1]

(Real GDP growth at market prices in percent, unless indicated otherwise)

	2023	2024	2025e	2026f	2027f	Percentage-point differences from June 2025 projections 2025e	2026f	2027f
Argentina	-1.9	-1.3	4.6	4.0	4.0	-0.9	-0.5	0.0
Bahamas, The	3.0	3.4	2.3	2.1	1.8	1.2	0.9	0.5
Barbados	4.1	4.0	2.7	2.0	2.0	-0.1	0.0	0.3
Belize	0.5	3.5	1.5	2.4	2.2	-1.3	0.0	-0.1
Bolivia	3.1	0.7	-0.5	-1.1	-1.5	-1.7	-2.2	-2.6
Brazil	3.2	3.4	2.3	2.0	2.3	-0.1	-0.2	0.0
Chile	0.5	2.6	2.6	2.2	2.1	0.5	0.0	0.0
Colombia	0.7	1.6	2.6	2.6	2.8	0.1	-0.1	-0.1
Costa Rica	4.9	4.2	4.1	3.6	3.7	0.6	-0.1	-0.1
Dominica	3.7	2.1	3.1	3.0	2.9	-1.2	-0.4	0.1
Dominican Republic	2.2	5.0	2.5	4.5	4.5	-1.5	0.3	0.1
Ecuador	2.0	-2.0	3.2	2.0	2.4	1.3	0.0	0.3
El Salvador	3.5	2.6	3.5	3.0	3.0	1.3	0.6	0.1
Grenada	4.5	3.7	4.4	3.3	3.0	0.6	-0.1	0.3
Guatemala	3.5	3.7	4.0	3.7	3.7	0.5	-0.1	-0.1
Guyana	33.8	43.6	14.6	19.6	21.9	4.6	-3.4	-2.4
Haiti [2]	-1.9	-4.2	-2.0	2.0	2.5	0.2	0.0	0.0
Honduras	3.6	3.6	3.8	3.5	3.7	1.0	0.1	0.0
Jamaica	2.7	-0.5	-1.3	-2.3	3.7	-3.0	-4.0	2.1
Mexico	3.4	1.4	0.2	1.3	1.8	0.0	0.2	0.0
Nicaragua	4.4	3.6	3.1	3.0	3.0	-0.3	-0.3	-0.3
Panama	7.4	2.9	3.9	4.1	4.1	0.4	0.3	-0.2
Paraguay	5.3	4.7	5.5	3.9	3.9	1.8	0.3	0.3
Peru	-0.4	3.3	3.0	2.5	2.5	0.1	0.0	0.0
St. Lucia	2.2	3.9	1.8	2.0	2.1	-1.0	-0.3	0.2
St. Vincent and the Grenadines	5.3	4.1	4.0	2.9	2.7	-0.9	0.0	0.0
Suriname	2.4	1.7	1.4	3.5	3.7	-1.7	0.2	0.2
Trinidad and Tobago	1.5	2.5	1.4	0.3	2.5	-1.4	-1.0	-0.7
Uruguay	0.7	3.1	2.3	2.2	2.2	0.0	0.0	0.0

Source: World Bank.

Note: e = estimate; f = forecast. World Bank forecasts are frequently updated based on new information and changing global circumstances. Consequently, projections presented here may differ from those in other World Bank documents, even if basic assessments of countries' prospects do not significantly differ at any given moment in time.

1. Data are based on GDP measured in average 2010–19 prices and market exchange rates.

2. GDP is based on fiscal year, which runs from October to September of next year.

MIDDLE EAST, NORTH AFRICA, AFGHANISTAN and PAKISTAN

Growth in the Middle East, North Africa, Afghanistan and Pakistan (MNA) is estimated to have increased to 3.1 percent in 2025 and is projected to strengthen further to 3.6 percent in 2026 and 3.9 percent in 2027, mainly because of an expansion of activity in oil exporters. Growth in oil importers is expected to rise to 4 percent in 2026–27, supported by easing inflation. However, structural constraints will likely continue to dampen job creation in the region. Downside risks to the growth outlook are a re-escalation of armed conflicts, a tightening of global financial conditions, further increases in trade restrictions and heightened global trade policy uncertainty, more frequent or severe disasters stemming from natural hazards, and, for oil exporters, lower and more volatile oil prices. Upside risks include faster-than-expected expansion of technology-led investment and a stronger commitment to implementing growth-enhancing structural reforms.

Recent developments

Geopolitical tensions have remained elevated in the Middle East, North Africa, Afghanistan and Pakistan (MNA) region, particularly in the Middle East. Since the ceasefire in October 2025, Gaza has seen a return to relative calm, though humanitarian needs remain acute on account of ongoing access constraints and elevated food insecurity. In the Republic of Yemen, reductions in foreign assistance have strained health systems, increasing exposure to famine and disease risks among vulnerable populations. The situation in Afghanistan has remained fragile amid large inflows of returnees from neighboring economies, reduced foreign assistance, and damaging impacts from an earthquake in August.

Activity in MNA has firmed, with growth estimated at 3.1 percent in 2025, with the pickup mainly driven by rising oil production in oil exporters and solid private sector activity in oil importers. Among oil exporters, member countries of the Organization of the Petroleum Exporting Countries and other affiliated oil producers (OPEC+) have increased oil production at a faster pace than announced in early 2025 (refer to figure 2.4.1.A). Growth in non-hydrocarbon activity, including manufacturing and services, has stayed resilient in member countries of the Gulf Cooperation Council (GCC), as their key contributor to growth, as well as in Algeria. However, in the Islamic Republic of Iran and Iraq, energy shortages and other supply constraints have disrupted non-oil activity. In Libya, despite persistent political divisions, an agreement was reached in November to unify spending mechanisms aimed at improving the management of public finances.

Growth in most oil importers has also strengthened, reflecting a broad-based improvement in activity (refer to figure 2.4.1.B). Private demand has been boosted in the Arab Republic of Egypt by the easing of import and foreign exchange restrictions, and in Lebanon by the stabilization of the political environment. Favorable weather conditions have contributed to a recovery in agricultural output in Morocco and Tunisia. In Pakistan, a relaxation of import restrictions and an expansion of bank credit, stemming partly from easing financial conditions, have contributed to the strengthening of activity, particularly in the industrial sector.

Note: This section was prepared by Naotaka Sugawara. The region name "Middle East and North Africa" has been changed to "Middle East, North Africa, Afghanistan and Pakistan" to reflect the inclusion of Afghanistan and Pakistan following the World Bank's regional reclassification effective July 1, 2025.

FIGURE 2.4.1 MNA: Recent developments

Growth in MNA's oil exporters picked up in 2025, with oil production increasing at a faster pace than initially announced, alongside robust expansion of non-oil activity. In most oil importers, growth strengthened, supported by an easing of macroeconomic policies, a softening of global financial conditions, and credit expansion. With broadly limited exposure to increases in U.S. import tariffs, merchandise exports have grown steadily. Despite generally receding inflationary pressures, inflation has remained elevated in some economies.

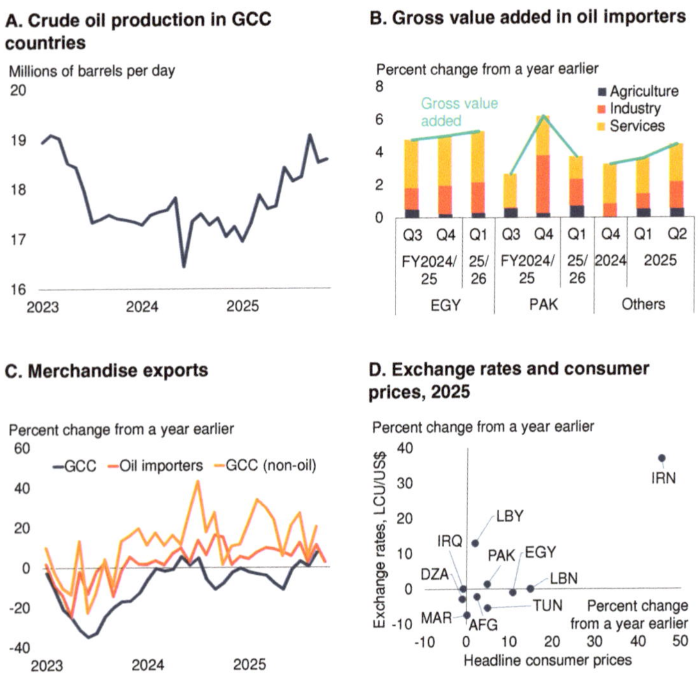

Sources: Haver Analytics; International Energy Agency; World Bank.

Note: AFG = Afghanistan; DZA = Algeria; EGY = Arab Republic of Egypt; FCS = fragile and conflict-affected situations; GCC = Gulf Cooperation Council; IRN = Islamic Republic of Iran; IRQ = Iraq; LBN = Lebanon; LBY = Libya; LCU = local currency unit; MAR = Morocco; MNA = Middle East, North Africa, Afghanistan and Pakistan; PAK = Pakistan; TUN = Tunisia.

A. Production of crude oil in six GCC countries. Last observation is November 2025.

B. Percent change in real gross value added from a year earlier, with sectoral contributions of the change, expressed in percentage points. The aggregate is computed as a weighted average, using gross value added at 2019 prices and market exchange rates as weights. Sample includes five non-FCS oil importers.

C. Percent change in non-seasonally adjusted merchandise export values, measured in U.S. dollars, from a year earlier. Last observation is October 2025. Sample includes up to four GCC countries and five non-FCS oil importers.

D. Vertical axis shows the percent change in the nominal exchange rate vis-à-vis the U.S. dollar from a year earlier, where positive (negative) values indicate depreciation (appreciation) of the local currency. Horizontal axis shows the percent change in the headline consumer price index from a year earlier. Data are for the second half of 2025 and presented as monthly averages from July to November 2025 in all economies except in Afghanistan, Algeria, Iraq, Lebanon, and Libya, where data are averaged from July to October 2025.

The region, on aggregate, has continued to record current account surpluses. In GCC countries, non-oil merchandise and services exports, particularly related to travel and transportation, have remained robust, alongside the recovery in oil exports (refer to figure 2.4.1.C). In Algeria, Iraq, and Libya, moderating oil prices and rising imports have led to an increase in external pressures. Libya's currency was devalued in April, though the divergence between official and market exchange rates has persisted (World Bank 2025h). Among oil importers, current account balances have improved in Morocco, Pakistan, and Tunisia, partly because of increases in remittances and tourism revenues.

Inflationary pressures across the region have receded, with several exceptions. Inflation has remained well-contained in GCC countries. However, among non-GCC oil exporters, inflation in the Islamic Republic of Iran has stayed elevated, alongside a currency depreciation, despite some tightening of monetary policy (refer to figure 2.4.1.D). Among oil importers, inflation has declined, particularly on account of softening food prices. This has led to multiple policy rate cuts, including in Pakistan, though monetary policies have still remained restrictive to tame inflation in several economies. Inflation in Gaza has remained persistently high, driven by acute supply constraints and shortages of essential goods, which have in turn exerted upward pressure on overall inflation in West Bank and Gaza (World Bank 2025i).

Outlook

Growth in MNA is projected to strengthen to 3.6 percent in 2026 and then 3.9 percent in 2027, mainly on account of rising growth in oil exporters, where the expansion of oil production is anticipated to outweigh the impact of lower oil prices (refer to figure 2.4.2.A; refer to table 2.4.1). Growth in the region will be supported by recovering export growth, with the contribution of net exports turning positive in 2026–27, alongside strengthening private investment growth. Nonetheless, forecasts for 2026 and 2027 have been marginally downgraded from June projections. This is primarily because the increase in oil production by OPEC+ countries in 2025 has been larger than previously assumed, suggesting less expansion to come in 2026–27. However, forecast downgrades for oil exporters are expected to be partly offset by upgrades for oil importers.

Crude oil prices are assumed to fall in 2026, given further production increases by OPEC+ countries and softening oil consumption growth, before a modest recovery in 2027. The growth outlook assumes a continued ceasefire in West Bank and Gaza without escalation in geopolitical tensions involving neighboring economies.

FIGURE 2.4.2 MNA: Outlook

Growth in MNA is expected to strengthen to 3.6 percent in 2026 and 3.9 percent in 2027, with the strengthening mainly reflecting rising oil production, particularly in GCC countries. Growth in oil importers is also projected to increase, backed by easing inflation. Contractionary fiscal policies will gradually reduce fiscal deficits in oil importers, whereas non-GCC oil exporters are forecast to face heightened deficits, mainly because of subdued oil exports and higher spending needs, alongside higher inflation. Poverty is set to decline in oil importers, with steady per capita income growth.

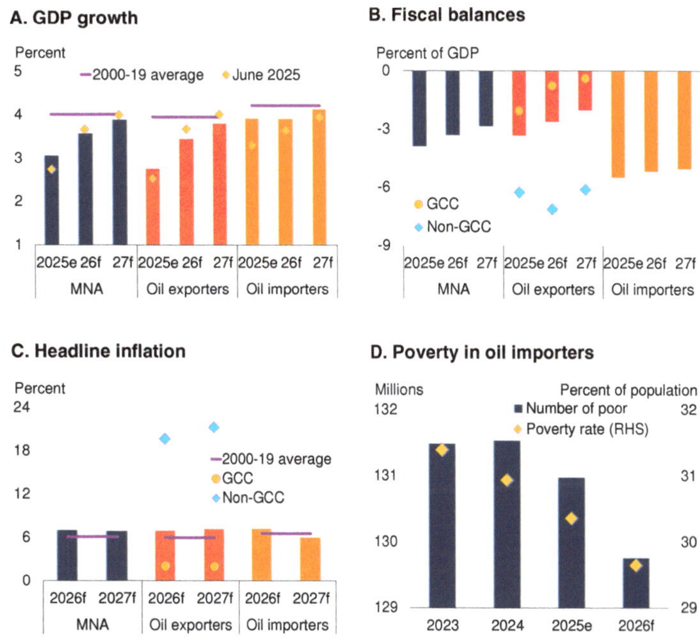

Source: World Bank.

Note: e = estimate; f = forecast. GCC = Gulf Cooperation Council; MNA = Middle East, North Africa, Afghanistan and Pakistan.

A. Aggregates are calculated as weighted averages using GDP at average 2010–19 prices and market exchange rates as weights. Diamonds for June 2025 refer to the rates computed with data in the June 2025 edition of the *Global Economic Prospects* report.

B. Aggregates are calculated as weighted averages, using nominal GDP in U.S. dollars as weights.

C. Aggregates are calculated as weighted geometric averages, using nominal GDP in U.S. dollars as weights.

D. Poverty is defined using the lower-middle-income poverty threshold of 4.20 international dollars per day in 2021 purchasing power parity. Sample includes six oil importers.

Growth in GCC countries is forecast to increase to 4.4 percent in 2026 and 4.6 percent in 2027, mainly reflecting a steady expansion of non-hydrocarbon activity, in addition to a further rise in hydrocarbon production. The strengthening of non-hydrocarbon activity—accounting for more than 60 percent of GCC countries' total GDP—is projected to be supported by expected large-scale investments, including in Kuwait and Saudi Arabia. Increases in OPEC+ oil production are expected to continue, contributing to the acceleration of growth, along with the expansion of natural gas production, including in Qatar (Chattha et al. 2025). Aluminum production and exports are anticipated to rise in Bahrain, despite increased U.S. import tariffs, partly reflecting sustained demand related to the energy transition.

Among non-GCC oil exporters, economic activity in the Islamic Republic of Iran is expected to contract by 1.5 percent in fiscal year (FY) 2026/27 (late-March 2026 to late-March 2027) and grow at a subdued pace of 0.6 percent in FY2027/28, mainly reflecting a decline in oil production amid the reintroduction of international sanctions and tighter trade restrictions (refer to table 2.4.2). In Algeria, despite a rise in oil production, dissipating fiscal support is anticipated to moderate growth and soften the pace of job creation (World Bank 2025j). In Iraq, oil production increases are projected to lift growth to an average of 5.2 percent in 2026–27. Growth in Libya is anticipated to stabilize in 2026–27, assuming the maintenance of security and political stability.

In oil importers, overall growth is projected to inch up to 4 percent a year, on average, in 2026–27, but prospects vary by economy.

In Egypt, growth is forecast to strengthen to 4.6 percent a year, on average, in FY2025/26 (July 2025 to June 2026) and FY2026/27, with robust net exports. Additionally, softening price pressures and easing global financial conditions will support private consumption, while private investment is projected to be solid, backed by monetary easing and continued structural reforms. In Pakistan, growth is expected to remain at 3 percent in FY2025/26 (July 2025 to June 2026) and then increase to 3.4 percent in FY2026/27, with a recovery of agricultural production and reconstruction following a series of floods in 2025 (World Bank 2025k). A steady strengthening of growth is anticipated in Jordan, with assumed geopolitical stabilization and lower oil prices outweighing the adverse effects of increased U.S. tariffs.

In contrast, growth in Morocco and Tunisia is expected to slow to average 4.4 percent and 2.4 percent, respectively, in 2026–27, with weaker expansion in agriculture and manufacturing, alongside softer employment growth (World Bank 2025l). In Djibouti, steady growth of 6.1 percent, on average, is projected for 2026–27, mainly reflecting the development of large infrastructure projects, which is anticipated to strengthen port and transportation activity.

The outlook for economies in fragile and conflict-affected situations (FCS) remains highly uncertain. Economic activity in Afghanistan is forecast to expand by 3.8 percent in FY2026/27 (late-March 2026 to late-March 2027) and 3.5 percent in FY2027/28, assuming that the labor market allows the absorption of returnees. In Lebanon, assumed progress in reforms is projected to strengthen growth to 4 percent in 2026. In West Bank and Gaza, growth is expected to rise to 5.1 percent in 2026 and 11.6 percent in 2027, given that reconstruction begins in 2026. However, activity will remain subdued in the Republic of Yemen, reflecting adverse security situations and limited foreign assistance (World Bank 2025m).

Fiscal positions across the region are expected to modestly improve over the forecast horizon. However, deficits will remain large among non-GCC oil exporters, reflecting subdued oil exports and spending pressures in several economies (refer to figure 2.4.2.B). Fiscal deficits in oil importers are set to narrow in 2026–27, partly because of contractionary policies, in Egypt, Morocco, Tunisia, and West Bank and Gaza, among others. In GCC countries, fiscal deficits are anticipated to shrink in 2026–27, as revenues will be boosted by increases in oil production, even though oil prices are expected to be lower, and by tax reforms, including in the United Arab Emirates.

The region, as a whole, is expected to maintain current account surpluses in 2026–27. In several oil importers, including Egypt and Jordan, current account deficits are anticipated to shrink, reflecting rising tourism receipts and remittances. However, in Pakistan, a current account deficit is projected to widen in FY2026/27, with a rise in import demand, alongside the strengthening growth, and post-flood normalization of remittance inflows. In Afghanistan, a reduction in foreign aid and weak remittance inflows will lead to a worsening of the current account balance (World Bank 2025n). In GCC countries, current account surpluses are expected to widen in 2026–27, with improving trade balances on account of increased oil exports.

Headline inflation rates in the region are forecast to be generally stable in 2026–27, at rates slightly higher than long-term averages (refer to figure 2.4.2.C). An expected increase in inflation in non-GCC oil exporters is likely to be accompanied by easing inflationary pressures in oil importers. A decline in inflation in several oil importers is anticipated to lead to an easing of monetary policies, supporting demand and activity. In GCC countries, headline inflation is forecast to remain contained in 2026–27.

Poverty is set to decline in oil importers over the forecast horizon, with steady per capita income growth (refer to figure 2.4.2.D). However, poverty will stay elevated in FCS economies, including the Syrian Arab Republic, and widespread informality will likely hinder poverty reduction in several economies. Job creation in the region is expected to remain weak, partly reflecting limited private sector dynamism, strict regulations, and skill mismatches—particularly among the youth. It is also projected to be outpaced by an increase in young people entering labor markets. In addition, the participation of females in the labor force is anticipated to remain limited, due in part to structural constraints, including legal barriers (World Bank 2025o).

Risks

Risks to the growth outlook are tilted to the downside. A re-escalation of armed conflicts in the region, or heightened violence and social unrest, could disrupt economic activity. Other downside risks include tighter global financial conditions, further increases in trade restrictions and tensions, or higher uncertainty about global trade policies, and more frequent or intense disasters resulting from natural hazards. In addition, in oil exporters, lower-than-expected oil prices or higher oil price volatility could diminish growth. However, there are also upside risks, including larger-than-expected technology-related productivity gains and a further commitment to structural reforms.

A re-escalation of armed conflicts in the region could cause a significant deterioration in consumer and business sentiment, not only in the economies directly affected but also in neighboring economies. It could spill over into a broader increase in policy uncertainty and a tightening of financial conditions, dampening investment and economic activity.

In economies with weak governance and institutional frameworks, particularly FCS, increases in conflict and social unrest could exacerbate food insecurity, weigh on job growth, and undermine long-term economic development (refer to figure 2.4.3.A; Gatti et al. 2024). Outcomes could be even worse if there is a larger decline in international support from donor countries than expected.

An abrupt decline in risk appetite in global financial markets and associated tightening of global financial conditions could result in substantial capital outflows and currency depreciations, particularly in economies exhibiting elevated fiscal and external vulnerabilities, including Egypt and Lebanon (World Bank 2025p). In oil importers, particularly those considered frontier markets, despite improving current account balances, external financing needs have risen (refer to figure 2.4.3.B). This partly reflects the accumulation of short-term debt, which has increased rollover risk (refer to chapter 4, forthcoming).

Further rises in import tariffs or other trade restrictions, or increased global trade policy uncertainty, could erode business confidence and dampen exports and economic activity in the region. In oil exporters, global demand for oil could weaken, reducing fiscal revenues and domestic investment. In several oil importers, particularly Pakistan and Tunisia, further increases in U.S. tariffs could lead to notable declines in exports (Gatti et al. 2025a). In addition, economies with a more concentrated export destination structure would be more vulnerable to trade-related shocks (Gatti et al. 2025b).

FIGURE 2.4.3 MNA: Risks

A re-escalation of regional conflict in MNA or a worsening of violence could aggravate food insecurity, especially in fragile economies. In oil importers, fiscal and external financing needs have remained high, making them vulnerable to an adverse shift in global financial conditions. Lower-than-expected crude oil prices and heightened oil price volatility could reduce revenues and soften growth prospects in oil exporters. However, the benefits for oil importers could be partly offset by weaker remittances from GCC countries, the major sources of these flows. GCC countries are better positioned to adopt new technologies, in terms of affordability and access, and reap their benefits, which could lead to faster productivity growth than assumed in the baseline.

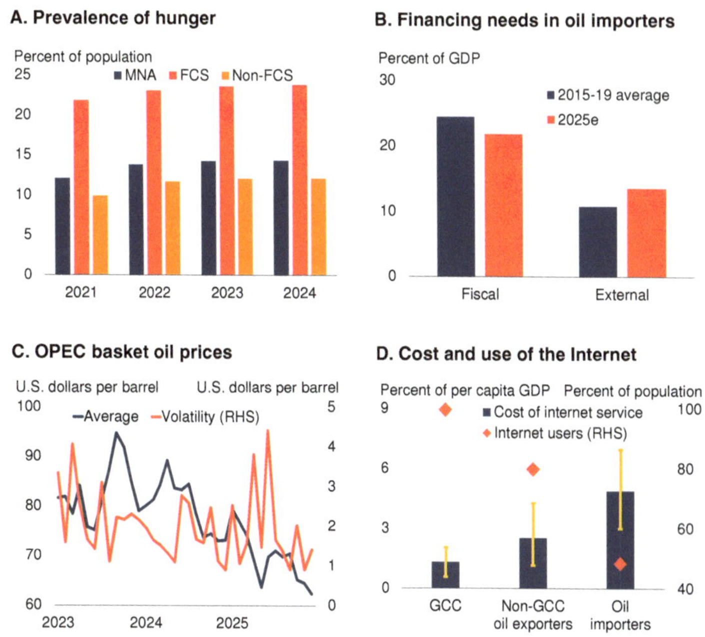

Sources: Food and Agriculture Organization; International Telecommunication Union; Kose et al. (2022); OPEC; World Bank (2025q); World Bank.

Note: e = estimate. FCS = fragile and conflict-affected situations; GCC = Gulf Cooperation Council; MNA = Middle East, North Africa, Afghanistan and Pakistan; OPEC = Organization of the Petroleum Exporting Countries.

A. Percent of the population that is undernourished, weighted by population in respective country groups. The numbers are presented as three-year moving averages, with, for example, a bar for 2024 covering data over 2023–25. Sample includes up to 14 economies, consisting of five FCS and nine non-FCS economies.

B. A fiscal financing need is defined as the sum of the fiscal deficit and short-term central government debt. An external financing need is defined as the sum of the current account deficit, principal repayments of long-term external debt, and the stock of short-term external debt at the end of the previous year. Aggregates are computed as weighted averages using nominal GDP in U.S. dollars as weights. Sample includes up to six non-FCS oil importers.

C. Monthly averages and standard deviations, defined as volatility, of daily OPEC basket prices. Last observation is December 2025, based on data until December 16, 2025.

D. The cost of internet service is represented by a fixed broadband Internet price basket, provided by each country's largest operator, and expressed in percent of nominal per capita GDP in U.S. dollars per month (that is, annual per capita GDP divided by 12). Data are averaged over 2023–24. Bars show medians across economies in each group, with vertical yellow lines showing the interquartile ranges. Diamonds show the percent of the population using the internet in 2023, and aggregates are computed as weighted averages using the total population as weights. Oil importers exclude FCS economies.

In oil exporters, weaker-than-expected global demand for oil and resulting declines in oil prices could depress government revenues, leading to reductions in growth-enhancing capital expenditures, diminishing growth prospects, and slowing economic diversification. In oil importers, the benefits of lower oil prices could be partly offset by weaker remittances from GCC countries. In addition, oil price volatility spiked in the first half of 2025 following surges in trade policy uncertainty and geopolitical stress (refer to figure 2.4.3.C). Any renewed increase in price volatility could raise macroeconomic uncertainty, reducing investment and decelerating job creation (Arroyo Marioli and Vasishtha 2025).

The region is vulnerable to severe weather events, including droughts, extreme heat, and floods. If such events become unexpectedly more frequent or severe, there could be large-scale humanitarian losses and damage to infrastructure, lowering growth and productivity. Food prices could also surge, exacerbating poverty and food insecurity. Other types of natural hazard-driven disasters, including earthquakes, could also impose humanitarian and economic costs.

Conversely, an upside risk to the growth forecast is the potential benefits from further investment in new technologies, including artificial intelligence (AI). For example, in GCC countries, AI investment is a key part of national development strategies, and these economies are better prepared to adopt such technologies (refer to figure 2.4.3.D). The diffusion of AI could raise productivity at a faster rate than expected. However, the materialization of AI-related growth gains hinges on the development of physical and human capital for technological adoption, including investment in digital infrastructure and the reskilling and upskilling of the workforce.

Another upside risk is a further commitment to implementing growth-enhancing structural reforms. In Morocco and Pakistan, the implementation of deeper-than-anticipated regulatory reforms to promote private sector activity could boost growth, reduce informality, and create jobs. In Djibouti, faster-than-expected reform efforts to improve climate resilience and lower energy costs could lead to increases in investment.

TABLE 2.4.1 Middle East, North Africa, Afghanistan and Pakistan forecast summary

(Real GDP growth at market prices in percent, unless indicated otherwise)

	2023	2024	2025e	2026f	2027f	Percentage-point differences from June 2025 projections: 2025e	2026f	2027f
EMDE MNA, GDP[1]	**2.1**	**2.6**	**3.1**	**3.6**	**3.9**	**0.4**	**-0.1**	**-0.1**
GDP per capita (U.S. dollars)	0.4	0.9	1.5	2.0	2.4	0.3	-0.1	-0.1
Excluding Afghanistan and Pakistan	2.3	2.5	3.0	3.6	3.9	0.3	-0.1	-0.2
(Average including countries that report expenditure components in national accounts)[2]								
EMDE MNA, GDP[2]	2.1	2.6	3.1	3.6	3.9	0.4	-0.1	-0.1
PPP GDP	2.3	2.8	3.0	3.4	3.8	0.3	-0.1	-0.1
Private consumption	4.6	4.0	3.5	3.5	3.5	-0.3	0.0	0.0
Public consumption	2.6	2.6	4.3	2.5	2.9	1.4	-0.3	0.1
Fixed investment	2.9	2.5	3.5	4.0	5.8	2.2	0.1	1.2
Exports, GNFS	2.0	3.2	5.0	5.6	6.7	1.4	-0.5	0.7
Imports, GNFS	5.5	6.1	5.8	5.5	6.8	1.4	-0.1	1.5
Net exports, contribution to growth	-1.0	-0.8	0.0	0.3	0.3	0.1	-0.2	-0.3
Memo items: GDP								
Oil exporters[3]	2.1	2.5	2.7	3.4	3.8	0.2	-0.3	-0.2
GCC countries[4]	1.0	2.5	3.8	4.4	4.6	0.6	-0.1	-0.2
Non-GCC oil exporters[5]	4.4	2.4	0.7	1.7	2.2	-0.6	-0.5	-0.3
Oil importers[6]	2.1	2.9	3.9	3.9	4.1	0.6	0.3	0.2
Excluding Afghanistan and Pakistan	2.8	2.6	4.3	4.3	4.5	0.7	0.4	0.2

Source: World Bank.

Note: e = estimate; f = forecast. EMDE = emerging market and developing economy; GCC = Gulf Cooperation Council; GNFS = goods and non-factor services; MNA = Middle East, North Africa, Afghanistan and Pakistan; PPP = purchasing power parity. World Bank forecasts are frequently updated based on new information and changing global circumstances. Consequently, projections presented here may differ from those in other World Bank documents, even if basic assessments of countries' prospects do not differ at any given moment in time. The region name "Middle East and North Africa" has been changed to "Middle East, North Africa, Afghanistan and Pakistan" to reflect the inclusion of Afghanistan and Pakistan following the World Bank's regional reclassification effective July 1, 2025.

1. GDP and expenditure components are measured in average 2010–19 prices and market exchange rates. Excludes Lebanon, the Syrian Arab Republic, and the Republic of Yemen because of the high degree of uncertainty. Aggregated growth rates based on data in the June 2025 edition of the *Global Economic Prospects* report are recomputed by including data for Afghanistan and Pakistan and therefore do not necessarily match those reported in the June 2025 publication.

2. Aggregate includes all economies in notes 3 and 6 except Jordan, for which data limitations prevent the forecasting of GDP components.

3. Algeria, Bahrain, the Islamic Republic of Iran, Iraq, Kuwait, Libya, Oman, Qatar, Saudi Arabia, and the United Arab Emirates.

4. Bahrain, Kuwait, Oman, Qatar, Saudi Arabia, and the United Arab Emirates.

5. Algeria, the Islamic Republic of Iran, Iraq, and Libya.

6. Afghanistan, Djibouti, the Arab Republic of Egypt, Jordan, Morocco, Pakistan, Tunisia, and West Bank and Gaza.

TABLE 2.4.2 Middle East, North Africa, Afghanistan and Pakistan economy forecasts

(Real GDP growth at market prices in percent, unless indicated otherwise)

	2023	2024	2025e	2026f	2027f	Percentage-point differences from June 2025 projections: 2025e	2026f	2027f
Calendar year basis								
Algeria	4.1	3.7	3.8	3.5	3.3	0.5	0.3	0.4
Bahrain	3.9	3.1	3.5	3.1	2.9	0.0	0.1	0.1
Djibouti	6.7	6.0	6.0	6.1	6.0	0.8	1.0	1.0
Iraq [1]	0.5	-1.5	-0.9	6.5	3.8	-2.1	2.1	0.7
Jordan	2.9	2.5	2.7	2.8	2.8	0.3	0.3	0.0
Kuwait	-3.6	-2.9	2.7	2.6	2.5	0.5	-0.1	-0.2
Lebanon [2 3]	-0.8	-7.1	3.5	4.0	..	-1.2	..	..
Libya	10.2	1.9	13.3	3.5	3.9	1.0	-2.9	-1.7
Morocco	3.7	3.8	5.0	4.4	4.4	1.4	0.9	0.8
Oman	1.2	1.7	3.1	3.6	4.0	0.1	-0.1	0.0
Qatar	1.5	2.4	2.8	5.3	6.8	0.4	-0.1	-0.8
Saudi Arabia	0.5	2.7	3.8	4.3	4.4	1.0	-0.2	-0.2
Syrian Arab Republic [2]	-1.2	-1.5	1.0	..	..	0.0	..	..
Tunisia	0.2	1.6	2.6	2.5	2.2	0.7	0.9	0.5
United Arab Emirates	2.9	3.9	4.8	5.0	5.1	0.2	0.1	0.2
West Bank and Gaza	-4.6	-26.6	3.9	5.1	11.6	5.5	1.1	-4.4
Yemen, Rep. [2]	-2.0	-1.5	-1.5	0.0	..	0.0	-0.5	..
Fiscal year basis [4]	2023/24	2024/25	2025/26e	2026/27f	2027/28f	2025/26e	2026/27f	2027/28f
Afghanistan	2.3	2.5	4.3	3.8	3.5	2.1	1.4	1.0
Iran, Islamic Rep.	5.3	3.7	-1.1	-1.5	0.6	-0.6	-1.8	-1.2
	2022/23	2023/24	2024/25e	2025/26f	2026/27f	2024/25e	2025/26f	2026/27f
Egypt, Arab Rep.	3.8	2.4	4.4	4.3	4.8	0.6	0.1	0.2
Pakistan [1]	-0.2	2.6	3.0	3.0	3.4	0.3	-0.1	0.0

Source: World Bank.

Note: e = estimate; f = forecast. World Bank forecasts are frequently updated based on new information and changing global circumstances. Consequently, projections presented here may differ from those in other World Bank documents, even if basic assessments of economies' prospects do not significantly differ at any given moment in time.

1. Data are reported on a factor cost basis.
2. Forecasts for Lebanon (beyond 2026), the Syrian Arab Republic (beyond 2025), and the Republic of Yemen (beyond 2026) are excluded because of a high degree of uncertainty.
3. Forecast for 2026 was not included in the June 2025 edition of the *Global Economic Prospects* report, and therefore the difference from the June 2025 projection is not computed.
4. Fiscal year runs from March 21 to March 20 in Afghanistan and the Islamic Republic of Iran; and from July 1 to June 30 in the Arab Republic of Egypt and Pakistan.

SOUTH ASIA

Growth in South Asia (SAR) is projected to moderate to 6.2 percent in 2026 before picking up to 6.5 percent in 2027. In the region excluding India, growth is expected to accelerate to 5 percent in 2026 and 5.6 percent in 2027, primarily on account of a projected recovery in Bangladesh. However, the pace of job creation in the region will likely remain subdued. Risks to the outlook are tilted to the downside and include further increases in trade restrictions and global trade policy uncertainty, a tightening of financial conditions amid banking sector vulnerabilities, increased social unrest, and extreme weather events. Upside risks include possible progress in bilateral trade negotiations; faster technology-led investment growth, particularly in India; and potential benefits from more resilient political environments after elections in several economies.

Recent developments

Growth in South Asia (SAR) is estimated to have strengthened to 7.1 percent in 2025, mainly because of resilient activity in India, which helped offset the effects of rising trade tensions and heightened policy uncertainty. In India, growth is estimated to increase to 7.2 percent in fiscal year (FY) 2025/26 (April 2025 to March 2026), as domestic demand has remained robust, reflecting strong private consumption, supported by earlier tax reforms and improvements in real household earnings in rural areas. Alongside resilient services exports, merchandise exports rose in November, despite increases in U.S. import tariffs on many Indian goods (refer to figure 2.5.1.A). This partly reflects buoyant demand from the United States and other trading partners, supported by efforts to diversify export markets to increase resilience.

Growth in SAR excluding India is estimated to have stabilized in 2025 at 4.2 percent. In Bangladesh—which accounts for more than three-quarters of GDP in the region when India is excluded—the recovery from earlier political turmoil continued in the second half of FY2024/25 (July 2024 to June 2025), though it lost some momentum, due in part to sluggish investment.

In contrast, activity in several other economies has been solid (refer to figure 2.5.1.B). In Maldives, the performance of the tourism sector has remained resilient. The commissioning of a new hydropower plant and the construction of new power plants have supported growth in Bhutan. However, in Nepal, political instability and economic policy uncertainty have been heightened following recent unrest and the subsequent formation of an interim government in September.

Headline inflation has declined in most economies (refer to figure 2.5.1.C). Policy rates have since been lowered in several economies, including India and Sri Lanka. However, in Bangladesh, inflation has remained above the target, and monetary policy has been tight. Inflation in Maldives has stayed high, particularly food price inflation, reflecting the impact of foreign exchange pressures.

Despite easier global financial conditions, the growth in credit to the private sector has been restrained in several economies in the region, either by policies designed to contain financial risks or on account of weakened demand. Credit growth has continued to be moderated in India by macroprudential policies aimed at containing banking sector risks, despite increases in financing from non-bank sources. In Bangladesh, demand for credit has been reduced amid subdued business

Note: This section was prepared by Naotaka Sugawara. As a result of the World Bank's regional reclassification effective July 1, 2025, Afghanistan and Pakistan are no longer included in the South Asia region.

FIGURE 2.5.1 SAR: Recent developments

Merchandise exports in India increased in November, despite a rise in U.S. import tariffs, partly reflecting resilient demand from the United States and other trade partners. In Bangladesh, the continued recovery from earlier political turmoil has lost some momentum, whereas activity in several other economies has remained firm. Inflation in most economies in SAR has moderated. In India, currency pressures have led to a depreciation of the rupee since May, whereas in Bangladesh the adoption of a more flexible currency regime has contributed to the stabilization of the exchange rate.

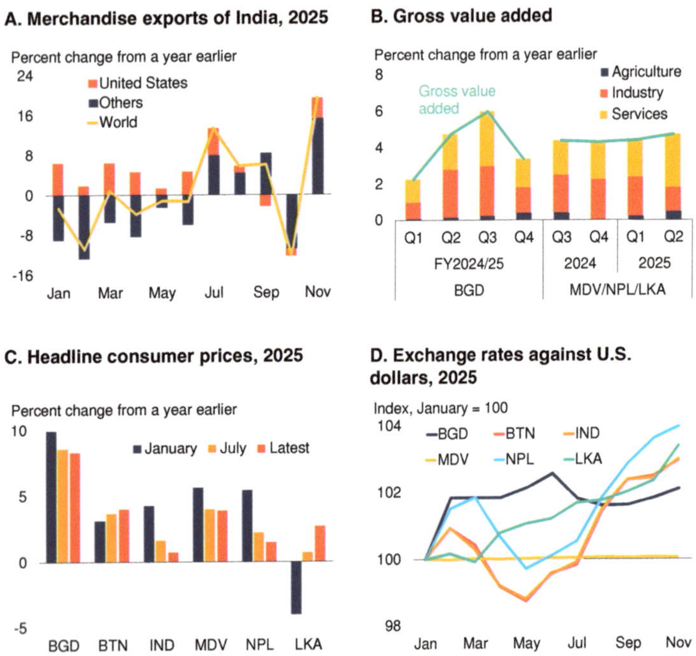

Sources: Haver Analytics; World Bank.

Note: BGD = Bangladesh; BTN = Bhutan; IND = India; LKA = Sri Lanka; MDV = Maldives; NPL = Nepal; SAR = South Asia.

A. Percent change in non-seasonally adjusted merchandise export values, measured in U.S. dollars, from a year earlier, with contributions of respective export destinations, expressed in percentage points. Last observation is November 2025.

B. Percent change in real gross value added from a year earlier, with sectoral contributions of the change, expressed in percentage points. The aggregate is computed as weighted averages, using gross value added at 2019 prices and market exchange rates as weights.

C. Percent changes in the headline consumer price index from a year earlier. Data for the latest month, as shown in red bars, refer to November for Bangladesh and India, and October for Bhutan, Maldives, Nepal, and Sri Lanka.

D. Nominal exchange rates with respect to the U.S. dollar, presented with a value in January 2025 equal to 100. An increase (decrease) in values reflects depreciation (appreciation) of local currency. Last observation is November 2025.

activity and heightened borrowing costs. Credit growth has also decelerated in Maldives, especially in fishing, construction, transport, and communications sectors. In contrast, in Sri Lanka, recovering domestic demand contributed to an expansion of credit.

External positions have strengthened in most economies in the region. Solid inflows of remittances and international tourists have contributed to improved current account balances and increased foreign exchange reserves. In contrast, India's currency has depreciated since May in the face of capital outflows amid higher U.S. tariffs and heightened trade-related uncertainty (refer to figure 2.5.1.D). In Bangladesh, the exchange rate has stabilized since mid-2025, partly reflecting the adoption of a more flexible currency regime in May.

Outlook

Growth in SAR is expected to slow to 6.2 percent in 2026, mainly reflecting the impact of increased U.S. import tariffs on India's export growth (refer to figure 2.5.2.A; refer to table 2.5.1). The forecast for this year has been downgraded by 0.2 percentage point compared with June projections. The revision reflects higher U.S. import tariffs than previously assumed and updated assumptions about the timing of the tariff effects—from 2025 to early- to mid-2026—and of subsequent recovery. Growth in the region is then set to increase to 6.5 percent in 2027, with firming domestic demand and recovering exports partly supported by strong services activity, as the effects of political uncertainty in several economies dissipate.

Growth in India is projected to slow to 6.5 percent in FY2026/27. This assumes that the 50-percent import tariffs by the United States remain in place throughout the forecast horizon. Even so, India is expected to maintain the fastest growth rate among the world's largest economies (refer to table 2.5.2). Despite higher tariffs on certain exports to the United States—which accounts for about 12 percent of India's merchandise exports—the growth forecast has remained unchanged relative to June projections, primarily because adverse impacts of higher tariffs will be offset by stronger momentum in domestic demand and more resilient exports than previously anticipated. Growth is set to inch up to 6.6 percent in FY2027/28, underpinned by robust services activity, as well as a recovery in exports and a pickup in investment.

Excluding India, growth in the region is forecast to strengthen to 5 percent in 2026 and 5.6 percent in 2027. Compared with June projections, growth is 0.3 percentage point higher for 2027, primarily reflecting an upward revision for Bangladesh. In

Bangladesh, growth is expected to increase to 4.6 percent in FY2025/26 and 6.1 percent in the following fiscal year, with private consumption strengthening alongside easing inflationary pressures. Reduced political uncertainty related to the general election in early 2026 and the expected implementation of structural reforms by a new government are projected to support stronger industrial activity in FY2026/27 (World Bank 2025r). These factors are also anticipated to lead to faster public spending and investment growth than previously projected.

Excluding Bangladesh and India, regional growth is expected to slow further in 2026, to 3.6 percent, and remain at that pace in 2027. Growth in Sri Lanka is expected to decelerate to 3.5 percent in 2026 and 3.1 percent in 2027, reflecting structural impediments to growth, including factor and product market inefficiencies, the scarring effects of the economic crisis, and global economic uncertainty hurting demand for exports.[1]

In Nepal, growth is projected to weaken in FY2025/26 (mid-July 2025 to mid-July 2026) to 2.1 percent, amid heightened political instability and policy uncertainty. The outlook is 3.1 percentage points below June projections, with expected sharp declines in tourist arrivals and services activity. In addition, subdued investor sentiment and heightened uncertainty are expected to lead to a slowdown in industrial output. Growth is then forecast to recover in FY2026/27, mainly reflecting progress in reconstruction and a rebound in the services sector, but the forecast is subject to heightened uncertainty (World Bank 2025s).

Growth in Bhutan will continue benefiting from the commissioning and construction of hydropower plants, strengthening to 7.3 percent in FY2025/26 (July 2025 to June 2026). Growth is projected to remain robust in FY2026/27, primarily because of strong electricity production and increased construction activity. Growth in Maldives is also expected to remain solid, averaging 4 percent a year in 2026–27, supported by increased tourist arrivals facilitated by the full opening of a new international airport terminal.

FIGURE 2.5.2 SAR: Outlook

Growth in SAR is expected to slow to 6.2 percent in 2026, mainly reflecting the impact of increased tariffs on India, and then recover to 6.5 percent in 2027, partly supported by strong growth in services activity as political uncertainty eases in several economies. Fiscal consolidation in India is forecast to continue, whereas primary deficits are set to be steady, on average, in the rest of the region. Inflation is projected to remain moderate over the forecast horizon. Steady per capita income growth, aided by solid remittance inflows, is expected to help reduce poverty.

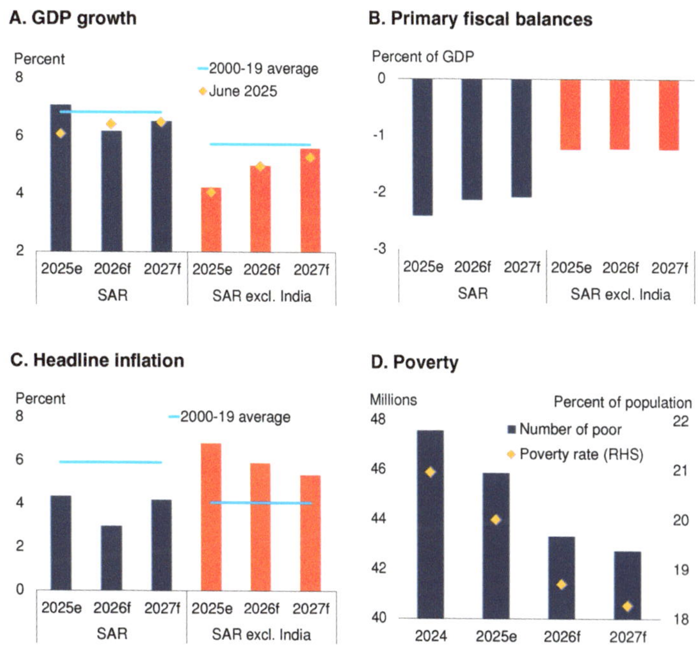

Source: World Bank.

Note: e = estimate; f = forecast. SAR = South Asia.

A. Aggregates are calculated as weighted averages, using GDP at average 2010–19 prices and market exchange rates as weights. Diamonds for June 2025 refer to the rates computed with data in the June 2025 edition of the *Global Economic Prospects* report.

B. Aggregates are calculated as weighted averages, using nominal GDP in U.S. dollars as weights.

C. Aggregates are calculated as weighted geometric averages, using nominal GDP in U.S. dollars as weights.

D. Poverty is defined using the lower-middle-income poverty threshold of 4.20 international dollars per day in 2021 purchasing power parity. Sample includes Bangladesh, Bhutan, Nepal, and Sri Lanka.

Fiscal policy is anticipated to vary across the region. Fiscal consolidation is set to continue in India over the forecast horizon, with the effects of tax cuts outweighed by a decline in current spending, resulting in a gradual reduction in the public debt-to-GDP ratio. Elsewhere in the region, primary deficits are forecast to be steady (refer to figure 2.5.2.B). In Bangladesh, an expected reform-driven increase in revenue collection is projected to offset a rise in expenditure following the formation of a new government. Strong revenue performance in Sri Lanka is

[1] In the growth projections, the impacts of Cyclone Ditwah in late 2025 have yet to be taken into account, given an ongoing assessment of its damage to the economy.

forecast to lead to reductions in fiscal deficits and public debt (World Bank 2025t). In contrast, Bhutan's fiscal deficit is anticipated to widen, reflecting the implementation of infrastructure projects despite expected tax reforms.

Current account deficits in the region are projected to remain moderate. In India, surpluses in services trade are expected to partly offset merchandise trade deficits. Elsewhere in the region, trade deficits are generally anticipated to widen in 2026–27, with some current account balances turning to deficit, reflecting strong growth in domestic investment. Current account deficits are projected to widen in Bhutan and Maldives, mainly because of increases in imports for investment. In Maldives, high external financing needs, including debt service requirements, are anticipated to sustain pressure on the balance of payments and official reserves. In contrast, Nepal and Sri Lanka are forecast to run current account surpluses, primarily reflecting lower global oil prices and resilient remittance inflows, particularly from member countries of the Gulf Cooperation Council, where activity is anticipated to remain robust.

Inflation in India is expected to converge to the target set by the central bank in FY2026/27, assuming stable seasonal conditions contain food price inflation. Excluding India, inflation in the region is set to decline over the forecast horizon (refer to figure 2.5.2.C). Inflation in Nepal is forecast to remain below the central bank's ceiling, given projections of weak global commodity prices and moderate inflation in India. Inflationary pressures are anticipated to soften in Bangladesh, leading to monetary policy easing, whereas rising demand and tight supplies of food are likely to contribute to price pressures in Maldives (World Bank 2025u).

Poverty is expected to decline in the region over the forecast horizon, supported by steady per capita income growth amid slowing population growth, moderate inflationary pressures, and solid remittance inflows (refer to figure 2.5.2.D). However, job creation, particularly in the non-agricultural sector, is anticipated to remain subdued in the region, likely insufficient for the youth who are expected to reach working age over the forecast horizon. In several economies, including Bhutan and Sri Lanka, emigration pressures are projected to remain heightened, especially among the young and highly skilled population.

Risks

Risks to the regional outlook are tilted to the downside. Further increases in trade restrictions or trade policy uncertainty could lower external demand relative to the baseline. Tighter-than-expected financial conditions amid heightened financial vulnerabilities, elevated violence and social unrest, or more frequent or intense disasters due to natural hazards could also reduce regional growth. However, there are multiple upside risks. Growth could exceed the baseline forecast if bilateral tariffs are, even partially, reversed in several economies in the region. Another upside risk is that new technologies could generate faster productivity and employment growth than assumed, particularly in India. In addition, the stabilization of the political environment in some economies could lead to growth-enhancing structural reforms.

A further rise in tariffs or other trade restrictions, or heightened uncertainty about global trade policies, could dampen export demand and economic activity in the region. Although openness to global trade is relatively limited in the region's economies, the risk is higher in those with larger exposure to the United States, including Bangladesh and Sri Lanka, than in other regional economies. Increases in tariffs, including through the removal of exemptions relating, for example, to electronics, or extensions to services, could directly weaken growth.

Tighter financial conditions in the region, resulting, for example, from a sudden shift in risk appetite, could weigh on private investment and raise public debt service burdens. It could also reduce access to foreign borrowing and trigger capital outflows from the region, particularly from frontier market economies with elevated debt levels and large external financing needs, including Maldives (refer to figure 2.5.3.A; refer to chapter 4, forthcoming).

Further increases in banking sector vulnerabilities could reduce the availability of credit to the private sector. In economies with weakened commercial bank balance sheets, further shocks to their financial systems could trigger financial disruptions. In Bhutan, the materialization of contingent liabilities associated with hydropower projects could disrupt the financial market and worsen the fiscal position (World Bank 2025v).

Increased violence and social unrest, as well as a surge in political instability—for example, surrounding elections—could disrupt economic activity and worsen investor confidence, reducing investment and capital inflows. This is more likely to occur in economies with weaker socioeconomic conditions, including in the provision of education and the promotion of employment (refer to figure 2.5.3.B).

More frequent or severe extreme weather events could result in substantial humanitarian and economic losses. The region is exposed to weather-related risks and has experienced a number of such events in recent years (refer to figure 2.5.3.C; Damania et al. 2025). Extreme weather events could also reduce food production, which could increase food inflation and households' living expenses.

In contrast, an upside risk to the outlook is the possible resolution of trade disputes, including a partial reversal of U.S. tariffs, in several economies, including India. Progress on bilateral negotiations to lower trade barriers and restrictions could lead to faster export growth and attract more foreign capital than assumed in the baseline. Business and consumer confidence could also be boosted, which would support stronger-than-expected increases in investment and consumption.

Another upside risk is that further investment in new technologies, including artificial intelligence, could enhance productivity at a faster pace than expected, especially in economies better prepared to adopt them, such as India (refer to figure 2.5.3.D). It could also raise potential growth and strengthen the economy's resilience to external shocks. However, the materialization of the benefits will likely require the implementation of reskilling initiatives (World Bank 2025w). It also hinges on the development of physical and human capital in neighboring economies. Investment to advance technological capacity and support digital transformation could help absorb skilled workers domestically.

FIGURE 2.5.3 SAR: Risks

Economies in SAR with large government financing needs, alongside elevated debt, are more prone to adverse shifts in global financial conditions. The share of youth not in employment, education, or training has risen in some countries, which could be a flashpoint for increased social unrest. Economic activity in the region could be disrupted by more frequent or severe weather events. Further investment in new technologies could lead to faster-than-expected productivity growth in economies that are better prepared to adopt such technologies.

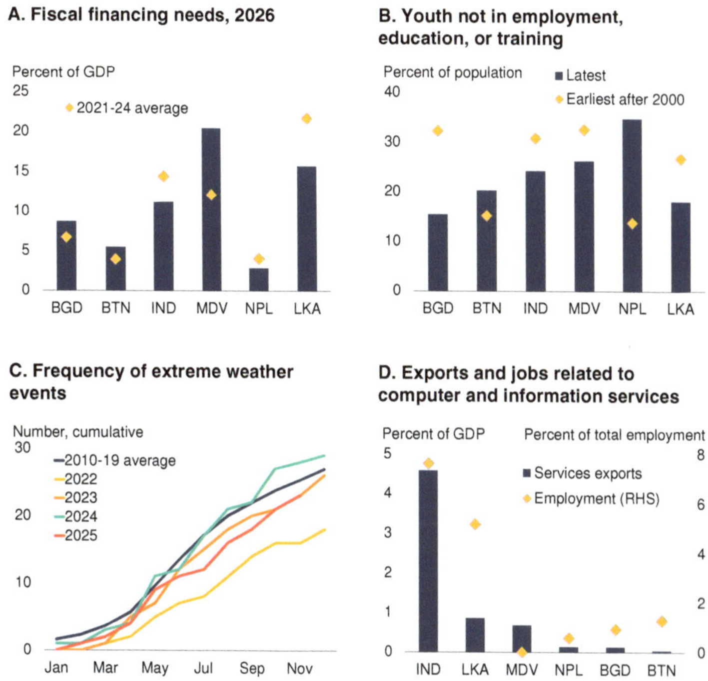

Sources: EM-DAT (database); International Labour Organization; International Monetary Fund; Kose et al. (2022); World Bank.

Note: BGD = Bangladesh; BTN = Bhutan; IND = India; LKA = Sri Lanka; MDV = Maldives; NPL = Nepal; SAR = South Asia.

A. A fiscal financing need is defined as the sum of the fiscal deficit and short-term central government debt. For Maldives and Sri Lanka, data refer to the 2026 projections, and for Bangladesh, Bhutan, India, and Nepal, the forecasts for FY2025/26 are presented. For the four economies where data are reported on a fiscal year basis, diamonds show averages of FY2020/21 to FY2023/24.

B. Percent of the youth, defined as the population aged 15–24, who are not in employment, education, or training, which is computed by the International Labour Organization with survey data from national sources. The latest year refers to: 2024 for Bangladesh, Bhutan, and India; 2022 for Sri Lanka; 2019 for Maldives; and 2017 for Nepal. The earliest year after 2000 refers to: 2006 for Bangladesh; 2008 for Nepal; 2009 for Maldives; 2010 for Sri Lanka; and 2018 for Bhutan and India.

C. Cumulative number of extreme weather events, including droughts, extreme temperatures, floods, storms, wildfires, and landslides. Last observation for 2025 is November. Sample includes six countries.

D. Bars show exports of computer and information services, as a percent of GDP. For Maldives, telecommunications are also included. Data are for 2024 in all countries except in Bhutan, where data refer to FY2023/24. Diamonds show the percent of employment in computer programming, consultancy and related activities, and information service activities—defined as codes 62 and 63 in the fourth revision of the International Standard Industrial Classification of All Economic Activities—among workers with advanced education. Data are computed by the International Labour Organization with survey data from national sources for the latest year: 2024 for Bangladesh, Bhutan, and India; 2022 for Sri Lanka; 2019 for Maldives; and 2017 for Nepal.

Finally, political transitions following the scheduled elections in Bangladesh and Nepal in early 2026 could improve economic stability, with better predictability in growth-enhancing reform efforts. If these transitions are accompanied by stronger macroeconomic management and a greater commitment to structural reforms, investor confidence and economic activity could be materially boosted.

TABLE 2.5.1 South Asia forecast summary

(Real GDP growth at market prices in percent, unless indicated otherwise)

	2023	2024	2025e	2026f	2027f	Percentage-point differences from June 2025 projections: 2025e	2026f	2027f
EMDE South Asia, GDP[1]	**8.0**	**6.3**	**7.1**	**6.2**	**6.5**	**1.0**	**-0.2**	**0.0**
GDP per capita (U.S. dollars)	7.1	5.4	6.1	5.2	5.6	1.0	-0.3	0.0
(Average including countries that report expenditure components in national accounts)[2]								
EMDE South Asia, GDP[2]	8.0	6.4	7.1	6.2	6.5	1.0	-0.2	0.0
PPP GDP	8.1	6.4	7.1	6.2	6.5	1.0	-0.2	0.0
Private consumption	5.4	6.5	7.1	7.1	7.0	0.3	0.4	0.2
Public consumption	6.9	4.0	4.1	5.3	7.4	-0.7	-0.1	1.9
Fixed investment	7.5	6.9	6.5	6.6	6.8	0.3	0.0	0.1
Exports, GNFS	3.1	4.6	5.8	4.7	5.4	-0.5	-1.5	-1.5
Imports, GNFS	7.4	0.8	6.5	7.6	7.5	1.1	0.1	0.0
Net exports, contribution to growth	-1.4	0.8	-0.5	-1.0	-0.9	-0.4	-0.4	-0.4
Memo items: GDP								
	2023/24	2024/25	2025/26e	2026/27f	2027/28f	2025/26e	2026/27f	2027/28f
India[3]	9.2	6.5	7.2	6.5	6.6	0.9	0.0	-0.1
	2023	2024	2025e	2026f	2027f	2025e	2026f	2027f
South Asia excluding India	3.7	4.2	4.2	5.0	5.6	0.1	0.0	0.3
Excluding Bangladesh	-0.5	4.7	4.3	3.6	3.6	0.2	-0.3	-0.2

Source: World Bank.

Note: e = estimate; f = forecast. EMDE = emerging market and developing economy; GNFS = goods and non-factor services; PPP = purchasing power parity. World Bank forecasts are frequently updated based on new information and changing global circumstances. Consequently, projections presented here may differ from those in other World Bank documents, even if basic assessments of countries' prospects do not differ at any given moment in time.

1. GDP and expenditure components are measured in average 2010–19 prices and market exchange rates. Aggregates are presented in calendar year terms. Because of the World Bank's regional reclassification effective July 1, 2025, aggregated growth rates based on the June 2025 edition of the *Global Economic Prospects* report are recomputed without data for Afghanistan and Pakistan and therefore do not necessarily match those reported in the June 2025 publication.
2. Aggregate excludes Maldives, for which data limitations prevent the forecasting of GDP components.
3. Fiscal year runs from April 1 through March 31.

TABLE 2.5.2 South Asia country forecasts

(Real GDP growth at market prices in percent, unless indicated otherwise)

	2023	2024	2025e	2026f	2027f	Percentage-point differences from June 2025 projections: 2025e	2026f	2027f
Calendar year basis								
Maldives	4.9	3.5	4.2	3.9	4.0	-1.5	-1.4	-0.7
Sri Lanka[1]	-2.3	5.0	4.6	3.5	3.1	1.1	0.4	0.0
Fiscal year basis[2]	2023/24	2024/25	2025/26e	2026/27f	2027/28f	2025/26e	2026/27f	2027/28f
India	9.2	6.5	7.2	6.5	6.6	0.9	0.0	-0.1
	2022/23	2023/24	2024/25e	2025/26f	2026/27f	2024/25e	2025/26f	2026/27f
Bangladesh	5.8	4.2	3.7	4.6	6.1	0.4	-0.3	0.4
Bhutan	4.9	6.1	7.0	7.3	6.1	0.4	-0.3	0.8
Nepal	2.0	3.7	4.6	2.1	4.7	0.1	-3.1	-0.8

Source: World Bank.

Note: e = estimate; f = forecast. World Bank forecasts are frequently updated based on new information and changing global circumstances. Consequently, projections presented here may differ from those in other World Bank documents, even if basic assessments of countries' prospects do not significantly differ at any given moment in time.

1. The impacts of Cyclone Ditwah in late 2025 have yet to be incorporated due to an ongoing damage assessment.
2. Fiscal year runs from April 1 to March 31 in India; from July 1 to June 30 in Bangladesh and Bhutan; and from July 16 to July 15 in Nepal.

SUB-SAHARAN AFRICA

Growth in Sub-Saharan Africa (SSA) is forecast to firm to 4.3 percent in 2026, supported by ongoing reforms in some large economies, solid domestic investment growth, and a continued easing of inflation. In many economies, fiscal consolidation efforts are being prompted by the narrowing of fiscal space resulting from cuts to official development assistance, elevated government debt, and higher debt-servicing costs. Despite the improved growth outlook, per capita income gains will remain inadequate for significant progress in reducing extreme poverty and boosting job creation. Risks to the outlook remain tilted to the downside. Weaker-than-expected external demand, lower commodity prices, increased regional political instability, and worsening conflict could dent growth prospects. Further declines in donor support could heighten the vulnerability of SSA economies to shocks, including public health risks and natural disasters.

Recent developments

Growth in Sub-Saharan Africa (SSA) picked up to an estimated 4 percent in 2025—0.3 percentage point higher than projected in June—as economic activity benefited from moderating inflation, while higher-than-expected commodity prices, particularly for gold, other precious metals, and coffee, boosted fiscal revenues in several countries. However, the growth performance of individual SSA economies last year was mixed, with the pace of growth picking up in about half of them and slowing elsewhere.[1] Most notably, growth diverged among the region's three largest economies—firming in Nigeria and South Africa but moderating in Ethiopia. Overall, high-frequency survey data indicate that regional economic activity in the second half of 2025 continued to expand (refer to figure 2.6.1.A).

In South Africa, growth strengthened in 2025 to 1.3 percent, supported by more reliable electricity supply, a bumper agricultural harvest, and a pickup in business confidence toward year-end. Fiscal consolidation efforts and a lower inflation target further bolstered investor sentiment. In Nigeria, growth edged up to 4.2 percent in 2025. The increase was driven by expansion in the services sector—especially the finance and information and communication technology sectors—a modest recovery in agriculture, and the country's emergence as a net exporter of refined petroleum products. In Ethiopia, growth moderated to a still-robust 7.2 percent, owing to strong agricultural sector performance, buoyant gold and electricity production, and the effects of comprehensive reforms, which have begun to ease long-standing structural constraints. However, Ethiopia remains in debt distress, with elevated sovereign spreads amid ongoing debt restructuring negotiations with bondholders.

Elsewhere in the region, growth in industrial-commodity-exporting countries excluding Sudan slowed significantly to 3.6 percent in 2025 from 4.3 percent in 2024. In Angola, despite gains in non-oil sectors, weakness in the oil sector weighed on output in 2025, with growth dampened by lower oil prices relative to the previous year, underinvestment in the sector, and the drag from aging oil fields. In the Democratic Republic of Congo, growth decelerated further, with industrial output growth weakening sharply following a temporary ban on cobalt exports. However, higher-than-expected cobalt prices partly offset the decline, while agricultural and services activity

Note: This section was prepared by Joseph Mawejje and Edoardo Palombo.

[1] Several countries rebased their GDP in 2025, lifting nominal GDP and highlighting the expanding role of services and the digital economy (Guinea, Nigeria, Rwanda, Senegal).

FIGURE 2.6.1 SSA: Recent developments

High-frequency data indicate that economic activity strengthened in SSA in the second half of 2025. In anticipation of the implementation of announced increases in tariffs, some firms front-loaded their exports to the United States in the first half of 2025. Headline inflation in SSA has continued to ease, but the relative price of food has increased. Monetary policies have remained cautious, with some central banks hiking policy rates.

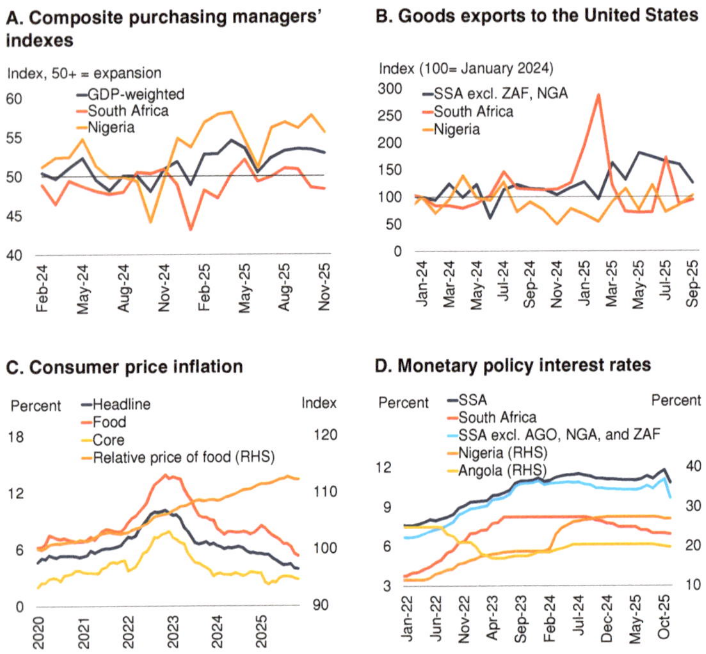

Sources: Haver Analytics; U.S. Bureau of Economic Analysis; World Bank.

Note: AGO = Angola; GDP = gross domestic product; NGA = Nigeria; RHS = right-hand scale; SSA = Sub-Saharan Africa; ZAF = South Africa.

A. Sample includes 7 SSA economies. Last observation is November 2025.

B. Data are export revenues in U.S. dollar terms, indexed to January 2024. Last observation is September 2025.

C. Median increases in consumer prices from 12 months earlier. Sample includes up to 44 countries for headline inflation, up to 40 for food inflation, and up to 12 for core inflation. Relative price of food is constructed relative to headline. Last observation is November 2025.

D. SSA refers to the unweighted average for at least 19 countries. Last observation is November 2025.

remained resilient. Similarly, growth continued to slow in Mozambique, weighed down by persistent investment weakness, mounting foreign exchange shortages, and the lingering effects of post-election unrest.

Growth in non-resource-rich countries edged up to 6.0 percent in 2025, mainly driven by favorable agricultural conditions and a surge in exports. Uganda's growth reached 6.3 percent, its highest rate since prior to the pandemic, boosted by higher government spending, a recovery in household consumption, robust investment growth, and buoyant coffee exports. In Côte d'Ivoire, growth strengthened to 6.3 percent—0.5 percentage point higher than projected in June—supported by strong investment and resilient private consumption. In Zimbabwe, growth increased sharply in 2025 to 6.6 percent, owing to a recovery in agricultural production, and investments in extractive sectors (gold, lithium, iron, and steel), which boosted industrial output. However, growth in 8 of the 23 non-resource-rich economies slowed in 2025.

Firms in several countries across the region front-loaded exports ahead of the implementation of increased U.S. import tariffs, resulting in a significant—albeit temporary—increase in exports to the United States (refer to figure 2.6.1.B). Since the United States is not a major export market for most countries in the region, and since a large part of the region's exports to the United States comprise energy and minerals, which are exempt from tariffs, the effect of the tariff increases has been modest and is expected to remain so—with a few exceptions. It is also being partly offset by the diversion of exports to China and other markets. Meanwhile, several SSA economies in 2025 benefited from stronger-than-expected FDI inflows. Median headline inflation in SSA continued to ease in 2025, reflecting lower global energy and food prices and strong agricultural harvests (refer to figure 2.6.1.C). However, food prices remain high, and their price relative to other consumer items continues to rise, while median core inflation has picked up for the first time in two years. Consequently, some central banks in SSA have paused monetary policy easing, while others have raised policy rates as underlying inflationary pressures re-emerged (refer to figure 2.6.1.D).

Severe food insecurity remained high across the region in 2025, affecting about one-fourth of the population—more than double the global average. In contrast to a declining global trend between 2021 and 2024, the number of undernourished people in SSA increased from about 250 million to nearly 280 million as food prices remained high (FAO et al. 2025). This partly reflects effects of the region's armed conflicts, as well as the aftermath of adverse weather events such as severe droughts in Southern Africa and floods elsewhere. Food insecurity in the region has been further exacerbated by transportation inefficiencies, with one-third of perishable food lost before reaching consumers (Kunaka et al. 2025; World Bank 2025x).

Financial conditions have generally eased in the region, with government bond yields declining, sovereign spreads narrowing, and SSA currencies appreciating against the U.S. dollar since the United States' announcement of tariffs last April. This has reduced pressure on debt repayments for many SSA economies, while helping to lower imported inflation. Nevertheless, debt vulnerabilities have remained elevated, with 20 SSA economies in, or at high risk of debt distress.

Outlook

Growth in SSA is forecast to firm to 4.3 percent in 2026 and 4.5 percent in 2027, supported by strengthening investment and exports. The pickup, however, is predicated on the external environment not deteriorating further and on substantial improvements in security assumed in several countries in fragile and conflict-affected situations (FCS) materializing. Relative to June 2025, growth projections for both 2026 and 2027 have been revised up by 0.2 percentage point (refer to figure 2.6.2.A; table 2.6.1). Despite the overall pickup in growth, projected growth rates for many economies in 2026–27 are still about one-half of a percentage point below their 2000–19 averages. They are also insufficient to generate enough jobs relative to the growth of the labor force, or to raise real per capita incomes enough to significantly reduce extreme poverty.

The modest exposure of most countries in SSA to U.S. markets is expected to limit the adverse effects on the region of the increases in import tariffs. The baseline projections assume that current levels of bilateral tariffs remain in place throughout the forecast horizon. Nevertheless, the increases in tariffs—including through the expiration in late 2025 of the United States' African Growth and Opportunity Act (AGOA), unless extended—are likely to have a notable impact on some countries (Kassa, Edjigu, and Hakobyan 2025). The effects will be felt particularly in economies reliant on exports of textiles

FIGURE 2.6.2 SSA: Outlook

Growth in SSA is forecast to firm to 4.3 percent in 2026 and 4.5 percent in 2027, with solid expansions in non-resource-rich countries. Primary fiscal deficits are expected to narrow with continued consolidation efforts and improving economic activity. Although public debt-to-GDP ratios are projected to decline somewhat, debt-servicing costs are envisaged to remain elevated in many countries. With fiscal space already limited, this will limit much-needed development spending. Real per capita incomes in the region are projected to rise in 2026–27, but by less than in other EMDE regions, so that the shortfall in SSA living standards relative to other EMDEs is set to widen further.

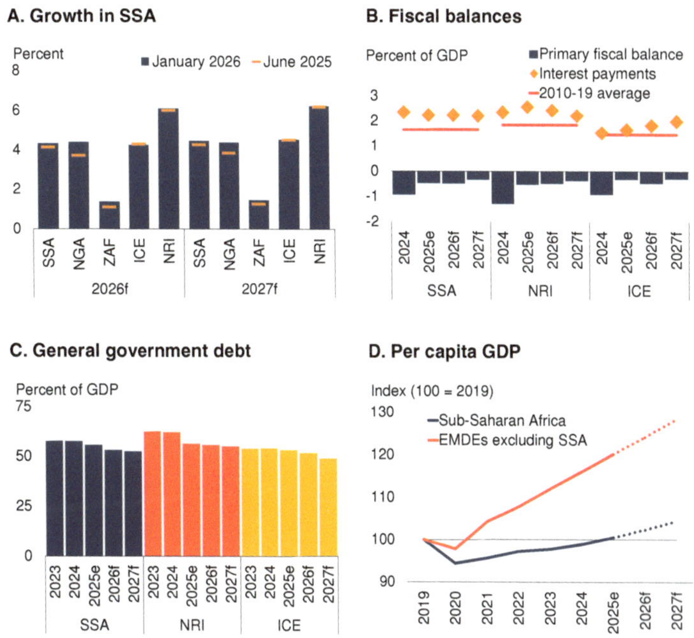

Sources: Haver Analytics; International Monetary Fund; World Bank.

Note: e = estimates; f = forecast. EMDEs = emerging market and developing economies; GDP = gross domestic product; ICE = industrial-commodity exporters; NGA = Nigeria; NRI = non-resource-rich countries; SSA = Sub-Saharan Africa; ZAF = South Africa. Industrial-commodity exporters exclude Nigeria, South Africa, and Sudan. Non-resource-rich countries represent agricultural-commodity-exporting and commodity-importing countries.

A. Aggregate growth rates are calculated using constant GDP weights at average 2010–19 prices and market exchange rates.

B. Median of country groupings. Sample includes 47 SSA economies.

C. Median of country groupings. Sample includes up to 45 SSA economies. Industrial-commodity exporters exclude Nigeria and South Africa. Non-resource-rich countries represent agricultural-commodity-exporting and commodity-importing countries.

D. Data are real per capita GDP in constant U.S. dollars at average 2010-19 prices and market exchange rates. Dotted lines represent estimates and forecasts. Sample includes 154 EMDEs, of which 47 are from SSA.

and vehicles, resulting in significant output and job losses. Nevertheless, continued progress in implementing the African Continental Free Trade Area (AfCFTA) is set to deepen regional trade integration further.

Monetary policy stances are likely to remain cautious, balancing efforts to contain inflation with the need to support growth. Primary fiscal deficits are envisaged to narrow during the forecast

FIGURE 2.6.3 SSA: Risks

Levels of violence in SSA remain high, weighing on economic activity and, in many instances, worsening food insecurity and intensifying humanitarian crises. ODA, having already declined in the past couple of years, is expected to fall further in 2026, increasing the vulnerability of many economies to shocks and risking a reversal of development gains. A more challenging external environment, including weakening prices for many commodities, could leave many SSA economies with depleted buffers. Recent SSA currency appreciations relative to the U.S. dollar have eased debt and inflation pressures but could erode export competitiveness and, if reversed, heighten vulnerabilities.

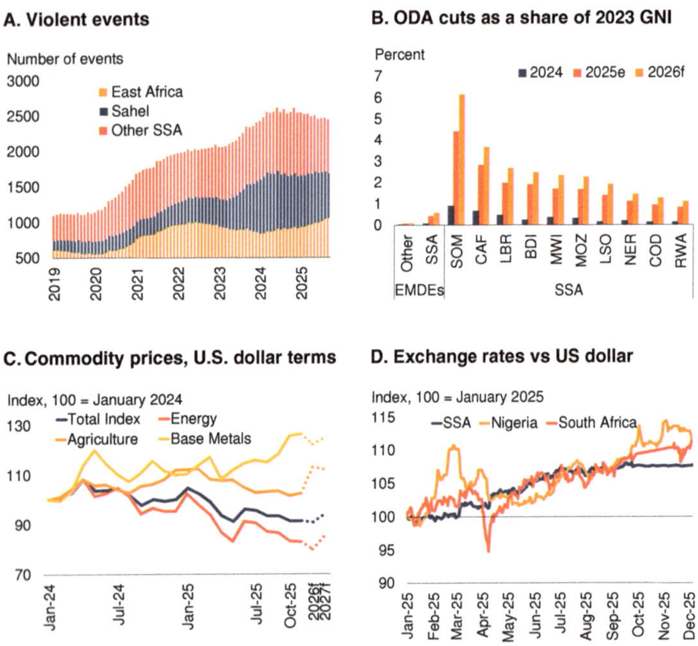

Sources: ACLED (database); Centre for Global Development; International Monetary Fund; World Bank.

Note: e = estimates; f = forecast. BDI = Burundi; CAF = Central African Republic; COD = Democratic Republic of Congo.; EMDEs = emerging market and developing economies; GNI = gross national income; LBR = Liberia; LSO = Lesotho; MWI = Malawi; MOZ = Mozambique; NER = Niger; ODA = official development assistance; RWA = Rwanda; SOM = Federal Republic of Somalia; SSA = Sub-Saharan Africa.

A. Twelve-month moving average. Violent events include battles, explosions, riots, and violence against civilians. Last observation is September 2025. Sahel sample includes Burkina Faso, Chad, Eritrea, Mali, Niger, and Sudan. East Africa sample includes Burundi, Democratic Republic of Congo, Ethiopia, Kenya, Rwanda, the Federal Republic of Somalia, South Sudan, Tanzania, and Uganda.

B. Bars show ODA cuts relative to 2023. "SSA" is the median of SSA economies and "Other" represents the median of non-SSA economies. The economies represented are the top 10 SSA economies most affected by ODA cuts in 2026.

C. Last observation is November 2025. Dotted lines represent forecasts.

D. U.S. dollar per local currency unit. Values less than 100 indicate depreciation. SSA sample comprises at least 44 economies. Last observation is December 5, 2025.

horizon, reflecting improved budgetary discipline, including in non-resource-rich economies. However, rising interest burdens are expected to partly offset the improvements in primary balances across the region (refer to figure 2.6.2.B). While public debt-to-GDP ratios are projected to decline somewhat, they are expected to remain elevated (refer to figure 2.6.2.C). Combined with high borrowing costs, this will necessitate continued fiscal consolidation, which will weigh on demand. In 2026, government interest payments in SSA are set to remain well above the 2010-19 average, reflecting a shift to less concessional terms and lagged effects of record debt accumulation in the aftermath of the COVID-19 pandemic. Increased reliance on riskier sources of financing can heighten vulnerabilities to currency, interest rate, and refinancing risks (Essl et al. 2019). Nevertheless, financing conditions have begun to improve, with several economies regaining access to international capital markets (Angola, the Republic of Congo, Kenya, and Nigeria).

Growth in South Africa is projected to increase to 1.4 percent in 2026 and 1.5 percent in 2027. Continued reform momentum— particularly in energy and logistics—alongside rising public investment is expected to crowd in private investment and support medium-term growth prospects. Private consumption and investment will remain the main growth drivers, aided by efforts to improve public-expenditure efficiency and ease supply-side constraints. Growth in Nigeria is forecast to strengthen to 4.4 percent in both 2026 and 2027—the fastest pace in over a decade. This further firming of growth is anticipated to be underpinned by a continued expansion in services and a rebound in agricultural output, with a modest acceleration in non-oil industry. Economic reforms, including in the tax system, along with continued prudent monetary policy, are expected to continue supporting activity. They are also expected to improve investor sentiment and reduce inflation further. Higher oil output is expected to offset lower international oil prices this year, helping to boost fiscal revenues and strengthen the external balance. In Ethiopia, growth is expected to moderate to a still-robust 7.1 percent in 2026 and pick up to 7.7 percent in 2027 driven by improved monetary conditions, productivity gains, and a recovery in investment (refer to table 2.6.2).

Growth is projected to diverge further between commodity exporters and other economies. In industrial commodity exporters, growth is projected to rise to 4.3 percent in 2026 and 4.5 percent in 2027, on account of solid mining-related investment and activity (Guinea, Liberia, and Zambia). In Guinea, exports from a new large

-scale iron ore project are anticipated to commence this year, providing a significant boost to output. Growth in non-resource-rich countries, however, is expected to outpace that of industrial commodity exporters, strengthening to 6.1 percent in 2026 and 6.2 percent in 2027. This outlook is underpinned by continued solid activity in Benin, Côte d'Ivoire, Ethiopia, Rwanda, and Uganda, while growth in other countries remains relatively steady.

Real per capita incomes in SSA are projected to grow by an average of 2 percent a year in 2026–27—a slightly faster pace than envisioned in June but still insufficient to create enough jobs to keep pace with labor force growth or to deliver significant reductions in extreme poverty. SSA, where an estimated 270 million youths resided in 2025, faces the world's largest rise in working-age population, yet the creation of productive employment remains limited (World Bank 2025y). The region is already home to more than 70 percent of the world's population living in extreme poverty, and the gap in living standards relative to other EMDEs is set to widen further, with the projected growth of real per capita incomes lower than in other EMDE regions (refer to figure 2.6.2.D). Real per capita income growth is also likely to remain uneven across the region, with lack of progress particularly in countries plagued by violent conflict (Chen et al. 2025). Even without escalation of conflicts, food insecurity in SSA will continue to exceed that of other regions through the 2030s (Cardell et al. 2024).

Risks

Risks to SSA's growth outlook remain tilted to the downside. Growth could be weaker than projected if trade barriers and related uncertainty increase further, reform implementation slows, violent conflict persists or worsens, weather shocks intensify, official development assistance (ODA) declines more rapidly, global growth weakens more than currently projected, commodity prices decline further, or global financial conditions deteriorate.

While the direct exposure of most SSA economies to global trade fragmentation remains limited, there are notable exceptions—such as Côte D'Ivoire, Kenya, Lesotho, Madagascar, Mauritius, and South Africa—which are heavily reliant on U.S. markets for their goods and commodity exports. Moreover, adverse shifts in trade policy may lead to a sharper-than-anticipated slowdown in global growth, which could be accompanied by further declines in global commodity prices and dampen demand—including for minerals and metals, which are the main exports of several SSA economies. Lower prices for these commodities would have particularly negative effects on the region through diminished economic activity and narrower fiscal space (Bolhuis et al. 2024).

Continuation or deterioration of civil unrest and violent conflict remain a key risk to SSA's outlook, especially in the Sahel and East Africa (refer to figure 2.6.3.A). Elevated civil discord often reflects persistent unemployment and failing state services (World Bank 2025z). Intensification of the conflicts in the Democratic Republic of Congo and Sudan could result in deeper humanitarian crises and intensified food insecurity, with potential spillovers to other countries.

Many countries remain highly vulnerable to climate change and related extreme weather events, not only because of their geographical location but also because of their economic structures, limited buffers, and lack of resources for adaptation (Damania et al. 2025). Particularly vulnerable are countries in the Horn of Africa, the Sahel, and Southern Africa. Recent events, including flooding in South Sudan, drought in the Federal Republic of Somalia, and landslides in Sudan's Darfur region, have devastated livestock and agricultural production and left large populations displaced. Natural disasters also interact with fragility in pernicious ways, such as by worsening food insecurity and intensifying humanitarian needs (FAO et al. 2025). How such developments deepen poverty has been seen in fragile nations like Mozambique, Niger, Sudan, and South Sudan, with subsistence farmers bearing the greatest burden. In addition, extreme climate events can exacerbate poverty and vulnerability by diminishing agricultural productivity, heightening food insecurity, worsening health risks, and adversely impacting jobs (World Bank 2025aa).

The sharp scaling back of ODA since 2024 is likely to undermine the resilience of SSA economies in the face of adverse shocks. ODA—largely directed to SSA economies—declined markedly in 2025 and is projected to fall further in 2026, reflecting shifts in policy priorities amid diminished fiscal space in donor countries (OECD 2025). Further cuts to ODA than assumed in the baseline could weaken growth prospects further. In an environment of already-limited fiscal space in most SSA economies, declining ODA will force governments to scale back shock prevention and mitigation measures, heightening their countries' vulnerability to the adverse impacts of extreme weather events and health emergencies. ODA cuts and resulting vulnerabilities vary by country. In some FCS economies—such as Burundi, the Central African Republic, and the Federal Republic of Somalia—cuts to donor aid are substantial (refer to figure 2.6.3.B). For some of these economies, cuts in aid could hit growth and living standards substantially, given their high dependence on these financial resources. In South Sudan, one of the countries most affected by conflict and fragility, aid amounted to an estimated annual average of 24 percent of GDP during 2020–24 (World Bank 2025ab).

Elevated long-term interest rates, reduced donor support, and limited fiscal headroom leave SSA countries—particularly those without access to non-concessional debt or facing extremely high market interest rates—at risk of increased financial stress and vulnerable to a tightening of global financial conditions. For the 50 percent of SSA economies that are industrial-commodity exporters, weaker-than-expected external demand or lower global commodity prices could dampen growth and government revenues (refer to figure 2.6.3.C).

Recent appreciations of SSA currencies against the U.S. dollar may ease financial conditions but could also have mixed effects (refer to figure 2.6.3.D). Stronger currencies reduce dollar-denominated debt burdens in domestic currency terms and reduce imported inflation, particularly for essential goods like fuel and food. However, real currency appreciation can undermine competitiveness in tradable sectors, posing risks to growth and weakening fiscal and external positions. Moreover, if recent currency appreciation proves temporary and reverses significantly, it could expose economies to renewed inflationary pressures, financial instability, and debt sustainability concerns.

On the upside, activity in SSA could be supported by duty-free access to China, stronger-than-expected global growth, firmer commodity prices, and progress in structural transformation and diversification, which would enhance value addition and resilience.

TABLE 2.6.1 Sub-Saharan Africa forecast summary

(Real GDP growth at market prices in percent, unless indicated otherwise)

	2023	2024	2025e	2026f	2027f	Percentage-point differences from June 2025 projections: 2025e	2026f	2027f
EMDE SSA, GDP [1]	**3.0**	**3.7**	**4.0**	**4.3**	**4.5**	**0.3**	**0.2**	**0.2**
GDP per capita (U.S. dollars)	0.5	1.2	1.6	1.9	2.0	0.4	0.2	0.2
(Average including countries that report expenditure components in national accounts) [2]								
EMDE SSA, GDP [2,3]	2.9	3.6	4.0	4.2	4.4	0.3	0.0	0.1
PPP GDP	2.3	3.6	4.2	4.5	4.6	0.2	0.0	0.0
Private consumption	2.7	3.1	4.6	4.1	4.1	0.6	0.1	0.1
Public consumption	1.7	3.9	4.3	3.3	2.3	1.2	1.1	-0.2
Fixed investment	9.5	6.0	4.7	6.4	6.5	0.3	-0.3	-0.1
Exports, GNFS [4]	2.4	4.8	3.6	5.0	6.0	1.2	0.4	0.8
Imports, GNFS [4]	7.2	2.5	5.2	5.7	5.6	1.7	0.4	0.4
Net exports, contribution to growth	-1.6	0.4	-0.7	-0.5	-0.3	-0.2	0.0	0.1
Memo items: GDP								
Eastern and Southern Africa	2.5	3.0	3.7	4.0	4.2	0.3	0.0	0.1
Western and Central Africa	3.6	4.6	4.5	4.7	4.8	0.4	0.4	0.3
SSA excluding Nigeria and South Africa	3.7	4.7	5.0	5.3	5.5	0.2	0.0	0.1
Oil exporters [5]	2.9	4.1	3.8	4.1	4.1	0.4	0.4	0.3
CFA countries [6]	3.9	5.0	4.9	4.9	5.1	0.1	0.0	0.1
CEMAC	1.9	3.0	2.9	3.3	3.5	0.4	0.1	0.3
WAEMU	5.0	6.1	6.1	5.8	5.9	0.0	0.0	-0.1
SSA2	2.1	2.5	2.9	3.0	3.1	0.6	0.4	0.4
Nigeria	3.3	4.1	4.2	4.4	4.4	0.6	0.7	0.6
South Africa	0.7	0.6	1.3	1.4	1.5	0.6	0.3	0.2

Source: World Bank.

Note: e = estimate; f = forecast. EMDE = emerging market and developing economy; PPP = purchasing power parity. World Bank forecasts are frequently updated based on new information and changing (global) circumstances. Consequently, projections presented here may differ from those contained in other World Bank documents, even if basic assessments of countries' prospects do not differ at any given moment in time.

1. GDP and expenditure components are measured in average 2010–19 prices and market exchange rates.

2. Subregion aggregate excludes the Central African Republic, Eritrea, Guinea, Nigeria, São Tomé and Príncipe, the Federal Republic of Somalia, and South Sudan, for which data limitations prevent the forecasting of GDP components.

3. Subregion growth rates may differ from the most recent edition of *Africa's Pulse* because of data revisions.

4. Exports and imports of goods and nonfactor services (GNFS).

5. Includes Angola, Cameroon, Chad, the Republic of Congo, Equatorial Guinea, Gabon, Ghana, Nigeria, and South Sudan.

6. The African Financial Community (CFA) franc zone consists of 14 countries in Sub-Saharan Africa, each affiliated with one of two monetary unions. The Central African Economic and Monetary Union (CEMAC) comprises Cameroon, the Central African Republic, Chad, the Republic of Congo, Equatorial Guinea, and Gabon; the West African Economic and Monetary Union (WAEMU) comprises Benin, Burkina Faso, Côte d'Ivoire, Guinea-Bissau, Mali, Niger, Senegal, and Togo.

TABLE 2.6.2 Sub-Saharan Africa country forecasts[1]

(Real GDP growth at market prices in percent, unless indicated otherwise)

	2023	2024	2025e	2026f	2027f	Percentage-point differences from June 2025 projections		
						2025e	2026f	2027f
Angola	1.3	4.4	2.3	2.6	2.8	-0.4	0.0	-0.4
Benin	6.4	7.5	7.3	7.0	7.0	0.1	-0.1	0.0
Botswana	3.2	-3.0	-3.0	2.3	3.8	-3.6	-1.9	0.0
Burkina Faso	3.0	4.8	4.7	4.9	5.1	0.4	0.2	0.1
Burundi	2.7	3.9	4.6	4.9	5.5	1.1	1.2	1.5
Central African Republic	0.7	1.5	2.7	3.0	3.1	0.6	0.8	0.3
Cabo Verde	4.8	7.2	5.4	5.2	5.0	-0.5	-0.1	0.1
Cameroon	3.2	3.5	3.7	3.7	3.9	0.0	-0.1	0.0
Chad	4.1	3.5	3.4	3.7	4.1	-0.1	-0.8	-0.3
Comoros	3.0	3.3	3.4	3.7	3.8	-0.3	-0.1	-0.2
Congo, Dem. Rep.	8.6	6.5	5.1	5.1	5.3	0.3	0.1	0.0
Congo, Rep.	1.9	2.6	2.9	3.2	3.0	0.1	0.0	0.1
Côte d'Ivoire	6.5	6.0	6.3	6.4	6.5	0.5	0.3	0.1
Equatorial Guinea	-5.1	0.9	-1.6	0.4	1.0	1.5	-0.2	2.1
Eritrea	2.6	2.9	3.2	3.5	3.6	0.1	0.1	0.1
Eswatini	3.5	3.0	4.2	3.8	2.9	-0.8	-0.2	0.1
Ethiopia[2]	7.2	8.1	7.2	7.1	7.7	0.8	0.6	0.5
Gabon	2.4	3.4	3.1	3.7	4.1	1.0	1.5	1.1
Gambia, The	5.0	5.3	5.7	5.5	5.3	0.1	0.2	-0.2
Ghana	3.1	5.7	4.3	4.6	4.8	0.4	0.0	0.0
Guinea	5.5	5.4	7.5	9.3	11.6	1.0	0.5	0.3
Guinea-Bissau	4.5	4.8	5.1	5.2	5.2	0.0	0.0	0.0
Kenya	5.7	4.7	4.9	4.9	5.0	0.4	0.0	0.0
Lesotho	1.8	2.9	1.3	0.7	1.1	-0.2	-0.2	0.5
Liberia	4.7	4.0	4.6	5.4	5.6	-0.5	-0.1	-0.1
Madagascar	4.2	4.2	4.0	4.0	4.4	0.3	0.1	0.0
Malawi	1.9	1.7	1.9	2.6	3.1	-0.1	0.2	-0.1
Mali	3.5	4.0	4.9	5.0	5.0	0.1	0.2	0.3
Mauritania	6.8	6.3	5.3	5.4	5.9	0.4	0.9	0.5
Mauritius	5.0	4.7	3.0	3.4	3.4	-0.2	0.4	0.5
Mozambique	5.5	2.1	1.1	2.8	3.5	-1.9	-0.7	0.0
Namibia	4.4	4.0	3.1	3.5	3.8	0.2	0.1	0.3
Niger	2.0	10.3	6.5	6.7	6.6	-0.6	1.6	2.1
Nigeria	3.3	4.1	4.2	4.4	4.4	0.6	0.7	0.6
Rwanda	8.6	7.2	7.0	7.2	7.6	0.0	-0.1	0.3
São Tomé and Príncipe	0.4	1.1	2.5	4.0	3.5	-0.6	-0.8	-0.6
Senegal	4.3	6.1	6.4	4.1	4.3	-1.5	-1.8	-2.4
Seychelles	2.3	2.9	3.2	3.2	3.4	0.1	0.2	0.5
Sierra Leone	5.7	4.3	4.3	4.4	4.6	0.2	0.2	0.4
Somalia, Fed. Rep.	4.2	4.1	3.0	3.5	3.5	0.0	0.0	0.0
South Africa	0.7	0.6	1.3	1.4	1.5	0.6	0.3	0.2
Sudan	-29.4	-14.0	6.1	5.1	3.7	1.1	-4.2	-0.4
South Sudan[2]	-1.3	-7.2	-23.8	48.8	0.8	10.9	7.7	-20.4
Tanzania	5.1	5.5	6.0	6.2	6.5	0.1	0.1	0.1
Togo	6.4	5.3	5.0	5.4	5.6	0.0	0.0	0.1
Uganda[2]	5.3	6.1	6.3	6.4	9.8	0.1	0.2	-0.6
Zambia	5.4	3.8	5.2	5.8	6.0	-0.6	-0.6	-0.5
Zimbabwe	5.3	1.7	6.6	5.0	5.0	0.6	0.4	1.4

Source: World Bank.

Note: e = estimate; f = forecast. World Bank forecasts are frequently updated based on new information and changing global circumstances. Consequently, projections presented here may differ from those contained in other Bank documents, even if basic assessments of countries' prospects do not significantly differ at any given moment in time.

1. Data are based on GDP measured in average 2010–19 prices and market exchange rates.

2. Fiscal-year-based numbers.

References

ACLED (Armed Conflict Location & Event Data) database. Accessed on September 30, 2025. https://acleddata.com/data-export-tool/.

Arias, O., D. Fukuzawa, D. T. Le, and A. Mattoo. 2025. *Future Jobs: Robots, Artificial Intelligence, and Digital Platforms in East Asia and Pacific. East Asia and Pacific Development Studies*. Washington, DC: World Bank.

Arroyo Marioli, F., and G. Vasishtha. 2025. "Fiscal Policy Procyclicality and Volatility in Commodity-Exporting Emerging and Developing Economies: Determinants and Implications for Growth." Policy Research Working Paper 11037, World Bank, Washington, DC.

Arroyo Marioli, F., and C. A. Vegh. 2023. "Fiscal Procyclicality in Commodity Exporting Countries: How Much Does it Pour and Why?" NBER Working Paper 31431, National Bureau of Economic Research, Cambridge, MA.

Bakker, B. B., S. Chen, D. Vasilyev, O. Bespalova, M. Chin, D. Kolpakova, A. Singhal, and Y. Yang. 2024. *What Can Artificial Intelligence Do for Stagnant Productivity in Latin America and the Caribbean?* Washington, DC: International Monetary Fund.

BCRP (Banco Central de Reserva del Perú). 2025. *Nota de Prensa: Programa Monetario de Setiembre 2025*. Lima: Banco Central de Reserva del Perú.

Bolhuis, M., H. Mighri, H. Rawlings, I. Reyes, and Q. Zhang. 2024. "How Vulnerable Is Sub-Saharan Africa to Geoeconomic Fragmentation?" IMF Working Paper 24/83, International Monetary Fund, Washington, DC.

Cardell, L., Y. A. Zereyesus, K. Ajewole, J. Farris, M. E. Johnson, J. Lin, C. Valdes, and W. Zeng. 2024. *International Food Security Assessment, 2024–34 (GFA-35)*. Washington, DC: U.S. Department of Agriculture, Economic Research Service.

Cazzaniga M., F. Jaumotte, L. Li, G. Melina, A. J. Panton, C. Pizzinelli, E. J. Rockall, and M. M. Tavares. 2024. "Gen-AI: Artificial Intelligence and the Future of Work." IMF Staff Discussion Note 2024/001, International Monetary Fund, Washington, DC.

Cerutti, E., A. Garcia Pascual, Y. Kido, L. Li, G. Melina, M. M. Tavares, and P. Wingender. 2025. "The Global Impact of AI: Mind the Gap." IMF Working Paper 25/76, International Monetary Fund, Washington, DC.

Chattha, M. K., A. N. Maseeh, A. Barone, A. Graupp, H. Youssef, D. Alsaleh, D. Richani, et al. 2025. *Gulf Economic Update: The Gulf's Digital Transformation—A Powerful Engine for Economic Diversification*. December. Washington, DC: World Bank.

Chen, W., M. Fornino, V. Maheshwari, H. Mighri, A. Sacco, and C. Sever. 2025. "Pushed to the Brink: Fragility and Conflict in Sub-Saharan Africa." IMF Note 2025/002, International Monetary Fund, Washington, DC.

Combes, J., and C. Ebeke. 2011. "Remittances and Household Consumption Instability in Developing Countries." *World Development* 39 (7): 1076–89.

Damania, R., E. Ebadi, K. Mayr, J. Russ, and E. Zaveri. 2025. *Reboot Development: The Economics of a Livable Planet*. Washington, DC: World Bank.

EBRD (European Bank for Reconstruction and Development). 2025. *Regional Economic Prospects: Under Pressure*. September. London: European Bank for Reconstruction and Development.

EM-DAT (Emergency Events Database). *EM-DAT: The International Disaster Database*. Centre for Research on the Epidemiology of Disasters (CRED), UCLouvain, Brussels. Accessed on December 17, 2025. https://www.emdat.be.

Essl, S. M., S. K. Celik, P. Kirby, and A. Proite. 2019. "Debt in Low-Income Countries: Evolution, Implications, and Remedies." Policy Research Working Paper 8794, World Bank, Washington, DC.

Estevao, M., V. Bonifacio, M. Castellano, M. P. Figueroa, and N. Raman. 2025. "U.S. Migration Shocks and Remittances." IIF Deep Dive, Institute of International Finance, Washington, DC.

FAO, IFAD, UNICEF, WFP, and WHO. 2025. *The State of Food Security and Nutrition in the World 2025. Addressing High Food Price Inflation for Food Security and Nutrition*. Rome: FAO.

Fitzgerald, D., S. Haller, and Y. Yedid-Levi. 2024. "How Exporters Grow." *The Review of Economic Studies* 91 (4): 2276–306.

Gatti, R., C. Ozden, J. Torres, L. Baghdadi, E. Sergenti, A. M. Islam, I. Gaddis, et al. 2025a. *Jobs and Women: Untapped Talent, Unrealized Growth. Middle East, North Africa, Afghanistan, and Pakistan Economic Update*. October. Washington, DC: World Bank.

Gatti, R., H. Onder, A. M. Islam, J. Torres, G. Mele, F. Bennett, S. Chun, R. Lotfi, and I. Suvanov. 2025b. *Shifting Gears: The Private Sector as an Engine of Growth in the Middle East and North Africa. Middle East and North Africa Economic Update*. April. Washington, DC: World Bank.

Gatti, R., J. Torres, N. Elmallakh, G. Mele, D. Faurès, M. E. Mousa, and I. Suvanov. 2024. *Growth in the Middle East and North Africa. Middle East and North Africa Economic Update*. October. Washington, DC: World Bank.

Kassa, W., H. Edjigu, and S. Hakobyan. 2025. Uncertainty in Preferential Trade Agreements: Impact of the African Growth and Opportunity Act (AGOA) Suspension on Exports. *Journal of African Economies* 34 (5): 569–83.

Kohn, D., E. Luttini, M. Szkup, and S. Zhang. 2024. "International Trade Finance and Learning Dynamics." Working Paper 1031, Central Bank of Chile.

Kunaka, C., A. M. Abera, L. T. Bougna, and M. K. Haile. 2025. *Transport Connectivity for Food Security in Africa: Strengthening Supply Chains*. Washington, DC: World Bank.

Hassan, G. M., and M. J. Holmes. 2016. "Do Remittances Facilitate a Sustainable Current Account?" *The World Economy* 39 (11): 1834–53.

IEA (International Energy Agency). 2025. *Oil Market Report*. December. Paris: International Energy Agency.

IMF (International Monetary Fund). 2025a. *Colombia: 2025 Article IV Consultation*. Washington, DC: International Monetary Fund.

IMF (International Monetary Fund). 2025b. *Mexico: 2025 Article IV Consultation*. Washington, DC: International Monetary Fund.

IMF (International Monetary Fund). 2025c. *Press Briefing Transcript: Regional Economic Outlook for the Western Hemisphere, Annual Meetings 2025*. Washington, DC: International Monetary Fund.

Kose, M. A., S. Kurlat, F. Ohnsorge, and N. Sugawara. 2022. "A Cross-Country Database of Fiscal Space." *Journal of International Money and Finance* 128 (November): 102682.

Loungani, P., E. Luttini, and H. Pallan. 2025. "Buffering Recessions: Labor Market Asymmetries and the Role of Self-Employment." Policy Research Working Paper Series 11089, The World Bank.

Mulabdic, A., and M. Ruta. 2018. *Effects of a Deeper Central European Free Trade Agreement*. Washington, DC: World Bank.

Mulabdic, A., and Y. V. Yotov. 2025. "Geopolitical Risks and Trade." Policy Research Working Paper 11219, World Bank, Washington, DC.

OECD (Organization for Economic Cooperation and Development). 2025. "Cuts in Official Development Assistance: OECD Projections for 2025 and The Near Term." *OECD Policy Brief No. 26*. Paris: OECD Publishing.

Rotunno L., S. Roy, A. Sakakibara, and P.-L. Vezina. 2024. "Trade Policy and Jobs in Vietnam: The Unintended Consequences of US-China Trade Tensions." IMF Working Paper 24/263, International Monetary Fund, Washington, DC.

World Bank. 2014. *Turn Down the Heat: Confronting the New Climate Normal.* Washington, DC: World Bank.

World Bank. 2025a. *Viet Nam Economic Update: Taking Stock. Special Focus: Nurturing Viet Nam's High-tech Talents*. September. Washington, DC: World Bank.

World Bank. 2025b. *Myanmar Economic Monitor: Economic Aftershocks*. June. Washington, DC: World Bank.

World Bank. 2025c. *Mongolia Economic Update: Building Resilience Amid Risks. Special focus: Strengthening Disaster Risk Management for Future Challenges*. May. Washington, DC: World Bank.

World Bank. 2025d. *Commodity Markets Outlook*. October. Washington, DC: World Bank.

World Bank. 2025e. *Europe and Central Asia: Jobs and Prosperity*. October. Washington, DC: World Bank.

World Bank. 2025f. *Towards Better Jobs. Western Balkans Regular Economic Report 28*. October. Washington, DC: World Bank.

World Bank. 2025g. *Unlivable: How Cities in Europe and Central Asia Can Survive and Thrive in a Hotter Future*. Washington, DC: World Bank.

World Bank. 2025h. *Libya Economic Monitor: Setting the Path towards Accountability and Transparency in Public Financial Management*. Fall. Washington, DC: World Bank.

World Bank. 2025i. *Impacts of the Conflict in the Middle East on the Palestinian Economy. World Bank Economic Monitoring Report*. September. Washington, DC: World Bank.

World Bank. 2025j. *Algeria Economic Update: Responding to Climate Challenges and Supporting*

Sustainable Development. Fall. Washington, DC: World Bank.

World Bank. 2025k. *Pakistan Development Update: Staying the Course for Growth and Jobs*. October. Washington, DC: World Bank.

World Bank. 2025l. *Tunisia Economic Monitor: Strengthening Social Safety Nets for Increased Efficiency and Equity*. Fall. Washington, DC: World Bank.

World Bank. 2025m. *Yemen Economic Monitor: Navigating Increased Hardship and Growing Economic Fragmentation*. Fall. Washington, DC: World Bank.

World Bank. 2025n. *Afghanistan Development Update: Sustaining Returns—Challenges and Opportunities*. November. Washington, DC: World Bank.

World Bank. 2025o. *Unlocking Potential: Legal Pathways to Boost Women's Labor Force Participation in the Middle East and North Africa Region*. Washington, DC: World Bank.

World Bank. 2025p. *Lebanon Economic Monitor: Turning the Tide?* Spring. Washington, DC: World Bank.

World Bank. 2025q. *International Debt Report 2025*. Washington, DC: World Bank.

World Bank. 2025r. *Bangladesh Development Update: Special Focus—Urbanization as a Pathway to Boost Job Growth*. October. Washington, DC: World Bank.

World Bank. 2025s. *Nepal Development Update: Reforms to Accelerate Public Investment*. November. Washington, DC: World Bank.

World Bank. 2025t. *Sri Lanka Development Update: Better Spending for All*. October. Washington, DC: World Bank.

World Bank. 2025u. *Maldives Development Update*. October. Washington, DC: World Bank.

World Bank. 2025v. *Bhutan Development Update: Bridging the Future—Addressing Challenges and Harnessing Opportunities of Migration*. Spring. Washington, DC: World Bank.

World Bank. 2025w. *Jobs, AI, and Trade. South Asia Development Update*. October. Washington, DC: World Bank.

World Bank. 2025x. *Food Security Update*. June. Washington, DC: World Bank.

World Bank. 2025y. *Africa's Pulse: Pathways to Job Creation in Africa*. October. Washington, DC: World Bank.

World Bank. 2025z. *Africa's Pulse: Improving Governance and Delivering for People in Africa*. April. Washington, DC: World Bank.

World Bank. 2025aa. *Jobs in A Changing Climate; Insights from World Bank Group Country Climate and Development Reports Covering 93 Economies*. Washington, DC: World Bank.

World Bank. 2025ab. *South Sudan Economic Monitor: A Pathway to Overcome the Crisis*. April. Washington, DC: World Bank.

CHAPTER 3

REBUILDING FISCAL SPACE

The Case for Fiscal Rules

At a time when global shocks have become more frequent and government debt among emerging market and developing economies (EMDEs) has climbed to a 55-year high, fiscal rules are an important policy tool for promoting fiscal discipline. More than half of EMDEs have at least one fiscal rule, up from about 15 percent in 2000. Fiscal rules are associated with improvements in budget balances that extend to the medium and long term. Among EMDEs, improvements in the cyclically adjusted primary balance (CAPB) peak five years after fiscal rules are adopted, reaching a cumulative 1.4 percentage points of trend GDP. The gains are more pronounced when institutions are strong and economic conditions are favorable at the time of adoption, and the use of a deficit rule is central to durable improvements. Fiscal rules are also associated with a greater likelihood of fiscal adjustment episodes—multiyear periods of improvement in the CAPB as a percent of trend GDP. During a fiscal adjustment episode, the CAPB in the typical EMDE improves by 1.6 percentage points of trend GDP per year. Fiscal rules with credible enforcement provisions are associated with a higher likelihood of expenditure-based adjustment. Further, fiscal rules need not be complex to be effective. Simple rule frameworks are associated with a higher likelihood of revenue-based adjustment. To enhance the effectiveness of fiscal rules, three policy efforts should be prioritized: designing fiscal rules to manage trade-offs, investing in the credibility of and commitment to the rules, and fostering a supportive, complementary policy environment.

Introduction

Emerging market and developing economies (EMDEs) have experienced deep and overlapping shocks in recent years, generating challenges for policy making. Yet EMDEs' resilience to these shocks has been bolstered by previous improvements in policy frameworks, including the introduction of fiscal rules, which set numerical limits on key budgetary aggregates or government debt (IMF 2025a; World Bank 2025).

As of 2024, 55 percent of EMDEs had at least one fiscal rule. The prevalence in EMDEs is far lower than in advanced economies, 90 percent of which have had fiscal rules for the past decade, but it has increased rapidly, from about 15 percent in 2000 (refer to figure 3.1.A). Fiscal rules have been adopted in all EMDE regions (refer to figure 3.1.B). Fiscal rules serve a variety of purposes—promoting fiscal discipline and debt sustainability, improving the credibility or transparency of fiscal policy, or supporting macroeconomic stability. In some cases, fiscal rules have been adopted in response to global developments, such as commodity price shocks, or as part of the frameworks of regional economic blocs.

There is substantial evidence that fiscal rules can lead to improved fiscal outcomes, including reduced fiscal deficits and narrower sovereign bond spreads (refer to annex 3.1; Heinemann, Moessinger, and Yeter 2018; Potrafke 2025). For many EMDEs, fiscal rules have been important in enabling them to provide countercyclical fiscal support for aggregate demand when needed, and in allowing them to dedicate public resources to critical needs, such as infrastructure and responses to shocks related to climate change. EMDEs with fiscal rules in place before the global recession of 2020 recorded smaller primary fiscal deficits in 2015–19 than those without fiscal rules and were able to implement larger countercyclical fiscal stimulus during 2020–21, while still reducing their fiscal deficits to pre-pandemic levels by 2024 (refer to figure 3.1.C).

Beyond fiscal outcomes, fiscal rules are linked to improved macroeconomic stability, higher private investment, lower external vulnerabilities, and enhanced financial sector stability—factors that can strengthen growth prospects in EMDEs (refer to annex 3.1). As a component of fiscal policy, fiscal rules can also affect jobs. Specifically, fiscal policy can influence employment by shaping economic activity, investment dynamics, and income distribution (Bova, Kolerus, and Tapsoba 2015; Combes et al. 2024; IMF 2014; Misra and Ranjan 2018; Sawadogo 2024). Fiscal rules can enhance the effectiveness of discretionary fiscal policy in reducing unemployment, including by strengthening the relationship between economic activity and labor market outcomes (Gehrke 2019). These effects, however, depend on the structure of the economy, its cyclical position, and

Note: This chapter was prepared by Bram Gootjes, Joseph Mawejje, and Dana Vorisek.

FIGURE 3.1 Fiscal conditions in EMDEs

The share of EMDEs and advanced economies with fiscal rules has increased substantially. EMDEs with fiscal rules recorded smaller average primary fiscal deficits in 2015–19 than those without fiscal rules. During the COVID-19 pandemic, these economies were able to provide more fiscal stimulus while still reducing their fiscal deficits to pre-pandemic levels by 2024. Yet fiscal challenges persist, including rising government debt burdens and interest payments. Extreme surges in government debt have been less common in EMDEs with fiscal rules than in those without rules, but debt accumulation since 2008 has been greater in EMDEs with rules.

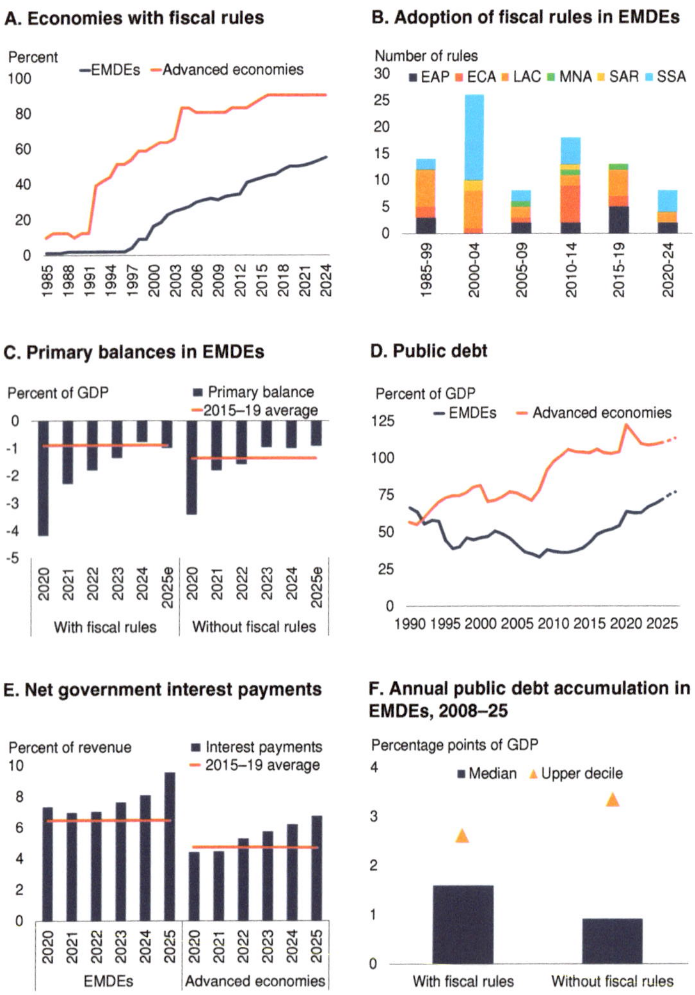

Sources: Haver Analytics; International Monetary Fund; World Bank.

Note: e = estimate. EAP = East Asia and Pacific; ECA = Europe and Central Asia; EMDEs = emerging market and developing economies; LAC = Latin America and the Caribbean; MNA = Middle East, North Africa, Afghanistan and Pakistan; SAR = South Asia; SSA = Sub-Saharan Africa.

A.B. Sample includes 154 EMDEs and 41 advanced economies.

C. Bars show medians in the indicated groups. Sample includes 154 EMDEs and 38 advanced economies.

D. Aggregates are computed with nominal GDP in U.S. dollars as weights, based on 154 EMDEs and 38 advanced economies.

E. Net interest payments are the difference between primary balances and overall fiscal balances. Aggregates are computed with government revenues in U.S. dollars as weights, based on 148 EMDEs and 36 advanced economies.

F. Sample includes 48 EMDEs.

other country-specific characteristics. The literature also highlights potential adverse consequences of fiscal rules that are poorly designed or implemented, including inducing procyclical policies that can heighten economic volatility and reduce potential growth.

Despite the widespread adoption of fiscal rules in EMDEs, fiscal space remains constrained in many economies. Since the global financial crisis of 2008–09, government debt in EMDEs has risen rapidly, to nearly 70 percent of GDP in 2024—the highest level in the last 55 years. Since 2023, interest payments on government debt relative to total government revenues have risen above the average of 2015–19 (refer to figures 3.1.D and 3.1.E). Among EMDEs with fiscal rules, the median economy experienced a faster debt buildup during 2008–25 than economies without rules, although rules may have helped avert the most extreme debt surges (refer to figure 3.1.F). In practice, countries with fiscal rules may have greater capacity to borrow by signaling a commitment to (future) fiscal discipline.

Borrowing can be development-enhancing when it funds productive investment. However, it becomes harmful when it turns unsustainable, as it erodes fiscal space, crowds out private investment, and depresses growth. Strong growth alone is unlikely to resolve fiscal pressures, and under the current outlook, growth in many EMDEs will remain weak. With debt rising and growth rates remaining mediocre, proactive fiscal adjustment may be increasingly important for safeguarding—or restoring—fiscal sustainability. In principle, fiscal rules are designed to guide policymakers toward prudent fiscal paths.

Against this backdrop, this chapter presents a comprehensive assessment of fiscal rules in EMDEs. It begins by evaluating the key characteristics of fiscal rules in EMDEs compared to those in advanced economies. It then explores the impact of fiscal rules on the fiscal balance—measured by the cyclically adjusted primary balance (CAPB) as a percent of trend GDP—highlighting how these effects evolve after rule adoption. It examines how these dynamics differ across countries, and how conditions at the time of rule adoption affect fiscal outcomes. Recognizing that even effective adoption does not guarantee enduring fiscal stability, the chapter further analyzes whether, and through which channels, fiscal rules are associated with episodes of fiscal adjustment, defined as multiyear improvements in the CAPB as a percent of trend GDP.

The chapter addresses the following questions:

- What are the key characteristics of fiscal rules in EMDEs?
- How do government budgets evolve after fiscal rule adoption?
- To what extent are fiscal rules associated with fiscal adjustment episodes?
- What policy interventions can foster the effectiveness of fiscal rules in EMDEs?

Contributions

This makes several contributions to the literature:

Comprehensive analysis of the use of fiscal rules in EMDEs. Most previous studies on fiscal rules focus on advanced economies, in part because they adopted fiscal rules before EMDEs (Brändle and Elsener 2024; Potrafke 2025). Yet in the current context of rapid debt accumulation, elevated global policy uncertainty, sluggish growth prospects, and dwindling official development assistance, it is important to understand how fiscal rules have performed in EMDEs. The chapter investigates the type of fiscal rules in a large set of EMDEs and advanced economies, with a focus on identifying the conditions and design features under which rules are effective.

Examination of the characteristics of fiscal rules. Many EMDEs face challenges in designing fiscal policy frameworks that provide the necessary guardrails and credible forward guidance to navigate policy trade-offs (Ardanaz, Cavallo, and Izquierdo 2023). The chapter examines the characteristics of fiscal rules in EMDEs, differences in design features between EMDEs and advanced economies, changes in rule design over time, and relationships between design features and outcomes.

Analysis of the effects of adopting fiscal rules. Fiscal rules are tools for strengthening fiscal discipline, but little is known about what drives and sustains their effects. The circumstances that spur the adoption of fiscal rules can shape the early effects of rules, but those circumstances change, and so too may the willingness of governments to respect the letter and spirit of fiscal rules. The context in which rules are adopted can also affect the credibility of rules. The chapter provides new evidence on how conditions at adoption influence the effectiveness of fiscal rules in the long term. This is particularly relevant for EMDEs, where institutional contexts vary widely.

Identification of fiscal adjustment episodes. Many countries, EMDEs included, have accumulated public debt at a rapid pace since the global financial crisis, despite the increasing use of fiscal rules. Even when fiscal rules are effective, they do not fully insulate countries from fiscal stress, and significant policy efforts are periodically required to reduce budget deficits, lower debt burdens, and restore fiscal sustainability. The chapter examines how fiscal rules can influence the likelihood of fiscal adjustment episodes—a question largely overlooked in previous studies (Di Lorenzo and Lacey 2024). The empirical evidence underscores how the design of fiscal rules involves trade-offs and choices that affect fiscal adjustment outcomes.

Policy priorities related to fiscal rules. The chapter distills three key policy priorities for effective fiscal rules: designing rules to manage trade-offs; investing in credibility and commitment; and fostering a supportive, complementary policy environment. It highlights how fiscal rules can be made more effective, while acknowledging that there is no single roadmap to success.

Main findings

The chapter presents the following main findings:

EMDEs have steadily expanded and upgraded their fiscal rule frameworks since 2000. More than half of EMDEs now have rule-based frameworks, compared with about one-sixth in 2000. Many EMDEs have shifted toward multi-rule frameworks, mirroring earlier trends in advanced economies. Deficit–debt rule combinations remain the most common frameworks, but the use of expenditure rules has expanded in recent years.

Rule design in EMDEs has improved, particularly through greater flexibility.

The adoption of fiscal rules in EMDEs tends to be followed by a medium-term improvement in fiscal balances, but the context in which rules are introduced has lasting implications for their effectiveness. In EMDEs, CAPB as a percent of trend GDP improves by a cumulative 1.4 percentage points five years after the adoption of a fiscal rule, compared with a counterfactual of no adoption. The persistence of improvements in CAPB following adoption of fiscal rules in the medium and long term depends critically on institutional capacity, as well as on economic conditions at the time of adoption, possibly because those conditions help build early credibility for the rules. Deficit rules are particularly effective in generating long-term improvements in fiscal balances following adoption, even in countries where institutions are weak.

The use of fiscal rules is associated with a higher likelihood of a fiscal adjustment episode—a multi-year period of sustained improvement in the CAPB as a percent of trend GDP. Fiscal adjustment episodes are less frequent and typically shorter in EMDEs than in advanced economies—lasting three years instead of four. However, these episodes are associated with larger annual budgetary improvements in EMDEs, where revenue increases and expenditure cuts together amount to 1.6 percent of trend GDP per year in the median fiscal adjustment episode. Fiscal rules significantly increase the likelihood of adjustment: in any given year, the probability of starting an episode is 14 percent in countries with fiscal rules, compared with 5 percent in countries without rules. This result hinges on the use of a deficit rule. Rule design also shapes how adjustment occurs: credible enforcement provisions are associated with a higher likelihood of expenditure-based adjustment, while broad public sector coverage and simple rule design are associated with a higher probability of revenue-based episodes.

Sound design, strong commitment by policy makers, and a supportive institutional environment can enhance the effectiveness of fiscal rules. Effective fiscal rules strike a balance between simplicity, enforceability, and flexibility. Design choices matter, both in shaping the likelihood and the composition of fiscal adjustment. Deficit rules, in particular, tend to deliver sustained fiscal improvements. Actively investing in rule credibility and building wide political consensus from the outset is also important, especially when rule adoption is motivated by short-term considerations. A supportive institutional environment—through complementary policy frameworks, sufficient administrative and statistical capacity for fiscal management and revenue mobilization, and sustained external support—can help ensure that fiscal rules contribute to fiscal sustainability. Most importantly, the selection of design features should be tailored to country-specific conditions and challenges.

Characteristics of fiscal rules

The number of countries with fiscal rules has risen sharply in recent decades. Among EMDEs, 55 percent—or 85 economies—had at least one fiscal rule as of 2024. Fiscal rules may be adopted at the national or supranational level. Supranational frameworks bring together a group of countries under a common agreement—often within an economic or monetary union—to promote fiscal discipline, policy coordination, and macroeconomic stability among member states.[1] The number of EMDEs in supranational frameworks has increased, from 14 in 2000 to 31 in 2024.

Types of fiscal rules

Fiscal rules are commonly classified by the budgetary variable they aim to constrain. Accordingly, there are four main types of fiscal rules: deficit rules (also known as budget balance rules), debt rules, expenditure rules, and revenue rules. In the early 2000s, most rules targeted either the fiscal balance or debt (refer to figure 3.2.A). After the global financial crisis, countries increasingly adopted expenditure rules. Revenue rules remain

[1] The most prominent example is the European Union (EU), where supranational rules are embedded in the Stability and Growth Pact. However, similar arrangements exist in several EMDE regions, including the West African Economic and Monetary Union (WAEMU), the East African Community (EAC), and the East Caribbean Currency Union (ECCU).

the least frequently used type of rule. Because no single type of rule addresses all objectives, most countries with rules have at least two simultaneously (refer to figure 3.2.B). Advanced economies, particularly those in the European Union (EU), pioneered such multi-rule frameworks; more recently, this practice has become more widespread among EMDEs, with almost one-third having three or more rules in place.

Deficit rules

Deficit rules are usually upper limits on overall or primary fiscal deficits, sometimes in cyclically adjusted terms. By constraining fiscal deficits, these rules aim to prevent excessive borrowing. Regarded as a straightforward and effective tool for promoting fiscal discipline, deficit rules formed the backbone of most early fiscal rule frameworks, including in EMDEs (refer to figure 3.2.C). The relative prevalence of deficit rules across rule frameworks peaked in 2004 in EMDEs, declined thereafter, and rose modestly after 2012 amid post-crisis reforms and supranational initiatives, particularly in Sub-Saharan Africa. As of 2024, 66 EMDEs (78 percent of those with fiscal rules) had a deficit rule. Nearly all advanced economies maintain such a rule (refer to figure 3.2.D). Deficit rules are typically adopted in conjunction with debt rules in both EMDEs and advanced economies (refer to figure 3.2.E).

Debt rules

Debt rules limit the stock of gross or net government debt, usually as a percent of GDP. In many cases, they are adopted alongside deficit rules, and they are increasingly common. Eight EMDEs added a debt rule to their fiscal frameworks after the global recession of 2020, as rising debt prompted several countries to strengthen fiscal discipline. At the end of 2024, 71 EMDEs—84 percent of those with fiscal rules—had a debt rule in place, making it the most prevalent type.

Expenditure rules

Deficit and debt rules do not directly address how governments should comply with them. Expenditure rules help fill this gap by setting limits on total, primary, or current government expenditure—either as a share of GDP or, more commonly, by limiting the growth rate of one of these aggregates. The adoption of expenditure rules surged after the global financial crisis, both in advanced economies (with the strengthening of the European fiscal framework in 2012) and in EMDEs, where the share of countries with fiscal rules using expenditure rules rose from 13 percent

FIGURE 3.2 Adoption of fiscal rules

As more countries adopted fiscal rules, they have increasingly adopted more than one, with many adopting three or more. The most common combination is a deficit ceiling with a debt ceiling, mirroring practice in advanced economies. An increasing number of countries have introduced expenditure rules, while revenue rules remain uncommon.

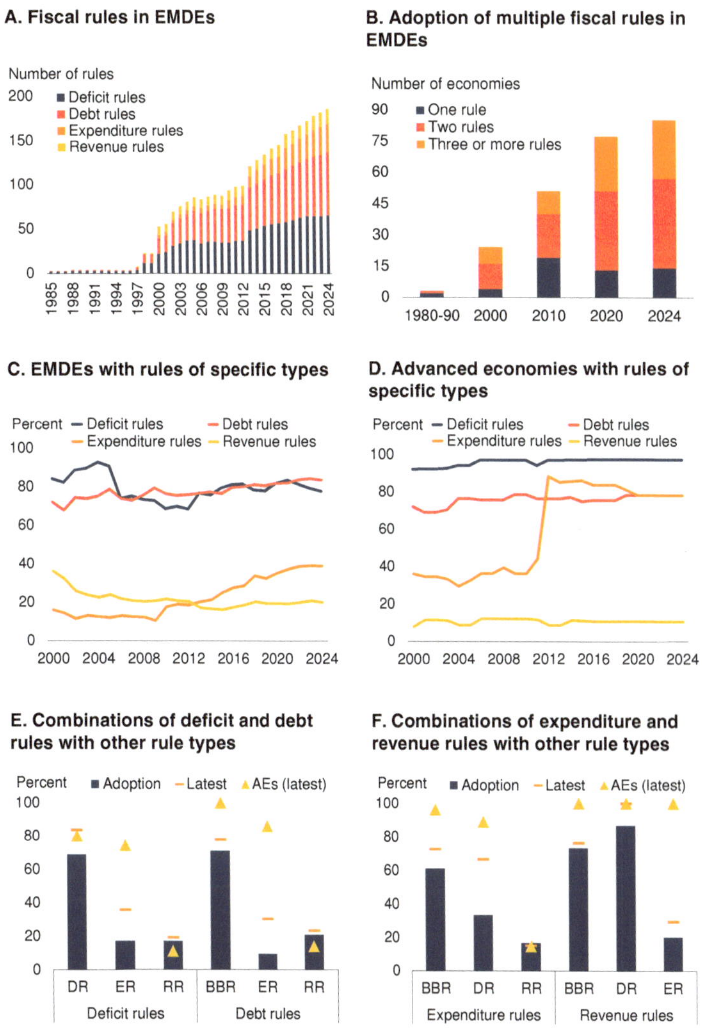

Sources: International Monetary Fund; World Bank.
Note: AEs = advanced economy; BBR = deficit rules; DR = debt rules; EMDEs = emerging market and developing economies; ER = expenditure rules; RR = revenue rules.
A. Number of fiscal rules in use in EMDEs. Sample includes 85 EMDEs with fiscal rules.
B. Number of EMDEs with fiscal rules, by number of fiscal rules. Sample includes up to 85 EMDEs.
C.-D. Charts show the share of each type of fiscal rule among countries with established rule frameworks. The sample includes 85 EMDEs and 37 advanced economies.
E.-F. Charts show the share of EMDEs (bars and dashes) and advanced economies (triangles).

before the crisis to 39 percent by 2024. Although some countries initially adopted only expenditure rules, more recent frameworks—and reforms to existing frameworks—have tended to combine expenditure rules with deficit rules, debt rules, or both (refer to figure 3.2.F).

Revenue rules

Revenue rules impose floors or ceilings on revenues to promote collection or prevent excessive tax burdens. They remain uncommon, partly because revenues are largely endogenous to economic activity and less directly controlled by governments. While a relatively large share of early rule adopters—particularly among EMDEs—incorporated revenue rules into their frameworks, more recent adopters have tended to avoid them. As of 2024, 17 EMDEs (20 percent of those with fiscal rules) had revenue rules, of which 10 are in Sub-Saharan Africa, where they form part of supranational fiscal frameworks. Only four advanced economies had revenue rules as of 2024. Revenue rules usually coexist with deficit and debt rules; joint use of expenditure and revenue rules is rare.

Design features of fiscal rules

Fiscal rules vary not just in terms of the variable to which they apply but also in their design. Three broad design features are important: institutional anchoring, enforceability, and flexibility. Over time, fiscal rule design has become more intricate, especially through the incorporation of technical elements intended to strengthen enforceability and flexibility. More complex rules, however, tend to require more calibration, which in turn requires stronger institutional capacity and coordination for effectively implemented.

Institutional anchoring

The institutional anchoring of fiscal rules determines their legal force and reach across the public sector. Fiscal rules can be "narrow," applicable to the central government, or "broad," applicable to the entire general government or public sector. Broader coverage tends to improve control over the overall fiscal balance by limiting opportunities to shift deficits between levels of government and by promoting shared fiscal discipline across central and local authorities and public sector enterprises. Narrow coverage—often adopted where central authorities lack control over local budgets or where timely data are scarce—can allow imbalances to be shifted to local governments, thus failing to contain the overall fiscal deficit. That said, rules targeting the central government can still impose meaningful discipline, as the central government typically accounts for the largest share of public sector activity.

The legal basis of a rule is another element of institutional anchoring that helps to determine its binding force. Fiscal rules can be formalized in a variety of ways—from political pledges and coalition agreements to legislation, constitutional provisions, and, in the supranational context, international treaties. A stronger legal basis can make fiscal rules more durable and credible (Asatryan, Castellón, and Stratmann 2018; van Eden, Khemani, and Emery 2013). By contrast, a weaker legal basis makes it easier for (new) governments to amend fiscal rules in response to changing circumstances.

The institutional anchoring of fiscal rules has been broadly stable over the past 25 years. Rules in advanced economies are generally broader in their public sector coverage and more firmly based in law than those in EMDEs (refer to figures 3.3.A and 3.3.B). Since 2000, the legal basis of fiscal rules in EMDEs has weakened slightly. Early fiscal rules in these economies were typically established through international treaties, driven by supranational frameworks in the context of regional monetary unions. More recent adoptions have mostly occured at the national level, typically with legal foundations that are weaker than those in international treaties, although most EMDEs still anchor their rules in legislation.

Enforceability

The effectiveness of fiscal rules depends partly on the mechanisms that promote compliance. Enforcement provisions typically specify formal actions to be taken in the event of non-compliance—such as corrective actions and penalties—and may assign oversight roles to independent fiscal institutions with responsibility for enforcement (Beetsma et al. 2019; Grembi,

Nannicini, and Troiano 2016). Enforceability of fiscal rules is particularly strong when there are explicit corrective mechanisms—with clear triggers, timelines, and policy responses in the event of breaches (Acalin et al. 2025).

In practice, many countries face challenges in enforcing fiscal rules. Fiscal policy is inherently political, and spending pressures tend to create a structural deficit bias (Velasco 1999, 2000). Moreover, when sustainability concerns arise, political dynamics can make it difficult for governments to agree on fiscal adjustments and pass the necessary legislation (Alesina and Drazen 1991; Gootjes 2025). Fiscal rules are intended to contain such political pressures, but they cannot remove them.

In recent decades, enforceability in fiscal rule design has strengthened, largely reflecting efforts to improve compliance. In advanced economies, the reforms of the EU's Stability and Growth Pact in 2005 and 2012 tightened implementation and monitoring, although these efforts have been stymied by the fiscal pressures arising from the COVID-19 pandemic and the repercussions of Russia's invasion of Ukraine (refer to figure 3.3.C). In EMDEs, fiscal rules have moderately increased explicit corrective mechanisms, but other enforcement provisions have not advanced, partly because of challenges in establishing independent fiscal institutions capable of overseeing compliance (refer to figure 3.3.D).

Flexibility

Flexibility features of fiscal rules are design elements that provide exemptions from numerical constraints or allow adaptation to economic conditions. Escape clauses give policy makers room to respond to large, unexpected shocks, without ad hoc suspensions or modifications of the rules (Davoodi et al. 2022). Flexibility can also be built into deficit rules by setting targets on a cyclically adjusted basis, so that departures from rules due to cyclical factors do not call for corrective action that would involve procyclical adjustment (Bova, Carcenac, and Guerguil 2014; Eyraud et al. 2018), although distinguishing cyclical from structural changes in fiscal aggregates is likely to be difficult, especially in the short term.[2] Finally, some rule frameworks provide

FIGURE 3.3 Fiscal rule design

Fiscal rules in EMDEs have a weaker legal basis and narrower coverage of the government sector than rules in advanced economies, on average. Fiscal rule design has become more intricate, increasingly incorporating elements that enhance enforceability and flexibility. Although these innovations aim to increase the rules' effectiveness, they can also increase complexity, requiring stronger institutional capacity and coordination to ensure effective implementation.

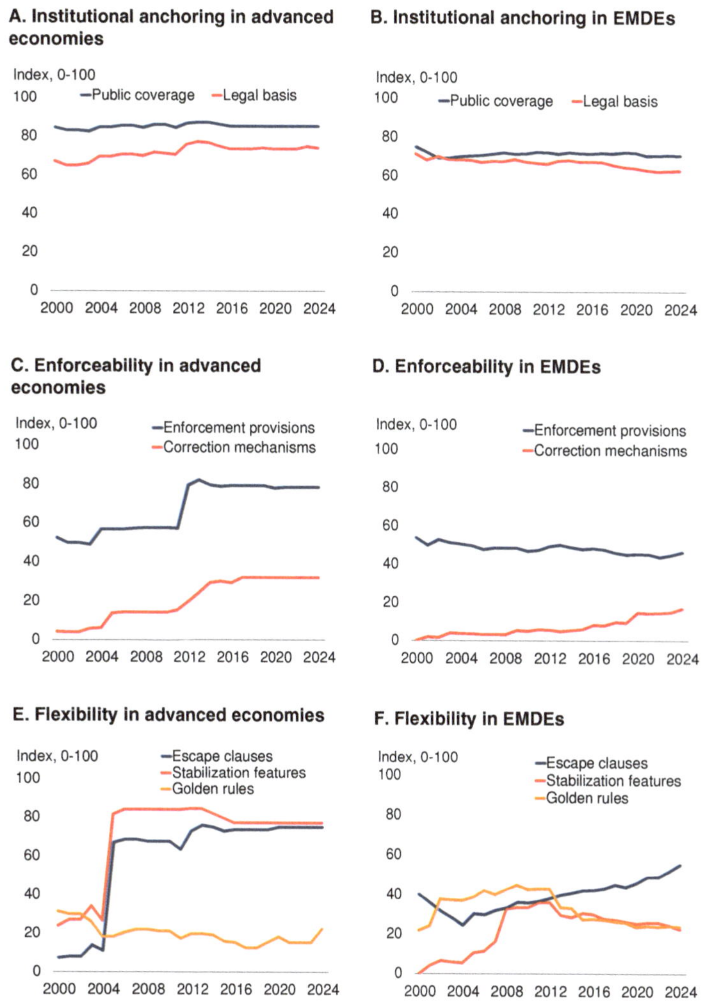

Sources: International Monetary Fund; World Bank.

Note: EMDEs = emerging market and developing economies. Lines show average index scores of fiscal rule design features, derived from IMF data and normalized on a 0–100 scale (100 = best). Higher values indicate greater use or sophistication of each feature. Sample includes and 85 EMDEs and 37 advanced economies.

[2] Chile's fiscal rule, for example, takes account of cyclical deviations from trend for GDP and of the price of the main export commodity, copper, through analysis by two expert panels (Frankel 2011a). Other countries' rules take account of the cycle by automatically correcting for past deviations with a view to avoiding the "ratcheting up" of debt (for example, Panama and Serbia).

flexibility by exempting priority spending items from numerical limits. Most notably, "golden rules" exclude public investment for long-term purposes, such as infrastructure, from deficit and expenditure constraints.

Early fiscal rules were often criticized for being overly rigid and economically destabilizing in the way they required adjustment to economic shocks (Buiter 2004). Over time, policy makers have increasingly incorporated escape clauses—notably, in 2005, when the European Commission introduced medium-term budgetary objectives for the structural balance for all EU countries (refer to figure 3.3.E). More EMDEs, as well, have adopted escape clauses since the mid-2000s (refer to figure 3.3.F). In both groups of economies, the use of cyclically adjusted fiscal targets is far more common than in the early 2000s. However, such targets remain less widespread in EMDEs, reflecting data and modeling limitations. As of 2024, 21 percent of EMDEs with deficit rules employed cyclically adjusted targets, compared with 78 percent of advanced economies. The use of golden rules remains limited in both groups and, in EMDEs, has declined since the global financial crisis.

The dynamic effects of fiscal rule adoption on primary balances

It is widely recognized that fiscal rules can foster fiscal discipline. Yet the literature has devoted scant attention to how their effects evolve after adoption. Most studies estimate a single "average" effect of fiscal rules—sometimes conditioned on select covariates—implicitly assuming that the short-, medium-, and long-term responses are identical. However, reforms to fiscal governance may take time to build credibility and take full effect, and their effectiveness may weaken subsequently if, for example, political support proves fragile.

To examine how the effects of fiscal rules evolve, the response of the CAPB-to-trend-GDP ratio is followed for 58 cases of fiscal rule adoption in a sample of 116 countries between 1984 and 2015. Using the CAPB filters out cyclical fluctuations in the primary balance, isolating changes beyond those driven by economic conditions. The CAPB is estimated following the methodology outlined by Fedelino, Ivanova, and Horton (2009), while local projection regressions are used to study the trajectory of the CAPB after fiscal rule adoption (refer to annex 3.2 for methodological details).

Fiscal rule adoption is modeled as a treatment effect, following the logic of difference-in-differences analysis. To mitigate concerns of policy endogeneity, a two-stage procedure is implemented: in the first stage, the likelihood of having a fiscal rule in place is estimated; in the second, these estimates are used as weights in the local projection regressions. The trajectory of the CAPB -to-trend-GDP ratio is examined over a ten-year horizon, chosen to capture the longer-term evolution of the effects of fiscal rule adoption. The initial build-up of credibility and subsequent evolution of a rule's effectiveness are assumed to depend on the initial conditions in which the rule is introduced.[3]

The regression estimates indicate that fiscal rules improve the CAPB, but with a lag, and the improvements vary across country groups. In EMDEs, the effects of fiscal rule adoption peak after five years, with the CAPB improving by a cumulative 1.4 percentage points of trend GDP relative to a counterfactual of no rule adoption (refer to figure 3.4.A). Thereafter, the effect fades, becoming statistically insignificant seven years after adoption. Advanced economies exhibit a response that is more delayed but also stronger at the peak, with improvements in the CAPB peaking six years after adoption at a cumulative 1.7 percentage points of trend GDP (refer to figure 3.4.B).

The role of institutional context

One explanation for the differences between EMDEs and advanced economies in the estimated effects on the CAPB of the adoption of fiscal rules could be differences in the quality of governance

[3] Post-adoption shifts in conditions may also affect the performance of fiscal rules, but they should not contaminate the regression estimates, because local projection regressions accommodate all possible future trajectories, including subsequent changes in the underlying state variables (Jordà and Taylor 2025).

and institutions. Many EMDEs introduced fiscal rules without a mature fiscal governance framework, history of fiscal discipline, or strong political commitment (Brändle and Elsener 2024). Such shortcomings may limit the effectiveness of fiscal rules. In addition, more limited state capacity in EMDEs may reduce the ability—or willingness—of policy makers in these economies to pursue sound fiscal policies (Calderón, Duncan, and Schmidt-Hebbel 2016). Weaker institutions and governance can weaken the credibility and enforcement of rules, undermining their impact, particularly in the long term.

A second version of the local projection estimates, which interacts the fiscal rule indicator with a measure of the strength of public institutions, suggests that the institutional envirionment has been an important determinant of the response of the CAPB to rule adoption. In EMDEs with strong institutions, fiscal rule adoption is followed by pronounced and durable improvements in the CAPB. The effect peaks five years after adoption at a cumulative 2.5 percentage points of trend GDP, before tapering to 0.9 percentage point after nine years (refer to figure 3.5.A). By contrast, in EMDEs with weak institutions, CAPB improves by 0.8 percentage point of trend GDP in the year of adoption, but the gains are not sustained in the medium to long term (refer to figure 3.5.B).[4]

Country experiences underscore the critical role of strong institutional foundations in determining the success of fiscal rules. Chile is a commonly cited example. The success of its structural-balance rule, introduced in 2001, rests on robust public institutions—most notably on transparent methodologies, applied by independent expert committees, for estimating potential GDP and long-run copper prices. These institutional arrangements have given the rule credibility and helped ensure that the application of the rule makes fiscal policy countercyclical rather than procyclical (Barreix et al. 2019).

For Chile, the introduction of the rule had sizeable effects. A modest CAPB deficit in 2000 became a surplus equivalent to about 7 percent of

FIGURE 3.4 Fiscal rule effectiveness

Fiscal rules tend to improve the cyclically adjusted primary balance (CAPB) following adoption, but the effects occur gradually and vary across country groups. In EMDEs, improvements in the CAPB peak after five years and diminish thereafter. In contrast, advanced economies experience more gradual but persistent improvements.

A. Change in CAPB following rule adoption in EMDEs

B. Change in CAPB following rule adoption in advanced economies

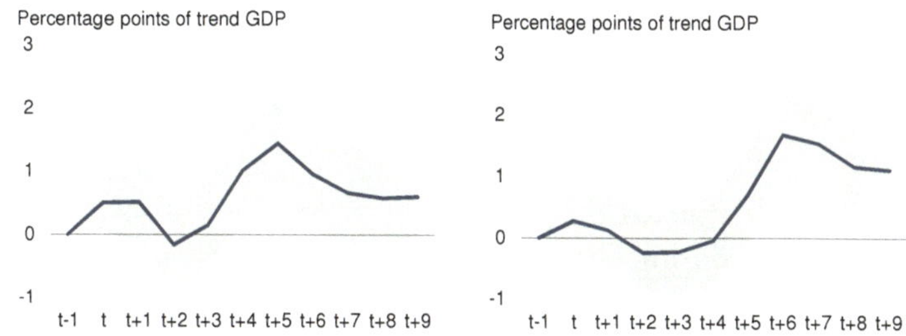

Source: World Bank.
Note: CAPB = cyclically adjusted primary balance; EMDEs = emerging market and developing economies. Results are from LP-AIPW regressions. Technical details are provided in annex 3.2. Lines show the cumulative change in the CAPB as percent of GDP in the years around fiscal rule adoption, compared to a counterfactual scenario of no rule adoption in year t. Shaded areas show 90 percent confidence intervals. Results are based on a sample of 116 countries (83 EMDEs and 33 advanced economies) with 58 cases of fiscal rule adoption (33 in EMDEs and 25 in advanced economies) between 1984 and 2015.

FIGURE 3.5 Institutional environment and fiscal rule effectiveness

In EMDEs with strong institutions, improvements in the cyclically adjusted primary balance (CAPB) are durable. In EMDEs with weak institutions, fiscal rule adoption leads to no significant improvement in fiscal outcomes.

A. Change in CAPB following rule adoption in EMDEs with strong institutions

B. Change in CAPB following rule adoption in EMDEs with weak institutions

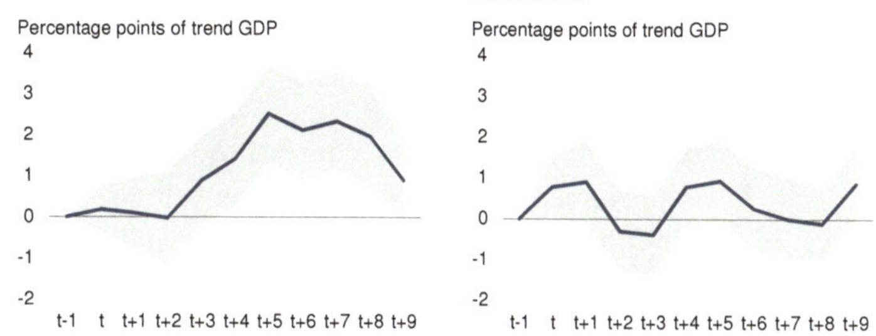

Source: World Bank.
Note: CAPB = cyclically adjusted primary balance; EMDEs = emerging market and developing economies. Results are from LP-AIPW regressions. Technical details are provided in annex 3.2. Lines show the cumulative change in CAPB as a percent of trend GDP in the years around fiscal rule adoption, with the rule(s) adopted at year t, compared with a counterfactual scenario of no rule adoption in year t. Shaded areas show 90 percent confidence intervals. Institutional strength is measured using principal component analysis of International Country Risk Guide data. Results are based on a sample of 83 EMDEs with 33 cases of fiscal rule adoption between 1984 and 2015.

[4] A similar institution-driven dynamic is observed for commodity exporters.

trend GDP by 2007, as copper revenue windfalls were saved to build fiscal buffers. When copper prices fell sharply in 2008 during the global financial crisis, the government was able to draw on these buffers to implement a large fiscal stimulus without jeopardizing fiscal sustainability. Anchoring fiscal policy in a rule-based countercyclical framework therefore not only bolstered public finances but also contributed to a significant reduction in output volatility (Céspedes, Parrado, and Velasco 2014). Chile's fiscal rules and prudent fiscal policy management also enabled the government to provide fiscal stimulus during the pandemic without undermining fiscal sustainability (Lam et al. 2023).

The experiences of Nigeria and Botswana are telling as well. Nigeria adopted fiscal rules in 2007 to delink public spending from oil revenue and improve macroeconomic stability. Weak institutional frameworks have constrained rule enforcement, however, and performance has been mixed despite early gains (Okonjo-Iweala and Osafo-Kwaako 2007; World Bank 2022). Botswana introduced fiscal rules in 2003 to secure long-term fiscal sustainability in anticipation of declining diamond revenues. In contrast with Nigeria, Botswana's relatively strong institutional environment—with established sound fiscal management and credible policy frameworks—has supported the successful implementation of these rules (Apeti, Basdevant, and Salins 2023).

The role of initial conditions

Beyond the institutional context, the durability of improvements in fiscal conditions following the adoption of fiscal rules may also reflect the motives for adoption. In many cases, these motives are signaled by the economic, fiscal, and political conditions at the time of adoption, which the literature identifies as determinants of fiscal rule adoption (for example, Badinger and Reuter 2017a). Initial conditions can act as a tailwind or a headwind for the effectiveness of rules, influencing not only their early effects but also the establishment and evolution of their credibility. Those conditions also evolve over time, however, and as they do, the government's compliance with rules may strengthen or wane. Fiscal rules may also be motivated by factors related to internal consensus building and policy communication. For example, a government may introduce a fiscal rule to frame a fiscal adjustment that it needs to make in any case. Such a rule may make little difference at first, but it may constrain policy later.

State of the economy

Fiscal rules are introduced under various economic conditions. To examine the influence of prevailing conditions, the state of the economy is classified by comparing a country's three-year average of lagged real GDP growth to its own long-term average, following a similar approach to Auerbach and Gorodnichenko (2012) and Alesina et al. (2024). By this metric, about half of adoptions during 1984–2015 occurred during periods of economic strength, a share that is similar in EMDEs and advanced economies (refer to figure 3.6.A).

Fiscal rules are found to be more effective at improving primary balances when they are adopted in a strong economy. Under such conditions, the impact on the CAPB builds gradually. Five years after adoption, the CAPB improves by a cumulative 1.3 percentage points of trend GDP relative to the preadoption level five years after adoption, compared with a counterfactual of no fiscal rule adoption (refer to figure 3.6.B). The improvement in primary balances following rule adoption in strong economic conditions is sustained in the long term, settling at 1.2 percentage points after a decade. When adopted in a weak economy, fiscal rules have no statistically significant effect on the CAPB.

One reason why fiscal rules yield different results depending on economic conditions at adoption could be that rule credibility is more difficult to establish in a weak economy. When rules are introduced in economic downturns, they are often rushed through and face pressure to deliver early, visible improvements. If such results fail to materialize, credibility can erode rapidly. Even among countries with strong institutional capacity, fiscal rules are more effective when adopted in a strong economy. This suggests that robust public institutions may not be sufficient to offset the headwinds associated with adverse economic conditions (Fatás, Gootjes, and

Mawejje 2026). Another possible reason for the finding of ineffectiveness of fiscal rules adopted during periods of economic weakness is that some EMDEs adopt fiscal rules during economic crises to meet the conditionality of international lenders. In such circumstances, domestic political support for the rules may be lacking.[5]

Argentina's experience in the early 2000s offers a cautionary tale about the adoption of fiscal rules in times of macroeconomic turbulence. The Fiscal Solvency Law of 1999 stipulated that primary expenditure could not grow faster than nominal GDP and, at most, stay constant in real terms in periods of negative nominal GDP growth. However, the rule was introduced just as the economy entered its most severe recession on record and quickly lost relevance because there was no time to build fiscal buffers before the downturn (Artana et al. 2021). A subsequent attempt by the government to install a deficit rule in 2001 rapidly lost credibility as fiscal and economic conditions deteriorated sharply during the 2002 crisis. Nevertheless, the implementation of fiscal rules has been more successful in recent years, reflecting stronger commitment by the authorities. This has resulted in primary fiscal surpluses since early 2024 and lower borrowing costs (IMF 2025b).

Debt levels

The introduction of fiscal rules since the 1980s has not been systematically associated with high levels of government debt, defined as being above the median ratio of government debt to government revenues in the sample.[6] Among EMDEs, 50 percent of rule adoptions have occurred in high-debt conditions (above 183 percent of revenues), compared with 27 percent in advanced economies (refer to figure 3.6.C).

When rules are introduced in low-debt conditions, the CAPB improves by a statistically significant amount. Five years after adoption, the cumulative improvement reaches 1.8 percentage points of trend GDP, moderating to 1.3 percentage points

FIGURE 3.6 Macroeconomic and political conditions and fiscal rule effectiveness

Fiscal rules are not more likely to be adopted during periods of economic weakness, nor, at least in EMDES, are they more likely to be adopted when government debt levels are high. However, rules adopted when domestic economic conditions are favorable or when government debt is low tend to be more effective at improving the cyclically adjusted primary balance (CAPB) than those adopted when economic conditions are weak and debt is high. show no significant effect. Fiscal rules adopted by governments with slim parliamentary majorities result in larger CAPB improvements in the longer term than those adopted with large majorities.

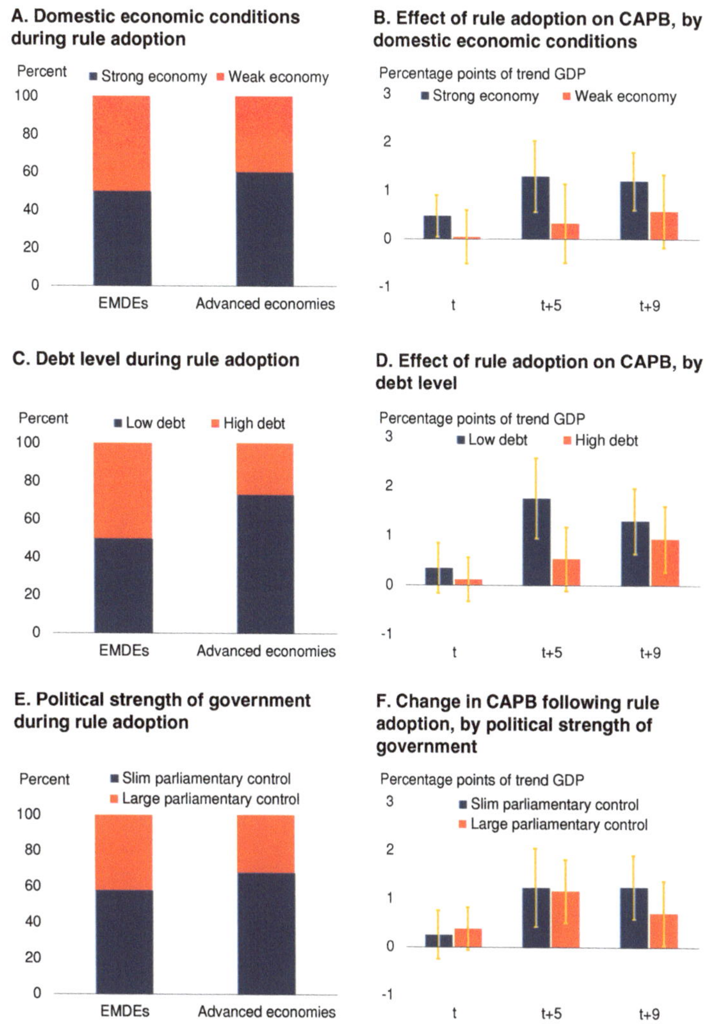

Source: World Bank.

Note: CAPB = cyclically adjusted primary balance; EMDEs = emerging market and developing economies.

A.B. The state of the economy is defined using a weighing function based on a country-normalized, 3-year average of lagged real GDP growth relative to its long-term average. Sample includes 116 economies (83 EMDEs and 33 advanced economies), with 57 cases of fiscal rule adoption (33 in EMDEs and 24 in advanced economies).

B.D.F. Figure show the results of LP-AIPW regressions. Technical details are provided in annex 3.2. Bars show the cumulative change in the CAPB as percent of trend GDP in the years around fiscal rule adoption, with the rule(s) adopted at year *t*, compared to a counterfactual scenario of no rule adoption in year *t*. Vertical lines show 90 percent confidence intervals.

C.D. Countries are classified as having low (high) debt if they are below (above) the median debt-to-revenue ratio in the sample. Sample includes 116 economies (83 EMDEs and 33 advanced economies), with 58 cases of fiscal rule adoption (33 in EMDEs and 25 in advanced economies).

E.F. Countries are classified as having a slim (large) parliamentary control if the margin of seats the government holds within parliament is above (below) the sample median. Sample includes 116 economies (83 EMDEs and 33 advanced economies), with 56 cases of fiscal rule adoption (32 in EMDEs and 24 in advanced economies).

[5] Results in Fatás, Gootjes, and Mawejje (2026) indicate that the adoption of fiscal rules under IMF-supported programs has made no long-run difference to changes in the CAPB after adoption.

[6] Similar regression results are obtained when the debt-to-GDP ratio is used.

after a decade (refer to figure 3.6.D). For rules adopted in high-debt settings, the impact takes longer to develop, and the long-run results are smaller, with an improvement in the CAPB after a decade of about 0.9 percentage point of trend GDP. Still, the effect is statistically significant. Overall, these results suggest that fiscal rules can both help low-debt countries avert future stress and enable high-debt countries to establish fiscal discipline.

Consensus building

A central theme in the literature on economic reforms is the importance of building domestic consensus and ownership for the success of the reforms, including through the "use of consultation, communication and mitigating strategies" (IMF 2024, p. 67). Partly for this reason, thorough preparation before implementing a fiscal rule is essential to ensure its credibility and effectiveness (Kopits and Symansky 1998). While the time required to prepare fiscal rules, communicate their rationale, and build consensus varies among countries and is difficult to quantify, governments with larger majorities in parliament may find it easier to introduce and legislate rules. As a result, they may have less incentive to build broader consensus, potentially weakening long-term support as new administrations take office.

The argument that narrow parliamentary majorities tend to increase the effectiveness of fiscal rules by promoting consensus-building is supported by the data. About 60 percent of fiscal rules in EMDEs and nearly 70 percent of those in advanced economies were adopted when the governing party or coalition held a slim (below-median) share of parliamentary seats (refer to figure 3.6.E). The regression results show that rules introduced by governments with narrow parliamentary majorities, the CAPB improves by a statistically significant 1.2 percentage points of trend GDP five years after adoption, and remains at about the same level after a decade (refer to figure 3.6.F). By contrast, when governments with relatively large parliamentary margins adopt fiscal rules, the short- to medium-term improvements are similar, but the effects tend to diminish over time—reaching only a 0.7 percentage point improvement in the long run. This pattern is not driven by composition effects, such as countries with weaker institutions (often EMDEs) being more likely to adopt rules under large majorities. It persists even among countries with comparatively strong institutional frameworks (Fatás, Gootjes, and Mawejje 2026).

Jamaica provides an example of how early investment in political consensus and durable commitment to fiscal rules can promote their success. In 2014, the country adopted a fiscal rule to address long-standing imbalances and restore debt sustainability. Since then, the rule has been instrumental in reducing public debt from a peak of more than 140 percent of GDP in 2012 to about 70 percent in 2025. This achievement was made possible not only by the rule itself but also through partnerships forged by the government with political and other social groups that built and sustained consensus for fiscal adjustment. Transparent monitoring and credible reporting on compliance with the rule and on the progress of the broader economic reform program reinforced commitment and accountability, helping to maintain reform momentum (Arslanalp, Eichengreen, and Henry 2024).

The role of fiscal rule design

In addition to conditions at the time of adoption, the design of the fiscal rules matters for effectiveness. Deficit rules appear essential: with other types of rules, improvements in the CAPB are not sustained in the long term (refer to figures 3.7.A and 3.7.B). Deficit rules tend to have positive effects on the CAPB, even in weak institutional environments, suggesting that these types of rules can provide a critical anchor for fiscal sustainability. However, the benefits of deficit rules emerge more slowly in the presence of weak institutions.

Turning to specific design features, the positive effects of broad public sector coverage of fiscal rules stand out most clearly (refer to figures 3.7.C and 3.7.D). Fiscal rules that encompass the general government tend to produce lasting fiscal gains in the long term, whereas those narrowly focused on the central government have more limited effects, even in countries with strong institutions. However, broad public sector coverage does not compensate for weak institutional environments. Other design features appear to be less critical. For instance, fiscal rules yield significant improvements regardless of enforcement strength, provided institutions are strong. Similarly, a strong legal basis tends to enhance effectiveness, but robust institutions have been able to compensate for weak legal foundations. Overall, these results show that good design alone does not ensure the effectiveness of fiscal rules.

Fiscal adjustment episodes and the role of fiscal rules

The preceding results indicate that the adoption of fiscal rules generally yields gradual improvements in fiscal balances, and that such improvements are more likely to persist when rules are supported by strong public institutions and introduced in favorable economic conditions. Yet stronger primary balances after rule adoption do not guarantee enduring fiscal stability. Deficits can re-emerge and debt can accumulate, especially after large shocks such as the global financial crisis or the COVID-19 pandemic. In such circumstances, periodic fiscal adjustments may still be necessary.

To better understand whether and how fiscal rules have promoted fiscal policy adjustments, it is useful to look beyond the factors that shape the gradual postadoption developments considered in the preceding section. This section examines whether fiscal rules have fostered fiscal adjustments and under what circumstances adjustments occur.[7] The direction of this effect is not obvious *a priori*. By imposing numerical constraints on key fiscal aggregates, fiscal rules are designed to trigger fiscal adjustment once limits are approached or breached. But if rules operate primarily as preventive guardrails—curbing deficit and debt build-ups—they could reduce the need for abrupt adjustment episodes. Moreover, enforcement may be difficult in practice, potentially weakening any disciplining effect. While a large literature has examined the determinants of the onset and success of fiscal adjustments, the role of fiscal rules has received surprisingly little attention. Even fewer studies examine the nature of fiscal adjustment—specifically, whether adjustment occurs largely through expenditure restraint or revenue measures.

FIGURE 3.7 Institutional environment, rule design, and fiscal rule effectiveness

Among rule types, deficit rules are particularly effective in improving primary balances in the medium and long term, whereas gains from other rules tend to be short-lived. Deficit rules yield significant effects even with weak public institutions. Broad coverage of the government sector also enhances the effectiveness of fiscal rules. When rules apply only to the central government, improvements in primary balances tend to fade in the long term, whereas broad coverage of the general government helps sustain these improvements. However, wide coverage does not compensate for institutional weakness.

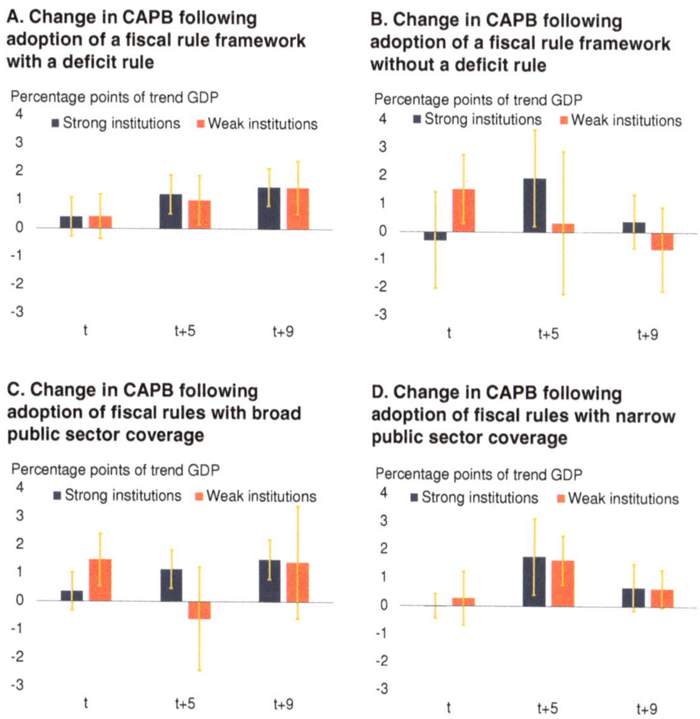

Source: World Bank.

Note: CAPB = cyclically adjusted primary balance; EMDEs = emerging market and developing economies. Results are from LP-AIPW regressions. Technical details are provided in annex 3.2. Bars show the cumulative improvement in the CAPB as a percent of trend GDP in the years around fiscal rule adoption, with the rule(s) adopted in year *t*, compared to a counterfactual scenario of no rule adoption in year *t*. Vertical lines show 90 percent confidence intervals. Institutional strength is measured using principal component analysis of International Country Risk Guide data. Results are based on a sample of 116 economies (83 EMDEs and 33 advanced economies) with 58 cases of fiscal rule adoption (33 in EMDEs and 25 in advanced economies).

Identification of fiscal adjustment episodes

Fiscal adjustment episodes are defined as multi-year increases in the CAPB as a percent of trend GDP, identified using Bai–Perron structural-break

[7] Wiese, de Haan, and Jong-A-Pin (2018) survey the literature on successful fiscal adjustments, finding that beyond policy measures, factors such as GDP growth and inflation can also contribute to debt reduction. However, the influence of fiscal rules is expected to operate primarily through fiscal policy itself, rather than through broader macroeconomic conditions.

testing (Bai and Perron 1998, 2003; refer to annex 3.3 for methodological details). Applying this approach to 125 EMDEs and 34 advanced economies over 1984–2022, 131 adjustment episodes are identified—89 in EMDEs and 42 in advanced economies. The characterization of these episodes as policy-driven efforts to improve fiscal positions is confirmed by their close alignment with episodes identified through narrative-based approaches (refer to annex 3.3).

Fiscal adjustment episodes are found to have occurred less frequently in EMDEs than in advanced economies. In the nearly 40 years covered by the data, 63 percent of EMDEs experienced at least one episode, compared with 85 percent of advanced economies. EMDEs were in an adjustment episode in about 8 percent of years, versus 14 percent in advanced economies. A notable wave of fiscal adjustments across EMDEs took place in the 2000s. This partly reflected actions to strengthen fiscal positions in the wake of successive financial crises in EMDEs in the 1990s (refer to figure 3.8.A). These adjustments occurred at approximately the same rate in commodity-exporting and commodity-importing EMDEs, suggesting that they were not primarily driven by the mid-2000s commodity boom. EMDEs also substantially strengthened their policy frameworks during this period, including through the adoption of fiscal rules.[8]

In addition to differences in the frequency of fiscal adjustment episodes in EMDEs and advanced economies, there are striking differences in the duration and magnitude of episodes. Fiscal adjustments are shorter in EMDEs, lasting three years in the median episode, compared with four years in the median episode in advanced economies (refer to figure 3.8.B). Yet the magnitude of adjustments is substantially larger in EMDEs. In the median adjustment episode in EMDEs, the primary balance improves by 1.6 percentage points of trend GDP per year, compared with 1.0 percentage point in the median episode in advanced economies (refer to figure 3.8.C). The difference between the two country groups stems mainly from an increase in revenues in EMDEs. In non-adjustment years, by contrast, the CAPB-to-GDP ratio deteriorates slightly in the median EMDE, entirely driven by an increase in expenditures. Advanced economies experience a deterioration of about half the size, equally split between increasing expenditures and deteriorating revenues (refer to figure 3.8.D).

Fiscal rules and fiscal adjustment

To formally test the effects of fiscal rules in fiscal adjustment episodes, discrete choice models are estimated (refer to annex 3.4 for methodological details). The empirical analysis first examines whether the presence of a fiscal rule affects the likelihood of starting a fiscal adjustment episode, and then considers the channels through which rules operate and the role of rule design. The specification includes half-decade time effects, country-group fixed effects, and controls for the fiscal stance, macroeconomic conditions, external support arrangements, and quality of public institutions.

Effect of fiscal rules on the likelihood of fiscal adjustment episodes

The unconditional probability of a fiscal adjustment episode starting in a given country-year in the sample is 9 percent. Results for the set of controls show that fiscal adjustment episodes are more likely in environments characterized by fiscal strain: larger primary deficits as a share of GDP, higher debt-to-GDP ratios, and higher interest payments relative to revenues (refer to table A3.4.1). Moreover, lower inflation and stronger current account balances are associated with a higher likelihood of fiscal adjustment. This likely reflects the fact that inflation reduces the urgency of adjustment by eroding outstanding debt in real terms, while stronger external balances provide a more supportive environment for adjustment. By contrast, real GDP growth does not significantly affect the likelihood of an adjustment episode, providing no evidence of an inherent procyclical bias in the initiation of fiscal adjustments. Other factors, such as the quality of public institutions or the presence of external support programs, are also

[8] Two major consolidation waves are observed in advanced economies. The first wave, in the mid-1990s, reflects efforts to stabilize public debt following recessions in the early 1990s and, in Europe, to meet the Maastricht convergence criteria for entry into the Economic and Monetary Union. The second wave, in the early 2010s, occurred when governments withdrew stimulus to contain debt surges after the global financial crisis.

not found to have a statistically significant effect on the initiation of fiscal adjustment.

Turning to the main variable of interest, the regression results indicate that fiscal rules are significantly associated with a higher likelihood of a fiscal adjustment episode. All else equal, countries without rules face a 5 percent probability of starting a fiscal adjustment, compared with 14 percent for countries with a fiscal rule framework (refer to figure 3.9.A). This implies that fiscal rules raise the probability of fiscal adjustment by about 9 percentage points.[9] Sample splits further show that fiscal rules significantly increase the likelihood of fiscal adjustment in both EMDEs and advanced economies (refer to table A3.4.1). Moreover, an interaction between fiscal rules and institutional quality is not significant, suggesting that the difference in the likelihood of an adjustment episode across country groups is not conditional on the institutional environment.

Not all fiscal rules are equally effective at prompting fiscal adjustment episodes, however. Rule frameworks that include a deficit rule raise the probability of fiscal adjustment by more than 9 percentage points, whereas frameworks without a deficit rule—those relying only on debt, expenditure, and revenue rules, or combinations thereof—do not significantly increase the likelihood of an adjustment episode (figure 3.9.B). The finding that deficit rules are integral in both exercises is informative, as the government budget is the key indicator of a country's fiscal stance. Other rule types may still serve important complementary objectives—for example, expenditure rules can help limit procyclical spending (Guerguil, Mandon, and Tapsoba 2017).

Effect of fiscal rule design on the likelihood of fiscal adjustment episodes

Fiscal rules may influence not only the likelihood of fiscal adjustment but also its composition. Understanding how fiscal rules shape the channels through which adjustment occurs is important, as

FIGURE 3.8 Fiscal adjustment episodes

Fiscal adjustment episodes have occurred in waves in EMDEs and advanced economies. Episodes in EMDEs are typically shorter but involve larger CAPB improvements than those in advanced economies. The median improvement in the CAPB in EMDEs during consolidations is 1.6 percentage points of GDP, 60 percent higher than in advanced economies. The composition of adjustment also differs: EMDEs tend to rely more on revenue-based measures, whereas adjustment in advanced economies occurs mainly through expenditure cuts.

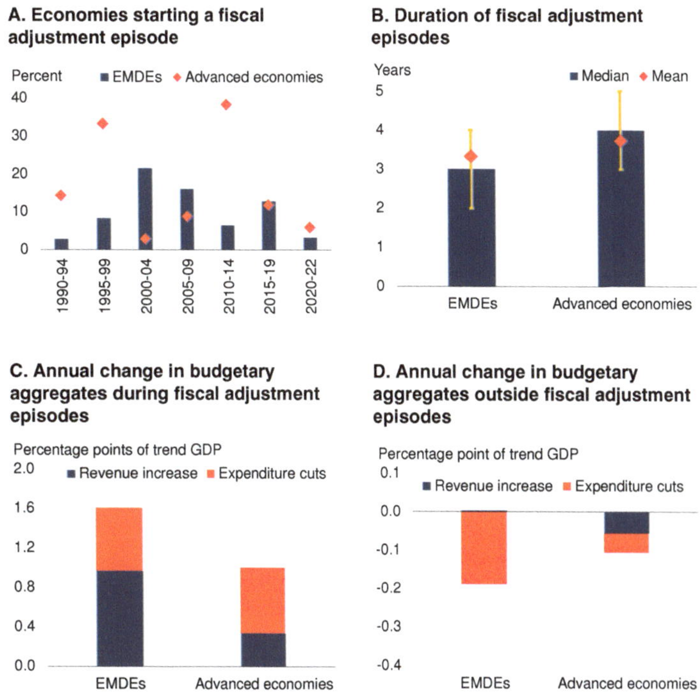

Sources: International Monetary Fund; World Bank.

Note: EMDEs = emerging market and developing economies. Fiscal adjustment episodes are identified using Bai–Perron structural break tests. Technical details are provided in annex 3.3. Sample includes 159 economies, of which 125 are EMDEs and 34 are advanced economies.

A. Panel shows the share of economies that started a fiscal adjustment episode.

B. Bars show the median duration of fiscal adjustment episodes. Vertical lines show the interquartile range.

C.-D. Bars show median annual change in cyclically adjusted government revenues and primary expenditures during and outside fiscal adjustment episodes.

countries face different fiscal challenges—some primarily on the expenditure side, others on the revenue side, and others on both.[10]

[9] Regression-based Granger causality tests show that fiscal rules helped forecast the start of fiscal adjustment, while adjustment onsets do not predict fiscal rules. This suggests that rules generally precede the identified episodes rather than being adopted in response to them.

[10] The consequences of different compositions of fiscal adjustment have long been debated in the literature (Balasundharam et al. 2023). Some research—largely based on advanced economy samples—argues that expenditure-based adjustments entailed smaller output losses than tax increases and are thus more successful in reducing debt-to-GDP ratios (Alesina and Ardagna 2010; Alesina and Perotti 1995). Other work shows that a balanced mix of spending and revenue measures generates more durable fiscal adjustment, especially when there is scope for increasing revenue mobilization (Gupta et al. 2004; Molnar 2012).

FIGURE 3.9 Effect of fiscal rules on the start of a fiscal adjustment episode

Fiscal rules substantially increase the likelihood of entering a fiscal adjustment episode in any given year—from 5 percent without rules to 14 percent with them. Yet this effect hinges on the presence of a deficit rule. Without explicit budget balance constraints, fiscal rules do not significantly increase the probability of initiating a fiscal adjustment.

A. Probability of a fiscal adjustment episode

B. Impact of fiscal rules on the probability of adjustment, by presence of a deficit rule

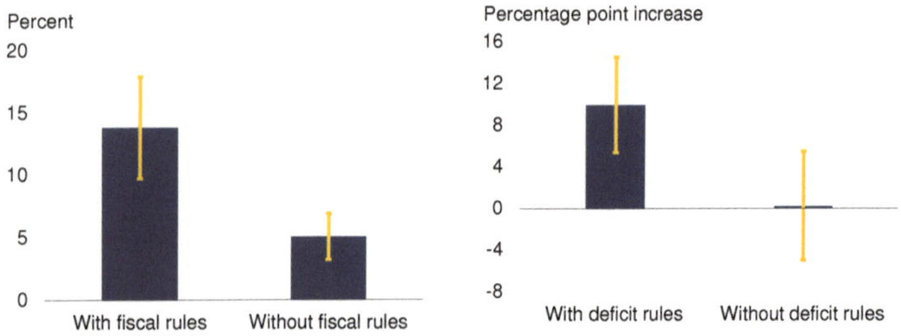

Sources: International Monetary Fund; World Bank.
Note: Results are from probit regressions. Technical details are provided in annex 3.4. Sample includes 122 economies, of which 89 are EMDEs and 33 are advanced economies.
A.B. Vertical lines show 90 percent confidence intervals.

In EMDEs with fiscal rules, expenditure-based adjustments—defined as episodes in which more than half of the adjustment comes from spending cuts—account for half of all episodes, compared with two-fifths in EMDEs without such rules (refer to figure 3.10.A). Thus, in the absence of fiscal rules, fiscal adjustment in EMDEs occurs mainly through revenue-based measures. In advanced economies, about half of adjustment episodes also occur through expenditure cuts when fiscal rules are present. When fiscal rules are not present, adjustments are still predominantly expenditure-based.

Estimating the likelihood of expenditure- and revenue-based adjustments separately shows that fiscal rules do not differentially favor one channel over the other (refer to table A3.4.1). Instead, the presence of a fiscal rule framework is associated with a higher probability of initiating both types of adjustment. After controlling for other factors that influence fiscal adjustment, fiscal rules raise the likelihood of revenue-based episodes by 5 percentage points and expenditure-based episodes by slightly less than 4 percentage points (refer to figure 3.10.B). The similarity of the results for the control variables suggests that expenditure- and revenue-led adjustments tend to occur under comparable macroeconomic and fiscal conditions, rather than being triggered at different times or for fundamentally different reasons.

While fiscal rules are associated with a higher likelihood of both revenue- and expenditure-based adjustments, the design of the rule framework can play a key role in shaping how fiscal adjustment is carried out. This influence can operate through the type of rule in place, as well as through specific design elements. To assess how different aspects of rule design influence the composition of adjustment, the fiscal rule indicator is interacted with alternative design dimensions in the empirical specification.

The results show that the presence of a deficit rule is associated with a higher likelihood of both revenue-based and expenditure-based fiscal adjustments (refer to figures 3.10.C and 3.10.D). The magnitude of each adjustment channel tends to be larger when the fiscal rule framework also includes rules targeting the relevant components—that is, a revenue or expenditure rule—although these additional rules do not appear to be decisive for the likelihood of initiating either type of adjustment. This likely reflects the fact that revenue and expenditure rules often coexist with deficit rules within broader fiscal frameworks. Nonetheless, the results highlight the importance of rule combinations: while deficit rules anchor adjustment, complementary rules can help shape how adjustment is carried out.

Specific design features of fiscal rules are also found to matter. For revenue-based adjustments, the breadth of institutional coverage appears particularly important (refer to figure 3.10.E). Fiscal rules targeting the general government (that is, with "wide coverage") are associated with a probability of revenue-based adjustments that is 9 percentage points higher than that under rules with narrow coverage. This finding is consistent with the notion that wide coverage helps align fiscal discipline across all levels of government, reducing the scope for efforts at the central level to be offset by subnational relaxation or slippages.

For expenditure-led adjustments, enforceability emerges as a key determinant (refer to figure 3.10.F). Rule frameworks with explicit enforcement mechanisms significantly raise the probability of an expenditure-based adjustment by 4 percentage points, while frameworks without such mechanisms do not significantly affect the likelihood of these episodes. This substantiates that the de jure existence of a rule can matter less than its de facto power. Moreover, the association between strong enforcement mechanisms and expenditure-led adjustments is consistent with the idea that such mechanisms typically demand swift fiscal improvements when numerical limits are approached or breached. In practice, this tends to favor expenditure restraint, as governments have greater direct control over spending, while revenues are more endogenous to economic conditions and tax reforms are often politically costly and difficult to pass through legislation.

Other design features can weaken the relationship between fiscal rules and adjustment. In particular, flexibility provisions are associated with a lower likelihood that fiscal rules trigger adjustment episodes. For example, rules that exempt priority spending items (such as public investment under "golden rules") render the effect of fiscal rules on expenditure-based adjustments statistically insignificant. This outcome does not necessarily imply poor design, provided broader fiscal adjustment still takes place through other channels. Consistent with this interpretation, empirical evidence suggests that golden rules can help protect public investment from cuts during fiscal consolidation episodes (Ardanaz et al. 2021).

Similarly, when escape clauses are included, the effect of fiscal rules on the onset of revenue-based adjustment is statistically insignificant. Although well-designed escape clauses are desirable during crises, the procedures for reactivating rules are often vague and left to the discretion of governments (or supranational authorities). This makes reinstatement prone to delay. As a result, the prolonged activation of escape clauses may weaken the disciplining effect of fiscal rules relative to frameworks that do not include them.

Simple rules versus complex frameworks

The results above underscore that fiscal rules matter for the likelihood of fiscal adjustment, and that the design features of fiscal rules help

FIGURE 3.10 Effect of fiscal rules on the channels of fiscal adjustment

In EMDEs, the use of fiscal rules tilts adjustment more toward expenditure-led episodes, whereas in advanced economies the fiscal rules tilt adjustment toward revenue-led episodes. Even so, fiscal rules significantly increase the likelihood of both expenditure- and revenue-led adjustments. Deficit rules are pivotal for both types of adjustment. Wide public-sector coverage raises the probability of revenue-led adjustment episodes, while excluding priority spending items from numerical constraints in fiscal rules lowers the probability of expenditure-based episodes. Escape clauses tend to lower the likelihood of revenue-led consolidations, whereas enforcement mechanisms significantly increase the likelihood of expenditure-led adjustments.

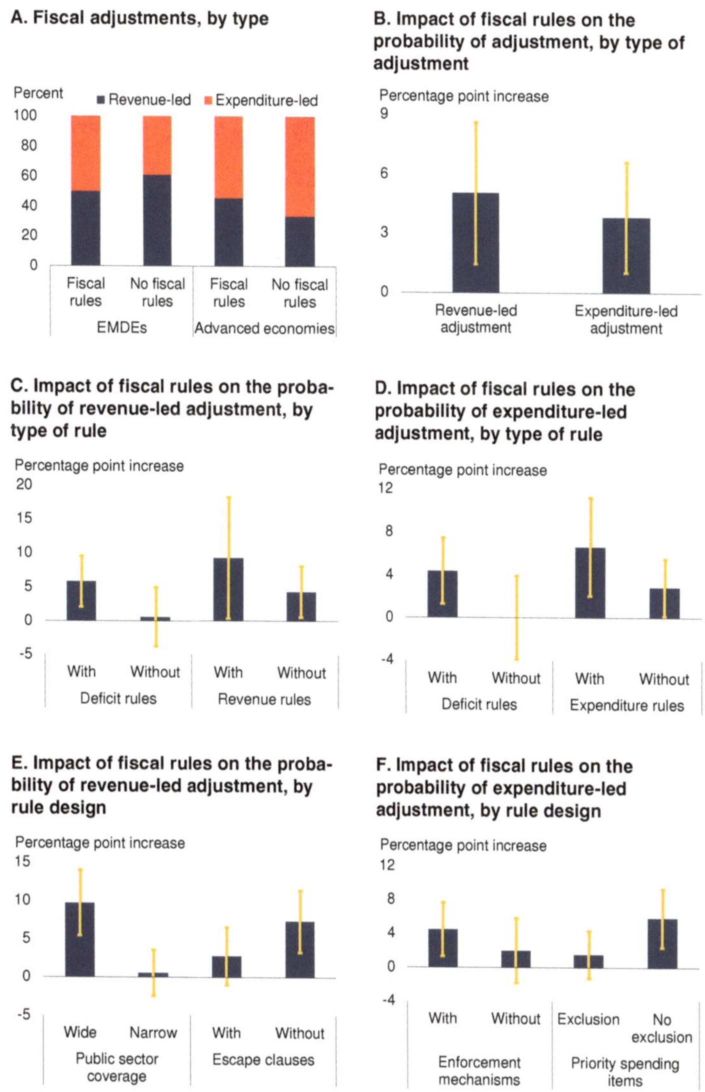

Sources: International Monetary Fund; World Bank.

Note: EMDEs = emerging market and developing economies.

A. Bars show the share of fiscal adjustments classified as expenditure-led and revenue-led. Sample includes 122 economies, of which 89 are EMDEs and 33 are advanced economies.

B-F. Results are from probit regressions. Technical details are provided in annex 3.4. Figures show the increase in the likelihood of fiscal adjustment. Vertical lines show 90 percent confidence intervals. Sample includes 122 economies, of which 89 are EMDEs and 33 are advanced economies.

determine whether an adjustment episode occurs through expenditure cuts or revenue increases. Taken together, these findings highlight that design features can interact in important ways—some reinforcing the effectiveness of fiscal rules, others potentially offsetting it. This interaction is particularly relevant given broader trends in fiscal frameworks. Over time, fiscal rule frameworks have become more intricate, often featuring multiple rule types, more elaborate enforcement tools, and flexibility provisions. While each rule or design feature may be justified on its own, together they can generate administrative challenges. Intricate rule may also increase the risk that policy becomes detached from objectives.

To investigate how some of these trends may have shaped the outcomes, the role of fiscal rule design complexity is measured in two ways: first, by the number of rules in place, and second, by the number of design features embedded in the rules—specifically, elements of enforceability and flexibility. Rules with no more than two such features are classified as having simple designs.

Expenditure-led adjustments typically occur in countries with multiple fiscal rules (refer to figure 3.11.A). This suggests that, although previous results highlight the importance of deficit rules for triggering fiscal adjustment, it is typically the combined presence of several rules that strengthens governments' operational leverage over spending. In contrast, the number of rules in place—whether single or multiple—does not appear to matter for the probability of a revenue-based adjustment (refer to figure 3.11.B).

The degree of rule design complexity appears to affect the likelihood of only revenue-based adjustments. For expenditure-based episodes, simple versus complex rule design shows no difference (refer to figure 3.11.C). By contrast, simple rule design is found to raise the likelihood of revenue-based adjustments by about 6 percentage points, whereas frameworks with more complex design show no statistically significant effect (refer to figure 3.11.D). This aligns with previous results: enforcement provisions tend to promote expenditure cuts—often the quickest adjustment channel—while flexibility features make rules less strict and can reduce the pressure to undertake sizeable fiscal adjustments.

Policy priorities

In recent decades, EMDEs have strengthened their fiscal policy frameworks through the increased use of fiscal rules. Nevertheless, fiscal space remains limited in many cases. Amid rising spending pressures and elevated debt levels, the need for significant fiscal adjustments is pressing in many EMDEs. Fiscal rules can help improve primary balances, but the type of rule used, the economic and institutional context in which they are introduced, and their design have important effects on outcomes. The evidence suggests that to enhance the effectiveness of fiscal rules in EMDEs, there are three policy priorities: designing fiscal rules to manage trade-offs; investing in the credibility of and commitment to rules; and fostering a supportive complementary policy environment.

Designing fiscal rules to manage trade-offs

Designing fiscal rules is inherently challenging and involves managing multiple trade-offs. Individual rule types and design features each have clear merits but combining multiple rules and features does not automatically lead to better policies. Designing and building an effective fiscal framework is a country-specific exercise that must begin with well-defined policy objectives and a sound diagnosis of underlying fiscal challenges.

A common principle, however, applies across contexts. To be successful, rule frameworks must strike a careful balance: they should be simple enough to be transparent and practicable, flexible enough to accommodate shocks, and credible enough to anchor expectations. It is up to policy makers to design and implement frameworks that achieve the best balance among these requisites in the contexts of their respective countries. In many cases, however, countries can fully achieve at most two of these requisites at once (Debrun and Jonung 2019). This underscores the need for prioritization to reach the appropriate balance, rather than mechanical adherence to every best practice.

Balancing enforceability, flexibility, and simplicity

Enforcement mechanisms can play an important role in ensuring compliance and strengthening the effective implementation of fiscal rules (Acalin, Martinez, and Roch 2025; Guerguil, Mandon, and Tapsoba 2017). This chapter shows that expenditure-based fiscal adjustments are more likely when such provisions are in place. Where pressures for excessive spending prevail, strengthening enforceability can be particularly important.

At the same time, enforcement mechanisms may place disproportionate emphasis on restraining expenditure, reflecting the fact that rapid budgetary actions are typically easier to implement on the spending side. Enforceability can therefore lose effectiveness, particularly in contexts where spending needs are rising. A more balanced framework—one that complements expenditure restraint with provisions supporting revenue mobilization—could improve the effectiveness of fiscal rules and the long-term sustainability of public finances.

Greater scope for adjustment within enforcement mechanisms, including longer adjustment paths, can also be important, as rapid fiscal improvements may come at the expense of productive expenditure. Public investment often bears a disproportionate share of fiscal adjustment (Servén 2007). Excluding priority items, such as public investment from numerical constraints, can protect growth-enhancing expenditure during periods of fiscal adjustment (Ardanaz et al. 2021). However, this should not undermine long-term fiscal sustainability. Exemptions from fiscal constraints carry the risk of creative accounting: the distinction between investment and consumption is blurred in many cases, and governments may exploit this ambiguity. Strong fiscal transparency and oversight are essential to prevent misuse and ensure that fiscal rule design remains effective in supporting credible fiscal adjustment (Gootjes and de Haan 2022; Milesi-Ferretti 2004).

Flexibility features can enhance the effectiveness of fiscal rules by allowing fiscal policy to adapt to changing economic conditions. To avoid procyclical policy adjustments, deficit limits can exclude cyclical effects and be set in terms of the cyclically adjusted or structural balance—if the country has the required administrative and statistical capacity and independent oversight. In the absence of such capacity and oversight, however, these adjustments risk encouraging strategic errors. Weaker institutions and less rigorous fiscal forecasting can allow cyclical estimates to be manipulated for political budgeting purposes, particularly when the numerical constraints of the fiscal rules are approached (Beetsma et al. 2013; Frankel 2011b).

One area where the design of fiscal rules could be improved is the specification of re-entry criteria following the use of escape clauses. Recent experience illustrates both the value and risks of

FIGURE 3.11 Effect of rule multiplicity and complexity on the start of a fiscal adjustment episode

Recent trends toward a greater number of fiscal rules per country and increasingly complex rule frameworks shape the channels through which rules induce fiscal adjustment—often in opposite ways. Expenditure-led consolidations tend to occur when multiple fiscal rules are in place, suggesting that expenditure restraint requires a more comprehensive rule architecture. Revenue-led adjustments are more likely under simpler rule frameworks.

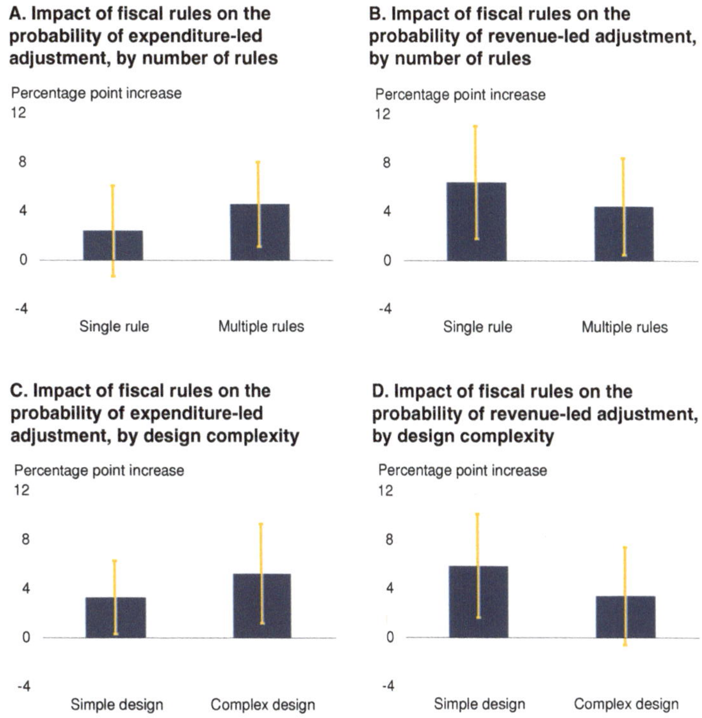

Sources: International Monetary Fund; World Bank.

Note: Results are from probit regressions. Technical details are provided in annex 3.4. Sample includes 122 economies, of which 89 are EMDEs and 33 are advanced economies. Vertical lines show 90 percent confidence intervals.

FIGURE 3.12 Suspension of fiscal rules

A large share of countries suspended their fiscal rules during the COVID-19 pandemic, largely by activating escape clauses, to allow critically needed fiscal stimulus. Many of these suspensions have lasted for several years. As of the end of 2024, one in eight fiscal rules remained suspended, with revenue rules most commonly inactive.

A. Suspension of fiscal rules | **B. Suspension of fiscal rules, by type of rule**

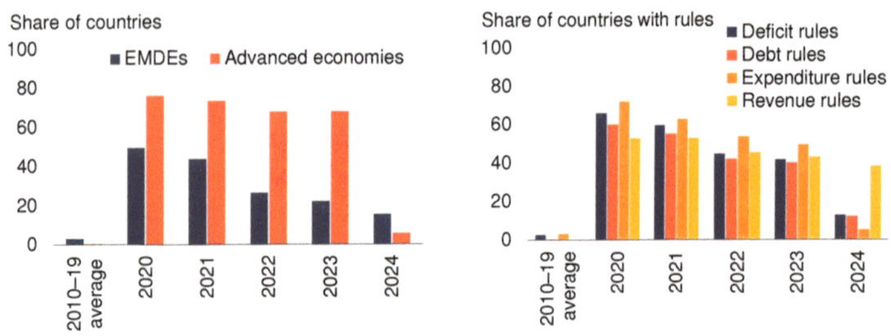

Sources: International Monetary Fund; World Bank.
Note: EMDEs = emerging market and developing economies. Sample includes 122 economies, of which 85 are EMDEs and 37 are advanced economies.

flexibility. In 2020, half of EMDEs and three-quarters of advanced economies suspended their fiscal rules countries to respond to shocks during the pandemic (refer to figure 3.12.A). Reactivation, however, has been uneven across countries. This largely reflects the fact that procedures for reactivating the rules are often vague and left to discretion. As of 2024, 15 percent of EMDEs still had inactive fiscal rules—three times the share in advanced economies. In advanced economies, EU rules were reactivated under a new framework that came into force in April 2024. Revenue rules have been particularly slow to be reactivated (refer to figure 3.12.B). In countries where rules are still inactive, the likelihood of timely fiscal adjustment is correspondingly lower.

One clear lesson is that layering multiple rules and numerous design features does not necessarily translate into stronger fiscal discipline or better fiscal outcomes. Preserving a degree of simplicity is therefore critical. Simple rules are easier to monitor, verify, and communicate than more complex ones, and they enhance accountability by making deviations more transparent and politically costly (Beetsma and Larch 2019; Hadfield and Weingast 2013). In addition, simpler—and, in many cases, clearer—rules can provide more effective guidance for investors, enabling markets to assess fiscal policy in relation to official objectives. In practice, the clarity of rules is typically a key driver of rule enforcement, sometimes more so than formal legal mechanisms (Kelemen and Teo 2014).

Rule design in challenging settings

Managing the trade-offs inherent in fiscal rule design is particularly challenging for countries with limited state capacity. Complex frameworks—for instance, multiple rules, each with several flexibility and enforcement provisions—are administratively demanding and require substantial statistical and technical capacity. Effective implementation also often relies on independent oversight, such as fiscal councils or expert panels, to monitor compliance and support credibility. Where state capacity is weak, countries may benefit from adopting a more streamlined fiscal framework that is clearer and easier to administer.

Evidence presented in this chapter shows that such streamlined frameworks can still be effective. Rule frameworks that preserve clarity and simplicity have been particularly important in enabling revenue-based fiscal adjustments. As many EMDEs face rising spending pressures, ensuring simplicity in fiscal rule design may be particularly important in fostering sound fiscal policy through revenue mobilization.

As to the choice of rules, deficit rules emerge as critical for both improving fiscal balances after adoption and for triggering fiscal adjustment episodes. Even in countries with relatively weak public institutions, deficit rules are found to be effective, helping to offset some of the challenges associated with adoption and implementation. In countries facing fiscal challenges beyond a deficit bias, complementary rule types may be useful for reinforcing the overall direction and credibility of the fiscal framework.

Design choices related to institutional coverage also matter for the effectiveness of fiscal rules. Fiscal rule frameworks that apply to the general government, rather than only the central government, are useful in limiting opportunities for deficit shifting across levels of government. Consistent with this, wider coverage of fiscal rules is associated with higher compliance, more so than any other design feature (Ardanaz, Ulloa-Suárez, and Valencia 2024). Although wider coverage does not fully offset institutional weaknesses, it can strengthen fiscal discipline without adding complexity. Notably, fiscal rules with broad government coverage significantly increase the likelihood of revenue-based adjustments.

Investing in credibility and commitment

Political constraints often hinder the implementation of fiscal rule frameworks, and fiscal governance reforms take time to yield results. Building and sustaining the credibility of fiscal rules is therefore essential. Credibility should be established early, when the momentum for implementing rules is strongest. Consequently, the context in which fiscal rules are adopted or reformed, including the state of the economy, matters. While certain circumstances may make rule adoption or reform politically expedient or practically feasible, achieving lasting gains in fiscal outcomes tends to be far more difficult. Especially when reforms are driven primarily by immediate pressures that call for rapid action, their long-term sustainability may be uncertain. Credibility can take time to build. A significant risk is that tangible results fail to materialize quickly enough to prevent the erosion of credibility before it takes root.

Policy makers should recognize that the usefulness and strength of fiscal rules depend on a long-term, broad-based, political commitment to fiscal discipline. The key to achieving such a commitment lies in actively building broad-based consensus, even—and perhaps especially—when the political strength of the government makes coalition-building unnecessary in the short term. Preparing well-designed fiscal rules that address structural challenges and that are backed by broad consensus usually requires time and careful negotiation among the government, opposition parties, and other stakeholders. But the benefits of such efforts for fiscal sustainability should far outweigh the costs of forgoing faster action whose effects are transitory.

Fostering a complementary policy environment

Fiscal rules are unlikely to be effective in promoting fiscal discipline or supporting macroeconomic stability in isolation. For rules to be effective, domestic policy makers and the international community must build complementary policy frameworks. This includes strengthening institutions, deepening revenue mobilization, enhancing spending efficiency, expanding access to concessional financing, and pursuing responsible debt management.

Complementary policy frameworks

The credibility of fiscal rules can be bolstered by complementary fiscal and monetary policy frameworks. Fiscal rules tend to be more effective when they are embedded in medium-term fiscal frameworks that align annual budgets with long-term fiscal objectives (Cangiano, Curristine, and Lazare 2013; Davoodi et al. 2022). Among EMDEs that have adopted fiscal rules, about one-quarter also have a medium-term fiscal framework, a far smaller share than among advanced economies (refer to figure 3.13.A). However, EMDEs have become far more likely to have both over the past decade. Fiscal councils can also strengthen the effectiveness of fiscal rules by overseeing compliance, assessing fiscal sustainability, and providing independent analysis (Beetsma et al. 2019). On this aspect of policy, EMDEs also lag advanced economies (refer to figure 3.13.B).

Supportive frameworks for monetary policy and the management of foreign assets, including inflation-targeting and sovereign wealth funds—and especially stabilization funds—can also enhance the effectiveness of fiscal rules (Keita and Turcu 2022). Thus, the joint use of fiscal rules and inflation targeting is associated with lower inflation and inflation volatility in developing countries than use of only one of these frameworks (Combes et al. 2018). However, inflation-targeting frameworks are used by only minorities of both EMDEs and advanced economies with fiscal rules (refer to figure 3.13.C). By contrast, the use of sovereign wealth funds in EMDEs is nearly as high as in advanced economies, with slightly more than half of EMDEs with fiscal rules also having established such funds (refer to figure 3.13.D).

Governance and institutions

Institutional and government effectiveness are generally lower in EMDEs than in advanced economies (refer to figure 3.14.A). Despite

FIGURE 3.13 Fiscal rules and complementary policy frameworks

About one-fourth of EMDEs with fiscal rules also had a medium-term fiscal framework at the end of 2024—a notable increase since 2010, though still well below the roughly three-fifths in advanced economies. The use of fiscal councils—independent public institutions that analyze, assess, and publicly report on fiscal policy—remains much less common in EMDEs than in advanced economies. About one-third of EMDEs with fiscal rules have adopted inflation targets, a slightly higher proportion than among advanced economies. Sovereign wealth funds have become increasingly common among both EMDEs and advanced economies with fiscal rules: More than half of countries in each group have adopted them.

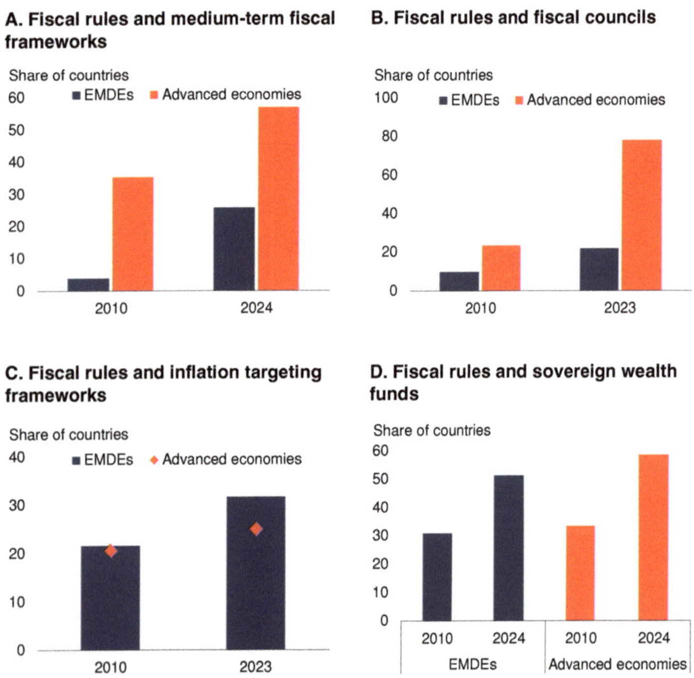

Sources: Global SWF (database); International Monetary Fund; World Bank.

Note: EMDEs = emerging market and developing economies.

A. Bars show the share of countries that have a fiscal rule in place and a medium-term fiscal framework. Sample includes up to 85 EMDEs and up to 37 advanced economies.

B. Bars show the share of countries with fiscal rules and fiscal councils in place in each period. Sample includes up to 82 EMDEs and up to 36 advanced economies.

C. Bars and markers show the share of countries with fiscal rules and an inflation targeting framework in each year. Sample includes up to 82 EMDEs and up to 36 advanced economies.

D. Bars show the share of countries with a fiscal rule and a sovereign wealth fund in the indicated years. Sample includes up to 85 EMDEs and up to 37 advanced economies.

notable progress in adopting modern fiscal policy frameworks, substantial capacity gaps persist in key areas of fiscal policy design and coordination. Institutions responsible for fiscal policy management remain fragile and, in many cases, have weakened in recent years—particularly in LICs (refer to figure 3.14.B). Statistical capacity remains low, on average, in EMDEs despite recent progress, and many remain data-poor, with limited capacity for the timely generation and analysis of reliable statistics (refer to figure 3.14.C). EMDEs also rank lower, on average, on measures of budget transparency (refer to figure 3.14.D). Such institutional and data weaknesses can undermine technical analyses, give rise to faulty policy decisions, and blunt the effectiveness of fiscal rules (Gatti et al. 2024; Gootjes and de Haan 2022). For EMDEs, priority areas for improving institutional effectiveness include establishing and adequately resourcing key fiscal institutions, improving budget transparency and accountability, and advancing the digitalization of core public financial management functions.

Revenue mobilization

Given the need to scale up productive public spending to close critical development gaps, improving revenue mobilization remains a priority in many EMDEs (McNabb, Danquah, and Tagem 2021). This is particularly important because tax collection continues to fall significantly short of potential in many countries. Improved revenue mobilization can also yield strong growth dividends, which can improve conditions for the effectiveness of fiscal rules (Choudhary, Ruch, and Skrok 2024). In general, revenue mobilization efforts should go hand in hand with measures to enhance spending efficiency and strengthen debt management practices.

Fiscal rules can support revenue mobilization by setting numerical constraints on government revenues. Fiscal rules can also regulate the treatment of windfall receipts, helping to strengthen fiscal discipline and reduce procyclical behavior by anchoring expectations and limiting persistent revenue shortfalls or the spending of unexpected gains. To improve revenue mobilization, revenue rules can be more tightly aligned with domestic resource mobilization strategies, particularly in countries where tax revenue performance is weak (Akitoby et al. 2018). The evidence presented in this chapter suggests that fiscal rules with broad coverage (targeting the general government) are more likely to lead to revenue-based fiscal adjustments, which may be preferable to expenditure-based adjustments, especially for LICs (Arizala et al. 2021; Cardoso and de Carvalho 2023).

Revenue mobilization can also be improved by broadening the tax base—particularly through the removal of exemptions, improved compliance, and greater reliance on underutilized taxes, such as property taxes (refer to figure 3.14.E). Advancing the use of technology and digitalization in tax administrations, including through e-filing, e-payments, e-invoicing, and the application of artificial intelligence and big data, can yield substantial efficiency and revenue gains (Junquera-Varela et al. 2022; Okunogbe and Santoro 2023).

Global policies

The international community can play a critical role in helping EMDEs strengthen their fiscal policy frameworks and advance needed reforms. This includes providing technical assistance, support for capacity-building programs, and greater concessional financing to alleviate financing constraints and help stabilize fiscal positions. Such assistance is essential for bolstering institutional capacity in EMDEs and promoting the use and effectiveness of fiscal rules. Official development assistance flows to EMDEs—and especially grants—have recently been declining rapidly (refer to figure 3.14.F). International coordination on tax matters is paramount for effective revenue mobilization in EMDEs. Closing loopholes in the treatment of international transactions and cross-border profits, including through the adoption of global tax transparency standards and strengthened transfer pricing rules, can further enhance revenue mobilization and limit base erosion (IMF 2023).

FIGURE 3.14 Governance and institutional challenges in EMDEs

Government effectiveness is weaker in EMDEs than in advanced economies. The institutions for fiscal policy management in EMDEs have deteriorated in recent years, particularly in LICs, and statistical capacity remains far weaker in EMDEs than in advanced economies, despite improvements. EMDEs have made limited progress in enhancing fiscal transparency since 2010. They have also made limited progress in strengthening tax revenue performance, collecting on average 18 percent of GDP, about half the level in advanced economies. Official development assistance flows to EMDEs—and especially grants—have declined markedly in recent years.

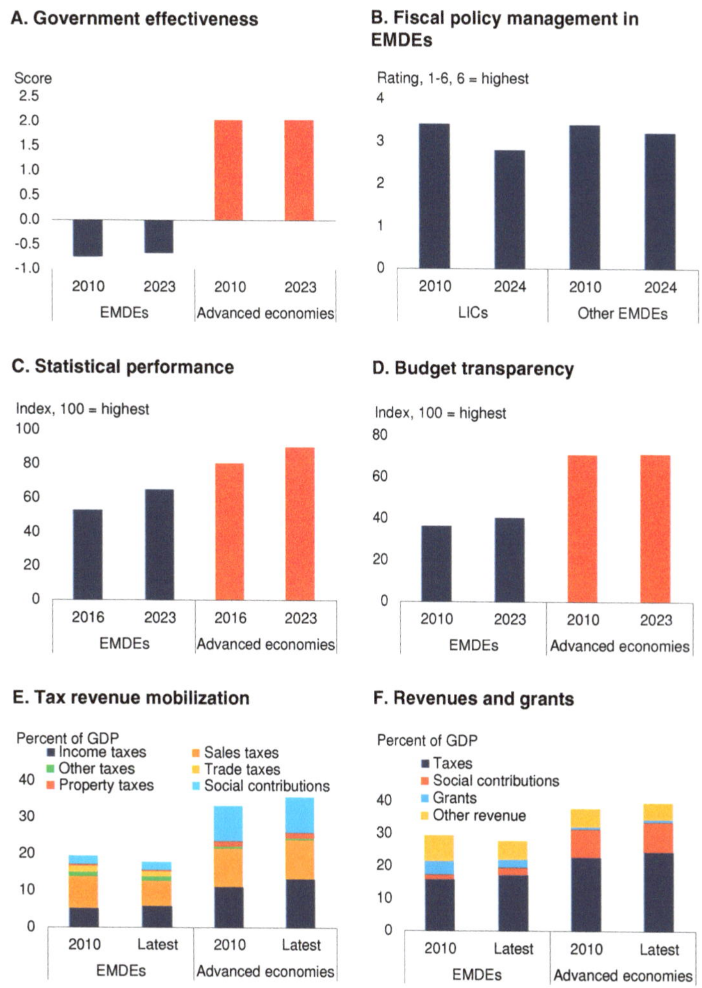

Sources: International Budget Partnership; International Monetary Fund; Organisation for Economic Co-operation and Development; World Bank.

Note: EMDEs = emerging market and developing economies; LICs = low-income countries.

A. Bars shows simple averages. Scores range from a minimum of –2.5 to a maximum of 2.5, where a higher value indicates better performance. Sample includes up to 100 EMDEs and up to 36 advanced economies.

B. Bars show unweighted averages of the CPIA fiscal policy management score. CPIA fiscal policy criterion assesses the quality of fiscal policy in its stabilization and allocation functions. Ratings range from 1 to 6, where 6 is the highest. Sample includes 62 EMDEs.

C. Bars show the unweighted average of the "overall" index in the World Bank's Statistical Performance Indicators, which cover five areas: data use, data services, data products, data sources, and data infrastructure. Sample includes up to 150 EMDEs and up to 37 advanced economies.

D. Aggregation by country group of the Open Budget Index is done using unweighted averages. Sample includes up to 107 EMDEs and up to 18 advanced economies.

E. Bars show unweighted averages. Sample includes up to 28 advanced economies and up to 36 EMDEs.

F. Aggregation of revenue components by country group is computed as unweighted average. Sample includes up to 100 EMDEs and up to 30 advanced economies.

ANNEX 3.1 The effects of fiscal rules in EMDEs: A literature review

Research on fiscal rules in EMDEs has increased steadily over the past 25 years (refer to figure A3.1.1.A). Much of the research in the 2010s focused on Latin America and the Caribbean (LAC), where several countries introduced fiscal rules in the late 1990s and early 2000s following financial and debt crises (refer to figure A3.1.1.B). A subsequent wave examined Sub-Saharan Africa (SSA), where the adoption of fiscal rules accelerated in the late 2000s and early 2010s. In the 2020s, as fiscal rules have become widespread, interest has shifted toward multiregional studies.

Evidence on whether fiscal rules have strengthened fiscal sustainability in EMDEs is mixed: most studies document positive effects, yet some find insignificant or even adverse effects, often attributed to contextual factors.[11] This annex synthesizes the literature on fiscal, macroeconomic, and distributional effects of fiscal rules in EMDEs and the institutional, economic, and political factors shaping their effectiveness.

Fiscal rules and fiscal sustainability

Fiscal discipline

Most studies find that fiscal rules improve fiscal performance in EMDEs, including by improving primary balances and reducing the prevalence of political budget cycles (refer to figure A3.1.1.C; Eklou and Joanis 2019; Strong 2023a). Rules are also associated with better debt outcomes (Andrián et al. 2024; Strong 2023b), lower borrowing costs (Afonso and Jalles 2019; Gomez-Gonzalez, Valencia, and Sánchez 2024), a lower likelihood of sovereign debt crises (Asatryan, Castellón, and Stratmann 2018), and lower reliance on foreign-currency borrowing (Apeti et al. 2024).

Fiscal procyclicality

Early work focused on whether fiscal rules have mitigated fiscal procyclicality—a persistent challenge in EMDEs (Gavin and Perotti 1997; Kaminsky, Reinhart, and Vegh 2004). Although initial findings showed mixed outcomes, more recent studies increasingly associate fiscal rules in EMDEs with macroeconomic stabilization, including through countercyclical policies (refer to figure A3.1.1.D; Combes, Minea, and Sow 2017; Jalles 2018; Keita and Turcu 2022). Even among commodity-exporting EMDEs and LICs, where the management of fiscal policy is often challenged by the volatility of commodity prices, fiscal rules have helped mitigate procyclicality.[12] In some cases, however, fiscal rules are found to induce procyclicality and volatility by forcing expenditures to follow revenues (Coulibaly 2015). Further, the patterns of such negative impacts differ across country groups and by the level of fiscal space, with particularly pernicious outcomes in countries with high debt, weak institutions, or weak fiscal and macroeconomic frameworks (Keita and Turcu 2022; Yelkesen and Iyidogan 2025).

Expenditure outcomes

Most studies find that fiscal rules help curb government consumption growth while leaving public investment largely unaffected (Vinturis 2023). Notably, they are found to protect public investment during fiscal consolidations (Ardanaz et al. 2021). By promoting predictability, fiscal rules can also reduce spending volatility (Cordes et al. 2015; Mendoza Bellido et al. 2021). Recent evidence suggests that fiscal rules can improve government spending efficiency (Apeti, Bambe, and Combes 2025).

Revenue mobilization

Evidence from as-yet limited literature suggests that fiscal rules can support domestic revenue mobilization efforts in EMDEs (Beyala 2025). Well-

[11] For recent comprehensive surveys of the literature on fiscal rules, refer to Brändle and Elsener (2024) and Potrafke (2025). Heinemann, Moessinger, and Yeter (2018) provide a useful meta-regression analysis. However, these studies focus primarily on advanced economies. In this annex, studies with samples limited to advanced economies or subnational rules are excluded, while those with samples including only EMDEs or a combination of EMDEs and advanced economies are retained.

[12] Apeti, Basdevant, and Salins (2023) and Céspedes and Velasco (2014) analyze the effects of fiscal rules in commodity-exporting EMDEs. Dessus, Diaz-Sanchez, and Varoudakis (2016) and Mawejje and Odhiambo (2024) study the effects in the West African Economic and Monetary Union and East African Community countries, respectively.

designed revenue can enhance the countercyclicality of tax policy, thereby improving the effectiveness of fiscal policy over the business cycle (Chrysanthakopoulos and Tagkalakis 2023a). Such rules tend to be more effective when implemented alongside other fiscal rules or when embedded within broader domestic fiscal frameworks (Jalles 2018).

Other macroeconomic outcomes

Recent studies extend the analysis beyond fiscal sustainability to assess a wider range of outcomes, including growth, investment, inequality, and external balances. Fiscal rules are associated with lower output volatility (Arroyo Marioli, Fatás, and Vasishtha 2024; Badinger and Reuter 2017b), and they can also reduce inflation risks by curtailing fiscal dominance (Zoumenou 2025).

Fiscal rules can strengthen sovereign creditworthiness, mitigate the sovereign-bank nexus, and foster broader financial sector stability (Coulibaly and Diallo 2025). Fiscal rules can foster cross-border financial integration (Ech-charfi 2024) and ease credit constraints, improving market access (Islamaj, Penaloza, and Sommers 2024; Sawadogo 2020; Thornton and Vasilakis 2020). Moreover, fiscal rules can enhance external sector sustainability (Afonso et al. 2022), lower sovereign risk (Gomez-Gonzalez, Valencia, and Sánchez 2022), and reduce the probability of a sudden reversal of capital flows (Buda 2024).

Evidence on growth and distributional effects is mixed (refer to figure A3.1.1.E). Some studies find sizable long-term growth gains (Grundler and Potrafke 2020; Misra and Ranjan 2018), while others show adverse effects, underscoring that their impacts can be context specific (Nabieu et al. 2021). At the same time, fiscal rules can affect income inequality through their differentiated effects on taxation, spending, and debt (Combes et al. 2024; Baret 2023).

Building on the literature on the effect of fiscal policy on employment, a small but growing body of research finds that fiscal rules can impact jobs and other labor market conditions in several ways, including by shaping economic activity, investment, and income inequality (Bova, Kolerus, and Tapsoba 2015; IMF 2014). Fiscal rules enhance the positive effects of discretionary fiscal policy on unemployment (Gehrke 2019).

FIGURE A3.1.1 Literature on the effectiveness of fiscal rules

There is growing interest in the impact and effectiveness of fiscal rules in EMDEs. Most studies are multiregional, while region-specific studies focus predominantly on LAC and SSA. The literature finds that the effectiveness of fiscal rules is conditional on rule design, institutional quality, and the economic environment in which they operate. Compliance with fiscal rules is a necessary condition for their effectiveness.

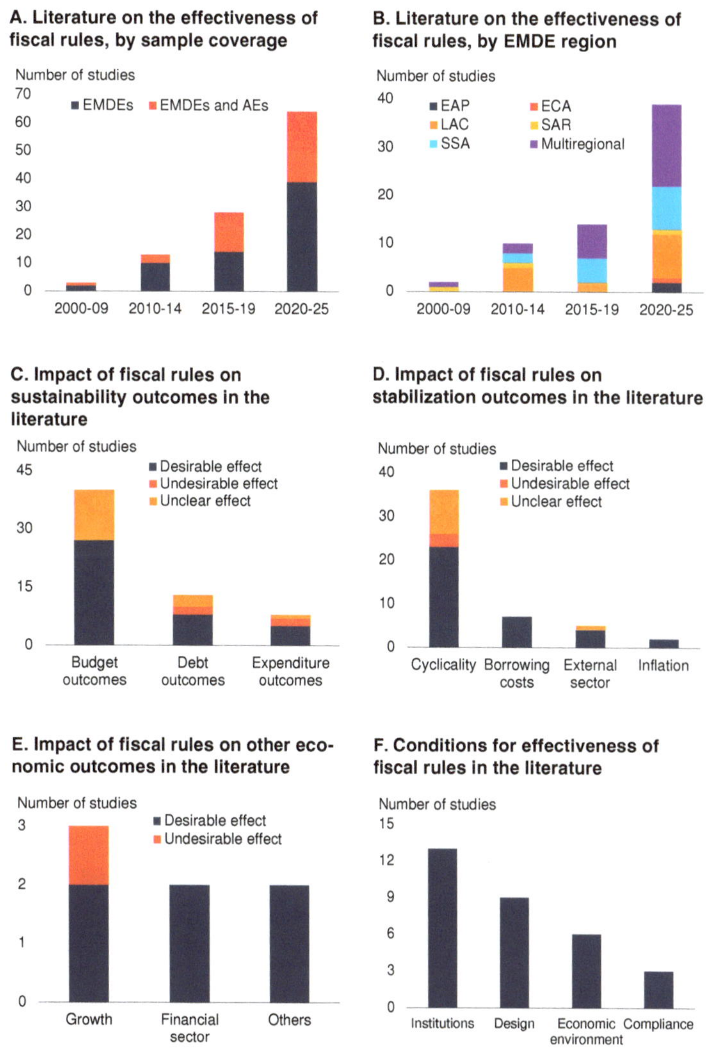

Source: World Bank

Note: AEs = advanced economies; EAP = East Asia and Pacific; ECA = Europe and Central Asia; EMDEs = emerging market and developing economies; LAC = Latin America and the Caribbean; SAR = South Asia; SSA = Sub-Saharan Africa. Results are based on 108 studies, including 65 using samples of only EMDEs and 43 using samples of EMDEs and advanced economies.

A.B. Year spans correspond with publication dates of the underlying studies.

C.-F. Bars show simple count of studies.

E. "Others" include inequality and private investment.

Conditions for effectiveness of fiscal rules

Broadly, the literature highlights the importance of the design of fiscal rules, supportive institutional frameworks, institutional quality, compliance, and macroeconomic conditions in fostering the disciplining effects of fiscal rules (refer to figure A3.1.1.F).

Design of fiscal rules

Rule design is central to effectiveness (Caselli and Reynaud 2020; Gootjes, de Haan, and Jong-A-Pin 2021). Rules with flexible mechanisms, well-designed escape clauses, effective monitoring, enforcement, and correction mechanisms, broad coverage, and a solid legal foundation tend to be more effective (Acalin et al. 2025; Ardanaz et al. 2021; Guerguil, Mandon, and Tapsoba 2017). By contrast, poorly designed rules can fail to improve fiscal discipline and, in some cases, may increase volatility or undermine growth (Afonso and Jalles 2015; Arezki and Ismail 2013; Nabieu et al. 2021).

Supranational frameworks

The literature on the effectiveness of supranational fiscal rules in EMDEs is limited but shows mixed results (for instance, Dessus, Diaz-Sanchez, and Varoudakis 2016; Mpatswe, Tapsoba, and York 2011). Supranational fiscal rules are typically anchored in a high legal framework and can enhance policy credibility. By imposing external commitments, they can help overcome political economy constraints that hinder national rule adoption or compliance. As such, supranational rules can outperform national rules (Lehtimäki 2025). However, these rules also face challenges. They are often less responsive to country-specific circumstances, harder to adjust in the face of economic shocks, and subject to enforcement dilemmas—especially when political will or institutional capacity to sanction noncompliance is limited.

Compliance with fiscal rules

Rules tend to be less effective when compliance is low or nonbinding (Blanco et al. 2020; Cordes et al. 2015). However, even partial adherence can yield benefits if rules serve as credible "benchmarks" (Reuter 2015). Compliance itself is shaped by macroeconomic and political conditions (Ulloa-Suárez 2023) and is reinforced by strong institutions, independent monitoring, and well-designed rule features (Andrián et al. 2024; Ardanaz, Ulloa-Suárez, and Valencia 2024).

Institutional quality

The effectiveness of fiscal rules is greater in countries with stronger governance, characterized by higher transparency, lower corruption, and tighter limits on bureaucratic discretion (Bergman and Hutchison 2015; Gootjes and de Haan 2022; Hansen 2020). In contrast, where such institutional foundations are weak, fiscal rules often lack the credibility and enforcement power needed to anchor fiscal discipline (Bova, Medas, and Poghosyan 2018). In countries with weak public financial management and low investment efficiency, fiscal rules can have unintended consequences—curbing public investment and heightening volatility (Basdevant et al. 2020).

Economic environment

The broader economic environment also matters for the effectiveness of fiscal rules. Several studies highlight that fiscal rules tend to be more effective during periods of favorable economic conditions, even when they are well designed and supported by strong political institutions (Andrián et al. 2024; Combes, Minea, and Sow 2017). Structural characteristics play a conditioning role as well: fiscal rules tend to be less effective in economies with high informality or commodity dependence (Guerguil, Mandon, and Tapsoba 2017; Mara and Maran 2024).

Complementary frameworks

Fiscal rules are more effective when embedded in or complemented by supportive institutional arrangements such as medium-term expenditure frameworks or stabilization funds (Beetsma et al. 2019; Pouokam 2021). Their credibility and impact are further enhanced when accompanied by independent fiscal councils (Hagemann 2011). Supportive macro–fiscal interactions, including inflation-targeting frameworks and sovereign wealth funds, also enhance fiscal rule effectiveness (Alsweilem and Rietveld 2018; Combes et al. 2018).

Political economy

Evidence on the role of politico-economic factors in shaping the effectiveness of fiscal rules is mixed. Some studies find that rules are less effective in contexts of government fragmentation (Tapsoba 2012). Conversely, political consensus and low polarization improve rule performance (Piguillem and Riboni 2021). In resource-rich countries, contestation over the distribution of revenues can weaken institutions and, in turn, undermine the effectiveness of fiscal frameworks (Eyraud, Gbohoui, and Medas 2023).

ANNEX 3.2 Local projections to estimate dynamic effects of fiscal rule adoption

To begin an assessment of whether changes in fiscal balances are attributable to discretionary policy decisions, the chapter constructs estimates of the cyclically-adjusted primary balance (CAPB)—that is, the fiscal balance stripping out interest payments and the effects of economic fluctuations—at the country level. The resulting CAPB series is used in a local projections (LP) model to estimate the dynamic effects of fiscal rule adoption. Data on fiscal rules are sourced from the IMF's Fiscal Rules dataset (Alonso et al. 2025). Annual data on macroeconomic variables are sourced from the IMF's October 2025 World Economic Outlook (WEO) database. This section provides a condensed overview of the CAPB estimation and LP framework; full details are available in Fatás, Gootjes, and Mawejje (2026).

Cyclically adjusted primary balance

The CAPB is estimated following the methodology outlined by Fedelino, Ivanova, and Horton (2009):

$$CAPB_t = r_t * \left(\frac{Y_t^*}{Y_t}\right)^{\varepsilon R} - g_t * \left(\frac{Y_t^*}{Y_t}\right)^{\varepsilon G} \qquad \text{(A.3.2.1)},$$

where r_t is government revenue as a share of GDP, g_t is primary expenditure (government expenditure excluding interest payments) as a share of GDP, Y_t is actual real output, and Y_t^* is trend output estimated using a Hodrick-Prescott (HP) filter.[13] The parameters ε_r and ε_g denote the elasticities of revenue and primary expenditure with respect to the output gap, respectively.

Following standard practice in the literature, it is assumed that government revenues respond one-for-one to deviations of actual output from trend ($\varepsilon_r = 1$), while government expenditure is assumed to be non-cyclical ($\varepsilon_g = 0$). However, advanced economies often have built-in automatic stabilizers on both the revenue and expenditure sides, such as unemployment benefits. Girouard and André (2005) estimate that government spending in OECD member countries typically exhibits a negative elasticity of approximately –0.25. Hence, for advanced economies, the elasticity ε_g is set to -0.25.

Local projections

The sample includes 116 countries, with 58 cases of fiscal rule adoption. The starting year is 1984, reflecting the earliest availability of all relevant data for the control variables. The response of the CAPB is studied over a 10-year period following the introduction of fiscal rules. With fiscal rules data available up to 2024, the effects of rules adopted up to 2015 are investigated.

The 10-year timeframe is chosen to observe the immediate, medium-term, and long-term effects of introducing fiscal rules. It is assumed that the impact of fiscal rule adoption stabilizes after 10 years. This rationale is also applied by Dube et al. (2025) in examining the effect of democratization on output.

The response of the CAPB after the adoption of fiscal rules is estimated using the LP approach of Jordà (2005):

$$\Delta_h f_{i,t+h} = \varphi^h FR_{it} + \sum_{j=-s, j\neq 0}^{h} \omega_j^h FR_{it+j} + \sum_{k=1}^{K} \beta_k^h X_{k,it} + \mu_i^h + \tau_t^h + \varepsilon_{it+h}; h = 0,1,\ldots,H \qquad \text{(A.3.2.2)},$$

[13] The HP filter is used because it yields results that are more consistent with those presented in the IMF's *Fiscal Monitor*, making it the preferable choice for reasons of comparability. Alternative filtering techniques proposed in the literature, such as the Hamilton filter, generate different outcomes.

where $\Delta_h f_{i,t+h} \equiv f_{i,t+h} - f_{i,t-1}$ represents the cumulative change in the CAPB (as a percent of trend GDP) from time t-1 to $t+h$, with fiscal rule adoption occurring in year t. As the response of the CAPB is examined for the first ten years after fiscal rule adoption, H is set to 9. Only countries with at least 10 observations per projection horizon h are included, ensuring a theoretical rolling window of at least 20 observations of the primary balance.[14] μ_i and τ_t control for country and time fixed effects (for each projection of the primary balance, time-fixed effects are included with leads equal to h), respectively. ε_{it+h} is an error term.

Two lags of the CAPB are included in $X_{k,it}$, with an additional lag added to address serial correlation in the regression residuals (Montiel Olea and Plagborg-Møller 2021). The fiscal rules indicator (FR_{it}) is set to one in the year a fiscal rule is introduced and zero in all other years, modeling rule adoption as a treatment effect akin to that in difference-in-difference event studies, following Afonso and Jalles (2019).

To mitigate potential endogeneity in fiscal rule adoption, the analysis relies on a doubly robust approach—augmented inverse-probability weighting (AIPW), as set out by Jordà and Taylor (2016). In the first stage, propensity scores are calculated to predict the probability of having a fiscal rule in place, using the full set of controls as specified in vector $\boldsymbol{X}_{k,it}$. In the second stage, weights are assigned in the LP regression based on these propensity scores: observations with fiscal rules in place are weighted by the inverse of the probability score (w =1/p), while observations without rules are weighted by the inverse of one minus the probability score [w = 1/(1–p)].

For the LP-AIPW regression to yield an unbiased estimate of the average treatment effect on the treated, several adjustments are required. First, to control for the initial impact of rule adoption on the CAPB, four lags of the fiscal rule indicator are included. Second, leads of the fiscal rule indicator are included to account for future adoptions (Teulings and Zubanov 2014). Results presented in Fatás, Gootjes, and Mawejje (2026) support the validity of the LP-AIPW estimates, by examining pre-treatment dynamics and potential anticipation effects, and by applying the clean control condition proposed by Dube et al. (2025).

Each of the 58 cases of fiscal rule adoption included in the regressions represents the implementation of one or more fiscal rules in a context where no such rule existed in the preceding year. The analysis thus focuses on cases of newly (re)installed fiscal rules, excluding subsequent adoptions or amendments. Later adoptions are instead treated as secondary treatment effects within the control set.

The vector $\boldsymbol{X}_{k,it}$ contains several control variables to account for other factors that may influence the CAPB. It includes measures capturing the broader macroeconomic environment: the debt-to-GDP ratio (in levels and in squared terms), real GDP growth, inflation, and current account balance (all lagged by one period to address endogeneity concerns). The regressions further control for the presence of an election year and the institutional environment, with the institutional environment measured using principal component analysis based on indexes of rule of law, democratic accountability, bureaucratic quality, and control of corruption from the International Country Risk Guide database (refer to Fatás, Gootjes, and Mawejje 2026). Controls for the presence of other economic policy frameworks affecting the CAPB are also included: specifically, the presence of an inflation targeting regime (from the IMF's Annual Report on the Exchange Arrangements and Exchange Restrictions database), the prevailing exchange rate regime (from Ilzetzki, Reinhart, and Rogoff 2019), capital account openness (from Chinn and Ito 2006), and the presence of an independent fiscal council (from the IMF Fiscal Council dataset). Finally, the model accounts for financial market development, which proxies a country's capacity to finance debt (measured using the IMF's Financial Development Index), and adds a dummy for participation in the Heavily Indebted Poor Countries initiative.

[14] The actual window may be smaller in some cases, as countries with extreme volatility are excluded from the sample. See Fatás, Gootjes, and Mawejje (2025) for more details.

ANNEX 3.3 Structural break tests to identify fiscal adjustment episodes

Fiscal adjustment episodes are identified by testing for structural breaks in fiscal variables using the approach developed by Bai and Perron (1998, 2003). The Bai–Perron approach enables the detection of statistically significant shifts in the underlying data-generating process. Therefore, it avoids reliance on arbitrary thresholds for fiscal variables that are uniformly applied across countries (Wiese, de Haan, and Jong-A-Pin 2018).

The procedure consists of two main steps. First, the null hypothesis of no structural breaks is tested against the alternative hypothesis of $1 \le m \le M$ breaks, where M denotes the predetermined maximum number of breaks. If the null hypothesis is rejected, sequential F-tests are conducted to compare models with m versus $m + 1$ breaks. At least 25 years of country-level data are required for a country to be included in the analysis. The potential number of breaks is constrained by assuming that, on average, only one break can occur every 10 years, setting the maximum number of breaks as $M = \text{int}\,(T/10)$, where T denotes the number of observations. In addition, a minimum spacing of four years between breaks is imposed. To address potential serial correlation, a heteroskedasticity- and autocorrelation-consistent covariance matrix estimator is used.

Once structural breaks are determined, fiscal adjustment episodes at the country level are identified when there is a positive change in the cyclically adjusted primary balance (CAPB) as a percent of trend GDP for at least two consecutive years, beginning in the year following a structural break. Adjustment episodes are considered to continue beyond the two-year threshold for as many years as the change in the CAPB-to-GDP ratio remains positive. If a structural break is detected but the fiscal stance does not continue in the same direction in the following year, the episode is not counted. Beyond the two-year threshold, a "gap year"—a year in which the trend temporarily stalls—is allowed, provided the trend persists for at least two additional years and that the first year following the interruption at least compensates for the deviation in the gap year.

Changes in the CAPB as a percent of trend GDP are used to identify fiscal adjustment episodes because they are more likely to reflect government policy. Other forces—such as macroeconomic conditions, exchange rate movements, and shifts in financial market conditions—also influence fiscal conditions, but are less likely to be under the direct control of the government.

To validate that the identified fiscal adjustment episodes reflect policy-driven efforts to strengthen fiscal sustainability, their overlap with studies employing narrative-based identification approaches is examined (Carrière-Swallow, David, and Leigh 2021; Devries et al. 2011; Gootjes 2025). The results correspond closely with those identified using structural break tests.

ANNEX 3.4 Discrete choice model to estimate the probability of starting fiscal adjustment episodes

To examine the probability of initiating a fiscal adjustment episode, a probit model is estimated:

$$y_{it} = 1 \; \textit{if} \; y_{it}^{*} > 0 \qquad \text{(A.3.4.1)},$$
$$y_{it} = 0 \; \textit{otherwise}$$

where the latent variable y_{it}^{*} is defined as:

$$y_{it}^{*} = \alpha + X_{it}'\beta + \mu_i + \varepsilon_{it}.$$

The dependent variable y_{it} takes the value of 1 if an episode begins in country i at time t, and 0 otherwise. The latent variable captures the underlying propensity to start such an episode and is modeled as a function of a constant (α), the set of observed covariates (X_{it}'), the unobserved country-specific characteristics (μ_i), and a stochastic error term (ε_{it}). The corresponding probability of a fiscal episode starting is given by:

$$P(y_{it} = 1) = P(y_{it}^{*} > 0) = P(\varepsilon_{it} > -\alpha - X_{it}'\beta - \mu_i)$$
$$= F(-\alpha - X_{it}'\beta - \mu_i) \qquad \text{(A.3.4.2)}.$$

To capture the start of a fiscal adjustment episode, a three-year window centered on the identified start year is used. Specifically, if an episode begins in year *t*, the years *t*-1, *t*, and *t*+1 are all assigned a value of one. This approach helps mitigate the risk of missing the true start of an episode on account of potential errors in the data or imperfections in the identification method. A similar strategy has been employed in the literature to examine the determinants of growth acceleration episodes (Hausmann et al. 2005). All subsequent years that are part of a fiscal adjustment episode beyond *t*+1 are excluded from the analysis. Additionally, the first four years following the end of an identified episode are omitted, as they cannot serve as starting points for new episodes.

In the baseline specification, a 0 or 1 indicator is included to capture whether fiscal rules are present. Further specifications include more detailed information on rule types and granular design elements, based on data from the IMF's Fiscal Rules dataset (Alonso et al. 2025). To control for potential confounding effects, half-decade fixed effects are included to account for global time-specific factors, while a set of country-group indicators (binary variables for EMDEs, energy exporters, metal exporters, agricultural exporters, and small states) accounts for unobserved heterogeneity across country types.

The model further incorporates key indicators of the fiscal and macroeconomic environment, including the primary balance (as a share of GDP), public debt (as a share of GDP), interest payments (as a share of government revenues), real GDP growth, inflation (measured using the GDP deflator), and the current account balance (as a share of GDP), using data from the IMF's World Economic Outlook database (October 2025). All these variables are lagged to mitigate potential endogeneity.

Finally, the specification includes indicators for whether a country received IMF credit and international support under the HIPC Initiative, along with a composite index of political-institutional quality to capture institutional capacity (Fatás, Gootjes, and Mawejje 2026). The results are shown in table A3.4.1. [15]

[15] Including political economy factors in the set of controls yields similar results but substantially reduces the country sample. For this reason, these variables are excluded from the baseline specification.

TABLE A3.4.1 Probit results on the likelihood of fiscal adjustment episodes

	All fiscal adjustments	EMDEs	Advanced economies	Interaction result	Expenditure-led episodes	Revenue-led episodes
	(1)	(2)	(3)	(4)	(5)	(6)
Fiscal rules (*t*)	0.76***	0.76***	0.87*	0.76***	0.81**	0.90**
	(0.24)	(0.28)	(0.51)	(0.25)	(0.34)	(0.40)
EMDE	-0.42			-0.41	-1.53	-0.87
	(0.42)			(0.43)	(1.09)	(0.89)
Primary balance (t_{-2})	-0.11***	-0.07***	-0.18***	-0.11***	-0.08***	-0.06**
	(0.02)	(0.02)	(0.03)	(0.02)	(0.02)	(0.03)
Public debt (t_{-2})	0.01***	0.01**	0.01	0.01***	0.01***	0.01***
	(0.00)	(0.00)	(0.01)	(0.00)	(0.00)	(0.00)
Interest payments (t_{-2})	0.05***	0.04***	0.14***	0.05***	0.07***	0.05***
	(0.01)	(0.01)	(0.05)	(0.01)	(0.02)	(0.02)
Real GDP growth (t_{-2})	0.00	0.01	0.02	0.00	-0.01	0.01
	(0.02)	(0.02)	(0.02)	(0.02)	(0.01)	(0.02)
Inflation (t_{-2})	-0.14***	-0.12***	-0.25***	-0.14***	-0.21***	-0.13***
	(0.04)	(0.04)	(0.09)	(0.04)	(0.06)	(0.05)
Current account balance (t_{-2})	0.05***	0.04***	0.05	0.05***	0.06***	0.06***
	(0.01)	(0.01)	(0.03)	(0.01)	(0.02)	(0.02)
HIPC (*t*)	-0.19	-0.32		-0.19		0.31
	(0.40)	(0.39)		(0.40)		(0.49)
IMF credit support (*t*)	0.15	0.03		0.15	1.06	0.31
	(0.39)	(0.40)		(0.39)	(0.74)	(0.83)
Public institutions (*t*)	0.11	0.07	-0.00	0.10	0.18	0.01
	(0.12)	(0.16)	(0.25)	(0.13)	(0.24)	(0.19)
Fiscal rules (*t*) * Public institutions (*t*)				0.01		
				(0.13)		
Half-decade time dummies	Yes	Yes	Yes	Yes	Yes	Yes
Country-group fixed effects	Yes	Yes	Yes	Yes	Yes	Yes
Observations	2,715	1,923	792	2,715	2,652	2,664
Number of economies	122	89	33	122	122	122
Log-likelihood	-680.1	-422.2	-219.4	-680.1	-396.7	-427.8

Source: World Bank.

Note: HIPC = Heavily Indebted Poor Countries Initiative. Table shows the probit regression estimates; robust standard errors are reported in parentheses. *** p<0.01, ** p<0.05, * p<0.1. Column (3) excludes HIPC and IMF credit support, and column (5) excludes HIPC, as HIPC perfectly predicts that no fiscal adjustment episode is initiated.

References

Acalin, J., V. Alonso, C. Arroyo, W. R. Lam, L. Martinez, A. D. M. Nguyen, F. Roch, G. Sher, and A. Solovyeva. 2025. "Fiscal Guardrails against Rising Debt and Looming Spending Pressures." Staff Discussion Note 2025/004, International Monetary Fund, Washington, DC.

Acalin, J., L. Martinez, and F. Roch. 2025. "Fiscal Rules, Robust Correction Mechanisms, and Sovereign Spreads." IMF Working Paper 25/195, International Monetary Fund, Washington, DC.

Afonso, A., and J. T. Jalles. 2015. "How Does Fiscal Policy Affect Investment? Evidence From a Large Panel." *International Journal of Finance and Economics* 20: 310–27.

Afonso, A., and J. T. Jalles. 2019. "Fiscal Rules and Government Financing Costs." *Fiscal Studies* 40: 71–90.

Afonso, A., F. Huart, J. T., Jalles, and P. Stanek. 2022. "Twin Deficits Revisited: A Role for Fiscal Institutions?" *Journal of International Money Finance* 121 (March): 102506.

Akitoby, B., A. Baum, C. Hackney, O. Harrison, K. Primus, and V. Salins. 2018. "Tax Revenue Mobilization Episodes in Emerging and Low-Income Countries: Lessons from a New Dataset." IMF Working Paper 18/234, International Monetary Fund, Washington, DC.

Alesina, A., and S. Ardagna. 2010. "Large Changes in Fiscal Policy: Taxes versus Spending." *Tax Policy and the Economy* 24 (1): 35–68.

Alesina, A., and A. Drazen. 1991. "Why Are Stabilizations Delayed?" *American Economic Review* 81(5): 1170–88.

Alesina, A., D. Furceri, J. Ostry, C. Papageorgiou, and D. Quinn. 2024. "Structural Reforms and Elections: Evidence from a World-Wide New Dataset." *Journal of the European Economic Association* 22 (4): 1936–80.

Alesina, A., and R. Perotti. 1995. "The Political Economy of Budget Deficits." *IMF Staff Papers* 42: 1–31.

Alonso, V., C. Arroyo, O. Aydin, V. Balasundharam, H.R. Davoodi, G. Hegab, A.M. Nguyen, N. Salazar Ferro, G. Sher, A. Solovyeva, and N. Tchelishvili. 2025. "Fiscal Rules and Fiscal Councils: Recent Trends and Revisions since the Pandemic." IMF Working Paper 25/198, International Monetary Fund, Washington, DC.

Alsweilem, K., and M. Rietveld, eds. 2018. *Sovereign Wealth Funds in Resource Economies: Institutional and Fiscal Foundations*. New York: Columbia University Press.

Andrián, L., J. Hirs-Garzón, I. L. Urrea, and O. Valencia. 2024. "Fiscal Rules and Economic Cycles: Quality (Always) Matters." *European Journal of Political Economy* 85 (December): 102591.

Apeti, A. E., B. W. W. Bambe, and J. L. Combes. 2025. "On the Macroeconomic Effects of Fiscal Reforms: Fiscal Rules and Public Expenditure Efficiency." *Public Choice* 205 (March): 1–29.

Apeti, A. E., B. W. W. Bambe, J. L. Combes, and E. D. Edoh. 2024. "Original Sin: Fiscal Rules and Government Debt in Foreign Currency in Developing Countries." *Journal of Macroeconomics* 80: 103600.

Apeti, A. E., O. Basdevant, and V. Salins. 2023. "Do Fiscal Rules Foster Fiscal Discipline in Resource-Rich Countries?" Working Paper WP/23/88, International Monetary Fund, Washington, DC.

Ardanaz, M., E. Cavallo, A. Izquierdo, and J. Puig. 2021. "Growth-Friendly Fiscal Rules? Safeguarding Public Investment from Budget Cuts Through Fiscal Rule Design." *Journal of International Money and Finance* 111 (March): 102319.

Ardanaz, M., E. Cavallo, and A. Izquierdo. 2023. "Fiscal Rules: Challenges and Reform Opportunities for Emerging Markets." IDB Working Paper 1443, Inter-American Development Bank, Washington, DC.

Ardanaz, M., C. Ulloa-Suárez, and O. Valencia. 2024. "Why Don't We Follow the Rules? Drivers of Compliance with Fiscal Policy Rules in Emerging Markets." *Journal of International Money and Finance* 142 (April): 103046.

Arezki, R. and K. Ismail. 2013. "Boom–Bust Cycle, Asymmetrical Fiscal Response and the Dutch Disease." *Journal of Development Economics* 101 (March): 256–67.

Arizala, F., J. Gonzalez-Garcia, C. G. Tsangarides, and M. Yenice. 2021. "The Impact of Fiscal Consolidations on Growth in Sub-Saharan Africa." *Empirical Economics* 61 (1): 1–33.

Arroyo Marioli, F., A., Fatás, and G. Vasishtha. 2024. "Fiscal Policy Volatility and Growth in Emerging Markets and Developing Economies." *International Review of Economics & Finance* 92 (April): 758–77.

Arslanalp, S., B. Eichengreen, and P. B. Henry. 2024. "Sustained Debt Reduction: The Jamaica Exception."

NBER Working Paper 32465, National Bureau of Economic Research, Cambridge, MA.

Artana, D., C. Moskovits, J. Puig, and I. Templado. 2021. "Fiscal Rules and the Behavior of Public Investment in Latin America and the Caribbean: Towards Growth-Friendly Fiscal Policy? The Case of Argentina." IDB Working Paper 1188, Inter-American Development Bank, Washington, DC.

Asatryan, Z., C. Castellón, and T. Stratmann. 2018. "Balanced Budget Rules and Fiscal Outcomes: Evidence from Historical Constitutions." *Journal of Public Economics* 167 (November): 105–19.

Auerbach, A. J., and Y. Gorodnichenko. 2012. "Measuring the Output Responses to Fiscal Policy." *American Economic Journal: Economic Policy* 4 (2): 1–27.

Badinger, H., and W. H. Reuter. 2017a. "Determinants of Fiscal Rules." *Applied Economics Letters* 24 (3): 154–58.

Badinger, H., and W. H. Reuter. 2017b. "The Case for Fiscal Rules." *Economic Modeling* 60: 334–43.

Bai, J., and P. Perron. 1998. "Estimating and Testing Linear Models with Multiple Structural Changes." *Econometrica* 66: 47–78.

Bai, J., and P. Perron. 2003. "Computation and Analysis of Multiple Structural Change Models." *Journal of Appied Econometrics* 18: 1–22.

Balasundharam, V., O. Basdevant, D. Benicio, A. Ceber, Y. Kim, L. Mazzone, H. Selim, and Y. Yang. 2023. "Fiscal Consolidations: Taking Stock of the Success Factors, Impact, and Design." IMF Working Paper 23/63, International Monetary Fund, Washington, DC.

Baret, K. 2023. "Fiscal Rules' Compliance and Social Welfare." *Annals of Economics and Statistics* 150 (June): 25–65.

Barreix, A. D., and L. F. Corrales, eds. 2019. *Reglas Fiscales Resilientes en America Latina* [Resilient Fiscal Rules in Latin America]. Washington, DC: Inter-American Development Bank.

Basdevant, O., T. Chaponda, F. Gonguet, J. Honda, S. Thomas. 2020. "Designing Fiscal Rules to Protect Investment." In *Well Spent: How Strong Infrastructure Governance Can End Waste in Public Investment*, edited by G. Schwartz, M. Fouad, T. S. Hansen, G. Verdier, 106–24. Washington, DC: International Monetary Fund.

Beetsma, R., B. Bluhm, M. Giuliodori, and P. Wierts. 2013. "From Budgetary Forecasts To Ex Post Fiscal Data: Exploring the Evolution of Fiscal Forecast Errors in the European Union." *Contemporary Economic Policy* 31 (4): 795–813.

Beetsma, R., X. Debrun, X. Fang, Y. Kim, V. Lledó, S. Mbaye, and X. Zang. 2019. "Independent Fiscal Councils: Recent Trends and Performance." *European Journal of Political Economy* 57: 53–69.

Beetsma, R., and M. Larch. 2019. "EU Fiscal Rules: Further Reform or Better Implementation?" CESifo DICE Report 17(2):7–11.

Bergman, U. M., and M. Hutchison. 2015. "Economic Stabilization in The Post-Crisis World: Are Fiscal Rules the Answer?" *Journal of International Money and Finance* 52: 82–101.

Beyala, B. C. N. 2025. "Do Fiscal Rules Enhance States' Fiscal Capacity?" *Kyklos* 78 (4): 1539–66.

Blanco, F., P. Saavedra, F. Koehler-Geib, and E. Skrok. 2020. *Fiscal Rules and Economic Size in Latin America and the Caribbean*. Washington, DC: World Bank.

Bova, M. E., N. Carcenac, and M. M Guerguil. 2014. "Fiscal Rules and the Procyclicality of Fiscal Policy in the Developing World." IMF Working Paper 14/122, International Monetary Fund, Washington, DC.

Bova, E., C. Kolerus, and S. J. Tapsoba. 2015. "A Fiscal Job? An Analysis of Fiscal Policy and The Labor Market." *IZA Journal of Labor Policy* 4 (13).

Bova, E., P. Medas, and T. Poghosyan. 2018. "Macroeconomic Stability in Resource-Rich Countries: The Role of Fiscal Policy." *Journal of Banking and Financial Economics* 1: 103–22.

Brändle, T., and M. Elsener. 2024. "Do Fiscal Rules Matter? A Survey of Recent Evidence." *Swiss Journal of Economics and Statistics* 160: 101186.

Buda, K. 2024. "Can Fiscal Rules Decrease the Probability of a Sudden Stop Crisis?" *Review of World Economics* 160 (1): 213–78.

Buiter, W. H. 2004. "Two Naked Emperors? Concerns about the Stability & Growth Pact and Second Thoughts about Central Bank Independence." *Fiscal Studies* 25: 249–77.

Calderón, C., R. Duncan, and K. Schmidt-Hebbel. 2016. "Do Good Institutions Promote Countercyclical

Macroeconomic Policies?" *Oxford Bulletin of Economics and Statistics* 78: 650–70.

Cangiano, M., T. Curristine, and M. Lazare, eds. 2013. *Public Financial Management and Its Emerging Architecture.* Washington, DC: International Monetary Fund.

Cardoso, D. S., and L. B. de Carvalho. 2023. "Effects of Fiscal Consolidation on Income Inequality: Narrative Evidence from South America." *Empirical Economics* 64 (3): 1177–218.

Carrière-Swallow, Y., A. C. David, and D. Leigh. 2021. "Macroeconomic Effects of Fiscal Consolidation in Emerging Economies: New Narrative Evidence from Latin America and the Caribbean." *Journal of Money, Credit and Banking* 53 (6): 1313–35.

Caselli, F., and J. Reynaud. 2020. "Do Fiscal Rules Cause Better Fiscal Balances? A New Instrumental Variable Strategy." *European Journal of Political Economy* 63: 101873.

Céspedes, L. F., E. Parrado, and A. Velasco. 2014. "Fiscal Rules and The Management of Natural Resource Revenues: The Case of Chile." *Annual Review of Resource Economics* 6 (1): 105–32.

Céspedes, L. F., and A. Velasco. 2014. "Was This Time Different? Fiscal Policy in Commodity Republics." *Journal of Development Economics* 106: 92–106.

Chinn, M. D., and H. Ito. 2006. "What Matters for Financial Development? Capital Controls, Institutions, and Interactions" *Journal of Development Economics* 81, 163–92.

Choudhary, R., F. U. Ruch, and E. Skrok. 2024. "Taxing for Growth: Revisiting the 15 Percent Threshold." Policy Research Working Paper 10943, World Bank, Washington, DC.

Chrysanthakopoulos, C., and A. Tagkalakis. 2023. "Fiscal Rules and Tax Policy Cyclicality." *Economics Letters* 225, 111035.

Combes, J.-L., X. Debrun, A. Minea, P. N. Sawadogo, and C. Vinturis. 2024. "On the Side Effects of Fiscal Policy: Fiscal Rules and Income Inequality." *European Journal of Political Economy*, 102534.

Combes, J.-L., X. Debrun, A. Minea, and R. Tapsoba. 2018. "Inflation Targeting, Fiscal Rules and The Policy Mix: Cross-Effects and Interactions." *Economic Journal* 128 (615): 2755–84.

Combes, J.-L., A. Minea, and M. Sow. 2017. "Is Fiscal Policy Always Counter-(Pro-) Cyclical? The Role of Public Debt and Fiscal Rules." *Economic Modelling* 65: 138–46.

Cordes, T., T. Kinda, P. Muthoora, and A. Weber. 2015. "Expenditure Rules: Effective Tools for Sound Fiscal Policy?" IMF Working Paper 15/29, International Monetary Fund, Washington, DC.

Coulibaly, M. 2015. "Fiscal Rules in WAEMU: Limiting Public Deficits." In *Regional Integration and Policy Challenges in Africa,* edited by A. B. Elhiraika, A. C. K. Mukungu, and W. Nyoike, 302–25. London: Palgrave Macmillan.

Coulibaly, Y., and A. C. Diallo. 2025. "Can Fiscal Rules Improve Banking System Stability in Developing Countries?" *Journal of Macroeconomics* 86: 103724.

Davoodi, H. R., P. Elger, A. Fotiou, D. Garcia-Macia, X. Han, A. Lagerborg, W. R. Lam, and P. Medas. 2022. "Fiscal Rules and Fiscal Councils: Recent Trends and Performance During the COVID-19 Pandemic." IMF Working Paper 22/11, International Monetary Fund, Washington, DC.

Debrun, X., and L. Jonung. 2019. "Under Threat: Rules-Based Fiscal Policy and How to Preserve It." *European Journal of Political Economy* 57: 142–57.

Dessus, S., J. L. Diaz-Sanchez, and A. Varoudakis. 2016. "Fiscal Rules and The Pro-Cyclicality of Public Investment in the West African Economic and Monetary Union." *Journal of International Development* 28 (6): 887–901.

Devries, P., J. Guajardo, D. Leigh, and A. Pescatori. 2011. "A New Action-Based Dataset of Fiscal Consolidation." IMF Working Paper 11/128, International Monetary Fund, Washington, DC.

Di Lorenzo, P., and E. A. Lacey. 2024. *A Primer on Restoring Fiscal Space and Sustainability.* Washington, DC: World Bank.

Dube, A., D. Girardi, Ò. Jordà, and A. M. Taylor. 2025. "A Local Projections Approach to Difference-In-Differences Event Studies." *Journal of Applied Econometrics* 40: 741–58.

Ech-charfi, N. E. 2024. "Fiscal Rules, Capital Controls, and Cross-border Financial Integration." *European Journal of Political Economy* 85: 102594.

Eklou, K. M., and M. Joanis. 2019. "Do Fiscal Rules Cause Fiscal Discipline Over the Electoral Cycle?" IMF Working Paper 19/291, International Monetary Fund, Washington, DC.

Eyraud, L., W. Gbohoui, and P. Medas. 2023. "A New Fiscal Framework for Resource-Rich Countries." IMF

Working Paper 23/230. International Monetary Fund, Washington, DC.

Eyraud, L., X. Debrun, A. Hodge, V. Lledó, and C. Pattillo. 2018. "Second-Generation Fiscal Rules: Balancing Simplicity, Flexibility, and Enforceability." Staff Discussion Note 18/04, International Monetary Fund, Washington, DC.

Fatás, A., B. Gootjes, and J. Mawejje. 2026. "Dynamic Effects of Fiscal Rules: Do Initial Conditions Matter?" *Journal of International Money and Finance* 161: 103499.

Fedelino, A., Ivanova, A., and M. Horton. 2009. "Computing Cyclically Adjusted Balances and Automatic Stabilizers." IMF Technical Notes and Manuals 09/05, International Monetary Fund, Washington, DC.

Frankel, J. 2011a. "A Solution to Fiscal Procyclicality: The Structural Budget Institutions Pioneered by Chile." NBER Working Paper 16945, National Bureau of Economic Research, Cambridge, MA.

Frankel, J. 2011b. "Over-optimism in Forecasts by Official Budget Agencies and Its Implications." *Oxford Review of Economic Policy* 27 (4): 536–12.

Gatti, R., D. Lederman, A. M. Islam, H. Nguyen, R. Lotfi, and M. E. Mousa. 2024. "Data Transparency and GDP Growth Forecast Errors." *Journal of International Money and Finance* 140: 102991.

Gavin, M., and R. Perotti. 1997. "Fiscal Policy in Latin America." *NBER Macroeconomics Annual* 12: 11–61.

Gehrke, B. 2019. "Fiscal Rules and Unemployment." *Macroeconomic Dynamics* 23 (8): 3293–326.

Girouard N., and C. André. 2005. "Measuring Cyclically Adjusted Budget Balances for OECD Countries." OECD Economics Department Working Paper 434, Organisation for Economic Co-operation and Development, Paris.

Gomez-Gonzalez, J. E., O. M. Valencia, and G. A. Sánchez. 2022. "How Fiscal Rules Can Reduce Sovereign Debt Default Risk." *Emerging Markets Review* 50: 100839.

Gomez-Gonzalez, J. E., O. M. Valencia, and G. A. Sánchez. 2024. "Debt Affordability in Developed and Emerging Market Economies: The Role of Fiscal Rules." *Journal of Economics and Finance*, 48 (2): 377–93.

Gootjes, B. 2025. "Kicking the Can Down the Road? A Real-Time Data Analysis of Delayed Fiscal Consolidation." *European Journal of Political Economy* 89: 102736.

Gootjes, B., and J. de Haan. 2022. "Do Fiscal Rules Need Budget Transparency to Be Effective?" *European Journal of Political Economy* 75: 102210.

Gootjes, B., J. de Haan, and R. Jong-A-Pin. 2021. "Do Fiscal Rules Constrain Political Budget Cycles?" *Public Choice* 188: 1–30.

Grembi, V., T. Nannicini, and U. Troiano. 2016. "Do Fiscal Rules Matter?" *American Economic Journal: Applied Economics* 8 (3): 1–30.

Grundler, K., and N. Potrafke. 2020. "Fiscal Rules: Historical, Modern, and Sub-National Growth Effects." CESifo Working Paper 8305, Center for Economic Studies and Ifo Institute, Munich.

Guerguil, M., P. Mandon, and R. Tapsoba. 2017. "Flexible Fiscal Rules and Countercyclical Fiscal Policy." *Journal of Macroeconomics* 52: 189–220.

Gupta, S., B. Clements, E. Baldacci, and C. Mulas-Granados. 2004. "The Persistence of Fiscal Adjustments in Developing Countries." *Applied Economics Letters* 11 (4): 209–12.

Hadfield, G. K., and B. R. Weingast. 2013. "Law without the State: Legal Attributes and the Coordination of Decentralized Collective Punishment." *Journal of Law and Courts* 1 (1): 3–34.

Hagemann, R. 2011. "How Can Fiscal Councils Strengthen Fiscal Performance?" *OECD Journal: Economic Studies* 2011 (1): 1–24.

Hansen, D. 2020. "The Effectiveness of Fiscal Institutions: International Financial Flogging or Domestic Constraint?" *European Journal of Political Economy* 63: 101879.

Hausmann, R., L. Pritchett, and D. Rodrik. 2005. "Growth Accelerations." *Journal of Economic Growth* 10: 303–29.

Heinemann, F., M. D. Moessinger, and M. Yeter. 2018. "Do Fiscal Rules Constrain Fiscal Policy? A Meta -Regression-Analysis." *European Journal of Political Economy* 51: 69–92.

Ilzetzki, E., C. Reinhart, and K. Rogoff. 2019 "Exchange Arrangements Entering the 21st Century: Which Anchor Will Hold?" *Quarterly Journal of Economics* 134 (2): 599–646.

IMF (International Monetary Fund). 2014. *Back to Work: How Fiscal Policy Can Help. Fiscal Monitor.*

October. Washington, DC: International Monetary Fund.

IMF (International Monetary Fund). 2023. *International Corporate Tax Reform.* Washington, DC: International Monetary Fund.

IMF (International Monetary Fund). 2024. *World Economic Outlook: Policy Pivot, Rising Threats.* October. Washington, DC: International Monetary Fund.

IMF (International Monetary Fund). 2025a. *World Economic Outlook: Global Economy in Flux, Prospects Remain Dim.* October. Washington, DC: International Monetary Fund.

IMF (International Monetary Fund). 2025b. "Argentina: First Review Under the Extended Arrangement Under the Extended Fund Facility, Requests for a Waiver of Nonobservance of a Performance Criterion, Rephasing of Access, Modification of Performance Criteria, and Financing Assurances Review—Press Release; Staff Report; and Statement by the Executive Director for Argentina." International Monetary Fund, Washington, DC.

Islamaj, E., A. S. Penaloza, and S. Sommers. 2024. "The Sovereign Spread Compressing Effect of Fiscal Rules during Global Crises." Policy Research Working Paper 10741, World Bank, Washington, DC.

Jalles, J. T. 2018. "Fiscal Rules and Fiscal Counter-Cyclicality." *Economics Letters* 170: 159–62.

Jordà, Ò. 2005. "Estimation and Inference of Impulse Responses by Local Projections." *American Economic Review* 95 (1): 161–82.

Jordà, Ò., and A. M. Taylor. 2025. "Local Projections." *Journal of Economic Literature* 63: 59–110.

Jordà, Ò., and A. M. Taylor. 2016. "The Time for Austerity: Estimating the Average Treatment Effect of Fiscal Policy." *The Economic Journal* 126 (590): 219–55.

Junquera-Varela, R. F., C. O. Lucas-Mas, I. Krsul, V. Calderon, and P. A. Arce. 2022. *Digital Transformation of Tax and Customs Administrations.* Washington, DC: World Bank.

Kaminsky, G. L., C. M. Reinhart, and C. A. Vegh. 2004. "When it Rains, It Pours: Procyclical Capital Flows and Macroeconomic Policies." *NBER Macroeconomics Annual* 19: 11–53.

Keita, K., and C. Turcu. 2022. "Promoting Counter-Cyclical Fiscal Policy: Fiscal Rules Versus Institutions." *Comparative Economic Studies* 10: 1–46.

Kelemen, R. D., and T. K. Teo. 2014. "Law, Focal Points, and Fiscal Discipline in the United States and the European Union." *American Political Science Review* 108 (2): 355–70.

Kopits, G., and S. Symansky. 1998. "Fiscal Policy Rules." Occasional Paper 162, International Monetary Fund, Washington, DC.

Lam, R. W., Y. Cao, A. Lagerborg, and A. Scipioni. 2023. "Chile Technical Assistance Report—Fiscal Considerations in Managing Stabilization Funds." IMF Country Report 23/249, International Monetary Fund, Washington, DC.

Lehtimäki, J. 2025. "The Fiscal and Macroeconomic Effects of Fiscal Rules." *Journal of Economics* 146: 379–441.

Mara, E. R., and R. Maran. 2024. "Are Fiscal Rules Efficient on Public Debt Restraint in The Presence of Shadow Economy?" *Finance Research Letters* 64: 105495.

Mawejje, J., and N. M. Odhiambo. 2024. "Fiscal Rules and the Cyclicality of Fiscal Policy in the East African Community." *Applied Economics Letters* 31 (15): 1429–32.

McNabb, K., M. Danquah, and A. Tagem. 2021. "Tax Effort Revisited: New Estimates from The Government Revenue Dataset." WIDER Working Paper 170, United Nations University World Institute for Development Economics Research, Helsinki.

Mendoza Bellido, W., M. Vega, C. Rojas, and Y. Anastacio. 2021. "Fiscal Rules and Public Investment: The Case of Peru, 2000-2019." IDB Working Paper 1186, Inter-American Development Bank, Washington, DC.

Milesi-Ferretti, G. M. 2004. "Good, Bad or Ugly? On The Effects of Fiscal Rules with Creative Accounting." *Journal of Public Economics* 88 (1–2): 377–94.

Misra, S., and R. Ranjan. 2018. "Fiscal Rules and Procyclicality: An Empirical Analysis." *Indian Economic Review* 53: 207–28.

Molnár, M. 2012. "Fiscal Consolidation: What Factors Determine the Success of Consolidation Efforts?" OECD Economics Department Working Paper 936, Organisation for Economic Co-operation and Development, Paris.

Montiel Olea, J. L., and M. Plagborg-Møller. 2021. "Local Projection Inference is Simpler and More Robust Than You Think." *Econometrica* 89 (4): 1789–823.

Mpatswe, G. K., S. J. A. Tapsoba, and R. C. York. 2011. "The Cyclicality of Fiscal Policies in the CEMAC Region." IMF Working Paper 11/205, International Monetary Fund, Washington, DC.

Nabieu, G. A. A., G. A. Bokpin, A. K. Osei, and P. O. Asuming. 2021. "Fiscal Rules, Fiscal Performance and Economic Growth in Sub-Saharan Africa." *African Development Review* 33 (4): 607–19.

Okonjo-Iweala, N., and P. Osafo-Kwaako. 2007. "Nigeria's Economic Reforms: Progress and Challenges." Working Paper No. 6, Brookings Global Economy and Development, Brookings Institution, Washington, DC.

Okunogbe, O., and F. Santoro. 2023. "The Promise and Limitations of Information Technology for Tax Mobilization." *The World Bank Research Observer* 38 (2): 295–324.

Piguillem, F., and A. Riboni. 2021. "Fiscal Rules as Bargaining Chips." *The Review of Economic Studies* 88 (5): 2439–78.

Potrafke, N. 2025. "The Economic Consequences of Fiscal Rules." *Journal of International Money and Finance* 153: 103286.

Pouokam, N. 2021. "Sharing Resource Wealth Inclusively Within and Across Generations." IMF Working Paper 21/97, International Monetary Fund, Washington, DC.

Reuter, W. H. 2015. "National Numerical Fiscal Rules: Not Complied with, but Still Effective?" *European Journal of Political Economy* 39, 67–81.

Sawadogo, R. F. 2024. "Do Fiscal Rules Shape Private-Sector Investment Decisions?" *Journal of Macroeconomics* 81: 103617.

Servén, L. 2007. "Fiscal Rules, Public Investment, and Growth." Policy Research Working Paper 4382, World Bank, Washington, DC.

Strong, C. O. 2023a. "Tying One's Hand: The Effect of Fiscal Rules on the Political Business Cycle in Africa." *Journal of African Economies* 32 (4): 438–67.

Strong, C. O. 2023b. "The Impact of Fiscal Rules on Government Debt: Evidence from the CFA Zone." *Empirical* Economics 65 (5): 2357–91.

Tapsoba, R. 2012. "Do National Numerical Fiscal Rules Really Shape Fiscal Behaviours in Developing Countries? A Treatment Effect Evaluation." *Economic Modelling* 29 (4): 1356–69.

Teulings, C. N., and N. Zubanov. 2014. "Is Economic Recovery a Myth? Robust Estimation of Impulse Responses." *Journal of Applied Econometrics* 29 (3): 497 –514.

Thornton, J., and C. Vasilakis. 2020. "Do Fiscal Rules Reduce Government Borrowing Costs in Developing Countries?" *International Journal of Finance & Economics* 25 (4): 499–510.

Ulloa-Suárez, C. 2023. "Determinants of Compliance with Fiscal Rules: Misplaced Efforts or Hidden Motivations?" *European Journal of Political Economy* 78: 102399.

van Eden, H., P. Khemani, and R. P. J. Emery. 2013. "Developing Legal Frameworks to Promote Fiscal Responsibility: Design Matters." In *Public Financial Management and its Emerging Architecture*, edited by M. Cangiano, T. Curristine, and M. Lazare, 79–105. Washington, DC: International Monetary Fund.

Velasco, A. 1999. "A Model of Endogenous Fiscal Deficits and Delayed Fiscal Reforms." In *Fiscal Institutions and Fiscal Performance*, edited by J. Poterba, and J. von Hagen. Chicago: University of Chicago Press.

Velasco, A. 2000. "Debts and Deficits with Fragmented Fiscal Policymaking." *Journal of Public Economics* 76: 105–25.

Vinturis, C. 2023. "How Do Fiscal Rules Shape Governments' Spending Behavior?" *Economic Inquiry* 61 (2): 322–41.

Wiese, R., R. Jong-A-Pin, and J. de Haan. 2018. "Can Successful Fiscal Adjustments Only Be Achieved by Spending Cuts?" *European Journal of Political Economy* 54: 145–66.

World Bank. 2022. "Nigeria Public Finance Review: Fiscal Adjustment for Better and Sustainable Results." World Bank, Washington, DC.

World Bank. 2024. *Global Economic Prospects*. January. Washington, DC: World Bank.

World Bank. 2025. *Global Economic Prospects*. June. Washington, DC: World Bank.

Yelkesen, O., and P. V. Iyidogan. 2025. "Do the Level of Government Debt and Economic Development Matter in the Impact of Fiscal Rules on Fiscal Performance? Evidence from the Dynamic Panel Threshold Model." *Empirical Economics* 69: 1751–78.

Zoumenou, J. M. 2025. "On the Impact of Fiscal Policy on Inflation: The Case of Fiscal Rules." *BE Journal of Macroeconomics* 25 (1): 191–240.

CHAPTER 4

FRONTIER MARKET ECONOMIES

Promise, Performance, and Prospects

Frontier market economies are a subset of emerging market and developing economies that have meaningful but limited access to international financial markets. For global investors looking for returns beyond advanced economies, frontier markets represent a middle ground: they are less integrated into international financial markets than emerging markets but more integrated than other developing economies. These economies are home to 1.8 billion people today, about one-fifth of the world's total, and are projected to account for a larger share of global population growth than the rest of the world combined over the next 25 years. With some 230 million young people expected to reach working age by 2035 in frontier markets, they will play a critical role in addressing the jobs challenge facing developing economies. Many frontier markets possess valuable natural resources, and their populations are, on average, better educated and longer-lived than those in other developing economies. Growing working-age populations could create a sizeable demographic dividend—provided that sufficient jobs can be generated. Together with progress in international financial integration, these strengths point to considerable potential for rapid growth, job creation, and development. Yet although growth in some frontier markets has been relatively strong in the past quarter century, the group as a whole has not fully realized its potential. Progress in financial integration has brought benefits but remains partial, and these economies have also experienced greater vulnerability to sudden stops in capital flows and an increased incidence of sovereign defaults. There is no single path to success, but frontier markets that have recorded stronger growth over the last quarter century share some key features, including faster investment growth, improved institutions, and more contained government debt. Advancing financial development, alongside policies to bolster macroeconomic stability and catalyze investment, productivity, and job creation, can help frontier markets harness the gains from global financial integration while mitigating associated risks. Realizing frontier markets' potential is essential not only for these economies, but also for global job creation and development progress.

Introduction

Frontier market economies (hereafter simply "frontier markets") are a diverse subgroup of emerging market and developing economies (EMDEs) characterized by their intermediate position in terms of international financial integration. They have gained some access to international financial markets—less than emerging market economies, but more than other developing economies—and are sometimes referred to as "pre-emerging" (refer to box 4.1).[1] This chapter identifies frontier markets primarily by their inclusion in some widely tracked financial market indexes. Frontier markets are distinguished from emerging markets, which are part of higher-grade equity indexes or have high-income status. The chapter identifies 39 frontier markets as of 2012, and these provide the baseline sample for the analysis. Parts of the chapter also consider new entrants to the class, which had grown to 56 as of 2025.[2]

Frontier markets have significant economic potential, in terms of demographics, natural resources, and gains from financial integration. Understanding the challenges and prospects of today's frontier markets is central to addressing the jobs challenge confronting EMDEs: these economies are home to roughly 1.8 billion people, over one-fifth of the world's population, but account for about 5 percent of global output. More than 230 million young people in today's frontier market economies are expected to reach working age between 2025 and 2035. Between 2025 and 2050, total and working-age populations in frontier markets are both projected to grow by more than those of the rest of the world

Note: This chapter was prepared by Tommy Chrimes, Philip Kenworthy, Jiwon Lee, Kate McKinnon, Takuma Tanaka, and Hamza Zahid.

[1] Definitions vary, but frontier markets are generally considered "pre-emerging" economies with financial markets that are usually smaller and less liquid than those in emerging markets but that are still investable (refer to, for example, Chowdhury, Edmonds, and Walker 2015). The classification used in this chapter is based primarily on economies' inclusion in several key financial market indexes, supplemented by a per capita income level filter. "Other developing economies" refers to EMDEs that are not classified as emerging markets or frontier markets. This taxonomy is intended solely for the analysis in this chapter; it carries no implications for the operations or policies of the World Bank Group. Box 4.1 and annex 4.1 give full details on the classification.

[2] By 2012, all indexes used in this classification had been established. Using 2012 (roughly the midpoint of the quarter century) for the baseline also allows for assessment of frontier market performance over time. Where the 2025 sample of frontier markets is more instructive, this is made clear in the text and chart notes.

combined. This represents a large demographic dividend, provided that working-age people can find productive jobs. People in frontier markets are better educated and live longer than in other developing economies. Many frontier markets also boast significant natural resources, including tourism potential as well as commodities crucial to new technologies and the energy transition.

Inclusion in major financial market indexes can have significant consequences for EMDEs. A direct benefit is that index inclusion attracts capital into an economy's bonds and equities through a so-called "benchmark effect" (Raddatz, Schmukler, and Williams 2017). Given the large amount of assets benchmarked to prominent indexes relative to the size of many EMDE financial markets, these effects can be substantial. In bond markets, inclusion in global indexes can lower borrowing costs, improve market liquidity, and broaden the investor base. Equity market index inclusion can lower firms' cost of capital, stimulate increased investment and innovation, and improve risk-sharing, but may also generate relative losses for producers of tradables through currency appreciation.[3]

Indirect benefits of index inclusion and international financial integration can stem from the reforms that they incentivize—including strengthening the rule of law, enhancing financial regulation, and improving macroeconomic policy frameworks. Such reforms bring their own economic benefits, supporting long-term growth by promoting investment, improving allocative efficiency, and boosting total factor productivity (Adarov 2025; Kose et al. 2010). Although such benefits should themselves encourage reforms, index inclusion and deeper integration into global financial markets can provide additional incentives to advance effective reform efforts.

Amid relatively easy global financial conditions, borrowing premia for many EMDEs have followed a declining trend since early 2023. Despite high geopolitical uncertainty over 2025, sovereign bond spreads at the start of January 2026 were lower than a year before in 90 percent of frontier markets; in 62 percent, they were also lower than on the eve of the pandemic in early 2020. This has prompted an uptick in frontier market bond issuance. However, in the past, such issuance has not consistently resulted in strong growth and development.

There have been many studies on EMDEs and on various EMDE sub-groups, such as low-income countries (LICs) and economies in fragile and conflict-affected situations (FCS).[4] Yet frontier markets as a subgroup have tended to be overlooked in economic analyses. This chapter presents the first comprehensive analysis of economic developments and prospects in frontier markets. It addresses three main questions:

- How have frontier markets performed in terms of macroeconomic and development outcomes, relative to emerging markets and other developing economies, since 2000?
- In what ways do macro-financial conditions shape macroeconomic and development outcomes in frontier markets?
- What policies can frontier markets pursue to raise growth and create jobs while containing vulnerabilities?

Contributions

The chapter makes several contributions to the literature.

Overview of frontier markets' characteristics and performance. The chapter provides an overarching

[3] On the benefits of index inclusion, refer to Arslanalp and Tsuda (2015) and Raddatz, Schmukler, and Williams (2017). On wider international financial integration benefits, refer to Bekaert, Harvey, and Lundblad (2005) and Kose et al. (2009). In sovereign bond markets, inclusion in global benchmarks such as J.P. Morgan's EMBI is linked to lower yields and spreads, deeper investor bases, and greater efficiency (Arslanalp, Bornhorst, and Poplawski-Ribeiro 2020; Broner et al. 2021; Romero et al. 2021). Equity index inclusion and market liberalization raise firm valuations, reduce the cost of capital, and foster innovation and productivity via increased investment and analyst coverage (Bena et al. 2017; Henry 2003; Kacperczyk, Sundaresan, and Wang 2021; Yang et al. 2025).

[4] On EMDEs or emerging markets, refer to, for example, Kose and Ohnsorge (2024) and Magnus (2010). Studies on EMDE subgroups include those of LICs, such as Collier (2007) and World Bank (2025a); of FCS economies, such as Ganson and Wennmann (2016) and World Bank (2025b); and of small states, such as World Bank (2024a).

BOX 4.1 Financial market classifications of frontier market economies

Financial market classifications of emerging market and developing economies (EMDEs), such as distinctions between emerging and frontier market economies, can lead to substantial capital inflows to upgraded economies by signaling progress in market reforms and institutional development. However, major financial market index compilers take different approaches to classification. There is no universally accepted definition of frontier or emerging markets. This box outlines a simple, transparent approach for identifying frontier and emerging market economies, based primarily on economies' inclusion in certain key financial market indexes (and also taking account of income levels). The resulting taxonomy provides the basis for this chapter's analysis of economies that are at early stages of integration into global capital markets.

Across financial markets and international institutions, countries are often grouped—for example, by region, income levels, trade patterns, policy frameworks, or other specific characteristics. The World Bank Group has been influential in this nomenclature, and the term "frontier market" was coined in the early 1990s by the International Finance Corporation (IFC) and is now used widely across financial markets (IFC 2016).[a] Yet while there is a broad general understanding that frontier markets are "pre-emerging" economies with some degree of financial market access, there is no precise common definition. Different, if overlapping, approaches adopted by financial market index providers create definitional challenges for cross-cutting analysis. Categories, tiers, criteria, and processes differ between index providers, often with some qualitative element to assessment.[b] With the rapid expansion of index-based investing, inclusion or exclusion from emerging market or frontier market indexes can be consequential, both as a signal of market development and reform progress, and as a direct shaping force on capital flows.

Robust analysis of frontier market prospects therefore requires an approach that captures the effects of inclusion in widely followed indexes, while drawing clear and transparent distinctions between emerging markets, frontier markets, and other developing economies. Against this backdrop, this box addresses the following questions:

- How do financial markets categorize EMDEs for the purpose of index creation?
- What is a simple and analytically robust definition of frontier markets to study their macroeconomic performance and prospects, including relative to other EMDEs?

Country classifications by financial markets

Financial market classifications of EMDEs into *frontier markets* and *emerging markets* reflect index providers' assessments of factors deemed relevant to international portfolio investors. The specific parameters differ across providers, but major equity market indexes primarily consider a combination of market characteristics (the size, breadth, and liquidity of domestic equity markets) and market accessibility (regulations involving the ease of financial market transactions). In addition to quantitative criteria, qualitative judgments—such as assessments of institutional and regulatory frameworks—also play a role in determining index inclusion (Quisenberry and Griffith 2010).[c] For more detail on the parameters used for index classifications, refer to annex 4.1.

Conceptually, emerging markets are more advanced along the dimensions emphasized by index providers,

Note: This box was prepared by Tommy Chrimes, Philip Kenworthy, and Takuma Tanaka.

a. IFC had previously developed the term "emerging markets" (IFC 2016). IFC also developed a frontier markets index, which was subsequently acquired and recast by Standard & Poor's (Chowdhury, Edmonds, and Walker 2013).

b. A financial market index provider is a firm that defines and maintains market classifications and benchmarks used by investors and asset managers to measure performance and allocate capital. For country group indexes, providers set rules and criteria for index inclusion—such as market size, liquidity, accessibility, and institutional quality—and monitor adherence. Classifications can influence investment decisions, capital flows, and market perceptions, particularly given the growing rise of index-tracking funds and other passive investment strategies. The four index providers used in this classification include J.P. Morgan, which produces the J.P. Morgan Emerging Market Bond Index; MSCI (Morgan Stanley Capital International), which provides the MSCI Emerging Markets and Frontier Markets indexes; FTSE Russell, which publishes the FTSE Emerging and Frontier Market indexes; and S&P Dow Jones Indices, which maintains the S&P Emerging and Frontier Broad Market Index series.

c. For instance, regular assessments against market accessibility criteria require incorporating and summarizing qualitative feedback from market participants. These may include judgments concerning areas such as the stability of institutional frameworks and the efficiency of operational frameworks (MSCI 2025).

BOX 4.1 Financial market classifications of frontier market economies (*continued*)

while frontier markets are at an earlier stage of financial development and integration. An economy may graduate from one index to another (for example, from a frontier market index to an emerging market index) if its markets deepen and become more accessible. EMDEs not included in either emerging or frontier market indexes—here called "other developing economies"—typically have a limited presence in global capital markets. These financial market classifications tend to broadly correlate with income levels: other developing economies are, on average, the poorest group, emerging markets the most affluent, and frontier markets occupy an intermediate position. However, exceptions exist where capital market development has outpaced income levels or, conversely, where higher-income economies remain less integrated into global capital markets, often because of limited market size.[d]

A simple, unified classification of frontier and emerging markets

Drawing on the classifications of several prominent index providers, this box presents a simple and coherent categorization of frontier market economies, emerging market economies, and other developing economies. It incorporates the taxonomies of four major index providers and categorizes EMDEs as follows (refer to annex 4.1 for full lists of economies):

- Economies included in at least one emerging or frontier market equity index are categorized as *frontier market economies* if they appear in more frontier than emerging market equity indexes, and as *emerging market economies* otherwise.[e]
- Economies not included in an emerging or frontier market equity index but included in the J.P. Morgan Emerging Markets Bond Index (EMBI) Global are categorized as *frontier market economies.*
- Any EMDE classified as a high-income country according to the World Bank Group is listed as an *emerging market economy.*
- After applying the above rules, remaining EMDEs are categorized as *other developing economies.*

This classification approach offers several advantages for the analysis in this chapter. First, by drawing clear distinctions among different groups of countries, it allows for clean and consistent cross-country comparisons. Second, the exclusion of high-income economies from both the frontier market and other developing economy groups enables a focused examination of how capital inflows can support growth from modest income levels. Third, the approach incorporates information from both equity and bond indexes, recognizing that different economic and market structures across EMDEs can channel capital flows through different instruments. Fourth, by drawing on indexes from four separate major index providers rather than a single index, the approach captures a broad view of market access.

Indexes classifying EMDEs have grown and evolved over time. Some of the indexes used in this chapter did not exist in their current form in 2000. Accordingly, this chapter uses index membership and income levels in 2012 to form the baseline sample. This is roughly the midpoint of the quarter century covered in this chapter, and from thereon data for all four indexes are available. There were 39 frontier markets as of 2012 under the definition used here. By 2025, this number had risen to 56 economies.

Many new entrants to the frontier market group between 2012 and 2025 achieved this status through inclusion in J.P. Morgan's EMBI Global bond index. Six economies were also added in 2016 following MSCI's decision to include the Western African Economic and Monetary Union (WAEMU) countries as frontier markets. For a full set of movements between EMDE groups, refer to annex 4.1. Economies identified as moving from frontier to emerging status between 2012 and 2025 have done so by reaching high-income status. Viet Nam's anticipated 2026 reclassification by FTSE Russell would buck this trend (LSEG 2025).

The approach applied here, based primarily on financial market index providers' assessments, yields intuitive

d. For example, some index providers classify some high-income countries such as Bahrain, Estonia, Iceland, and Mauritius as frontier markets. Meanwhile, large but less affluent economies, such as India and Indonesia, are commonly classified as emerging markets by index providers.

e. Some index providers maintain additional distinctions between different tiers of emerging markets. The groupings in this chapter do not draw on these distinctions within the emerging markets group.

BOX 4.1 Financial market classifications of frontier market economies (*continued*)

patterns across various measures of economic development and financial integration. For example, per capita income in the median frontier market economy is less than one-third of that in the typical emerging market economy and more than double that of other developing economies. Similarly, portfolio liabilities—a measure of de facto financial openness—are negligible in other developing economies, about 7 percent of GDP in the median frontier market economy, and 33 percent of GDP in the typical emerging market economy.

analysis of the characteristics of frontier market economies. It documents how they have evolved since 2000, in terms of macroeconomic, structural, and development metrics. The chapter puts these characteristics and developments in context by comparing them with those of emerging markets and other developing economies. It also considers the movement of countries between these groupings.

Analysis of frontier markets' global financial integration. Despite their financial market access, there has been little analysis of frontier markets' exposure to global financial conditions. This chapter's analytical exercises address this gap. First, a study documents the exposure of frontier markets to surges and stops in capital inflows. Second, a dynamic factor model assesses the integration of frontier markets with the global financial cycle, highlighting vulnerabilities when global financial conditions tighten sharply. The chapter also examines the evolution and composition of debt in frontier markets.

Assessment of frontier market success cases and identification of policy priorities. The chapter examines which frontier markets have had stronger economic growth over the past 25 years, and the macroeconomic, financial market, and structural features that have been associated with this success. Selected case studies also consider economic characteristics and policies that may have contributed to strong performance. Drawing on lessons from these cases, together with an assessment of the advantages and challenges facing today's frontier markets and insights from the econometric exercises, the chapter identifies policy priorities to drive better growth outcomes and development progress in these economies.

Main findings

The chapter presents the following main findings:

Despite the considerable economic potential of frontier markets, as a group, their progress in growth and development over the past quarter century has been modest. Half of frontier markets recorded slower per capita GDP growth than the EMDE average. Real GDP per capita in the median frontier market is now less than one-third of that in the typical emerging market—a wider gap than in 2000. In the five-year period from the onset of the pandemic, high-income status moved further away for about 40 percent of frontier markets. Growth of per capita investment has more than halved since the 2000s. Poverty rates in frontier markets have reduced by more than half this century, but remain at about five times those in emerging markets, and progress has slowed in the past decade. Life expectancy has risen, as have other human development indicators, such as education levels. These indicators have also risen in other EMDEs.

Frontier markets' financial development and integration into the global economic and financial system remain partial—and modest in some respects—leaving opportunities and potential gains unrealized, as well as some notable vulnerabilities. Frontier markets' de jure financial openness has increased but remains below that of emerging markets. Meanwhile, the partial nature of frontier markets' financial development and international integration tends to heighten their vulnerabilities:

- First, frontier markets have more limited capacity than emerging markets to translate financial inflows into productive investment, given their relatively weak absorptive capacity.

This is reflected in relatively underdeveloped and shallow domestic financial markets, with wider lending–deposit rate spreads than in emerging markets, as well as institutional and governance weaknesses. Accordingly, growth in capital stock per capita has been disappointing.

- Second, thin policy buffers (for example, in terms of fiscal flexibility and foreign exchange reserves) and credibility gaps in governance and policy frameworks in frontier markets increase uncertainty for firms and investors, raise external financing costs, and amplify the adverse effects of shocks.

- Third, the nature of frontier markets' external exposures is unfavorable relative to emerging markets. Portfolio flows tend to be more volatile; export baskets are more concentrated; and more debt is denominated in foreign currencies, alongside lower reserves cover. These features generally increase balance-sheet risks.

Output growth in frontier markets has tended to rise substantially around capital inflow surges. Stops in capital flows see a slowing of output growth (though this impact appears to be larger in emerging markets than in frontier markets). This suggests that financial integration is good for growth, even though stop events are more likely in the wake of a surge. In recent years, there have been more sovereign defaults in frontier markets than in all other countries combined.

Some frontier markets have achieved more rapid economic progress than others; although routes to success have varied, some common themes emerge from their experiences. The frontier markets that recorded the fastest average growth in GDP per capita over the last quarter century recorded strong increases in capital stock per person relative to other frontier markets. They also improved governance, and their banks' lending–deposit spreads narrowed significantly. In addition, these faster-growing frontier markets were more effective in containing growth in government debt and debt-service burdens. These top-performing frontier markets are a diverse group that have adopted different development approaches: from encouraging investment into energy and commodities sectors (Kazakhstan), to pursuing value-added manufacturing and exports (Viet Nam), to focusing on services- and tourism-driven growth (Rwanda). Four economies (Bulgaria, Costa Rica, Panama, and Romania) reached high-income status and therefore graduated from frontier market status to emerging market classification between 2012 and 2025.

Policy makers in frontier markets should strive to leverage the benefits of financial market access and growing populations effectively, including by:

- *Advancing financial and trade integration while mitigating associated risks.* Furthering integration while improving oversight capacity, developing local financial markets, and enhancing policy buffers can help harness international investment, while expanding and diversifying exports can support resilience and development objectives.

- *Bolstering macroeconomic stability.* Macroeconomic stability and credibility strengthen the underpinnings of financial integration, including by reducing the risk premia sought by investors, and are important components of economic progress more broadly. Sound monetary and fiscal policies to cement price stability and fiscal sustainability are key for frontier markets' future prospects (as in other EMDEs).

- *Catalyzing investment, productivity growth, and job creation.* Taking full advantage of access to international finance requires investment in infrastructure and human capital. Structural reforms are needed to help generate high-return investment opportunities and set the stage for sustained productivity growth and job creation. Effective physical and digital infrastructure can lay the foundations for accelerating private investment, and better human capital can help ensure that growing working-age populations secure productive jobs. Enhancing governance and the business environment can also support these objectives. These are priorities across many EMDEs, but they are particularly important to enable frontier markets to capitalize on their demographic and resource endowments.

Given the heterogeneity of frontier markets, policy design must account for individual economies' particular advantages and vulnerabilities; this will shape the relative importance of these themes. Inclusion in major global financial market indexes is not a magic bullet, but it can incentivize reform and attract investment, thereby helping to sustainably boost job creation and living standards. The international community has an important role to play in fostering an environment in which these economies can thrive. With potential growth slowing elsewhere and working-age populations plateauing or declining in many advanced and emerging market economies, frontier markets will play a growing role in shaping global economic and development outcomes. The extent to which they can convert financial integration into sustained output growth and job creation will be critical.

Characteristics of frontier markets

The baseline set of frontier markets in this chapter—those that met the criteria in 2012, midway through the period under analysis—comprises 39 economies that are diverse in their geographies and economic structures. Frontier markets are found in all six EMDE regions, with the largest numbers in Sub-Saharan Africa and the Latin America and the Caribbean region (refer to figure 4.1.A). Six frontier markets are classified as small states, and four as FCS (refer to figure 4.1.B). Frontier markets are generally middle-income countries, although this masks significant dispersion in income per capita. About one-quarter of frontier markets are members of the International Development Association (IDA).

Compared to other developing economies, frontier markets typically exhibit higher levels of market access and financial development. The median frontier market has more than double the physical capital stock per capita of the typical other developing economy. In addition, human capital—in terms of education and health metrics—is stronger in frontier markets than in other developing economies. Relative to emerging markets, however, important gaps persist across all of these areas.

FIGURE 4.1 Basic characteristics of frontier markets

Frontier markets exist in all six EMDE regions. They are mostly middle-income countries. About half of frontier markets are commodity exporters, many specializing in energy exports. The population of frontier markets, about 1.8 billion today, is set to rise to 2.6 billion by 2050. Frontier markets' share of the global population is projected to rise substantially over 2025–50, unlike that of emerging markets.

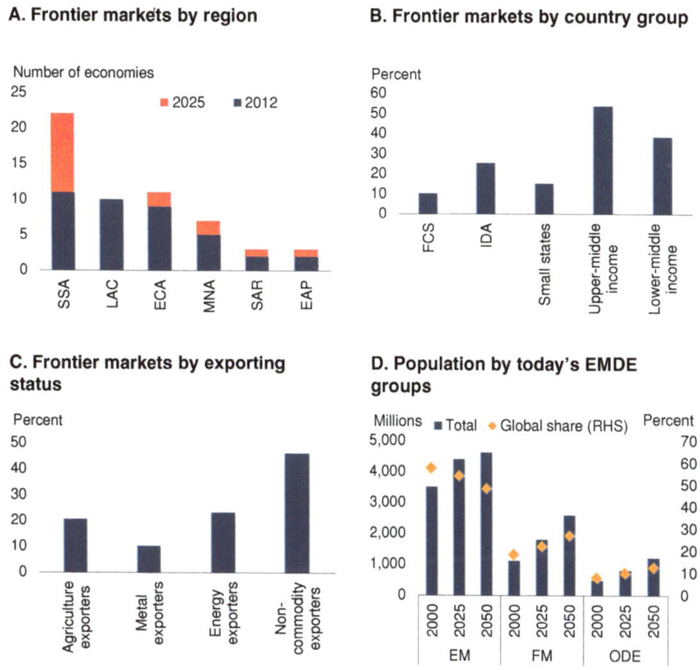

Sources: UN Population Prospects (database); World Bank.

Note: EAP = East Asia and Pacific; ECA = Europe and Central Asia; EM = emerging markets; FCS = fragile and conflict situations; FM = frontier markets; IDA = International Development Association; LAC = Latin America and the Caribbean; MNA = Middle East, North Africa, Afghanistan and Pakistan; ODE = other developing economies, neither EM nor FM; SAR = South Asia; SSA = Sub-Saharan Africa.

A. Sample includes 39 FMs in baseline 2012 classification, and 56 FMs as of 2025 classifications.

B.C. Sample includes 39 FMs, using baseline 2012 classification of economies based primarily on membership of key equity and bond market indexes. Income, FCS, IDA, and small states markers are based on 2025 World Bank Group classifications. Commodity exporters are economies where 2019 exports in the named area accounted for over 20 percent of total exports.

D. Sample includes 37 EMs, 56 FMs, and 57 ODEs, as of 2025 classification status. Bars show total population in millions. Orange diamonds show the share of total population.

About half of frontier markets have exports that are dominated by primary commodities, with the majority exporting industrial commodities, such as energy commodities and metals (refer to figure 4.1.C). Industrial activity in these economies is often substantially geared toward commodity extraction, and commodity revenues form an important part of tax bases. Relative to GDP, resource rents are especially large in frontier market energy exporters, although they are also sizeable in metal exporters—a pattern shared with other EMDE groups. Many frontier markets possess significant commodity endowments that

FIGURE 4.2 Frontier markets in the global economy

The baseline sample of frontier markets accounted for about 5 percent of global GDP in 2025, up from less than 4 percent in 2000, but their contribution to global growth remains small. Frontier markets' exports as a share of the global total also remain small, especially relative to emerging markets. Although the share of global capital flows to frontier markets remains modest, it has almost quadrupled since the early 2000s.

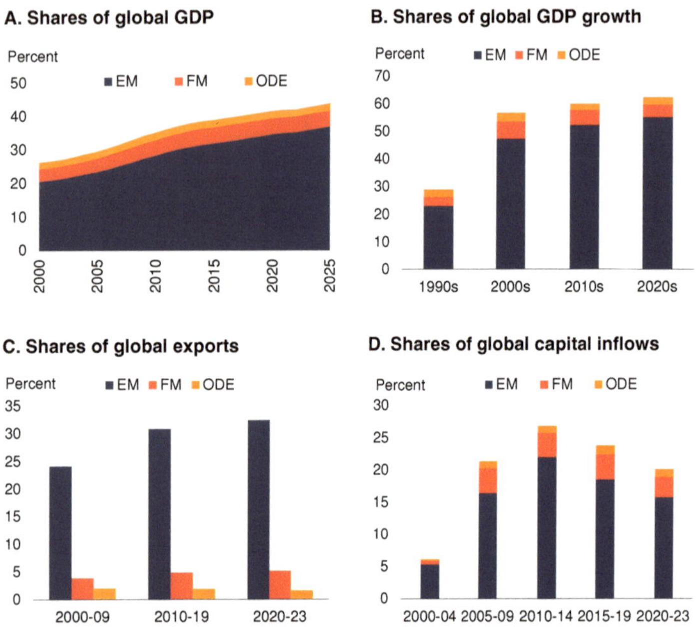

Sources: IMF Balance of Payments and International Investment Position (database); WDI (database); World Bank.

Note: EM = emerging markets; FM = frontier markets; ODE = other developing economies, neither EM nor FM. Sample includes 34 EMs, 39 FMs, and 80 ODEs, as of the 2012 baseline (the midpoint of the quarter century), unless otherwise specified.

A.B. Panels show the share of global GDP and GDP growth respectively. GDP aggregates are calculated using real U.S. dollar GDP weights at average 2010–19 prices and market exchange rates.

C. Panel shows exports of goods and services for each group of countries as share of total world exports during each average period. Sample includes up to 31 EMs, 38 FMs, and 66 ODEs.

D. Stacked bars show total capital inflows per country group as a share of the global total. Based on an unbalanced sample, including up to 32 EMs, 39 FMs, and 74 ODEs.

are globally relevant for new technologies and the energy transition. Solar energy potential is also generally high in frontier markets. However, their solar energy output remains quite modest. In addition, frontier markets often have significant natural capital that could support tourism.

Share of global population

The population of frontier markets as a group is large and growing. About 1.8 billion people live in frontier markets in 2025—over one-fifth of the global population (refer to figure 4.1.D). More than 230 million young people in these economies will reach working age between 2025 and 2035. While population growth is slowing in emerging markets, an increase of 783 million is projected for today's frontier markets over the next quarter century. This exceeds the increase projected for the rest of the world combined. It is about 100 million more than frontier markets' increase in the previous quarter century. By 2050, the population in today's frontier markets is forecast to grow to almost 2.6 billion—27 percent of the global total.

Growing populations represent large economic potential for both frontier markets and other developing economies. While the number of working-age people is expected to fall in both advanced economies and emerging markets between 2025 and 2050, in frontier markets it is expected to rise by 568 million. This is an increase of more than 50 percent, and more than three-quarters of the projected increase in the global working-age population.

Global economic footprint

Frontier markets' share of global output edged up from 3.8 percent in 2000 to 4.8 percent in 2025 (refer to figure 4.2.A). Compared to emerging markets, this remains modest: between 2000 and 2025, emerging markets' contribution to global GDP rose from 21 percent to 37 percent, largely driven by China and India. Despite the slight increase in their share of the global economy since 2000, frontier markets' contribution to global growth has declined, although it remains larger than that of other developing economies (refer to figure 4.2.B).

Frontier markets are relatively open to international trade. However, their share of global exports remains small. Between the 2000s and the early 2020s, it increased only from 4 to 5 percent, whereas that of emerging markets grew from 23 to 33 percent (refer to figure 4.2.C).

There has been a notable shift in the distribution of global capital inflows since the start of this century: EMDEs' share more than tripled, from 6 to 20 percent, between the early 2000s and the early 2020s (refer to figure 4.2.D). The share received by frontier markets grew fivefold but remained modest, rising from 0.6 to 3.1 percent (with the increase concentrated early in the quarter century). Emerging markets account for most of the shift in EMDEs as a whole. The share of other developing economies increased, but only to just over 1 percent.

Frontier markets continue to lag behind both advanced economies and emerging markets in terms of openness to financial flows, in part owing to capital account restrictions. However, unlike other developing economies, frontier markets have liberalized their capital accounts significantly since 2000. A measure of de jure financial integration rose from 0.18 in 2000 to 0.45 in 2022—slightly above the level in the median emerging market in 2000 (refer to figure 4.3.A). Since the start of this century, frontier markets have maintained high levels of trade openness. Exports and imports together amounted to 78 percent of GDP in the median frontier market as of 2023, similar to ratios observed in both emerging markets and other developing economies (refer to figure 4.3.B).

Inward FDI positions in frontier markets increased from 17 percent to 21 percent of GDP between 2009 and 2023—significant, but smaller than the increases in emerging markets and in other developing economies (refer to figure 4.3.C). However, in the median frontier market, inward portfolio liabilities relative to GDP more than tripled over 2001–23, from 2 to 7 percent—a larger proportional rise than that in emerging markets (refer to figure 4.3.D).

Financial integration and financial development

Access to global financial markets confers benefits on frontier markets, facilitating capital inflows to support investment, growth, and development. However, the composition and volatility of capital flows to frontier markets, together with the limited development of their financial markets and financial systems, can leave them vulnerable to shifts in sentiment, particularly in periods of global stress. This is the case even though their integration with the global financial cycle remains relatively limited.

Composition and volatility of capital inflows

The composition and dynamics of capital flows in frontier markets have evolved over the last 25 years. Total capital inflows to these economies, in proportion to GDP, jumped in the late 2000s. Over that decade as a whole, they were higher than in both emerging markets and other developing economies, but they have trended lower since then (refer to figure 4.4.A; Lane and Milesi-Ferretti 2018). In fact, in the first half of the 2020s, total capital inflows as a share of GDP

FIGURE 4.3 Financial and trade openness

There has been a pronounced increase in the de jure financial openness of frontier markets since 2000, leading to higher foreign direct investment and portfolio investment liability positions. Although frontier markets have not increased their openness to international trade significantly since 2000, they remain more open than emerging markets and slightly more open than other developing economies.

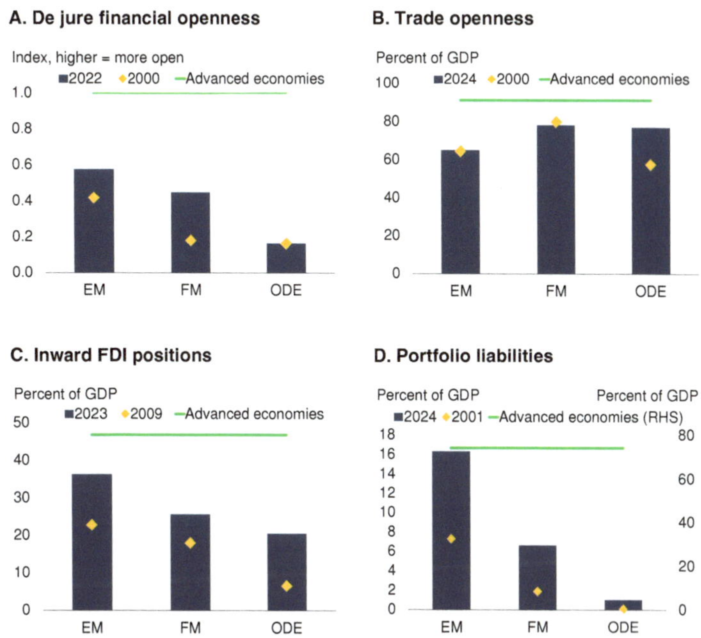

Sources: Chinn and Ito (2006); IMF Coordinated Direct Investment Survey (database); IMF Coordinated Portfolio Investment Survey (database); WDI (database); World Bank.

Note: EM = emerging markets; FM = frontier markets; FDI = foreign direct investment; ODE = other developing economies, neither EM nor FM. Green line shows the median value for advanced economies in the latest data available for each panel.

A. Financial openness is proxied by the Chinn–Ito Index, which measures a country's degree of capital account openness using the first principal component of variables on regulatory controls over current or capital account transactions, with a normalized value of 1 indicating the most open (Chinn and Ito 2006). Values are regional medians for 2000 and 2022, based on a balanced sample comprising 32 advanced economies, 34 EMs, 37 FMs, and 69 ODEs.

B. Trade openness is the sum of exports and imports of goods and services, expressed as a share of GDP. Values are aggregate medians, based on a balanced sample of 33 advanced economies, 26 EMs, 36 FMs, and 51 ODEs.

C. Inward direct investment positions represent the value of equity and debt instruments held by nonresident direct investors or their affiliated enterprises in resident enterprises. Positions are based on reported data where available, supplemented with derived data constructed from partner-reported outward investment to fill gaps. Values are aggregate medians for 2023 and 2009, based on a balanced sample of 33 advanced economies, 28 EMs, 31 FMs, and 54 ODEs.

D. Portfolio liability positions reflect the value of foreign-held equity and debt securities and are based on derived data constructed from partner-reported holdings of these instruments. Values are aggregate medians for 2001 and 2024, based on a balanced sample of 32 advanced economies, 34 EMs, 38 FMs, and 68 ODEs.

FIGURE 4.4 Capital inflows

Relative to GDP, capital inflows to frontier markets have trended downward since the 2000s. Portfolio inflows picked up in the 2010s but have been negligible in recent years, and FDI inflows have declined over time. Portfolio inflows have consistently been most volatile in frontier markets. Capital flow surges are often followed by stops, especially for frontier market portfolio flows.

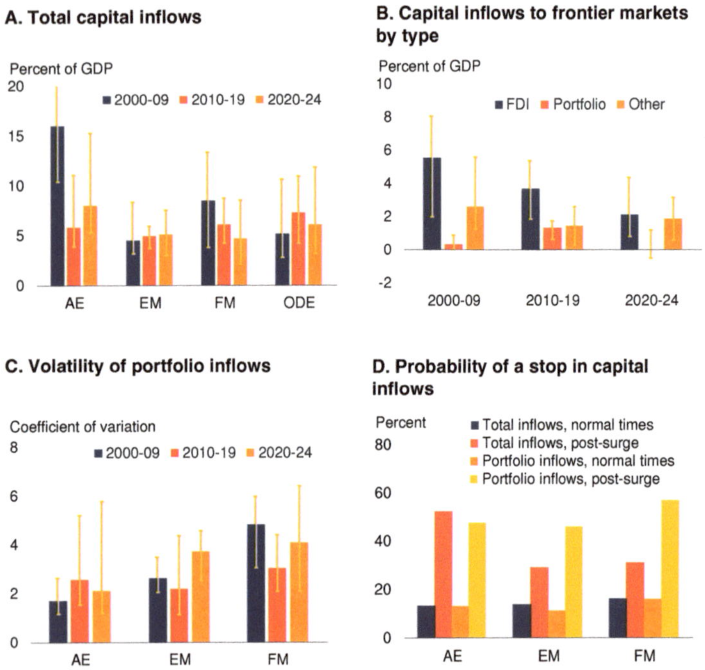

Sources: Haver Analytics; World Bank.

Note: AE = advanced economies; EM = emerging markets; FM = frontier markets; ODE = other developing economies, neither EM nor FM. Sample includes up to 33 AEs, 25 EMs, 33 FMs, and 40 ODEs.

A. Bars show group medians of country-level period averages, given the unbalanced nature of the underlying time series. Orange whiskers indicate the interquartile range. Upper interquartile value for AEs is truncated.

B. Bars show the median value for frontier markets based on country-level period averages, given the unbalanced nature of the underlying time series. Orange whiskers indicate the interquartile range.

C. Bars show the median coefficient of variation, and orange whiskers indicate the interquartile range. The coefficient of variation is obtained as the standard deviation of quarterly capital inflows to each country over the specified period, divided by the absolute value of the mean inflows during the same period. Bar and interquartile range for ODEs are omitted due to negligible portfolio inflows.

D. Post-surge probability refers to the share of surge episodes followed by a stop within the subsequent 8 quarters after the surge ends, benchmarked against the probability of a stop during normal times—that is, within any forward-looking 8-quarter window outside surge and post-surge periods.

were lower in frontier markets than in all other country groups.

Foreign direct investment (FDI), which tends to be less volatile than other capital flows, has shrunk significantly, relative to GDP, in the median frontier market, to 2.1 percent in the first half of the 2020s, from 5.5 percent in the 2000s (refer to figure 4.4.B). Portfolio investment—the form of capital flow with the most direct link to financial market index inclusion—exhibits more volatility, reflecting greater sensitivity to short-term developments and shifts in global risk appetite (Forbes and Warnock 2012). Portfolio inflows to the median frontier market were close to zero in the early 2000s, increased to 1.3 percent of GDP in the 2010s, but fell back in the early 2020s, briefly turning negative during the global monetary tightening of 2022. Other inflows to frontier markets—primarily cross-border bank lending—have been somewhat more stable. Differences in the volatility of total capital inflows among the main country groups in the periods 2000–09, 2010–19, and 2020–24, appear unremarkable. However, the volatility of portfolio inflows was greater in frontier markets than in emerging markets or advanced economies in each of these periods (refer to figure 4.4.C).

Extreme movements in capital inflows—"surge" and "stop" episodes—have tended to be highly synchronized across different country groups (refer to box 4.2). They have been shaped both by global "push" factors and by domestic "pull" factors. Inflow surges have often been ignited by domestic factors. Higher credit ratings—often reflecting structural policy improvements—and stronger domestic growth both increase the chances of a surge in capital inflows. Surges can be beneficial to growth when channeled into productive investment, but they can also raise the chances of a stop, which can disrupt economic activity. For frontier markets in the period since 2000, the probability of a stop in aggregate capital inflows was almost twice as high (39 percent) in the aftermath of a surge episode than around non-surge periods (refer to figure 4.4.D).

Frontier markets become especially susceptible to capital flow stops during periods of global financial stress. This was evident during the 2008–09 Global Financial Crisis and in other episodes of tightening financial conditions, such as following U.S. monetary tightening shocks and spikes in risk aversion. Frontier markets are also vulnerable to contagion through financial and trade channels from stress in peer markets. For portfolio inflows specifically, the probability of a frontier market experiencing a stop rises from 16 percent in normal times to 57 percent after a surge. The share of frontier markets experiencing stops in portfolio inflows remained high in the 2010s, even

BOX 4.2 Incidence and drivers of surges and stops in capital inflows

Frontier markets have experienced frequent and pronounced surges and stops in capital inflows, especially in portfolio investment, reflecting deeper integration into global financial markets. Surges are common and are often followed by stops, highlighting heightened vulnerability to abrupt shifts in capital inflows. Capital inflow surge and stop episodes are shaped by both global "push" factors and domestic "pull" factors. For frontier market portfolio inflows, key global push factors include global risk sentiment and global growth, while domestic financial market depth is a significant pull factor. Contagion across country groups and through trade linkages further amplifies risks. Overall, the findings underscore the need for tailored policies that strengthen resilience to volatile capital inflows in response to global conditions, domestic fundamentals, and systemic spillovers.

While capital inflows—in the form of foreign direct investment (FDI), portfolio investment, or other investment—can support growth and development in emerging market and developing economies (EMDEs), their volatility can undermine macroeconomic stability, with long-term consequences (CGFS 2021). In particular, the risks associated with sudden "stops" in capital inflows are well recognized, including restricted access to external financing, depressed asset prices, financial sector stress, and declines in output growth (Gelos et al. 2022). Sharp increases in capital inflows—"surges"—are often associated with higher GDP growth for a time. They can also pose challenges by fueling credit booms and asset bubbles and by driving currency appreciations that erode export competitiveness. Surges may further increase the likelihood of abrupt stops and, in some cases, culminate in financial crises.[a]

A substantial body of research has examined extreme movements in gross capital flows—including surges and stops—and their macro-financial implications. Much of this literature has focused on understanding the incidence, synchronization, and drivers of such episodes across advanced economies and emerging markets. In contrast, frontier markets have received little attention, even as their financial integration has deepened. This box addresses the following questions:

- How does the incidence of extreme capital inflow movements in frontier markets compare with that in advanced economies and emerging markets?
- What are the roles of global "push" factors and domestic "pull" factors in influencing the likelihood of surges and stops?

Surges and stops in frontier market capital inflows

Extreme movements in capital inflows—namely, surges and stops—denote a sharp increase or decrease in gross capital inflows relative to a country's historical reference level.[b] To distinguish extreme shifts from cyclical swings, the analysis follows a statistical approach used in Forbes and Warnock (2012, 2021). A surge episode begins when the year-over-year change in four-quarter gross inflows exceeds two standard deviations above its 20-quarter rolling mean (threshold condition) and continues for all consecutive quarters while the change remains more than one standard deviation above the mean (continuation condition). Episodes are required to last more than one quarter (duration condition) and end when the change falls below one standard deviation above the mean (ending condition). Stop episodes are defined symmetrically, using the same conditions in the direction of sharp reductions in gross capital inflows.

The incidence of surges and stops highlights the synchronized nature of these episodes across country groups. For advanced economies, emerging markets, and frontier markets alike, the share of countries in surge episodes peaked in the last quarter of 2007 (refer to figure B4.2.1.A). The subsequent shift was rapid: amid the Global Financial Crisis, stops reached their highest incidence between 2008Q4 and 2009Q2 (refer to figure B4.2.1.B). During this period, over three-quarters of advanced economies, 60 percent of emerging markets, and about half of frontier markets experienced a sharp drop in capital inflows. Extreme capital inflow movements fell markedly after the crisis, but stop episodes picked up in the mid-2010s—particularly

Note: This box was prepared by Jiwon Lee and Kate McKinnon.

a. For evidence on the macro-financial risks associated with capital inflow surges—including increased vulnerability to abrupt stops and crises—refer to Blanchard et al. (2017); Forbes and Warnock (2021); Ghosh, Ostry, and Qureshi (2016); and Sula (2010).

b. Gross capital flows refer to total transactions between residents and nonresidents, usually measured as the net incurrence of liabilities (gross inflows) and the net acquisition of foreign assets (gross outflows). This contrasts with net capital flows, which refer to the balance of inflows and outflows.

BOX 4.2 Incidence and drivers of surges and stops in capital inflows (*continued*)

FIGURE B4.2.1 Share of countries experiencing surges and stops in capital inflows

Surges and stops in capital inflows have occurred in synchronized waves across country groups. Portfolio inflows in frontier markets have shown the highest incidence of surges and stops across most flow types and country groups, but the share of frontier markets experiencing surges has dipped in the 2020s.

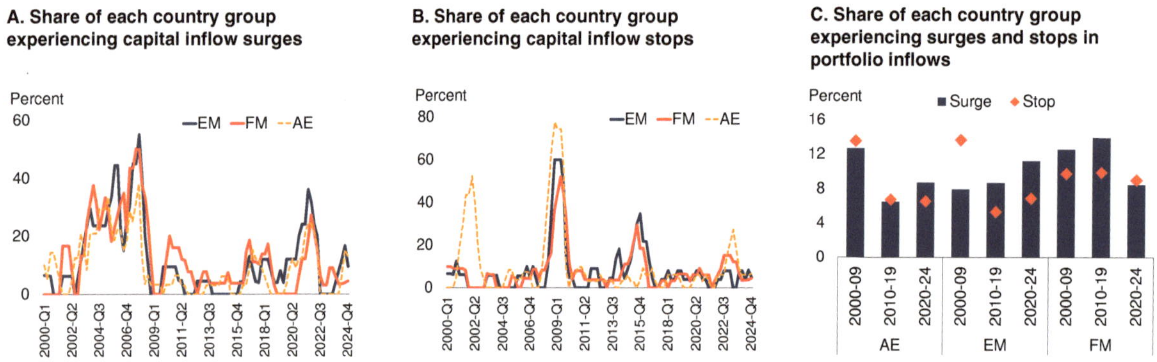

Sources: Haver Analytics; World Bank.

Note: AE = advanced economies; EM = emerging markets; FM = frontier markets. Surge and stop episodes are identified following the methodology of Forbes and Warnock (2012; 2021), based on unbalanced quarterly data on capital inflows. The sample includes up to 34 AEs, 25 EMs, and 33 FMs.

A.B. Panels show the share of economies experiencing a surge or stop episode in each quarter during 2000Q1–2024Q4.

C. Bars show the average share of economies experiencing a surge episode in portfolio capital inflows in each quarter over the given time period; diamond markers indicate stop episodes.

among emerging and frontier markets. More recently, surge activity re-emerged under the accommodative financial conditions of the immediate post-pandemic period.

Portfolio inflows to frontier markets displayed distinct dynamics in the period after the Global Financial Crisis window, both relative to other flow types (FDI and other investment), and to patterns in advanced economies and emerging markets. In the 2010s, the share of frontier markets experiencing a portfolio surge or a stop in a given quarter averaged 14 percent and 10 percent, respectively, nearly double the rate in other groups (refer to figure B4.2.1.C). In the 2020s so far, the incidence of stops in frontier markets has remained elevated, while the incidence of surges fell sharply—unlike in advanced economies and emerging markets.

Surges can raise the risk of sudden stops by fueling overheating, risk-taking, and macroeconomic imbalances. These risks are amplified by shifts in global financial conditions, as surges often occur during periods of abundant liquidity and may reverse abruptly when conditions tighten. Consistent with this, the probability that surges in capital flows are followed by a stop within eight quarters varies markedly over time, exceeding 70 percent for surges ending in 2007 and 2008. For all country groups, stop episodes are more likely to occur following the end of a surge than during periods with no preceding surge. Surges in portfolio inflows to frontier markets are particularly prone to reversals, with the probability of a stop rising from 16 percent to 57 percent.

These patterns—particularly the elevated incidence of surges—align with the expansion of portfolio inflows into frontier markets during the 2010s, driven in part by their inclusion in global equity and bond indexes and investors' growing search for yield and diversification. These extreme episodes highlight the vulnerability of frontier markets to volatile portfolio movements and associated risks. While total inflows in frontier markets tend to move more closely with global trends, portfolio inflows exhibit a more idiosyncratic pattern.

Drivers of surges and stops in capital inflows

To examine the drivers of surges and stops in capital inflows across countries, a regression model links these

BOX 4.2 Incidence and drivers of surges and stops in capital inflows (*continued*)

episodes to a broad set of global "push" and domestic "pull" factors, in line with those commonly identified in the related literature.[c] "Push" factors comprise indicators reflecting global risk, global economic policy uncertainty, oil prices, world GDP growth, U.S. long-term interest rates, and U.S. monetary policy surprises. "Pull" factors comprise domestic structural and macroeconomic indicators, including domestic real GDP growth, financial depth as measured by stock market capitalization, de jure financial openness, sovereign credit ratings, and exchange rate arrangements.

Two variables are added to capture potential contagion effects influencing the transmission of shocks within country groups or through trade linkages. First, a group-based dummy variable is constructed, which equals one if another country in the same group—advanced economy, emerging market, or frontier market—has an episode in the previous quarter. Second, a trade-contagion variable is constructed as the trade-weighted share of episodes among each country's trading partners. The regressions are estimated using a complementary log-log model (data and methodological details are provided in annex 4.3).[d]

The role of global push factors. Higher long-term U.S. interest rates lower the likelihood of capital inflow surges, consistent with tighter global financial conditions reducing the attractiveness of cross-border investment (Ghosh, Qureshi, and Sugawara 2014; Rey 2015). A rise in the U.S. monetary policy surprise measure—capturing shifts toward tighter-than-expected policy—is associated with a significantly higher likelihood of stop episodes. This aligns with related literature emphasizing the key role of monetary policy shocks in driving the global financial cycle (Miranda-Agrippino and Rey 2020).

Global sentiment is also strongly associated with the likelihood of extreme capital inflow episodes. Rising global risk—measured by the CBOE VIX—significantly increases the likelihood of an economy having a stop episode, consistent with literature highlighting the importance of push factors in explaining capital flow dynamics (Calderon and Kubota 2019; Forbes and Warnock 2012, 2021).[e] Domestic policy makers in frontier markets have little control over these global forces, underscoring the need for resilience-focused strategies.

The role of domestic pull factors. Domestic macroeconomic conditions and structural features also influence the probability of extreme capital inflow episodes. GDP growth is positively and significantly associated with surges, implying that stronger domestic performance increases the likelihood of capital inflow booms. When excluding the GFC and COVID periods, higher growth also significantly lowers the likelihood of stops. While not significantly linked to surges, more rigid exchange rate regimes are associated with a higher probability of stops.[f] The finding that better sovereign ratings are significantly associated with surges is intuitive: stronger credit quality lowers perceived risk and broadens investor demand (Emara 2015). De jure financial openness—the extent of capital account liberalization—is significantly associated with a higher likelihood of stops, once other variables are controlled; this heightened risk may be due to larger external positions and greater reliance on non-resident investors.

Contagion effects. The group-level contagion variable is positively and significantly associated with both surges and stops, indicating that capital flow episodes tend to cluster within country groups. This likely reflects structural commonalities across similarly classified economies, with vulnerabilities amplified by the "pipes"

c. For instance, refer to Calderon and Kubota (2019); CGFS (2021); Forbes and Warnock (2012, 2021); Ghosh, Ostry, and Qureshi (2016); and Ghosh, Qureshi, and Sugawara (2014).

d. Table A4.3.1 presents the baseline regression results, estimated using the full panel of countries between 2000Q1–2024Q4. A robustness exercise is carried out, whereby observations falling within the Global Financial Crisis (2008Q3–2009Q4) and the COVID-19 shock (2020Q1–2021Q2) are excluded; results are shown in table A4.3.2. For many push and pull variables, the direction and significance of the estimated effects show little change.

e. While oil price growth is not found to play a significant role in this specification, related work using different sample periods has found that higher oil prices are significantly associated with a greater likelihood of surges and a lower likelihood of stops (Forbes and Warnock 2021).

f. Further, exchange rate flexibility has been found to enhance resilience by supporting a faster recovery in capital inflows following external shocks and, more generally, to mitigate vulnerability to financial crises (Claessens and Kose 2017; Gelos et al. 2022).

BOX 4.2 Incidence and drivers of surges and stops in capital inflows (*continued*)

of the international financial system—global investors, asset managers, and other intermediaries whose activities can transmit shocks across borders (Carney 2019).[g] The trade-contagion variable is significant, underscoring that shocks can spread through financial channels and through real economic linkages. Overall, the results suggest that exposure to extreme capital flow episodes is shaped by global and domestic factors, as well as spillovers across peers.

The drivers of portfolio inflows to frontier markets

Unlike capital inflows to all economies, neither U.S. long-term yields nor monetary policy surprises have a significant effect on the likelihood of surges or stops in portfolio inflows to frontier markets. Increased global risk significantly reduces the likelihood of surges, while weaker global activity raises the likelihood of stops. Domestic characteristics also matter for stops: larger stock market capitalization is associated with a higher likelihood.

However, the effects of stock market capitalization and global GDP growth appear to be largely driven by major global stress episodes. Once observations from the GFC and COVID periods are excluded, these relationships disappear: in the non-crisis sample, higher stock market capitalization becomes positively associated with surges rather than stops.[h] Exchange rate arrangements do not significantly impact portfolio surges or stops in frontier markets, although in the non-crisis sample, more rigid exchange rate regimes are associated with fewer surges. Consistent with the broader sample, trade-weighted surges in partner countries remain significant correlates of frontier market portfolio surges, underscoring the role of trade partner spillovers; however, this relationship loses significance once global stress periods are excluded.

g. Active fund strategies often exhibit procyclical behavior, such as return-chasing and herding (Raddatz and Schmukler 2012). Benchmark-tracking funds, meanwhile, adjust exposures in response to market movements and follow mechanical index reweightings and reclassifications that can prompt large capital reallocations disconnected from underlying fundamentals (CGFS 2021; Puy 2016). These effects may be pronounced for frontier markets. Inclusion in benchmark indexes and limited analyst coverage may lead investors to see them as a homogeneous group, raising the risk of contagion when sentiment shifts or a shock hits one country.

h. This pattern could reflect boom–bust dynamics: rapid growth and buoyant equity markets often coincide with inflow surges that later reverse abruptly when global conditions deteriorate.

as it declined in advanced economies and emerging markets. This underscores the importance of resilience-enhancing policies to help cushion the disruptive impacts of capital flow reversals.

Limited financial market development

Financial market depth (the size and liquidity of credit and capital markets) is a key determinant of an economy's absorptive capacity—that is, its ability to channel domestic and foreign savings into capital accumulation. Across frontier markets, financial openness has risen, but financial market depth varies widely. In many cases, it has not kept pace with increasing access to international investors. Underdeveloped domestic-currency markets, constraints on the supply of domestic credit to the private sector, and institutional gaps all hinder the efficiency and breadth of financial intermediation. As a result, and despite improvements in some areas, funding costs remain high, bond spreads wide, and maturities relatively short. In turn, limited risk-bearing financing tends to slow capital accumulation in non-stress periods and limit shock absorption under stress.

Across EMDEs, there has been progress in utilizing financial markets: between 1990 and 2021, the number of firms issuing bonds or equity annually more than tripled, with domestic markets accounting for most of that issuance. Firms that gained access to capital markets accounted for almost two-thirds of the estimated employment gains from expanding capital markets (Meh and Schmukler 2025).

Broad indexes of financial institutions' and financial markets' development show that the median frontier market remains behind the median emerging market but ahead of other developing economies. Frontier markets made notable advances in the development of financial institutions over the century's first two decades but made no progress in the development of financial markets (refer to figure 4.5.A). These overarching indexes assessing financial development are broadly consistent with specific market and financial data. Stock market capitalization as a ratio to GDP was 18 percent in the median frontier market in 2020–23, far lower than in the median emerging market (51 percent) and comparable with the typical other developing economy (refer to figure 4.5.B). Domestic credit to the private sector was equivalent to 37 percent of GDP in the median frontier market in the early 2020s, lower than the median emerging market but higher than in other developing economies (refer to figure 4.5.C).

Banking sector efficiency indicators suggest continued constraints in frontier markets. Bank loan–deposit rate spreads in frontier markets have narrowed since 2010 but still generally exceed those in emerging markets, although they tend to be smaller than in other developing economies (refer to figure 4.5.D). Non-performing loans account for a larger proportion of banks' assets in the median frontier market than in emerging markets, though a smaller proportion than in other developing economies. Differences relative to emerging markets likely reflect a range of structural challenges in frontier markets, such as limited competition among lenders and large information asymmetries and monitoring costs (Ahokpossi 2013). More broadly, frontier markets' limited progress with financial development suggests that their access to external finance has not always translated into stronger domestic lending (IMF 2020; Ashraf 2018; Hauner, Prati, and Bircan 2013).

Integration with the global financial cycle

Frontier markets offer investors opportunities for portfolio diversification, particularly given evidence that variation in equity returns in these economies has been less correlated with the global financial cycle than in advanced economies or emerging markets (refer to box 4.3). Global factors explain only about 12 percent of the variance in equity returns in frontier markets during the period since 2000—several times lower than in both advanced economies (64 percent) and emerging markets (46 percent). A similar pattern exists for domestic credit growth: the global factor explains only 13 percent of its variance in frontier markets, compared with 51 percent in advanced economies and 25 percent in emerging markets. Country-specific factors explain most of the

FIGURE 4.5 Financial development

Frontier markets score lower than emerging markets but higher than other developing economies on the International Monetary Fund's Financial Development Index measures. Relative to GDP, stock market capitalization has remained low in the median frontier market, even compared with that in other developing economies, whereas domestic credit to the private sector ranks between levels in the other country groups. Interest rate spreads have narrowed in frontier markets, while remaining wider than those in emerging markets.

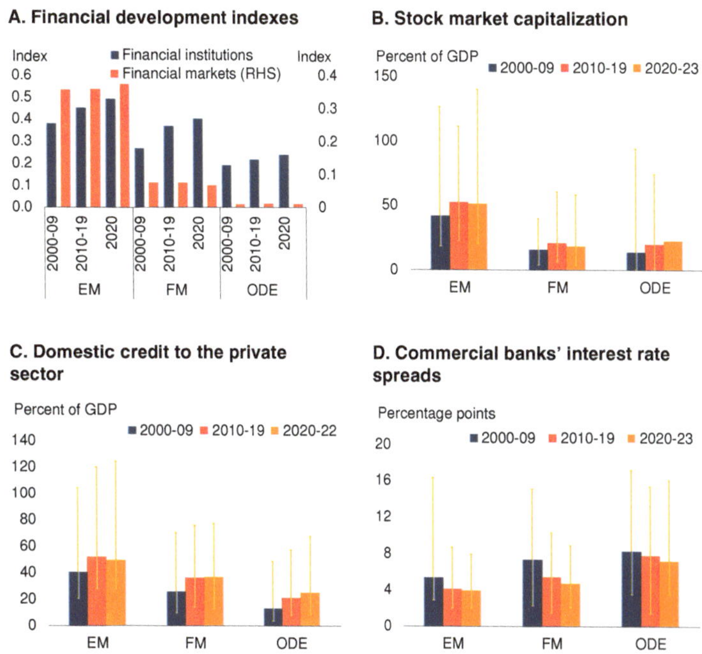

Sources: IMF Financial Development (database); WDI (database); World Bank.

Note: EM = emerging markets; FM = frontier markets; ODE = other developing economies, neither EM nor FM. Bars show period averages of country group medians, unless otherwise specified. Whiskers define the 10th and 90th percentile interval.

A. Indexes assess the development of financial institutions (such as banks and insurance firms) and financial markets (such as stock and bond markets), with a scale from 0 to 1 Sample includes up to 34 EMs, 38 FMs, and 72 ODEs for the institutions index and up to 23 EMs, 28 FMs, and 51 ODEs for the markets index.

B. Latest data available is 2023. Sample includes up to 26 EMs, 23 FMs, and 7 ODEs. The range in ODEs for the 2020–23 period is excluded for readability because of outliers in the data.

C. Latest data available is 2022. Sample includes 33 EMs, 39 FMs, and 72 ODEs.

D. Interest rate spread is the interest rate charged by banks on loans to private-sector customers minus the interest rate paid by commercial or similar banks for demand, time, or savings deposits. Latest data available is 2023. Sample includes 25 EMs, 32 FMs, and 58 ODEs.

BOX 4.3 The global financial cycle: Asset prices and credit growth

The comovement of frontier markets' equity returns and domestic credit growth with global financial conditions is limited relative to that in advanced economies and emerging markets. However, this comovement increases during global financial stress episodes. Across country groups, equity markets are more responsive than domestic credit growth to the global financial cycle.

Frontier markets have attracted increasing external investment, in part due to benchmark-driven portfolio inflows associated with index inclusion, but their exposure to the global financial cycle has received little specific research attention.[a] The global financial cycle—the tendency for asset prices, credit growth, and capital flows to move in tandem across economies—has become an important concept in international finance since the early 2000s.[b] This synchronization has been driven by increased global financial integration, which, in benign periods, can lower risk premia and ease financing, supporting cross-border capital allocation and some international risk-sharing (Kose et al. 2009). The same linkages, however, can make countries vulnerable during global stress episodes, when spikes in risk aversion and tighter global liquidity can feed through quickly to domestic financial conditions via wider sovereign and corporate spreads, sharp retrenchments and reversals in capital flows, and deleveraging by global banks and other intermediaries (Bruno and Shin 2015; Miranda-Agrippino and Rey 2022).

Frontier markets, where foreign investor participation has risen against a backdrop of shallow financial systems and thin domestic investor bases, may be particularly vulnerable to swings in global risk appetite, especially during periods of widespread stress such as the 2008–09 Global Financial Crisis and the COVID-19 pandemic (IMF 2020; Prates, Fritz, and de Paula 2023). The extent of such vulnerabilities and the conditions under which they crystallize have important implications for policy making. Against this backdrop, this box analyzes the influence of the global financial cycle on frontier markets by examining the comovement of equity returns and domestic credit growth. It addresses three questions:

- To what extent are frontier market financial conditions synchronized with global financial cycles?
- How has this exposure evolved over time?
- Do equity and credit channels differ across country groups and over time?

This analysis estimates two monthly dynamic factor models—one for equity returns and one for domestic credit growth—covering 63 economies (21 advanced economies, 24 emerging markets, and 18 frontier markets) over 2000–25. Each series is decomposed into a global factor, a group factor, and a country-specific component using a Bayesian state-space approach.[c]

- **Global factor** (common to all countries): captures universal drivers—for example, global risk appetite, major central bank policies, widespread commodity price shocks, and episodes of systemic financial stress that reverberate worldwide.
- **Group factor** (common within advanced economies, emerging markets, and frontier markets): captures shocks with more pronounced effects within a group—for example, the 2013 taper tantrum (emerging markets), euro-area sovereign debt crisis (advanced economies), and index inclusion and benchmark-driven portfolio reallocations (frontier markets).
- **Country-specific factor**: captures residual idiosyncratic components—for example, reflecting domestic policy decisions, institutional characteristics, political events, and localized economic shocks.

The results reveal three key patterns. First, compared with advanced economies and emerging markets, frontier market financial conditions are far less synchronized with global equity and credit cycles. Over 2000–25, global factors explain only 12 and 13 percent of the

Note: This box was prepared by Kate McKinnon and Hamza Zahid.

a. One recent example which bucks this trend is Prates, Fritz, and de Paula (2023).

b. A wide body of literature documents this comovement and examines constraints it places on policy makers—refer to, for example, Cerutti and Claessens (2024), Claessens, Kose, and Terrones (2011), and Rey (2015).

c. Refer to annex 4.3 for more detail on the methodology and data sources.

BOX 4.3 The global financial cycle: Asset prices and credit growth (*continued*)

FIGURE B4.3.1 Frontier markets' exposure to the global financial cycle

An estimated global factor extracted from a large sample of equity returns and credit growth is closely connected to global market risk, especially during periods of global financial stress, consistent with evidence of a pronounced global financial cycle. Frontier markets are only moderately exposed on average, with most of the variance in equity returns and credit growth driven by idiosyncratic factors. However, during major global stress episodes such as the Global Financial Crisis, the euro area debt crisis, and the COVID-19 pandemic, frontier markets' equity markets—and, with a lag, their credit growth—move much more in step with this global factor.

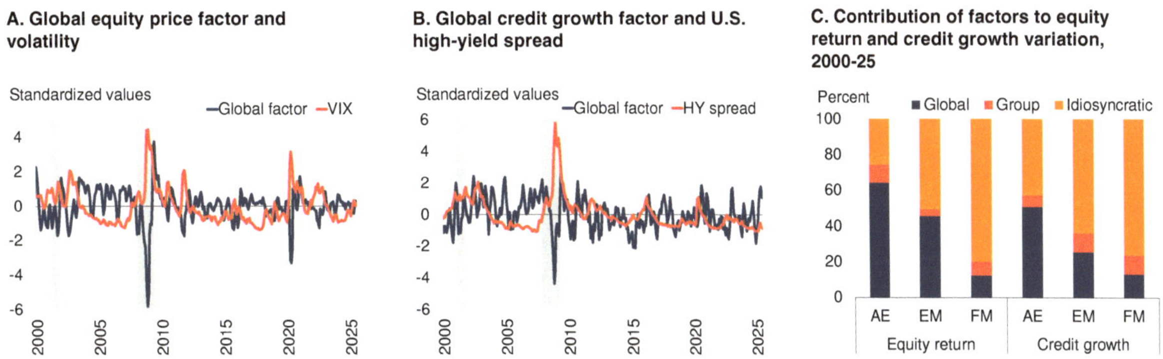

Sources: CEIC Data (database); Federal Reserve Economic Data (FRED) (database); World Bank.

Note: AE = advanced economies; EM = emerging markets; FM = frontier markets. The global, group-specific, and idiosyncratic factors are estimated using a dynamic factor model with 21 AEs, 24 EMs, and 18 FMs.

A.B. Lines are standardized (z-scores). The estimated global factors are 3-month centered moving averages. Higher values of the Chicago Board Options Exchange Volatility Index (VIX) and the Intercontinental Exchange BofA U.S. High Yield Index option-adjusted spread (HY spread) indicate greater global risk and tighter global credit conditions, respectively. Gray bands denote NBER-dated United States recessions.

C. Bars show the share of variance in equity returns and domestic credit growth attributed to global, group-specific, and idiosyncratic factors, averaged across countries in each group.

variance in frontier market equity returns and domestic credit growth, respectively, compared with 64 and 51 percent for advanced economies and 46 and 25 percent for emerging markets. Second, frontier market synchronization with both global equity and credit cycles increases during global financial stress episodes, though it still lags that of other groups. Third, global influences are more cyclical in equity markets, including for frontier markets, where the global factor's variance share more than triples in the 2007–12 crisis period (covering the Global Financial Crisis and the euro-area debt turmoil), whereas comovement in domestic credit growth is more stable over time across all country groups. This may reflect country-specific credit market features—including regulatory constraints and lending standards—that buffer cyclical global shocks, while domestic equity prices can respond rapidly to global financial conditions (Cerutti and Claessens 2024).

Global factors

Estimates of the global equity price factor (GEPF) and the global credit growth factor (GCGF) capture related but distinct aspects of the global financial cycle. The GEPF, extracted from cross-country equity returns, primarily reflects global risk appetite (though looser funding can also lift equities). The GCGF, derived from credit growth, captures the availability and cost of international funding (yet still moves with broad sentiment). Together, these factors show how quickly investors reprice risk and how broadly global credit expands or contracts.

The GEPF plunges during major global stress episodes—the 2008–09 Global Financial Crisis, the euro-area sovereign debt crisis of 2011, and the onset of COVID-19 in 2020—before rebounding just as sharply (refer to figure B4.3.1.A). Extreme movements occur in only a small share of months but are more common than under a normal distribution; when they do occur, they are disproportionately large on the downside (Muir 2017; Rey 2015).[d] Correlation between the GEPF and the VIX reaches about –0.80 during stress episodes,

d. This finding is robust to smoothing the GEPF.

BOX 4.3 The global financial cycle: Asset prices and credit growth (*continued*)

consistent with evidence that global risk aversion dominates comovement in asset prices and credit conditions, especially amid global financial market stress (Miranda-Agrippino and Rey 2022). After the Global Financial Crisis, GEPF swings narrowed, reflecting compressed risk premia amid prolonged monetary policy easing in major advanced economies (Arteta et al. 2015). Correlation between the GEPF and the VIX falls to roughly –0.30 during the liquidity-abundant 2013–19 period, suggesting that while ample liquidity in key advanced economies can depress volatility indexes, it does not necessarily generate tighter global equity return comovement.[e]

The GCGF exhibits a similar boom-bust pattern and a high degree of persistence, indicating that peaks in the cycle tend to decay only gradually. The factor fell by almost three standard deviations during the late 2008 funding market freeze, dipped again during the euro-area sovereign debt episode, and fell briefly at the onset of COVID-19 (refer to figure B4.3.1.B). Its correlation with the U.S. high-yield spread was near –0.90 at the height of the Global Financial Crisis but close to zero during more benign periods. As with the GEPF, the GCGF features more frequent and severe contractions than a normal distribution would suggest, consistent with historical evidence (Jordà, Schularick, and Taylor 2013).

Global factor comovement by country group

For equity returns, all three country-group average series converge on the GEPF during the 2008–09 and early-2020 crises. Outside stress windows, average equity returns of advanced economies and emerging markets have tracked the GEPF fairly closely since 2000. Frontier market returns initially diverged markedly, but the gap with the GEPF has narrowed since 2009, suggesting gradual but still limited financial integration. For domestic credit growth, there is starker differentiation in the overall trajectories of the country group average series, which track the GCGF less closely and exhibit more limited convergence during crises.

e. The VIX, a U.S.-focused volatility measure, may overstate global risk perceptions if stress is focused on advanced economies, while the latent factor synthesizes information from more than 60 economies. This may explain the modest decoupling between the two series after the Global Financial Crisis.

Country-group differences are highlighted by variance decompositions (refer to figure B4.3.1.C):

Equity markets: The GEPF explains 64 percent of the variance in returns for advanced economies, 46 percent for emerging markets, and 12 percent for frontier markets. Idiosyncratic factors account for 25 percent of the variation in advanced economies, 50 percent in emerging markets, and 80 percent in frontier markets. Group-specific factors play a modest role (4 percent for emerging markets; 8 percent for frontier markets).

Credit markets: The GCGF captures 51 percent and 25 percent of domestic credit growth for advanced economies and emerging markets, respectively. In frontier markets, global factors explain only 13 percent of the credit variance, compared with about 76 percent for idiosyncratic forces. Group factors play a slightly larger role in credit growth than in equity returns (roughly 11 percent for emerging markets and frontier markets).

These results align with differences in market structure and integration channels. Advanced economies, with large and liquid financial markets and deep cross-border capital investment linkages, are tightly linked to global cycles in both equity and credit. Emerging markets have a sizeable but more limited global component and a larger role for country-specific forces. Frontier markets remain largely segmented, in line with more nascent financial integration; however, exposure to the global factors tends to rise during periods of global financial stress.

Changes in comovement over time

To trace how synchronization in equity markets and domestic credit conditions has evolved since the start of this century, variance decompositions are computed for four distinct phases of the global cycle: the pre-Global Financial Crisis period (2001–06), the Global Financial Crisis and euro-area debt turmoil (2007–12), the post-crisis low-rate period (2013–19), and the COVID-19 shock and subsequent tightening cycle (2020–25).

Frontier markets remain less connected to the global cycle in equity markets, but the role of the GEPF more than tripled, to almost 30 percent, during the 2007–12 window (refer to figures B4.3.2.A-C). Comovement in credit markets also peaked in this period, with the GCGF accounting for almost 22 percent of credit

BOX 4.3 The global financial cycle: Asset prices and credit growth (*continued*)

FIGURE B4.3.2 Variance decompositions of equity returns

In frontier markets, equity return variance is typically dominated by idiosyncratic shocks over longer windows, but vulnerability to global stress is underscored by the roughly tripled contribution of the global factor during the subperiod that includes the Global Financial Crisis. Equity returns in advanced economies and emerging markets are much more tightly tied to the global factor.

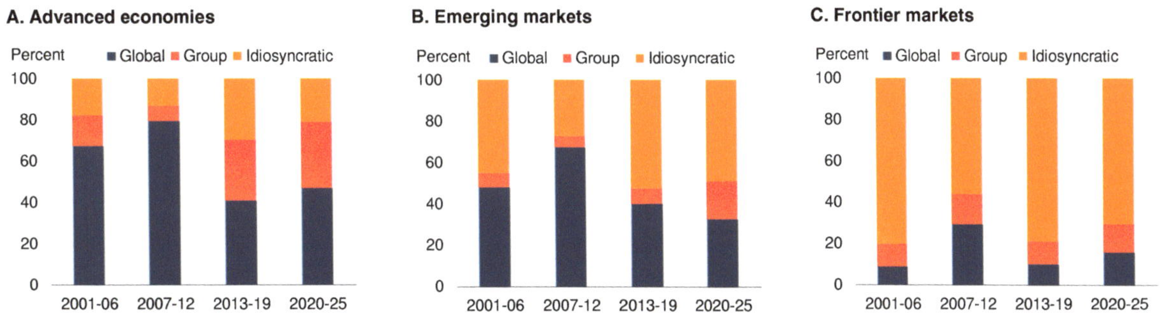

Sources: CEIC Data (database); World Bank.

Note: The global, group, and idiosyncratic factors are estimated using a dynamic factor model with monthly equity return data for 21 advanced economies, 24 emerging markets, and 18 frontier markets.

A.-C. Bars show variance attributed to global, group-specific, and idiosyncratic factors, averaged by country group.

growth variance. Across country groups, the GCGF's role in domestic credit growth was more stable over time (refer to figures B4.3.3.A-C).

Pre-Global Financial Crisis period (2001–06): Global factors accounted for about two-thirds of equity return variance and nearly 60 percent of credit growth variance in advanced economies, reflecting deep financial integration. Exposure was markedly lower in frontier markets: 9 percent in equity and 19 percent in credit markets. Emerging markets ranked in between.

Crisis era (2007–12): Synchronization increased across all groups, especially in equity markets, amid the common shock of the Global Financial Crisis. Frontier markets saw the most dramatic shift: the GEPF explained 29 percent of equity return variance, more than triple the pre-crisis share, while credit growth synchronization rose more modestly, to 22 percent.

Post-crisis low-rate period (2013–19): Group-specific influences became more visible in advanced economy equity markets, where regulatory reforms and monetary policies followed similar paths. In frontier markets, the global variance share for equities fell to near its pre-crisis level. Local credit conditions saw some decoupling across country groups.

COVID-19 period and beyond (2020–25): The pandemic triggered short-lived re-synchronization but with a more heterogeneous aftermath than the Global Financial Crisis: rapid monetary and fiscal support helped stabilize local conditions, while the pace of reopening varied. Over the window, frontier market equity synchronization rose 5 percentage points, to 16 percent, while credit synchronization increased to 21 percent.

Three findings emerge from this analysis. First, frontier markets' local financial conditions remain relatively insulated from the global financial cycle. Country-specific forces account for almost four-fifths of equity return variance over the full period, highlighting substantial diversification opportunities for international investors. However, there is evidence of increasing integration over time, with frontier market equity returns more influenced by the global factor since the Global Financial Crisis; this trend will likely continue as benchmark-driven capital flows expand and domestic markets deepen. Second, while generally more insulated, frontier markets exhibit episodic vulnerability to the global financial cycle: exposure increases during widespread financial stress. Third, there is pronounced asset-class asymmetry in shock transmission, with global influences showing much greater cyclicality in equity

BOX 4.3 The global financial cycle: Asset prices and credit growth (*continued*)

FIGURE B4.3.3 Variance decompositions of credit growth

Frontier markets' credit growth is largely driven by idiosyncratic forces, with the global factor explaining around one-fifth of variance across periods. This global factor share rises modestly in windows that include the Global Financial Crisis and the COVID-19 pandemic. By contrast, on average, the global factor accounts for more than one-half of credit growth variance in advanced economies and about one-third in emerging markets.

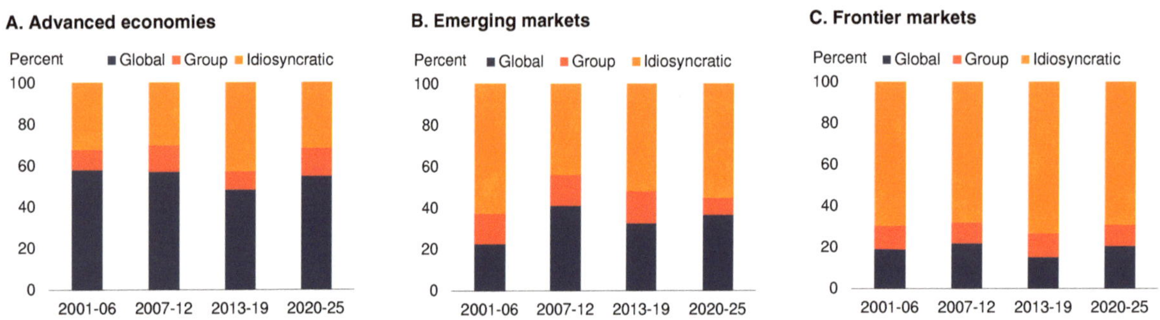

Sources: CEIC Data (database); World Bank.

Note: The global, group, and idiosyncratic factors are estimated using a dynamic factor model with monthly credit growth data for 21 advanced economies, 24 emerging markets, and 18 frontier markets.

A.-C. Bars show variance attributed to global, group-specific, and idiosyncratic factors, averaged by country group.

returns than credit growth, including in frontier markets.

This episodic pattern—long periods of decoupling punctuated by sharp synchronization—poses complex macroeconomic stabilization challenges and requires a two-pronged policy approach. During calm periods, limited integration reduces the pass-through of external shocks. This provides scope to build resilience: strengthening oversight; building countercyclical capital and liquidity buffers; accumulating reserves; sharpening macroprudential tools; and developing deeper local-currency debt markets and a more stable domestic investor base. When global financial stress emerges, deploying such buffers and tools can help contain shocks, reducing the risk of sharp changes in domestic financial conditions.

variance in equity returns and domestic credit growth in frontier markets, with the global factor and group-specific factors accounting for the remainder.

The role of the global factor in frontier markets appears to have been markedly higher during global shock periods, though still lower than in other country groups. For frontier market equity returns, the share of variance explained by the global factor rose to 30 percent in the 2007–12 window that spanned the Global Financial Crisis and its immediate aftermath, about two-and-a-half times higher than its share over the 2000–24 period as a whole. The influence of the global factor on frontier market credit growth also appears to have been greater during global stress episodes, though to a lesser extent than equity returns.

Consistent with frontier markets' rising international financial integration, their sensitivity to the global financial cycle has increased somewhat over time, and spillovers from global financial turbulence onto frontier markets may intensify in future. Frontier markets' vulnerability to external shocks will vary, depending on factors such as the liquidity and currency denomination of an economy's external liabilities, the economy's institutional capacity, and its available policy space. If domestic financial conditions are shaped more by the global financial cycle than by domestic policies and economic conditions, policy makers face a different challenge in developing effective responses (Rey 2015).

Fiscal positions, debt, and institutional quality

The ability of frontier markets to capitalize on their partial access to international financial markets, while mitigating associated risks, is constrained partly by their limited macroeconomic resilience. This limited resilience often reflects relatively weak institutional and fiscal capacity. Government debt has risen in the median frontier market, and the composition of frontier market liabilities suggests particular vulnerabilities.

Rising debt is not necessarily undesirable if it finances productive investment. The ability to borrow is an opportunity afforded by market access, and the costs of debt may be justified by the returns, which can drive economic development. However, when rising debt burdens coincide with modest and declining growth in the capital stock per head and frequent sovereign defaults—traits exhibited more frequently among frontier markets—this is a concern. In addition, governance has improved in some areas over the last 25 years, but gaps relative to emerging markets and advanced economies remain large.

Fiscal positions and debt

In the median frontier market, expenditures as a proportion of GDP have risen, while revenues have remained flat (and are lower than in the typical emerging market). The result has been widening fiscal deficits and rising total government debt, with a sharp uptick in the early 2020s (refer to figure 4.6.A). There has also been a notable rise in debt-service ratios in frontier markets over time, with the median frontier market spending 2.5 percent of GDP on net interest payments, on average, in 2020–24, more than both emerging markets (1.8 percent) and other developing economies (1.2 percent) (refer to figure 4.6.B).

FIGURE 4.6 Government and external debt

Total government debt as a share of GDP has risen in the median frontier market, as have debt-servicing costs. Short-term external debt and foreign currency-denominated general government debt have also risen. Frontier market sovereign bond maturities have lengthened, but credit ratings have weakened since the early 2010s. There have been more sovereign defaults in frontier markets in recent years.

Sources: Asonuma and Trebesch (2016); Erce, Mallucci, and Picarelli (2022); Fitch ratings (2025); Kose et al. (2022); Moody's Ratings (2025); S&P Global (2025); WDI (database); World Bank.

Note: EM = emerging markets; FM = frontier markets; ODE = other developing economies, neither EM nor FM. Bars show period averages of country group medians, unless otherwise specified.

A. Bars represent general government gross debt as a share of GDP. Sample includes up to 34 EMs, 39 FMs, and 78 ODEs.

B. Debt-servicing costs are represented by net interest payments in percent of GDP. Net interest payments are computed as the difference between primary and overall fiscal balances. Sample includes up to 34 EMs, 39 FMs, and 75 ODEs. Whiskers show the 10th and 90th percentiles.

C. Short-term external debt is all debt having an original maturity of one year or less and interest in arrears on long-term debt owed to non-residents, in percent of total reserves. Sample includes up to 22 EMs, 35 FMs, and 61 ODEs.

D. Bars represent shares of general government debt denominated in foreign currency (percent of GDP). Sample includes up to 12 EMs, 14 FMs, and 14 ODEs.

E. Bars represent median maturity years of sovereign debt for EMDEs, derived from the J.P. Morgan EMBI Global index, for each group. The index covers sovereign and quasi-sovereign instruments denominated in U.S. dollars with a minimum issue size of $500 million and a maturity of at least 2.5 years at the time of entry. Sample includes up to 25 EMs and 18 FMs. Diamonds represent median sovereign ratings (index ranging from 1 to 21, with higher values indicating better ratings) that are averaged among Moody's, Standard & Poor's, and Fitch Ratings. Sample includes up to 30 EMs and 39 FMs.

F. Data cover sovereign defaults and restructurings with private creditors that occurred between 2000 and 2024 as documented in Asonuma and Trebesch (2016), Erce, Mallucci, and Picarelli (2022), Fitch Ratings (2025), Moody's Ratings (2025), and S&P Global (2025).

Moreover, frontier markets have relied relatively heavily on external, sometimes short-term funding. Short-term external debt as a share of total reserves and the share of foreign currency-denominated general government debt relative to GDP have both surged in frontier markets in recent years, and are higher than in emerging markets or other developing economies (refer to figures 4.6.C and 4.6.D). These developments may increase the vulnerability of frontier markets to risks, including shifts in global financial conditions and currency mismatches on government or corporate balance sheets.

At the same time, the average maturity of sovereign bonds has risen since the early 2010s in frontier markets—a broadly positive trend, with average maturity approaching the duration in emerging markets by the early 2020s. However, sovereign credit ratings in frontier markets have remained well below those in emerging markets, declining in both absolute and relative terms since 2010–14 (refer to figure 4.6.E). Together, these developments reflect frontier markets' greater access to capital markets relative to other developing economies, but their generally weaker macroeconomic policy frameworks and debt management capacity relative to emerging markets.

The upshot is that sovereign debt defaults and restructurings have been increasingly concentrated in frontier markets. Nearly two-fifths of frontier markets defaulted at least once between 2000 and 2024. There have been more sovereign defaults since 2020 in frontier markets than in all other countries combined (refer to figure 4.6.F).[5] Repeated defaults are also more common in frontier markets than in other country groups. History suggests that economies with a record of defaults are more likely to default again in the future than other economies with similar debt-to-GDP ratios (Asonuma 2016). Sovereign defaults lead to a range of negative outcomes, including wider spreads, reduced access to external finance, and damaged confidence among investors, firms, and consumers (Farah-Yacoub et al. 2022).

Institutional quality

Strong legal and institutional foundations are critical for an economy's ability to attract external financing, manage associated risks, and translate investment opportunities into sustained improvements in growth and development outcomes. Conversely, institutional weaknesses can reinforce financial market constraints by raising the risk premia required by investors, domestic or foreign, thus elevating financing costs and hindering the deepening of the domestic financial system (Adarov 2025).[6] Weak legal and institutional frameworks can also facilitate rent-seeking behavior. Such shortcomings can hamper the effective use of natural resource endowments. This is relevant across EMDEs, including frontier markets, where commodity exports typically account for a higher share of GDP than in other EMDEs (refer to figure 4.7.A). Attracting investment that can facilitate the responsible use of natural resources hinges partly on the stability, efficiency, and transparency of the policy environment, including regulatory systems and enabling infrastructure.

Frontier markets' performance since 2000 in raising institutional quality has been mixed. Between 2000 and 2025, estimates of bureaucratic quality in the median frontier market saw no improvement, even as emerging markets and other developing economies made some gains (refer to figure 4.7.B). The median frontier market did make progress in both the control of corruption and the investment climate (refer to figures 4.7.C and 4.7.D). However, as with other EMDEs, significant gaps relative to advanced economies persist on all three measures.

[5] These calculations draw on all sovereign defaults and restructurings between 2000 and 2024, as documented in Asonuma and Trebesch (2016), Erce, Mallucci, and Picarelli (2022), Fitch Ratings (2025), Moody's Ratings (2025), and S&P Global (2025). They use the 2012 classification of 39 frontier markets, of which 15 experienced a default episode between 2000 and 2024. In addition to this result, three more economies obtained frontier market status after 2012 and have subsequently experienced a default episode.

[6] Gaps in contract enforcement, creditor rights, and insolvency frameworks curtail lending volumes and raise risk premia (Djankov, McLiesh, and Shleifer 2007). Weaker enforcement and resolution frameworks reduce the value lenders attach to pledged assets, constraining credit and slowing recoveries (Haselmann, Pistor, and Vig 2010; Baldacci, Gupta, and Mati 2011). Political uncertainty and opacity can generate large risk premia, leading external lenders and investors to require extra compensation (Adarov 2025; Bekaert et al. 2014).

Macroeconomic and development outcomes

Over the past 25 years, macroeconomic and development performance across frontier markets has been mixed. Per capita GDP growth in the typical frontier market has been slightly higher than in emerging markets. However, after much progress early in the quarter century, poverty reduction has slowed over the last decade. The World Bank's high-income threshold has moved further away for a rising share of frontier markets. Growth of investment per capita has fallen since the 2000s, with capital stocks typically much lower than in emerging markets. Yet some key human development indicators have improved.

Headline macroeconomic performance

Over the past quarter century, GDP growth has weakened across country groups. In the median frontier market, average annual output growth halved from 5.0 percent in the 2000s to 2.5 percent in the first half of the 2020s (refer to figure 4.8.A). Growth of output per capita has also declined, and by more in frontier markets than in other EMDEs. In the median frontier market, it averaged 3.2 percent annually in the 2000s and 2.6 percent in the 2010s, both higher than in the typical emerging market or other developing economy. During the first half of the 2020s, however, median frontier market per capita GDP growth was 1.2 percent a year, the same as in both emerging markets and other developing economies (refer to figure 4.8.B).

Investment growth, a major driver of output growth, has followed a similar downward trajectory. Per capita investment growth more than halved between the 2000s and the first half of the 2020s across all EMDE groups, averaging just 2.0 percent in the median frontier market over 2020–24 (refer to figure 4.8.C). Export growth in the typical frontier market has also been subdued, weaker over the quarter century as a whole than in both emerging markets and other developing economies, with declining trends across all country groups (refer to figure 4.8.D).

Inflation has typically been somewhat higher in frontier markets than in emerging markets (refer to figure 4.8.E). The volatility of inflation has also often been higher in frontier markets. This partly reflects exchange rate pass-through dynamics: exchange rate volatility has risen sharply in recent years in both frontier markets and other developing economies, in part due to terms-of-trade shifts and thin policy and reserves buffers to counter currency pressures (refer to figure 4.8.F). Shocks that lead to currency pressures can then trigger larger exchange rate movements. These movements can pass through rapidly to domestic prices and balance sheets (Carstens 2019; Caselli and Roitman 2016). Many frontier markets are vulnerable to exchange rate instability given their limited capacity to hedge foreign-exchange risk,

FIGURE 4.7 Economic structure and institutional quality

Commodity exports are a larger share of GDP in frontier markets than in emerging markets or other developing economies. Institutional progress in frontier markets has been mixed, with no change in bureaucratic quality since 2000 and modest improvements in control of corruption and the investment climate. Across EMDEs, significant institutional gaps remain relative to advanced economies.

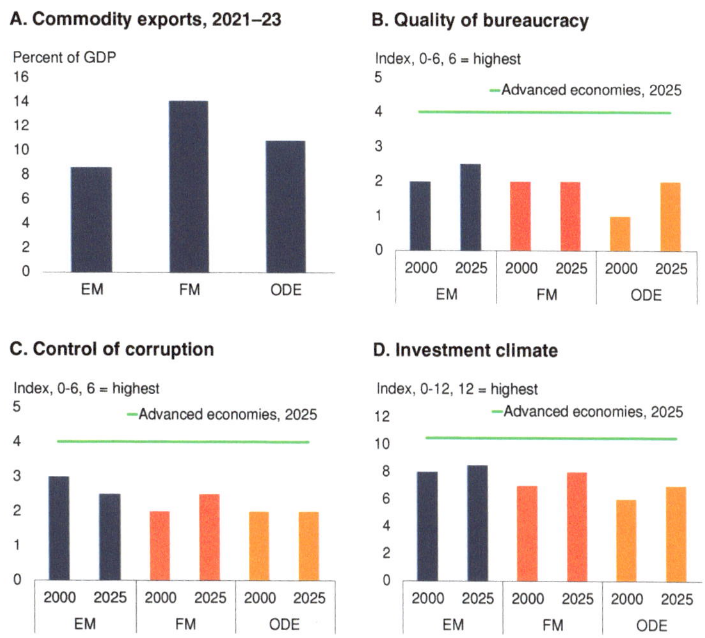

Sources: ICRG (database); WITS (database); World Bank.

Note: EM = emerging markets; FM = frontier markets; ODE = other developing economies, neither EM nor FM.

A. Bars show GDP-weighted commodity exports as a share of GDP for each country group, average of 2021–23. Sample includes 30 EMs, 35 FMs, and 49 ODEs.

B.–D. Sample includes 34 AEs, 31 EMs, 35 FMs, and 37 ODEs. ODE medians should be interpreted cautiously, given the sample includes less than half of the 80 ODEs in the baseline classification. Bars show median index values across country groups for each year. The green line shows the median value across advanced economies for 2025. A higher index score is associated with (B) stronger, more independent, and capable bureaucracy, (C) lower corruption risk in ICRG's scheme, and (D) better investment climate (contract viability, profit repatriation, payment delays).

FIGURE 4.8 Economic growth, inflation, and volatility

Growth of both aggregate output and output per capita has followed declining trends across all country groups since the 2000s. Growth of per capita investment in frontier markets weakened less than in other EMDEs in the 2010s, but the slowdown has since become more pronounced. Export growth has slowed in frontier markets and in other EMDEs. Inflation has generally been higher in frontier markets than in emerging markets. Real effective exchange rate volatility has also risen sharply in frontier markets in recent years.

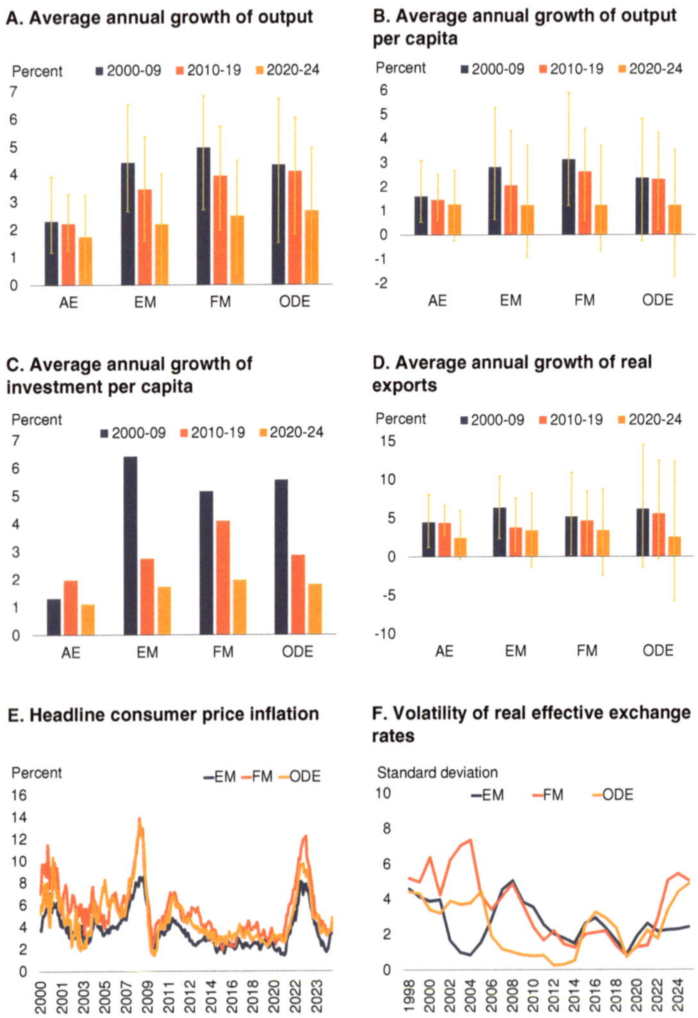

Sources: BIS (database); Ha, Kose, and Ohnsorge (2023); Haver Analytics; World Bank.

Note: AE = advanced economies; EM = emerging markets; FM = frontier markets; ODE = other developing economies, neither EM nor FM. Bars show period averages of country group medians, unless otherwise specified. Whiskers show the interquartile range.

A.B. Sample includes 34 AEs, 34 EMs, 38 FMs, and 78 ODEs.

C.D. Sample includes 34 AEs, 30 EMs, 34 FMs, and 42 ODEs.

E. Lines show median headline consumer price inflation from 12 months earlier, using monthly data. Last observation is March 2025. Sample includes up to 34 EMs, 39 FMs, and 72 ODEs.

F. Volatility is the 5-year rolling standard deviation of the annual group real effective exchange rate index. Lines are group medians. Sample includes 34 EM, 39 FMs, and 80 ODEs.

and particularly to currency depreciation given high levels of foreign-currency-denominated debt.

Convergence and poverty reduction

Growth in per capita output, even as it has moderated, has translated into large increases in real per capita GDP across EMDEs. Between 2000 and 2025, real annual GDP per capita in the median frontier market rose from $3,081 to $5,108. Over the same period, per capita output in the typical emerging market surged from $7,958 to $15,294 (refer to figure 4.9.A). The ratio of per capita GDP in frontier markets to that in emerging markets slipped from 39 to 32 percent. Beneath these overall trends, there is considerable diversity in both GDP per capita and population sizes across frontier markets (refer to figure 4.9.B).

Since 2000, most frontier markets have moved closer to the World Bank's high-income threshold. However, over the last decade, this convergence has slowed and, in many cases, reversed. In 2025, 45 percent of the 39 frontier markets in the baseline sample were further from high-income status than at the onset of the COVID-19 pandemic, underscoring the economic scars left by the series of shocks since 2020. The share of non-converging frontier markets had also jumped in the 2015–19 period amid commodity price weakness (refer to figure 4.9.C). In the median frontier market, per capita income is currently below 40 percent of the high-income threshold.

Frontier markets have made meaningful progress in reducing poverty since 2000. The share of people living on $3 per day or less more than halved between 2000 and 2024 (refer to figure 4.9.D). Yet poverty reduction in frontier markets has not been as rapid as in emerging markets, where poverty rates fell from levels somewhat above those in frontier markets in 2000 to levels far below them in 2024, largely reflecting advances in China and India. Over the past decade, as per capita GDP growth has slowed, reductions in poverty rates have tailed off in both frontier markets and other developing economies. Poverty rates remain significant in both groups, at 16 percent and 33 percent, respectively.

Physical capital accumulation and human development

Reflecting positive but moderating growth in per capita investment, the stock of physical capital per head in the typical frontier market rose by 61 percent over 2000–23. This was less than the increases experienced in both emerging markets (from a much higher base) and in other developing economies (refer to figure 4.10.A).

Frontier markets, like other EMDEs, have made progress in human capital development in recent years, though considerable gaps remain relative to emerging markets. The World Bank Group's composite Human Capital Index (HCI) measures the human capital a child is expected to acquire by age 18, relative to a benchmark of full health and education (on a 0–1 scale). In the typical frontier market, the HCI increased from 0.72 in 2010 to 0.75 in 2023. This remains below the level in emerging markets but above that in other developing economies (refer to figure 4.10.B).

Life expectancy in the median frontier market rose by six years between 2000 and 2023, reaching 74 years. This is closer to the 77 years recorded in emerging markets than to the 68 years in other developing economies (refer to figure 4.10.C). Average years of completed education have risen across all EMDE groups. In the median frontier market, they increased from 6.9 years in 2000 to 9.4 years in 2023 and remain positioned between emerging markets and other developing economies (refer to figure 4.10.D). These basic indicators of health and education standards have limitations but illustrate both progress and scope for further improvement among frontier markets.

FIGURE 4.9 Per capita GDP, convergence, and poverty rates

Since 2000, GDP per capita in the median frontier market has grown, but by less than in the median emerging market. In terms of both population size and per capita GDP, there is wide dispersion among frontier markets. Most frontier markets have made some progress toward high-income status since 2000, but the share failing to make such progress has increased in recent years. In 2000, frontier markets had lower poverty rates than both emerging markets and other developing economies. Poverty rates have declined since then, but progress has slowed in the second half of the period.

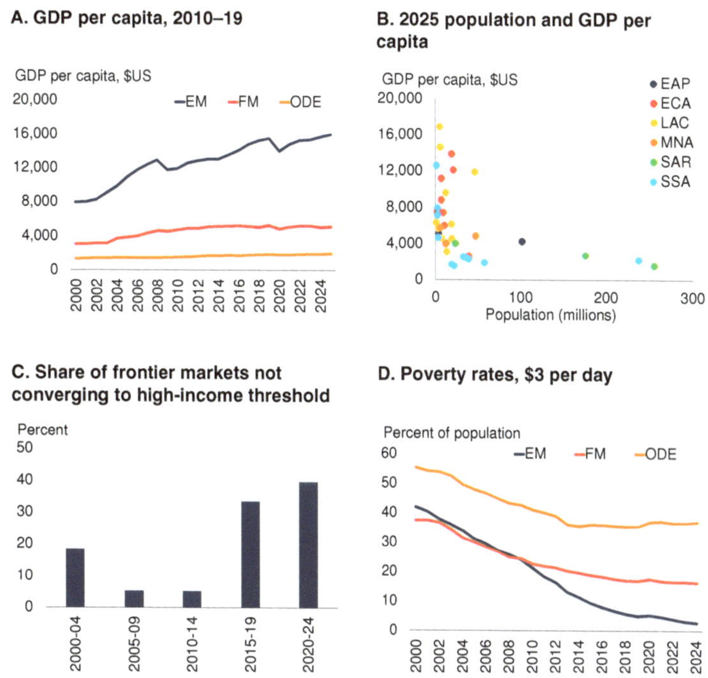

Sources: World Bank Poverty and Inequality Platform (database); WDI (database); World Bank.

Note: EAP = East Asia and Pacific; ECA = Europe and Central Asia; EM = emerging markets; FM = frontier markets; LAC = Latin America and the Caribbean; MNA= Middle East, North Africa, Afghanistan and Pakistan; ODE = other developing economies, neither EM nor FM; SAR = South Asia; SSA = Sub-Saharan Africa. Sample includes 34 EMs, 39 FMs, and 80 ODEs.

A. Lines show median real GDP per capita over time in average 2010–19 constant U.S. dollars, by country group.

B. Panel shows FM economies' real GDP per capita in average 2010–19 U.S. dollars and population in millions in 2025.

C. Bars show the share of FM economies in the baseline sample not converging to high-income status over each time range. An economy is converging if its per capita income, relative to the World Bank Group's annually updated high-income threshold, is rising.

D. Lines represent population-weighted poverty rates, measured using the $3 poverty line (2021 PPP), by country groups. Last observation is 2024.

Sectoral composition of output and employment

Sectoral shares of output in frontier markets have shifted only gradually over time. The share of agricultural output in GDP averaged 8 percent in the median frontier market in the early 2020s. This was less than half the share in other developing economies but double the share in the typical emerging market. The share of services output in the median frontier market, at 62 percent, was similar to that in emerging markets but above that in other developing economies. The share of manufacturing output in GDP in frontier markets, at 28 percent, was similar to that in other developing economies but below that in emerging markets.

Effective shifts of resources both across these broad sectors and within them to more productive sub-sectors and firms can help drive aggregate job

FIGURE 4.10 Physical capital stock and human development

Since 2000, physical capital stocks per capita in frontier markets have been consistently smaller than in emerging markets but larger than in other developing economies, with emerging markets experiencing the fastest growth. Human capital indicators, including the World Bank's Human Capital Index, life expectancy, and years of schooling, have improved across all three EMDE groups, with frontier markets again positioned between emerging markets and other developing economies.

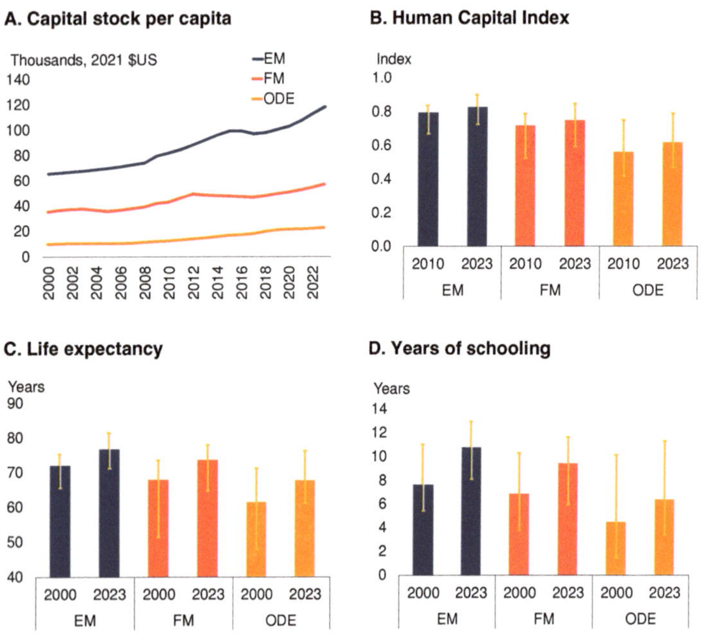

Sources: Feenstra, Inklaar, and Timmer (2015); UN Population Prospects (database); WDI (database); World Bank Human Capital Data Project; World Bank.

Note: EM = emerging markets; FM = frontier markets; ODE = other developing economies, neither EM nor FM.

A. Lines represent the median value of capital stock by capita per country group. Sample includes 34 EMs, 39 FMs, and 62 ODEs. Last data available is 2023.

B. Bars show median Human Capital Index (scale 0 to 1) within each group. Whiskers show the 10th and 90th percentiles. Original data source starts in 2010. Sample includes up to 34 EMs, 38 FMs, and 78 ODEs.

C. Bars represent median values of life expectancy in each group. Sample includes up to 34 EMs, 39 FMs, and 80 ODEs.

D. Bars show median of mean years of schooling within each group. Whiskers show the 10th and 90th percentiles. Sample includes up to 34 EMs, 39 FMs, and 70 ODEs.

creation, productivity improvements, and output growth (Bhorat et al. 2025; Meh and Schmukler 2025). Well-designed policies that promote the appropriate development of specific sub-sectors, including agribusiness, energy and infrastructure, healthcare, tourism, and value-added manufacturing, could offer routes to more resilient local growth and jobs (Development Committee 2025). An important challenge for all EMDEs, and for frontier markets in particular, is to adapt to, and take advantage of, technological, trade, and other developments in the global economy in ways that promote stronger growth, job creation, and development.

Burgeoning working-age populations could generate a significant demographic dividend in frontier markets, but this hinges on strong job creation. Amid slowing output growth (both globally and in frontier markets), this represents a major challenge for policy makers: average employment growth in frontier markets in the 2010s was lower than the projected growth in the working-age population over the coming decade, underscoring the importance of a focus on job creation. However, relative to other developing economies, frontier markets have advantages, including healthier and better educated populations, larger capital stocks, and better international market access. These advantages can provide a strong platform to meet these challenges and achieve better economic and development outcomes.

Features of frontier market success

Macroeconomic performance has varied among frontier markets over the past quarter century. As a group, frontier markets have struggled with weak investment and episodic vulnerability to global shocks. Yet some frontier markets have fared notably better than others.[7] Despite differing circumstances and growth models, quantitative analysis and case studies reveal some common distinguishing features among the frontier markets in which growth of per capita output has been relatively stronger over the past quarter century. These include faster investment growth and greater capital accumulation, larger improvements in governance, and better management of government debt.

Features of faster-growing frontier markets

Economies in the top quartile of frontier markets in terms of per capita GDP growth since 2000 display diverse characteristics. They are located in five of the six EMDE regions. Their population sizes vary widely. Faster growth of per capita GDP in the top-quartile frontier markets between 2000

[7] This analysis combines the baseline 2012 sample of 39 frontier markets plus those economies that had become frontier markets by 2025, for a sample of 62 economies. The top quartile in terms of growth performance consists of 15 economies (refer to annex 4.1).

and 2024 translated into much larger output increases across the period as a whole. In the median top-quartile frontier market, real GDP per capita almost quadrupled, rising from $1,522 in 2000 to $5,851 in 2024—more than double the increase in other frontier markets, where it rose from $2,111 to $3,810. Quantitative analysis shows that developments in the top-quartile frontier markets share several distinguishing features.

The median top-quartile frontier market registered more than twice the growth rate of investment per capita as other frontier markets over the quarter century since 2000 (refer to figure 4.11.A). Investment growth was higher in almost every individual year. This fed into much higher per capita capital stocks, which grew almost twice as fast in the top quartile as in other frontier markets, from an already higher base.

The top quartile of frontier markets is also characterized by larger improvements in institutional quality. Over 2000–25, the median top-quartile frontier market registered notable improvements in bureaucratic quality, control of corruption, and investment climate, while in the median other frontier economy there was scant progress on these measures (refer to figure 4.11.B). This is consistent with wider evidence linking institution-building and economic development (Acemoglu and Robinson 2012; Collier 2019).

Financial intermediation costs were notably lower among the faster-growing frontier markets. Spreads between banks' lending and borrowing rates narrowed by 2.8 percentage points, to 4.1 percent, in the median top-quartile frontier market between the 2000s and the early 2020s. This represents a larger decline than in other frontier markets (refer to figure 4.11.C).

Government debt burdens have grown across frontier markets in recent years, but the increases among faster-growing frontier markets have been more modest. Government debt-to-GDP ratios averaged 41 percent in the median top-quartile frontier market in the first half of the 2020s, compared with 68 percent in the median other frontier market (refer to figure 4.11.D). In part, this reflects higher revenues, relative to GDP, in the typical top-quartile frontier market, even as expenditures have risen across both groups.[8]

FIGURE 4.11 Characteristics of faster-growing frontier markets

In faster-growing frontier markets, per capita investment growth has also been higher. These faster-growing frontier markets have also registered improvements across governance indicators. Declines in banks' interest rate spreads have been larger, and increases in government debt-to-GDP ratios have been smaller than in other frontier markets.

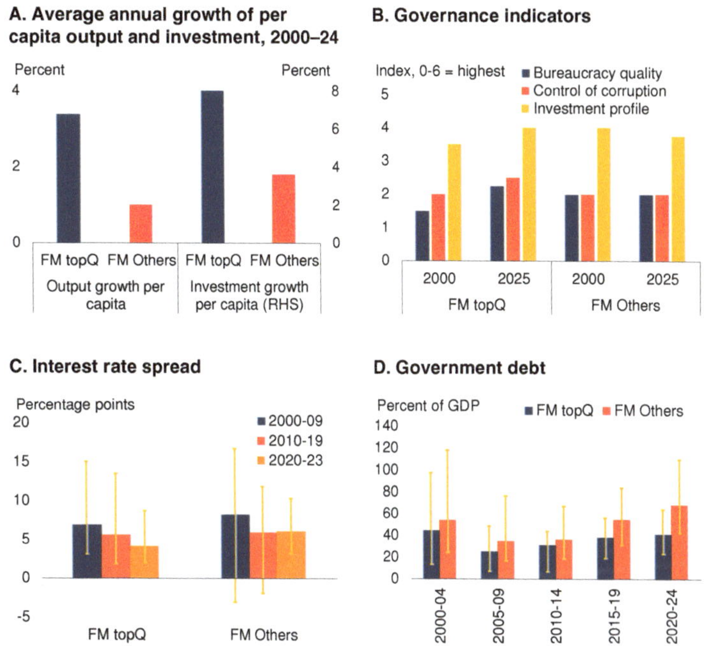

Sources: ICRG (database); Kose et al. (2022); WDI (database); World Bank.

Note: FM topQ = frontier markets in the top quartile for average per capita GDP growth over 2000–24; FM Others = remaining frontier markets in the sample. This captures economies that were frontier markets in 2012 and those that have subsequently achieved frontier market status. Bars represent period averages of medians for each group, unless otherwise specified. Whiskers show the 10th and 90th percentiles.

A. Sample includes 11 FM topQ and 39 FM Others for output per capita, and 15 FM topQ and 47 FM Others for investment growth per capita.

B. The bureaucracy quality and control of corruption indexes range from 0 to 6, with 6 representing the highest score. The investment profile index was originally on a 0–12 scale, with 12 the highest score; for ease of comparison, it has been normalized to a 0–6 scale, with 6 the highest value. Sample includes 12 FM topQ and 40 FM Others.

C. Interest rate spread is the interest rate charged by banks on loans to private sector customers minus the interest rate paid by commercial or similar banks for demand, time, or savings deposits. Latest data available is 2023. Sample includes up to 13 FM topQ and 40 FM Others.

D. Data for 2024 is an estimate. Sample includes up to 15 FM topQ and 47 FM Others.

Lessons from case studies of faster-growing frontier markets

The experiences of five top-quartile frontier markets—Kazakhstan, Panama, Rwanda, Uzbe-

[8] This observation does not imply an absence of debt concerns among the top-quartile group, nor does it suggest that lower debt necessarily means faster growth. Debt-increasing fiscal positions were recorded in almost half of top-quartile frontier markets and over half of other frontier markets in 2020–24.

kistan, and Viet Nam—illustrate different paths to successful growth. They also point to the importance of mutually reinforcing financial, macroeconomic, and structural policies and reforms (refer to annex 4.2). Viet Nam has focused on strengthening export-oriented manufacturing, deepening its integration into global value chains. The growth strategies of Kazakhstan and Uzbekistan have been geared to their large resource endowments. Panama and Rwanda have both pursued services sector-focused development, but in different ways. Panama has done so as a small open economy with a relatively advanced financial sector, while Rwanda has developed services from a low base. Rwanda and Uzbekistan are both relatively new entrants to the frontier markets group, having been included in J.P. Morgan's EMBI Global bond index in 2022 and 2020, respectively. Meanwhile, Panama was classified as a high-income country (and thus an emerging market) for the first time in 2017, while FTSE Russell is poised to reclassify Viet Nam as an emerging market in 2026 (LSEG 2025).

Financial reforms in the case-study economies, including around the attainment of frontier status, have tended to focus on both reducing restrictions on foreign capital flows and enhancing financial market infrastructure, depth and regulation—balancing attracting new foreign financing with containing associated vulnerabilities. In several cases, country authorities prioritized the development of domestic stock markets, alongside the establishment of securities regulatory bodies, prior to index inclusion—Kazakhstan and Panama even before 2000, and later in Rwanda and Viet Nam. All five economies sought to attract FDI, with initiatives including loosening restrictions on foreign ownership and capital repatriation, establishing special economic zones, and enhancing investors' legal protections.

Portfolio inflows increased significantly following index inclusion in several of the case studies. Viet Nam experienced a marked rise in portfolio inflows after being added to global bond and equity indexes, with annual growth in these inflows peaking at 8.1 percent in 2007. More recent entrants to the frontier markets group—Rwanda (2022) and Uzbekistan (2020)—also saw large increases in portfolio inflows following index inclusion. However, FDI and bank lending have remained the dominant forms of external financing in all five cases, with FDI accounting for nearly half of all capital inflows since 2000.

Prudent macroeconomic policies are a further shared feature. Several countries have implemented reforms to bolster macroeconomic stability and the credibility of policy frameworks, attenuating risks to investors and reinforcing buffers. Monetary policy frameworks have been strengthened in some cases, enhancing the credibility of inflation control and potentially allowing more exchange rate flexibility for the absorption of shocks. For example, Kazakhstan and Rwanda adopted inflation targeting regimes in the second half of the 2010s, following preparatory reforms, while Uzbekistan unified its multiple exchange rates in 2017. Cautious fiscal management has also boosted investor confidence in several instances. Panama and Uzbekistan significantly reduced government debt-to-GDP ratios in the 2000s. Kazakhstan has maintained relatively low debt levels while using its oil fund as a countercyclical tool. Viet Nam's prudent debt management—and its maintenance of ample international reserves relative to external short-term debt—has kept debt -service costs manageable even as debt has increased.

Structural reforms, including trade liberalization, as well as investment in human capital and foundational infrastructure, have raised prospective returns on private investment, helping financial opening to support productivity and output growth. Trade liberalization has played a role, albeit to differing degrees across the cases. Viet Nam acceded to the WTO in 2007 and has signed multiple trade agreements, while Kazakhstan joined the WTO in 2015. Uzbekistan, in a late 2010s liberalization drive, lowered import tariffs and rationalized non-tariff barriers and customs procedures.

The World Bank Group has highlighted five sectors with particular potential for resilient job creation: infrastructure (including energy), agribusiness, healthcare, tourism, and value-added manufacturing (Development Committee 2025). Some of these sectors have been influential in driving broader economic growth. For example, services, including tourism, have played a growing role in Rwanda's economy, while value-added manufacturing has been vital in Viet Nam. Development of energy resources has been important in Kazakhstan and Uzbekistan. In most of the five cases, infrastructure investment has formed a substantial part of public expenditure. It has been a key driver of growth in Rwanda, while infrastructure megaprojects in Panama have supported growth in the logistics sector. In Viet Nam, investment in education has been given particular emphasis, with strong outcomes, though there is scope for more improvement (OECD 2025).

Sustained output growth often coincided with efforts to improve governance, including via regulatory quality and legal frameworks, which boosted confidence among foreign investors and domestic firms. Rwanda's steps to streamline regulation and build state capacity have made it one of the most welcoming business environments in its region (Boyce et al. 2025). Panama has maintained a competitive tax and regulatory environment, while also recently taking steps to improve financial transparency. Viet Nam's multifaceted Doi Moi drive, starting in the 1980s, included actions to rationalize regulations and reduce price controls.

Policy priorities for frontier markets

Debate over policy reforms to advance economic development has evolved over recent decades (Besley, Bucelli, and Velasco 2025). There is consensus that macroeconomic stability and economic efficiency are crucial for sustainable growth, and policy reforms have significantly improved economic performance in EMDEs (Chari, Henry, and Reyes 2021). Greater access to international financial markets provides options to advance economic development. Additional financing is vital for frontier markets, where significant investment gaps persist. Despite the promise conveyed by demographics, natural resources, and partial market access, economic progress in frontier markets has been mixed and has slowed. Unlocking additional financing and using it effectively to boost growth, increase resilience, and advance development can help frontier markets achieve their economic potential.

Priorities to unlock this potential span three related areas: advancing integration with international financial markets while minimizing associated risks through appropriately designed reforms; bolstering macroeconomic stability via improvements to policy frameworks and institutional capacity, addressing domestic imbalances and building resilience to external shocks; and catalyzing investment and productivity growth, including through investment in foundational infrastructure and human capital, to enhance potential output and job creation prospects. The hierarchy of these themes and the specific measures within them, as well as optimal sequencing, will hinge on country circumstances. Progress across these areas can reduce uncertainty for investors, attract financing, and help translate market access into greater private investment, higher productivity, and strong job creation. International support will remain important to help these efforts in frontier markets.

Advancing financial and trade integration while managing external vulnerabilities

Across EMDEs, investment growth has tended to be faster in economies with larger capital inflows (Adarov 2025). Capital inflows tend to ease financing constraints, lower funding costs, foster technology transfer, and promote risk sharing. Such benefits are more likely to materialize in economies with sufficient financial depth, strong institutional quality, and credible policies (IMF 2022; Kose et al. 2009; Prasad, Rajan, and Subramanian 2007). Several emerging markets that have experienced sustained high growth, including Chile, the Republic of Korea, Malaysia, and Uruguay, have done so partly on the basis of reforms that opened the capital account and deepened the financial sector (World Bank 2024c).

Larger capital inflows tend to be associated with substantial increases in output and investment growth. However, surges in capital inflows also raise the risk reversals and sudden stops, which depress economic activity and investment (refer to figures 4.12.A and 4.12.B; Ghosh et al. 2014).

FIGURE 4.12 Growth during capital inflow surges and stops

Both emerging markets and frontier markets have experienced pronounced swings in economic activity around extreme movements in capital inflows. Frontier markets have experienced sharper rises in real GDP growth than emerging markets during surges: nearly three-quarters higher than normal. Sudden stops have been associated with weaker output and investment growth across country groups.

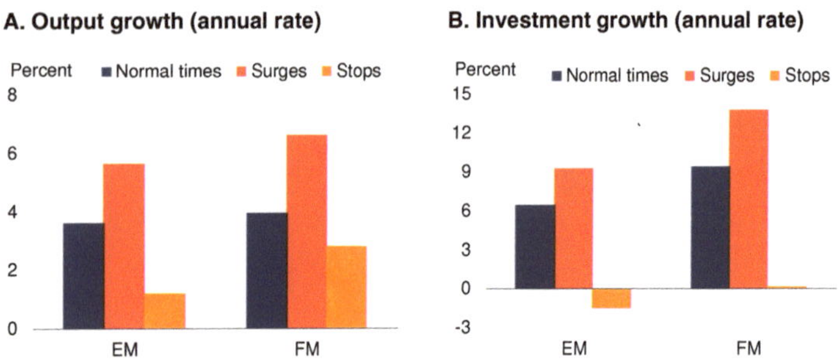

Sources: Haver Analytics; Organisation for Economic Co-operation and Development; World Bank.

Note: EM = emerging markets; FM = frontier markets.

A.B. Surges and stops in capital inflows are identified using an algorithm described in annex 4.2. GDP and investment growth are seasonally adjusted annualized growth rates based on real quarterly GDP and investment data in local currency terms. Sample includes 24 EMs and 27 FMs for GDP, and 21 EMs and 16 FMs for investment growth.

Thin financial markets in many frontier markets mean that even a moderate retrenchment by foreign investors can trigger sharp asset-price adjustments. Stop events in frontier markets become more likely both during periods of global financial stress, when frontier market conditions become more closely correlated with the global financial cycle, and when other frontier markets face crises. These developments are generally outside domestic policy makers' direct control. However, frontier markets can reduce the risk of sudden stops and limit costs when they occur through policies that reduce domestic and external imbalances and build effective buffers and toolkits during good times.

Building domestic financial market depth and resilience

Greater financial market depth—reflecting larger and more liquid credit and capital markets—together with more robust institutions and stronger legal and regulatory foundations, is associated with lower borrowing costs; in turn, this supports investment and growth (Bekaert et al. 2014). Policies to develop local financial markets and encourage domestic investor participation can help mitigate exposures to external financial market volatility (IMF 2020; IMF and World Bank 2021). Gains from capital market liberalization also tend to be larger where local institutional investors are already active (Cortina et al. 2023).

The depth and liquidity of capital and credit markets can be enhanced by policies that strengthen financial intermediary capacity and infrastructure (World Bank 2024b). Actions that reduce trading costs in capital markets—such as developing exchanges, streamlining trading processes, and investing in market infrastructure—can also help, as shown, for example, in Kazakhstan and Rwanda. Frontier markets' elevated interest rate spreads can be curbed by policies to promote competition among lenders, including privatization of state banks. Kazakhstan and Uzbekistan both made progress on this. Development of domestic capital markets can be particularly helpful for smaller, more capital-constrained firms, which are important in frontier markets. Constraints facing small firms specifically can also be eased by policies such as exemptions or ramp-up periods in the application of regulations, or even, in some cases, the establishment of size-segmented stock exchanges (Meh and Schmukler 2025).

Developing domestic-currency debt markets and lengthening bond maturities can improve external debt dynamics, alleviating balance-sheet currency mismatches and rollover risks and thereby helping to contain fiscal vulnerabilities. Key elements of domestic-currency bond market development include establishing a benchmark yield, maintaining secondary market liquidity, and expanding a retail investor base (IMF and World Bank 2020). Technical assistance by international organizations and domestic-currency debt issuances by international financial institutions may be helpful (IMF and World Bank 2021).

Adjusting to evolving international trade patterns

Trade has helped fuel rapid expansions in many EMDEs since 2000. Amid declining potential growth globally, uncertainty about the labor implications of artificial intelligence, and a proliferation of trade-restrictive measures, export-led growth models that powered EMDE structural transformations in the past may be harder to execute now. Nonetheless, increasing openness to international trade can boost growth, including by reducing input costs and promoting efficiency gains. Higher exports increase earned foreign exchange, which can help manage exposures associated with financial integration. Developing exports could also help attract FDI, which is generally a more stable form of financing and can also facilitate technology and skills infusions that support development (World Bank 2024d). Frontier markets may be able to unlock new trade opportunities by reducing regulatory and trade barriers in domestic markets, pursuing agreements with regional and other partners, and leveraging digital technology to expand services trade (World Bank 2025a).

FIGURE 4.13 External buffers and policy tools

Macroprudential tightening became more common in the 2010s across all country groups but remains relatively infrequent in frontier markets. Frontier markets tend to hold smaller foreign exchange reserves, relative to imports, than emerging markets, though holdings have trended up in all three EMDE groups since the 1980s. Most frontier markets retain some form of currency peg, although inflation targeting has become more common in recent years.

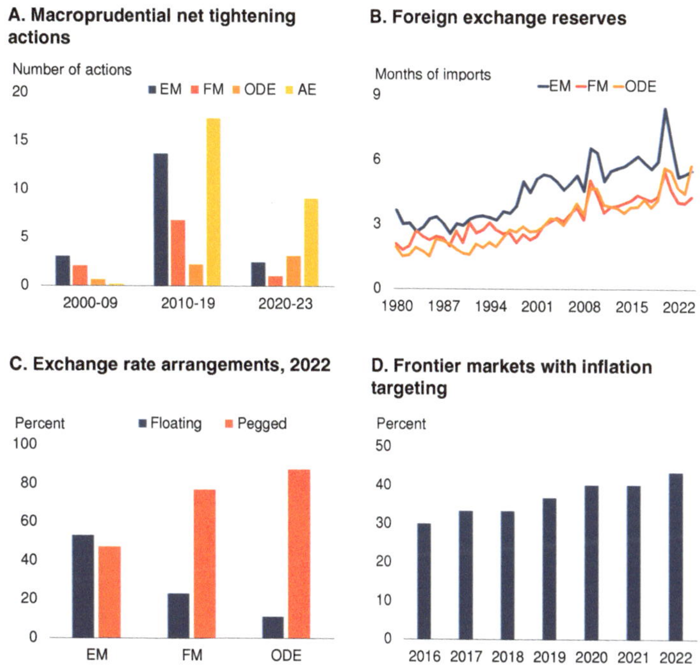

Sources: IMF AREAER (database); IMF Integrated Macroprudential Policy (iMaPP) (database), originally constructed by Alam et al. (2019); WDI (database); World Bank.

Note: AE = advanced economies; EM = emerging markets; FM = frontier markets; ODE = other developing economies, neither EM nor FM. Sample includes 34 AEs, 34 EMs, 39 FMs, and 80 ODEs, unless otherwise specified.

A. Net tightening actions are calculated as the sum of policy action indicators across 17 macroprudential policy instruments in a given period, where each instrument is coded 1 for a tightening, −1 for a loosening, and 0 for no or neutral action. Bars show the average number of net tightening actions by country group.

B. Lines show median foreign exchange reserves in total months of imports. Sample includes up to 27 EMs, 23 FMs, and 41 ODEs.

C. Bars show the share of economies with floating versus pegged exchange rate regimes in 2022.

D. Bars show the share of FMs with inflation targeting regimes for each year.

Policies that support diversification of exportable production, including through services development, can reduce exposure to terms-of-trade shocks. This is particularly relevant to frontier markets, where in many cases exports are concentrated in specific products or markets, leaving vulnerabilities should adverse shocks crystallize in these areas. Diversification can reduce exposure both in terms of products and destinations. Successful export diversification is contingent on other interlocking reform areas, with links to governance, education, and infrastructure improvements (Salinas 2021).

Buffering exposure to external shocks

In the event of financial shocks, buffers developed in good times can be deployed to dampen transmission to domestic financial conditions and the real economy. These may include financial buffers for addressing disorderly financial tightening, foreign exchange reserves to absorb currency pressures, and fiscal and monetary policy tools, underpinned by credible macroeconomic policy frameworks. Effective financial supervision and regulation, including capital buffer requirements, are cornerstones of effective risk management. In addition, rapid deployment of liquidity support and macroprudential easing can limit forced deleveraging when shocks hit. Macroprudential frameworks also offer tools to lean against credit booms and contain foreign-currency mismatches before they become systemic risks. However, perhaps reflecting more limited toolkits and capacity, frontier markets have tightened macroprudential policies less frequently than emerging markets (refer to figure 4.13.A).

Adequate foreign exchange reserves should form part of an economy's financial resilience toolkit. Such reserves, in proportion to imports, have been on a rising trend across EMDEs, but have been consistently lower in frontier markets than in emerging markets (refer to figure 4.13.B). Holding reserves is costly and using them to manage exchange rates is unlikely to be effective unless the exchange rate objective is consistent with economic fundamentals, including macroeconomic policies. Moreover, deploying reserves effectively in pursuit of such objectives is not always straightforward. However, reserves can be useful in helping to contain exchange rate volatility; in signaling, and buying time for, policies of macroeconomic adjustment; and in limiting the risk of self-reinforcing financial sector strains.

Appropriate levels of foreign exchange reserves depend on the structural and institutional characteristics of individual economies, particularly their exchange rate arrangements. With a credible inflation targeting regime, a flexible exchange rate, and limited foreign currency debt, large reserve buffers may not be necessary to mitigate risks. However, most frontier markets have some form of pegged currency arrangement (refer to figure 4.13.C). The credibility of such a regime may require significant reserve holdings, particularly if the economy is relatively open to capital flows. Reserves are also more likely to be needed if foreign currency liabilities are sizeable, to mitigate domestic currency depreciation risks.

Approaches to international financial integration

There is wide dispersion in the extent of capital account controls among frontier markets, with little change overall since the early 2000s. The speed and extent of liberalization, and its sequencing with related measures, must be carefully calibrated and tailored to country conditions. Some large emerging markets have made strong economic progress while retaining some restrictions on capital flows. Episodes such as the Asian financial crisis show that rapid integration into global financial markets can allow economic imbalances to build up and give rise to instability (World Bank 2017). Although not a substitute for necessary macroeconomic adjustments, certain capital flow management measures can be useful in specific circumstances, including to contain financial stability risks (IMF 2022).

Yet experience also shows that capital account liberalization can be successful when appropriately designed, implemented, and sequenced alongside macroeconomic and structural reforms. A crisis can act as a catalyst for such processes: Korea's reforms from the late 1990s saw extensive restructuring of the banking sector, strengthening of supervisory systems, development of the domestic-currency bond market, and the accumulation of foreign exchange reserves, all of which enabled Korea to rejoin global financial markets from a position of greater resilience (Batten and Szilagyi 2007). Malaysia's Financial Sector Masterplan and Capital Market Masterplan showcase the importance of appropriate sequencing—particularly ensuring that domestic financial markets and regulatory capacity are sufficiently robust before gradually expanding cross-border linkages (World Bank 2017).

Bolstering macroeconomic stability

Access to external capital markets is likely to durably lower financing costs and promote stronger growth only when accompanied by macroeconomic stability and associated policy frameworks. These are pillars of strong and durable growth for all economies, but especially for frontier markets, where they can help in establishing investor confidence, reducing risk premia, attracting additional financing, and containing instability during episodes of stress. Credible fiscal and monetary policies are thus critical complements to an effective strategy to take advantage of access to international markets while mitigating associated risks.

Monetary policy

Low and stable inflation is key to macroeconomic stability and is the primary responsibility of monetary policy. Monetary policy frameworks have been enhanced in many frontier markets, but credibility gaps remain larger and more common than in emerging markets and advanced economies. Central bank independence in frontier legislative frameworks has risen, and a growing share of frontier markets use inflation targeting (refer to figure 4.13.D). Experience across EMDEs suggests that stronger monetary frameworks support lower inflation volatility, better-anchored inflation expectations, and consequently less pass-through from external shocks to domestic inflation (Ha, Kose, and Ohnsorge 2019).

However, most frontier markets have not adopted inflation targeting. In these cases, exchange rate policies are more important for inflation and output stabilization efforts, and exchange rate stabilization may provide an anchor to secure macroeconomic stability (Carstens 2019). In some cases, such as small economies that are very open to international trade or economies with exports dominated by a dollar-denominated commodity, a prudently managed peg to a major, stable currency or currency basket may be viable. That said, in commodity exporters, shifts toward greater flexibility have often taken place in the aftermath of commodity price shocks, with more disruptive effects than a planned transition (Al-Sadiq, Bejar, and Ötker 2021). More generally, pegged exchange rates can easily lead to currency misalignments, which can be difficult and costly to correct. Indeed, pegged exchange rates are associated with more sudden stops. Country circumstances matter, but in many cases, a gradual move toward more exchange rate flexibility—when the technical capacity of the central bank and broader financial system allow—with an independently-administered inflation target as the nominal anchor, is a desirable long-term objective.

Fiscal policy

High public-sector debt and large budget deficits limit fiscal flexibility, reducing scope to provide countercyclical support to demand and activity when adverse shocks occur. Adverse debt dynamics are associated with higher sovereign risk premia, creating a feedback loop in which elevated borrowing costs further constrain fiscal headroom (Baldacci, Gupta, and Mati 2011; Jaramillo and Weber 2013). Frontier market sovereign bond issuance has risen over time, averaging 3 percent of GDP in the median frontier market in the early 2020s, notably higher than in the typical emerging market (refer to figure 4.14.A). Rising debt is not necessarily problematic if it funds initiatives that foster durably higher growth. Well-managed borrowing can create opportunities to advance development. However, high debt and large

FIGURE 4.14 Fiscal developments

Sovereign bond issuance has risen in frontier markets. Government revenues, relative to GDP, in the median frontier market have changed little since the early 2000s, even as expenditures as a proportion of GDP have increased. As a result, a majority of frontier markets have debt-increasing fiscal positions. Frontier markets also experienced more default events than other EMDEs over 2000–24; these were often external defaults, accompanied by sudden stops in capital flows.

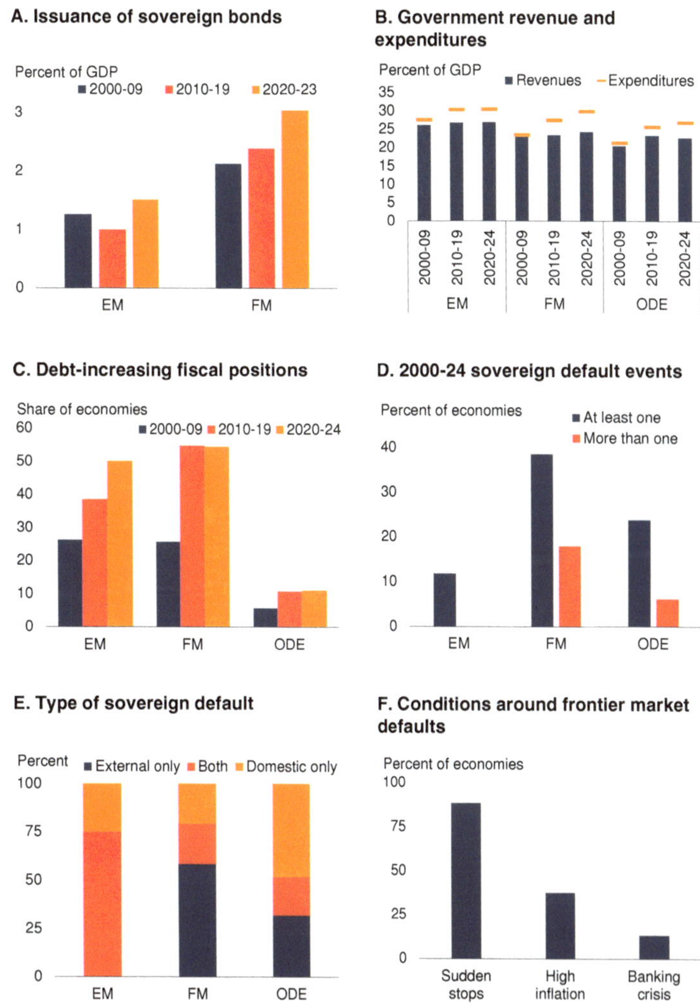

Sources: Asonuma and Trebesch (2016); Dealogic (database); Erce, Mallucci, and Picarelli (2022, 2024); Fitch ratings (2025); Kose et al. (2022); Laeven and Valencia (2020); Moody's Ratings (2025); World Economic Outlook (database); S&P Global (2025); World Bank.

Note: EM = emerging markets; FM = frontier markets; ODE = other developing economies, neither EM nor FM. Sample includes 34 EMs, 39 FMs, and 80 ODEs, using 2012 classifications, unless otherwise specified.

A. Bars show the median value of sovereign bonds issued in percent of GDP for each country group. Sample includes up to 30 EMs and 26 FMs.

B. Bars (dashes) represent period averages of median government revenue (expenditure) as a percent of GDP in each group. Sample includes up to 34 EMs, 39 FMs, and 77 ODEs.

C. Bars show the share of economies in each group with a primary balance sustainability gap of less than zero. The primary balance sustainability gap is calculated as the difference between the primary balance and the debt-stabilizing primary balance. Sample includes 29 EMs, 38 FMs, and 18 ODEs.

D.–F. Data cover sovereign defaults and restructurings with private creditors that occurred between 2000 and 2024 as documented in Asonuma and Trebesch (2016), Erce, Mallucci, and Picarelli (2022), Fitch Ratings (2025), Moody's Ratings (2025), and S&P Global (2025).

E. "Both" indicates simultaneous external and domestic defaults.

F. Bars show the share of sudden stops, high inflation, and banking crises that occurred in the same year as, or one year before or after, a default. Where samples are smaller than the number of default cases (24), this reflects data limitations. A sudden stop of capital inflows is defined as two standard deviations from the historical average, as defined in box 4.2 (15 out of 17 cases). High inflation is defined as annual consumer price inflation exceeding 20 percent (9 out of 24 cases). Data on systemic banking crises are for 2000–17, based on Laeven and Valencia (2020) (2 out of 15 cases).

deficits may become unsustainable, undermining macroeconomic stability.

Large deficits, growing debt, and rising debt-servicing costs have been a feature of many EMDEs in recent years, including many frontier markets. Government expenditures as a share of GDP have risen, averaging 30 percent in the median frontier market over the early 2020s, on a par with emerging markets (refer to figure 4.14.B). Revenues, however, have remained at a lower level, about 24 percent of GDP. Most frontier markets have therefore recorded debt-increasing fiscal positions in the 2010s and the early 2020s (refer to figure 4.14.C).

Frontier markets have been more prone to default or restructuring events than emerging markets or other developing economies: almost two-fifths experienced default between 2000 and 2024 (compared with one-eighth of emerging markets and one-quarter of other developing economies); frontier markets have also been more likely to experience multiple defaults (refer to figure 4.14.D). Many sovereign defaults are precipitated by a confluence of pre-existing macroeconomic vulnerabilities and imbalances (IMF 2021). External defaults are often linked to capital flight, while domestic defaults are often associated with financial instability and banking crises (Erce, Mallucci, and Picarelli 2024). Most frontier market defaults have included an external element (refer to figure 4.14.E).

Sudden stops of capital inflows have occurred in most of these frontier market defaults, while more than one-third of frontier market defaults coincided with high inflation (over 20 percent annually, usually alongside sharp capital outflows), with external defaults often linked to currency depreciation (refer to figure 4.14.F). A few frontier market default instances were accompanied by banking crises (refer to Laeven and Valencia 2020). Sovereign debt defaults and restructurings have serious implications for macroeconomic and development outcomes, as well as future credibility with potential investors (Farah-Yacoub et al. 2022).

Securing fiscal sustainability should therefore be prioritized in many frontier markets. Sustainably boosting domestic revenue mobilization can reduce fiscal risks and create space for investment in key services and infrastructure to enhance long-run productivity and growth. This may include expanding the tax base, strengthening tax administration, reducing exemptions, and selectively increasing tax rates while minimizing distortions (IMF and World Bank 2024). On expenditures, policy makers should seek to improve the efficiency of government services and replace broad subsidies with support targeted to the vulnerable. Medium-term budget frameworks, fiscal rules, and independent fiscal councils can help promote fiscal credibility and sustainability. However, the effectiveness of such policies hinges on their design and implementation (chapter 3; Fatas, Gootjes, and Mawejje 2025).

Commodity-exporting EMDEs, including many frontier markets, face distinct fiscal challenges because of commodity prices' volatility and their impact on fiscal revenues. Commodity exporters often exhibit procyclical fiscal policy, sometimes reflecting overly optimistic reassessments of potential growth during commodity booms (Arroyo Marioli and Vasishtha 2025). Establishing formal, transparent stabilization funds to save windfalls can bolster stability and resilience. Botswana (a frontier market) and Chile (an emerging market) are examples that have been relatively successful at converting resource rents into lasting economic gains. In some cases, natural resource booms have helped expedite graduation to higher income classifications (World Bank 2025a).

Catalyzing productivity growth through structural reforms

Macroeconomic stability, institutional capacity, and sound financial sector policies would help ensure that frontier markets' integration into international financial markets promotes growth and development. Alongside these, policy makers can take complementary steps to generate investment growth and enhance productivity. Structural reform is important for all EMDEs. When combined with policies to harness the benefits of financial integration, it could be catalytic in driving investment and job creation in frontier markets.

Such reforms include strengthening institutions and governance; developing effective foundational infrastructure and human capital; improving the functioning of markets, including by increasing competition and reducing monopoly power (including that of state-owned enterprises); and raising openness to international trade. Private investment can also be boosted by steps to develop strong physical and digital capital, particularly infrastructure, alongside improved human capital. These measures can raise prospective returns on private investment, making it more likely that frontier markets' access to international finance will translate into investment that boosts output, productivity, and job creation.

Governance, institutions, and the investment climate

Building effective and efficient governance systems is critical for a business-enabling environment, reducing uncertainty and building investor confidence, which can in turn generate growth and job creation. Improvements in economies' sovereign credit ratings, rising net capital inflows (as a share of GDP), and reforms enhancing investment profiles have a positive effect on investment growth (Adarov 2025). Enabling reforms are multifaceted and context-specific, but they encompass areas such as increasing regulatory quality, enhancing market-based competition (including for state-owned enterprises), ensuring predictable, well-implemented legal frameworks that avoid placing unnecessary burdens on firms, and delivering reliable public services (World Bank 2024b).

Substantial gaps in governance persist between frontier markets and emerging markets. The benefits of good governance are indicated, for example, by evidence that more robust institutions and legal foundations, along with greater market depth, are associated with lower borrowing costs and longer maturities of domestic-currency debt (Bekaert et al. 2014). Emerging markets that have experienced sustained periods of high investment growth and economic transformation, including Chile, Korea, Malaysia, and Uruguay, show common reform themes, including measures that deepen the financial sector, restore liquidity, and open the capital account (World Bank 2024c).

In addition, faster-growing frontier markets have tended to make more progress on governance indicators than other frontier markets. Further governance-related reform options include strengthening financial regulation and oversight, digitizing interactions between the private and official sectors, and boosting transparency to reduce corruption risks. Transparency can also help showcase potential returns to investors, for example in equity investments in infrastructure (Chari, Henry, and Mauro 2025). Better governance and institutions are key to boosting investment, including FDI, which has been in retreat globally in recent decades (Adarov and Pallan 2025). Attracting more FDI to complement portfolio and debt flows can ameliorate external vulnerabilities (Ghosh, Ostry, and Qureshi 2016; Sula 2010).

Strengthening physical and human capital

Strong investment growth is a vital ingredient for raising output. The private sector has a vital role, given limited public resources in frontier markets; this role hinges on risk-adjusted returns justifying the needed investments (Adarov 2025). The enabling environment, including effective government services, infrastructure, and human capital, is key.

There is substantial scope to improve foundational infrastructure in frontier markets, which can unlock private investment and foster job creation (Development Committee 2025). Public sector support for, or direct investment in, well-executed foundational infrastructure can expand accessible markets, increase connectivity, and reduce transaction costs for firms, consumers, and workers (World Bank 2024a). Infrastructure investment can underpin development gains linked to natural capital and resource wealth, including tourism. Tourism's contribution to frontier markets' GDP has risen since 2000 (refer to figure 4.15.A). Connectivity could unlock more growth in the sector; benefits include job creation, greater inclusion, and poverty reduction, including via ancillary activities (Christie et al. 2013).

Enhanced infrastructure could also help frontier markets capitalize on energy opportunities. Many

FIGURE 4.15 Natural resources

Tourism's contribution to frontier markets' GDP has risen since 2010, but the sector may have greater potential. Today's frontier markets, particularly in Africa and South Asia, have strong solar energy potential, but production remains limited. A sizable share of today's frontier markets are dependent on energy exports. Some frontier markets supply large shares of the global output of various minerals important for new technologies and the energy transition.

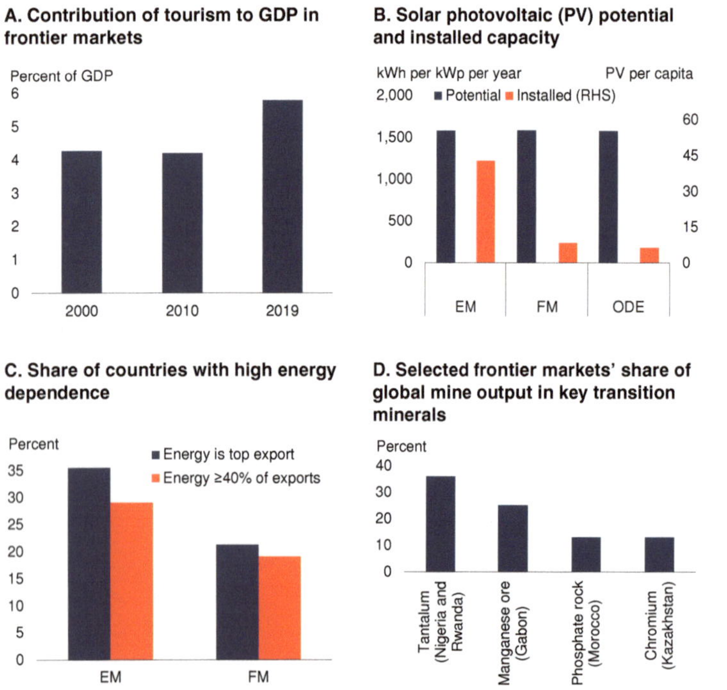

Sources: SolarGIS World Bank Global Solar Atlas; U.S. Geological Survey (USGS); World Bank.

Note: EM = emerging markets; FM = frontier markets; ODE = other developing economies, neither EM nor FM based on 2025 classifications. Sample size varies based on data availability.

A. International tourism receipts as a share of GDP; unweighted average for FMs in 2000 (36 FMs), 2010 (49 FMs), and 2019 (46 FMs), based on available data from the 2025 sample of 56 FMs.

B. PV potential measures solar resource quality (yield): the estimated annual electricity generated by a standard 1-kWp PV installation, based on sunlight and environmental factors (SolarGIS PVOUT; kWh/kWp/year, left axis). Installed PV is installed solar PV capacity per person in 2018 (Wp per capita, right axis). Bars show group means for EMs, FMs, and ODEs.

C. Share of countries based on 2021–23 average export composition. Sample includes only economies with data on GDP, total exports, and energy, metals, and agriculture breakdowns (31 EMs and 47 FMs).

D. Selected frontier markets' share of global mine output in the respective commodity; latest USGS year available (2023). Shares are computed as the sum of output across the frontier market(s) shown divided by world total (rounded).

frontier markets have substantial solar energy potential that, if realized, could help close energy deficits and support development. Yet infrastructure shortfalls, together with limited institutional capacity, have kept frontier market solar energy production well below potential, and low relative to emerging markets (refer to figure 4.15.B). Solar -generating capacity can be installed at relatively modest scale in a decentralized manner, utilizing mature technologies. With the right infrastructure and institutional strengthening, challenges to broad solar adoption in frontier markets should be surmountable.

Enhanced transport infrastructure can help with the discovery, development, and export of fuels and mineral deposits. Energy commodities represent at least 40 percent of exports in about one-fifth of today's frontier markets, less than emerging markets but still substantial (refer to figure 4.15.C). In addition, many new technologies—from renewable energy and electric vehicles to telecommunications infrastructure and consumer electronics—require inputs of particular metals and minerals (World Bank 2023).

Frontier markets already account for significant shares of global mining output in several key transition minerals. For example, Gabon accounts for almost one-quarter of global manganese output, a key input for battery technology and steel production; Morocco produces about one-eighth of mined phosphate rock, relevant for fertilizer and battery chemistry; and Nigeria and Rwanda between them provide over one-third of global tantalum, an important metal for digital technologies (refer to figure 4.15.D). Beyond current production, meanwhile, Bolivia and Argentina are home to the world's largest lithium resources (USGS 2025). Lithium has become a priority for many technology firms and electric vehicle manufacturers. Increasing demand for specific commodities could provide new opportunities for growth and development in relevant economies (Andreoni and Avenyo 2023; IEA 2022). Effective development of these resources will depend on adequate infrastructure, as well as on institutions, transparent revenue management, and appropriate skills development.

A healthy, educated, and skilled labor force is also vital to investment and output prospects. Investment in human capital to foster a productive workforce can include short-term interventions, such as the retraining of displaced workers, as well as longer-term policies on education and healthcare. Frontier markets have made some notable progress in these areas, but educational attainment, for example, generally remains lower than in emerging markets. A focus on integrating underrepresented groups, particularly women, into the workforce, by developing skills and opportunities and addressing restrictive social norms, could significantly boost growth and development, especially in some regions (Gatti et al. 2025). Optimal education and training in any economy will necessarily depend on the evolution of labor demand. Ensuring that growing working-age populations are equipped to find productive work must be a key objective for frontier market policy makers.

Productivity-enhancing shifts of resources across and within sectors have been a feature of economic progress in frontier markets and beyond. Economies that have made sustained progress often deployed different strategies at different income levels. (World Bank 2024d). At low income levels, boosting investment alone may succeed, but as incomes rise the focus often shifts toward investment combined with technology infusion, and later toward innovation. Amid global shifts in trade patterns and policies, technological innovation, and climate change, growth models will need to continue to adapt and evolve.

Support for frontier markets from the international community

Frontier markets generally remain eligible for official development assistance but are increasingly transitioning away from the most concessional forms of international support. Continued targeted external support, including via market development initiatives such as the World Bank Group's Joint Capital Markets Program (which includes several frontier markets), can support private sector growth and job creation. Development finance, including through the IDA private sector window where relevant, can help raise private investment by supporting new sectors and financing structures, providing guarantees, and showing the viability of innovative transactions, setting examples for private investors.

International partners have a vital role in supporting capacity development in frontier markets. Drawing on cross-country expertise, they can help develop appropriately tailored and robust policy approaches and institutions that foster credibility and investor confidence, including through stronger macroeconomic and financial sector policy frameworks. Beyond capacity development and financing, the international community can help to foster a global economic environment in which frontier markets can thrive. Spillovers from large economies and shifts in global sentiment can have large impacts on frontier markets, given their limited and sometimes fragile market access. Policy and regulatory consistency among large actors can help limit volatility that could be particularly destabilizing for frontier markets. With their potential for greater economic and financial integration, frontier markets would be beneficiaries of a more stable and predictable global trading system.

ANNEX 4.1 Classification of economies

This chapter classifies EMDEs into three groups: emerging markets, frontier markets, and other developing economies. As detailed in box 4.1, the classification approach is based primarily on economies' categorization by four prominent index providers—three for equity markets (FTSE Russell, MSCI, S&P Dow Jones Indices) and one for bond markets (from J.P. Morgan). In addition, EMDEs that are high income are automatically classified as emerging markets.[9]

Countries can enter or exit an index or category at different points in time, reflecting changes in their classification by index providers or income level (refer to tables A4.1.1-5 for full classification details). Unless indicated otherwise, this chapter uses country groupings in 2012 as the baseline sample. This year is roughly the midpoint of the quarter century covered in the chapter, and data for all four indexes are available from this point. This approach allows frontier market performance to be tracked over time. In some cases, use of the 2025 sample is more informative; this is noted explicitly in the text and chart notes.

Across equity index providers, classification criteria are primarily based on the size and liquidity of domestic equity markets and market accessibility, augmented by additional criteria—such as income levels and credit ratings—that are indicative of broader development.[10] The index provider categorizations that are used to determine the classifications in this chapter are:

FTSE Russell equity market classifications: Economies are classified as frontier, emerging (with a further subdivision between secondary emerging and advanced emerging), or developed. In the FTSE Russell classifications, the change from unclassified to frontier depends on market quality criteria and a credit rating no lower than speculative grade. The change from advanced emerging to developed depends on meeting minimum investable market capitalization and securities count, as well as achieving high income status under World Bank Group thresholds and holding an investment-grade credit rating.

MSCI equity market classifications: Economies are classified as frontier, emerging, or developed. In the MSCI classifications, the change from unclassified to frontier depends on market accessibility criteria and having at least one investable firm meeting size and liquidity requirements. A transition from emerging to developed depends on a per capita income threshold, complying with more stringent market accessibility criteria, and having at least five investable firms that meet higher size and liquidity requirements.

S&P equity market classifications: Economies are classified as frontier, emerging, or developed. In the S&P classifications, the change from unclassified to frontier depends on meeting market structure and accessibility criteria, as well as criteria indicating a sufficient degree of macroeconomic stability. The change from emerging to developed depends on meeting a per capita income threshold for two consecutive years, as well as more advanced market structure and accessibility criteria.

J.P. Morgan EMBI membership: This broad bond index captures both emerging and frontier market economies. Securities are included if they represent outstanding issuance of sovereign or quasi-sovereign debt with a face value of at least $500 million, denominated in U.S. dollars, and with at least six months until maturity. In addition, initial maturity must be at least 2.5 years, and daily pricing must be available. An exclusion criterion based on GNI per capita and purchasing power parity cost of living omits countries considered too affluent to be emerging markets.[11]

[9] Economies for which forecasts are not provided in the *Global Economic Prospects* report—because of, for example, a lack of data—are also excluded from the sample.

[10] The details of assessment frameworks nonetheless vary across index providers (FTSE Russell 2024; MSCI 2025; S&P Dow Jones 2024).

[11] J.P. Morgan also maintains an external bond index dedicated to frontier markets—NEXGEM, a subsection of EMBI. However, NEXGEM is not used as a classification input in this chapter because the index was new in 2012—the chapter's baseline sample year—having been launched in December 2011, with many EMBI economies also being added to NEXGEM in the subsequent years.

TABLE A4.1.1 Classification of frontier markets, emerging markets, and other developing economies: 2012 baseline sample

Region	Frontier markets	Emerging markets	Other developing economies	
East Asia and Pacific	Mongolia Viet Nam*^z	China Indonesia Malaysia Philippines Thailand	Cambodia Fiji Kiribati Lao PDR Marshall Islands Micronesia, Fed. Sts. Myanmar Nauru	Palau Papua New Guinea Samoa Solomon Islands Timor-Leste Tonga Tuvalu Vanuatu
Europe and Central Asia	Azerbaijan Belarus Bulgaria*^z Georgia Kazakhstan*^ North Macedonia* Romania*^z Serbia*^ Ukraine*^	Croatia Hungary Latvia Lithuania Poland Russian Federation Türkiye	Albania Armenia Bosnia and Herzegovina Kosovo	Kyrgyz Republic Moldova Montenegro Tajikistan Uzbekistan
Latin America and the Caribbean	Argentina*^z Belize Bolivia Costa Rica Dominican Republic Ecuador*^ El Salvador Guatemala Jamaica*^ Panama*^	Antigua and Barbuda Bahamas, The Barbados Brazil Chile Colombia Mexico Peru St. Kitts and Nevis Trinidad and Tobago Uruguay	Dominica Grenada Guyana Haiti Honduras	Nicaragua Paraguay St. Lucia St. Vincent and the Grenadines Suriname
Middle East, North Africa, Afghanistan and Pakistan	Iraq Jordan*^z Lebanon*^ Pakistan*^z Tunisia*	Bahrain Egypt, Arab Rep. Kuwait Morocco Oman Qatar Saudi Arabia United Arab Emirates	Afghanistan Algeria Djibouti Iran, Islamic Rep.	Libya Syrian Arab Republic West Bank and Gaza Yemen, Rep.
South Asia	Bangladesh* Sri Lanka*^z	India	Bhutan Maldives	Nepal
Sub-Saharan Africa	Angola Botswana* Côte d'Ivoire*^ Gabon Ghana*^ Kenya* Mauritius* Namibia*^ Nigeria*^z Senegal Zambia*^	Equatorial Guinea South Africa	Benin Burkina Faso Burundi Cabo Verde Cameroon Central African Republic Chad Comoros Congo, Dem. Rep. Congo, Rep. Eritrea Eswatini Ethiopia Gambia, The Guinea Guinea-Bissau Lesotho	Liberia Madagascar Malawi Mali Mauritania Mozambique Niger Rwanda São Tomé and Principe Seychelles Sierra Leone South Sudan Sudan Tanzania Togo Uganda Zimbabwe
Total	39	34	80	

Source: World Bank.

Note: For the frontier markets column, * indicates classification as a frontier market based on membership of at least one frontier equity index; ^ indicates economies that are included in J.P. Morgan's EMBI Global and at least one frontier equity index; z indicates frontier markets that are members of all four providers' indexes. Frontier markets without a superscript are classified solely on the basis of their membership in J.P. Morgan's EMBI Global.

TABLE A4.1.2 Classification of frontier markets, emerging markets, and other developing economies: 2025 sample

Region	Frontier markets	Emerging markets	Other developing economies	
East Asia and Pacific	Mongolia*^ Papua New Guinea Viet Nam*	China Indonesia Malaysia Nauru Palau Philippines Thailand	Cambodia Fiji Kiribati Lao PDR Marshall Islands Micronesia, Fed. Sts. Myanmar	Samoa Solomon Islands Timor-Leste Tonga Tuvalu Vanuatu
Europe and Central Asia	Armenia Azerbaijan Georgia Kazakhstan*^z Kyrgyz Republic Montenegro North Macedonia* Serbia*^ Tajikistan Ukraine Uzbekistan	Bulgaria Hungary Poland Romania Russian Federation Türkiye	Albania Belarus Bosnia and Herzegovina Kosovo Moldova	
Latin America and the Caribbean	Argentina*^ Bolivia Dominican Republic Ecuador*^ El Salvador Guatemala Honduras Jamaica*^ Paraguay Suriname	Antigua and Barbuda Bahamas, The Barbados Brazil Chile Colombia Costa Rica Guyana Mexico Panama Peru St. Kitts and Nevis Trinidad and Tobago Uruguay	Belize Dominica Grenada Haiti Nicaragua St. Lucia St. Vincent and the Grenadines	
Middle East, North Africa, Afghanistan and Pakistan	Iraq Jordan*^z Lebanon Morocco*^z Pakistan*^z Tunisia* West Bank and Gaza*	Bahrain Egypt, Arab Rep. Kuwait Oman Qatar Saudi Arabia United Arab Emirates	Afghanistan Algeria Djibouti Iran, Islamic Rep. Libya Syrian Arab Republic Yemen, Rep.	
South Asia	Bangladesh* Maldives Sri Lanka*^z	India	Bhutan Nepal	
Sub-Saharan Africa	Angola Benin*^ Botswana* Burkina Faso* Cameroon Côte d'Ivoire*^z Ethiopia Gabon Ghana*^ Guinea-Bissau* Kenya*^z Mali* Mauritius* Mozambique Namibia*^ Niger* Nigeria Rwanda Senegal*^ Tanzania* Togo* Zambia*^	Seychelles South Africa	Burundi Cabo Verde Central African Republic Chad Comoros Congo, Dem. Rep. Congo, Rep. Equatorial Guinea Eritrea Eswatini Gambia, The Guinea	Lesotho Liberia Madagascar Malawi Mauritania São Tomé and Principe Sierra Leone South Sudan Sudan Uganda Zimbabwe
Total	56	37	57	

Source: World Bank.

Note: For the frontier markets column, * indicates classification as a frontier market based on membership of at least one frontier equity index; ^ indicates economies that are included in J.P. Morgan's EMBI Global and at least one frontier equity index; z indicates frontier markets that are members of all four providers' indexes. Frontier markets without a superscript are classified solely on the basis of their membership in J.P. Morgan's EMBI Global.

TABLE A4.1.3 Number of economies in each classification (as of 2012 and 2025)

	Frontier markets	Emerging markets	Other developing economies	Advanced economies
2012	39	34	80	34
2025	56	37	57	37

Source: World Bank.

TABLE A4.1.4 Classification changes between 2012 and 2025

Classification changes	Economies
From EM to AE[a]	Croatia (2023), Latvia (2014), Lithuania (2015)
From EM to ODE[b]	Equatorial Guinea (2015)
From EM to FM[c]	Morocco (2014)
From FM to EM[d]	Bulgaria (2023), Costa Rica (2024), Panama (2017)*, Romania (2019)*
From FM to ODE[e]	Belarus (2023), Belize (2022)
From ODE to EM[f]	Guyana (2022), Nauru (2015)*, Palau (2016)*, Seychelles (2014)
From ODE to FM[g]	Armenia (2014), Benin (2016), Burkina Faso (2016), Cameroon (2017), Ethiopia (2015), Guinea-Bissau (2016), Honduras (2014), Kyrgyz Republic (2025), Maldives (2022), Mali (2016), Montenegro (2025), Mozambique (2014), Niger (2016), Papua New Guinea (2018), Paraguay (2014), Rwanda (2022), Suriname (2016), Tajikistan (2018), Tanzania (2014), Togo (2016), Uzbekistan (2020), West Bank and Gaza (2017)

Source: World Bank.

Note: Years in parentheses following economy names are the years the classification changed for that economy. An asterisk following the year indicates that, for one or more years after the initial classification change, an economy reverted to upper-middle-income status; however, these economies are all classified as high-income as of 2025. AE = advanced economy; EM = emerging market; FM = frontier market; ODE = other developing economy that is neither EM nor FM.

a. All these economies were reclassified as advanced economies in the respective years upon joining the euro area.

b. The economy's status was changed from high-income to upper-middle-income in 2015.

c. All three equity index providers moved Morocco to their frontier indexes between 2013 and 2015, citing declining liquidity or access.

d. All these economies reached high-income status.

e. Both economies were removed from J.P. Morgan's EMBI Global.

f. All these economies reached high-income status.

g. MSCI granted frontier market status to the Western African Economic and Monetary Union (WAEMU) economies in 2016, meaning that Benin, Burkina Faso, Guinea-Bissau, Mali, Niger, and Togo became frontier markets under this chapter's classification. Côte d'Ivoire and Senegal were already frontier markets as of 2012. FTSE Russell added West Bank and Gaza to its equity index. The remaining economies joined J.P. Morgan's EMBI Global in the years in parentheses following their names.

TABLE A4.1.5 Top quartile analysis for combined 2012 and 2025 frontier market samples

Category	Count	Economies
Frontier markets top quartile	15	Armenia, Azerbaijan, Bangladesh, Belarus, Bulgaria, Ethiopia, Georgia, Kazakhstan, Mongolia, Panama, Romania, Rwanda, Tajikistan, Uzbekistan, Viet Nam
Other frontier markets	47	Angola, Argentina, Belize, Benin, Bolivia, Botswana, Burkina Faso, Cameroon, Costa Rica, Côte d'Ivoire, Dominican Republic, Ecuador, El Salvador, Gabon, Ghana, Guatemala, Guinea-Bissau, Honduras, Iraq, Jamaica, Jordan, Kenya, Kyrgyz Republic, Lebanon, Maldives, Mali, Mauritius, Montenegro, Morocco, Mozambique, Namibia, Niger, Nigeria, North Macedonia, Pakistan, Papua New Guinea, Paraguay, Senegal, Serbia, Sri Lanka, Suriname, Tanzania, Togo, Tunisia, Ukraine, West Bank and Gaza, Zambia

Source: World Bank.

Note: This table combines the baseline 2012 sample of 39 frontier markets (including those which subsequently moved to other groupings), plus those economies that had attained frontier market status as of 2025. The top 25 percent in terms of average per capita GDP growth over 2000–24, 15 economies, are included in the "top quartile."

ANNEX 4.2 Frontier market case studies

This annex examines selected frontier markets that have delivered relatively strong per capita output growth over 2000–24. The examples are drawn from the top quartile of economies in terms of per capita GDP growth since 2000 (refer to annex 4.1). Country circumstances matter: factors that contributed to success in one context may not be applicable in another. Nevertheless, lessons for other frontier markets do emerge. For each economy considered, the case study addresses the following questions:

- How did the economy evolve?
- How did capital flows and financial development evolve, and was this associated with inclusion in major indexes?
- What policy choices supported these outcomes?

The five case studies represent a diverse set of economies in terms of geography, economic structure, and per capita income—Kazakhstan, Panama, Rwanda, Uzbekistan, and Viet Nam.[12]

Kazakhstan

Economic performance

Kazakhstan's growth over the past 25 years has been driven by abundant oil and gas resources, alongside a gradual shift toward more market-oriented institutions. Per capita growth has moderated over time—from 8 percent in the 2000s to 3 percent in the 2010s, weighed down by lower oil prices and subdued domestic demand. It subsequently slowed further to 1.6 percent over 2020–24. Compared to regional oil-exporting peers, Kazakhstan has nonetheless sustained higher per capita growth overall since 2000.

Over the past two decades, Kazakhstan's growth has been driven by large-scale investment—especially in energy and infrastructure—and productivity gains following post-Soviet reforms (OECD 2016). In the 2000s, demand was supported by strong investment fueled by foreign direct investment in oil and gas, public infrastructure spending, and expanding domestic credit. Consumption also benefited from rising real wages and consumer loans. Employment and economic activity shifted away from agriculture toward extractive and service sectors. Buoyed by unusually rapid investment growth in the early 2000s and further solid gains thereafter, capital stock per capita rose by 48 percent between 2000 and 2023, reaching among the highest levels in upper-middle -income countries (refer to figure A4.2.1.A). Favorable external conditions and fiscal restraint saw government debt rise only gradually—from 10 percent of GDP in the 2000s to 25 percent over 2020–24.

Alongside robust growth, Kazakhstan has achieved substantial reductions in poverty (World Bank 2025c). By 2008, the share of people living in extreme poverty ($3.00 in 2021 PPP) had fallen below 1 percent and has since remained close to zero, while income inequality also declined. The Human Development Index (HDI) rose from 0.69 in 2000 to 0.84 in 2023, placing the country in the "very high" category. This represents a key competitive advantage. Over this period, life expectancy increased by around 10 years, tertiary education enrollment nearly doubled, and access to clean water improved. Internet access also grew rapidly, supporting digital inclusion.

Capital flows, financial development, and index inclusion

Kazakhstan was included in J.P. Morgan's EMBI Global in 2007. It was added to the MSCI and S&P Frontier Markets indexes in 2007 and 2008, respectively, and was subsequently included in the FTSE Frontier Index in 2017, the year in which the Astana International Exchange was launched. However, market liquidity, sectoral diversity, and investor participation remain limited, hampering progress toward emerging market status. Capital inflows have fluctuated significantly since 2000, influenced by commodity cycles, global financial

Note: Case study preparation was led by Jiwon Lee and Takuma Tanaka, with contributions from Marie Albert, Tommy Chrimes, Alen Mulabdic, Edoardo Palombo, and Collette Wheeler.

[12] Data on poverty and inequality are drawn from the World Bank's Poverty and Inequality Platform. Where decade averages are used in the text, these are based on a simple average of years for which data is available within the given time range. This public, survey-based data is not always strictly comparable over the full time span presented.

conditions, regional shocks, and FDI in large-scale oil and gas developments (ADB 2021). Inflows peaked at 42.5 percent of GDP in 2006, driven by cross-border bank lending amid high oil prices and strong growth expectations (refer to figure A4.2.1.B). The 2008–09 Global Financial Crisis triggered a sharp drop in short-term flows and exposed vulnerabilities in the banking sector. Since then, aggregate portfolio flows have been limited or negative, with inflows dominated by sovereign and state-owned enterprise borrowing.

Financial development progressed rapidly in the early 2000s, foreshadowing index inclusions in 2007 and 2008, but progress has since stalled. The Financial Development Index rose from 0.16 in 2000 to 0.39 in 2007, and private sector credit expanded to 59 percent of GDP (refer to figure A4.2.1.C). However, the 2008–09 Global Financial Crisis exposed structural weaknesses, including high non-performing loans, related-party lending, and overreliance on foreign funding. These weaknesses left a lasting impact on the country's financial development. Despite policy efforts to deepen capital markets in recent years—such as the creation of the Astana International Financial Centre—the financial sector remains dominated by state-owned banks, with limited SME financing and highly concentrated credit markets (IMF 2024a).

Policy drivers

Kazakhstan's policy approach combined state-led development with gradual liberalization, supporting financial market integration while enhancing buffers to external shocks. Policy efforts, including the "Kazakhstan 2050 Strategy" in 2012, have aimed to build a resilient, diversified economy by bolstering macroeconomic stability, enhancing trade integration, improving institutions, and deepening financial markets. Macroeconomic frameworks have evolved significantly, with the 2015 adoption of inflation targeting and a floating exchange rate boosting monetary policy credibility and flexibility. The prudent management of oil revenues through the National Fund has helped support countercyclical fiscal policy.

Trade integration accelerated with Kazakhstan's 2015 accession to the World Trade Organization (WTO) and the Eurasian Economic Union, expanding market access and committing the country to tariff reductions and trade facilitation reforms (WTO 2019). Non-oil exports—particularly agriculture, metals, and manufacturing—have expanded gradually, supported by improved regional connectivity. Institutional reforms have focused on the business environment, legal frameworks, and governance improvements (OECD 2023). Efforts include enhancing contract enforcement, reducing regulatory

FIGURE A4.2.1 Kazakhstan: Economic performance

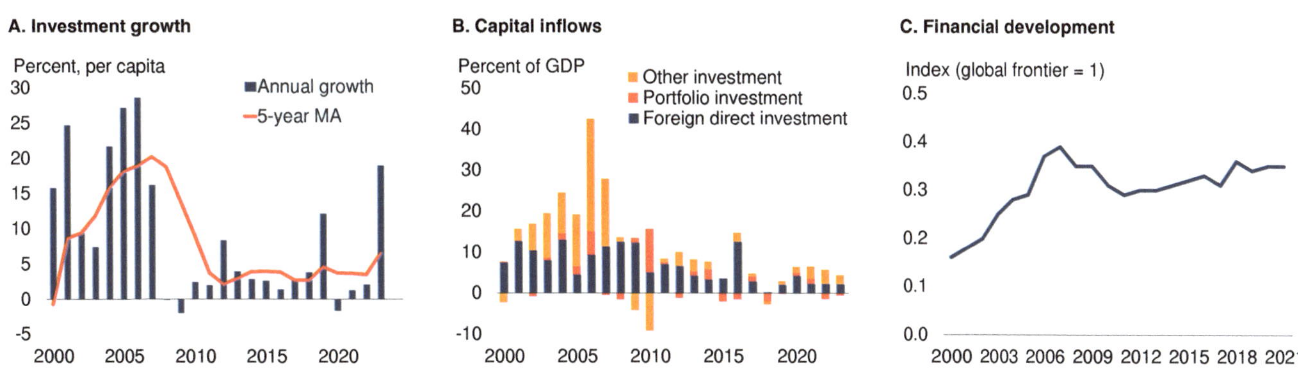

Sources: Haver Analytics; International Monetary Fund; WDI (database); World Bank.

Note: MA = moving average.

A. Bars show annual growth of per capita investment; lines represent the 5-year moving average of the annual growth rate.

B. Bars show annual gross capital inflows from balance of payments data in percent of GDP. Positive values indicate an increase in foreign liabilities, while negative values indicate repatriation of capital.

C. Bars show Financial Development Index, normalized so that 1 = intertemporal frontier and 0 = the lowest intertemporal reading.

burdens, expanding e-governance, and promoting transparency, but the consistent implementation of reforms remains a challenge.

Kazakhstan made progress on capital market development through phased capital account liberalization, alongside measures to ease foreign ownership restrictions and to strengthen market infrastructure. Post-independence reforms before 2000—including bank privatization, development of a multi-pillar pension system, and the creation of the Kazakhstan Stock Exchange—fostered market depth. Targeted reforms ahead of Kazakhstan's 2017 inclusion in the FTSE Frontier Index eased capital repatriation restrictions. Subsequent reforms included a framework for the Astana International Financial Centre based on English common law and the creation of a new regulatory agency to improve supervisory clarity.

Panama

Economic performance

At almost $17,000 (in 2010–19 constant prices) in 2025, Panama has the highest per capita GDP among the frontier markets in this chapter. This reflects the country's generally strong growth between 2000 and 2019, averaging more than 4 percent per capita. Panama reached high-income status by 2017 and therefore graduated from the frontier markets grouping. However, per capita growth and convergence have slowed over the last decade, and Panama's economy was hit hard by the COVID-19 pandemic (World Bank 2024e). Investment, including from abroad, has fueled significant capital deepening: capital stock per capita more than quadrupled between 2000 and 2023 (refer to figure A4.2.2.A). Government debt dynamics improved through much of the 2010s before the pandemic-related surge. Public debt service as a share of GDP also declined from the mid-2000s, remaining below 2 percent for most of the 2010s.

Panama was an open trading economy at the turn of the century and has remained so, although trade openness—total exports and imports as a share of GDP—has declined somewhat from 140 percent in 2000 to 90 percent in 2023. The economy is services-oriented, with the share of workers engaged in the services sector remaining stable over the period at about two-thirds. This economic structure reflects the country's status as both a transport and logistics hub and a regional financial center.

Panama has made substantial progress across several important development measures over the past 25 years. The share of the population living in extreme poverty ($3.00 in 2021 PPP) has fallen by three-quarters, from 15 percent in the 2000s to less than 4 percent.[13] Inequality has also fallen, with the Gini score declining from 57 in 2000 to 49 in 2023. Life expectancy has risen from 73 in 2000 to 80 in 2023, and electricity access is now close to universal, up from 81 percent in 2000. However, human capital remains low by regional and international standards (World Bank 2024e).

Capital flows, financial development, and index inclusion

Panama was an early member of J.P. Morgan's EMBI and was included in the S&P Frontier Market Index from its launch in 2008. S&P also launched a Panama-specific equity index in 2008. Panama is not included in the MSCI or FTSE frontier equity indexes.[14]

Capital inflows have been substantial in Panama, averaging about 15 percent of GDP over the period (refer to figure A4.2.2.B). Foreign direct investment (FDI) has formed a large part of these inflows and was positive in every year since 2000, except in 2020. Portfolio flows have also been substantial, at more than 3 percent of GDP in the average year, reflecting Panama's integration into global financial systems. Other capital inflows have also been relatively large.

Even in 2000, Panama scored well on financial development relative to most frontier markets, and progress has largely continued (refer to figure A4.2.2.C). Domestic credit to the private sector had risen above 100 percent of GDP by 2020,

[13] The income aggregate in Panama includes imputed rent only from 2008 onward; earlier welfare aggregates are therefore not directly comparable to more recent aggregates.

[14] MSCI launched a standalone Panama index as part of its May 2017 semi-annual index review.

although much of this is to established companies. Small firms still report challenges in accessing credit, and individuals' access to financial products remains limited (World Bank 2024e).

Policy drivers

Panama's macroeconomic success has been underpinned by a long period of macroeconomic stability, together with an outward-looking economic model. The geography of the Panama Canal (of which Panama assumed full control in 2000) and the development of associated infrastructure has helped establish the country as a hub for trade, transport, and logistics, consistently attracting investment (World Bank 2024e). Aside from 2020, Panama has run a current account deficit every year since 2000, financed by steady capital inflows, including the reinvestment of foreign-owner dividends.

The authorities have maintained a growth-friendly macroeconomic environment, with low inflation and declining government debt prior to a debt surge due to the COVID-19 pandemic (World Bank 2024e). As a dollarized economy for more than a century, Panama does not operate an independent monetary policy. Nevertheless, inflation has remained below 2 percent for most of the period since the mid-2010s. Dollarization has likely aided monetary stability, but other idiosyncratic and policy factors also play important roles. Dollarization may have been more effective in Panama because the economy is not a large producer of goods (Moreno-Villalaz 2005).

The financial sector in Panama has long been open and competitive, without restrictions on entry or capital flows, and the banking system is large relative to the economy (Moreno-Villalaz 2005). Lacking currency-issuing powers, deposit insurance, or a lender of last resort, Panama relies on banks self-insuring through large capital and liquidity buffers. The generally smooth functioning of this system has avoided major banking crises over the past three decades (IMF 2024b). A range of measures to enhance financial transparency contributed to Panama's removal from the list of jurisdictions under enhanced monitoring by the Financial Action Task Force in 2023 (World Bank 2025d).

Low taxes and a competitive regulatory environment have historically contributed to Panama's attractiveness as an investment destination. In addition, public investment, including several infrastructure "megaprojects," propelled rapid growth in the construction sector from the late 2000s and further strengthened the trade and logistics sectors (World Bank 2024e). However, amid growing spending pressures, government revenues may need to increase; the tax-to-GDP ratio is the lowest in the region. More broadly, slowing growth suggests the country's growth

FIGURE A4.2.2 Panama: Economic performance

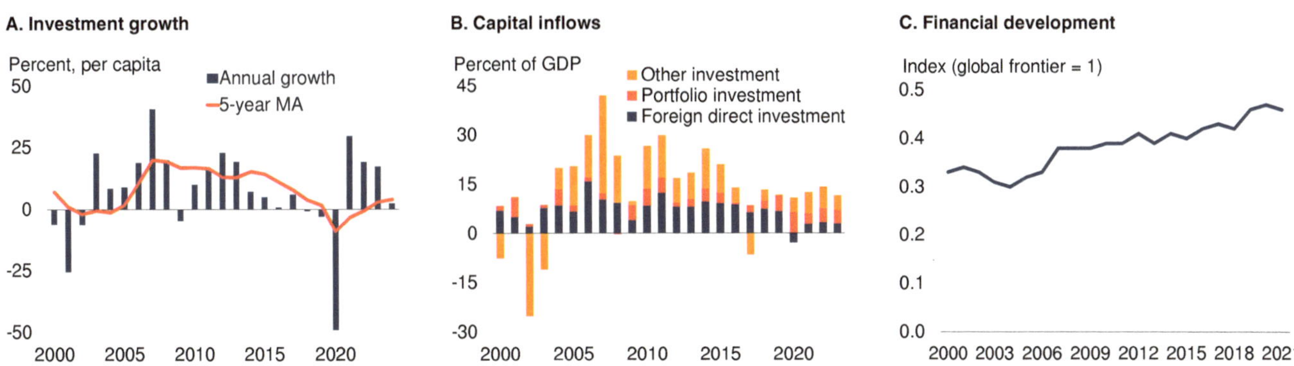

Sources: Haver Analytics; International Monetary Fund; WDI (database); World Bank.

Note: MA = moving average.

A. Bars show annual growth of per capita investment; lines represent the 5-year moving average of the annual growth rate.

B. Bars show annual gross capital inflows from balance of payments data in percent of GDP. Positive values indicate an increase in foreign liabilities, while negative values indicate repatriation of capital.

C. Bars show Financial Development Index, normalized so that 1 = intertemporal frontier and 0 = the lowest intertemporal reading.

model may need to evolve further, with renewed focus on productivity growth, human capital development, and diversification likely to be important.

Rwanda

Economic performance

Rwanda has made substantial economic progress since 2000, emerging as one of Africa's most dynamic economies. Real GDP per capita has grown by 245 percent since 2000, propelling Rwanda to the brink of middle-income status (World Bank 2025a). Per capita growth has nonetheless moderated, declining from 6.1 percent in the 2000s to 4.6 percent in the 2010s, and to 4.2 percent over 2020–24. Even so, Rwanda has continued to grow considerably faster than Sub-Saharan Africa as a whole, reflecting a diversified economic base and relatively strong institutional capacity (Aragie et al. 2024).

Sustained economic progress has been supported in part by a strategic focus on infrastructure investment. Investment as a share of GDP rose from 12 percent in 2000 to 23 percent in 2022, reflecting strong per capita investment growth for much of the period (refer to figure A4.2.3.A). As a result, capital stock per capita increased fivefold between 2000 and 2023. This investment drive was accompanied by higher government borrowing, particularly from the mid-2010s and again during the post-pandemic recovery, with government debt averaging 66 percent of GDP over 2020–24. Rwanda has also made progress in poverty reduction and various social development metrics, including schooling attainment, life expectancy, and maternal and child health. Extreme poverty ($3.00 in 2021 PPP) fell from 82 percent in 2000 to 64 percent in 2016, while inequality, as measured by the Gini index, fell materially between the 2000s and 2010s. Despite these gains, poverty rates remain high relative to some comparable economies.

Capital flows, financial development, and index inclusion

As of 2025, Rwanda features in an Africa-focused equity index and a standalone country index of S&P, but is not included in the major global frontier market equity indexes considered in this study. This absence likely reflects constraints related to market size, liquidity, and accessibility. However, Rwanda debuted in J.P. Morgan's EMBI in August 2021, with $620 million of issuance. Issuance of $400 million in 2013 was below the threshold for EMBI inclusion.

Rwanda has sustained robust growth in capital inflows, which rose from an average of 7.5 percent of GDP in 2010–19 to 9.3 percent in 2020–23 (refer to figure A4.2.3.B). Almost two-thirds of Rwanda's capital inflows in the 2020–23 period have been classified as "other investments,"

FIGURE A4.2.3 Rwanda: Economic performance

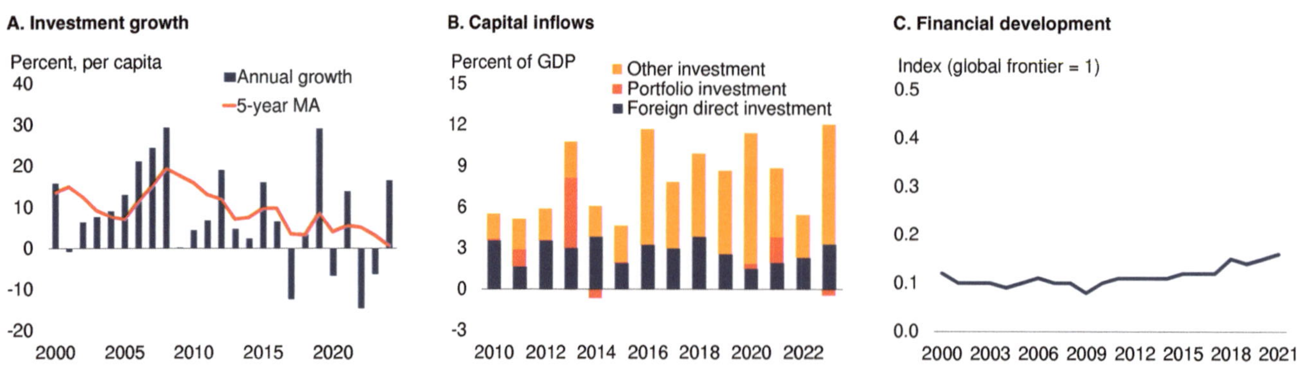

Sources: Haver Analytics; International Monetary Fund; WDI (database); World Bank.

Note: MA = moving average.

A. Bars show annual growth of per capita investment; lines represent the 5–year moving average of the annual growth rate.

B. Bars show annual gross capital inflows from balance of payments data in percent of GDP. Positive values indicate an increase in foreign liabilities, while negative values indicate repatriation of capital.

C. Bars show Financial Development Index, normalized so that 1 = intertemporal frontier and 0 = the lowest intertemporal reading.

reflecting bank transactions. Foreign direct investment (FDI) has also been a consistent source of capital, accounting for 2.8 percent of GDP on average between 2010 and 2023, signaling confidence in Rwanda's business environment and long-term prospects. Rwanda's capital inflows have been more volatile than those of some peer economies, reflecting shallow capital markets (Tang et al. 2022). Portfolio inflows exceeded 1 percent of GDP in three years since 2010. The largest increase occurred in 2011, reaching 5.1 percent, when the stock exchange began operations, despite its exclusion from major global frontier market indexes. The other two large portfolio inflows occurred in 2013 and 2021 and were mainly driven by international sovereign bond issuance.

Rwanda has made some gains in financial development, with the Financial Development Index rising from 0.12 in 2000 to 0.16 by 2021 (refer to figure A4.2.3.C). Domestic credit to the private sector as a share of GDP more than doubled, from 11 percent in the 2000s to 24 percent over 2020–24, mainly explained by progress in the early 2010s that coincided with financial market reforms. While the financial sector remains nascent, the gradual trajectory toward deeper intermediation reflects efforts to expand access to financial services.

Policy drivers

Rwanda's development path so far this century has reflected wide-ranging macroeconomic, structural, and financial reforms. Early efforts to improve efficiency in the banking sector, liberalize the capital account, and reduce trade barriers helped raise productivity by steering the economy toward a more market-based allocation of resources (Coulibaly, Ezemenari, and Duffy 2008; Malunda and Musana 2012). Milestones in capital market development were reached with the incorporation of Rwanda Stock Exchange Limited in 2005, the establishment of the regulatory Capital Market Authority in 2007, and the exchange's launch for trading in 2011. Over this period, Rwanda also implemented comprehensive investment liberalization measures, with no limits on foreign ownership or control, or capital transfers. Further reforms sought to reduce excessive tax and regulatory burdens on firms. The country has become one of the more competitive business environments in the region.

Policy frameworks have provided a clear roadmap for Rwanda's transformation into a knowledge-based, services economy, including through the government's Vision 2020 and Vision 2050 strategies (IMF 2005). Rwanda adopted a public investment strategy focused on high-potential sectors: health and education, growth-enhancing physical infrastructure, and agro-processing and tourism services (Redifer et al. 2020). These are all sectors which the World Bank Group has highlighted as having particular potential for resilient job creation globally (Development Committee 2025). Participation in the East African Community also helped to bolster regional trade integration. Rwanda's service-led growth has also benefited from skill upgrades and digital skills training.

Fiscal policy has supported growth via a focus on infrastructure and human capital investment, albeit at the cost of rising debt levels over the 2010s. Earlier, debt forgiveness in the mid-2000s had dramatically reduced the debt burden, generating fiscal headroom that enabled the subsequent government-led investment drive (IMF 2005; Redifer et al. 2020). Debt levels have surged further in the 2020s, reflecting the economic costs of the COVID-19 pandemic and subsequent shocks. Inflation eased and stabilized in the 2010s compared to the 2000s, though it jumped following the pandemic due largely to supply shocks. As financial deepening progressed, the link between reserve money and inflation weakened, leading the central bank to switch its monetary policy targeting from monetary aggregates to inflation in 2019, coupled with greater exchange rate flexibility (IMF 2019).

Uzbekistan

Economic performance

Uzbekistan recorded average annual per capita growth of 4.7 percent between 2000 and 2024, high relative to other current frontier markets. This included a period between 2004 and 2015 when per capita GDP increased by between 5 and 8 percent each year. Uzbekistan has a longstanding goal of achieving upper-middle-income status by 2030.

Since a new president took office in 2016, the government has advanced a rapid reform agenda aimed at transitioning to a new growth model (World Bank 2022). During this period, Uzbekistan unified the exchange rate, eliminated exchange rate restrictions, and liberalized trade and many prices for goods and services—all of which helped attract sizable capital inflows. Output growth has benefited from these reforms, as well as from favorable commodity prices and strong remittances, with per capita investment growth generally buoyant since the mid-2000s (refer to figure A4.2.4.A). Meanwhile, inflation has trended downward from about 20 percent annually in early 2018 to high single digits by the end of 2023. Headline government debt appears manageable, but broader external borrowing needs to be contained to ensure debt sustainability (IMF 2025).

Robust growth in both output and employment—the latter growing at an average of 3.7 percent annually during 2018–23—has underpinned a sharp decline in official estimates of extreme poverty. Extreme poverty ($3.00 in 2021 PPP) fell from an estimated 94 percent in the early 2000s to under 5 percent in the early 2020s.

Capital flows, financial development, and index inclusion

Uzbekistan is a relatively recent entrant into global financial indexes. The country's first international bond issuance, totaling $1 billion, prompted its inclusion in J.P. Morgan's EMBI Global in March 2019. Uzbekistan is not included in the major equity indexes.

Capital inflows have surged in recent years. Total inflows jumped to 14 percent of GDP in 2019 and have since stabilized at above 10 percent, having previously been in the -2 to 5 percent range (refer to figure A4.2.4.B). FDI inflows have been relatively stable, averaging 2 percent of GDP between 2005 and 2023. Increases in portfolio inflows have been linked to occasional bond issuances. Following more than a decade of limited portfolio inflows, a jump in 2019 (2.0 percent of GDP) reflected international sovereign bond issuance linked to inclusion in J.P. Morgan's EMBI. This inclusion paved the way for subsequent international issuance of corporate bonds by state-owned enterprises, including banks and energy companies. Uzbekistan also issued Sustainable Development Goal bonds in 2021, becoming the second country in the world to do so (UNDP 2021). Other investment inflows accounted for most of the increase in total capital inflows since 2019, driven largely by loans, particularly from multilateral institutions. Given this composition, aggregate capital flows to Uzbekistan have not been significantly affected by global shocks to date.

Progress in financial development picked up in the late 2010s, in conjunction with wider economic reforms (refer to figure A4.2.4.C). The headline Financial Development Index increased from 0.20 in the early 2010s to 0.29 in 2021. This trend was driven largely by increasing sophistication of financial institutions rather than capital markets. Amid rising bond issuance and capital market reforms, domestic credit to the private sector climbed to above 30 percent of GDP in the 2020s, from about 10 percent in the early 2010s. Recent macroprudential measures have targeted consumer lending to help bolster financial stability (IMF 2025). Despite gradual reforms of state-owned enterprises, state banks continue to dominate the financial sector, accounting for about two-thirds of banking system assets as of 2024 (IMF 2024c).

Policy drivers

Uzbekistan's development has had multiple phases over the past quarter century, reflecting an evolving development process underpinned by significant reform efforts. In the early 2000s, the economy was characterized by limited integration with the global economy, but benefited from supportive prices for key commodities—notably gold, gas, and cotton—exported to a relatively small number of partners. Despite an "unorthodox" economic strategy, relative macroeconomic stability was a feature of this period; reliance on the Russian Federation as a trading partner also declined significantly (Anderson, Ginting, and Taniguchi 2020).

FIGURE A4.2.4 Uzbekistan: Economic performance

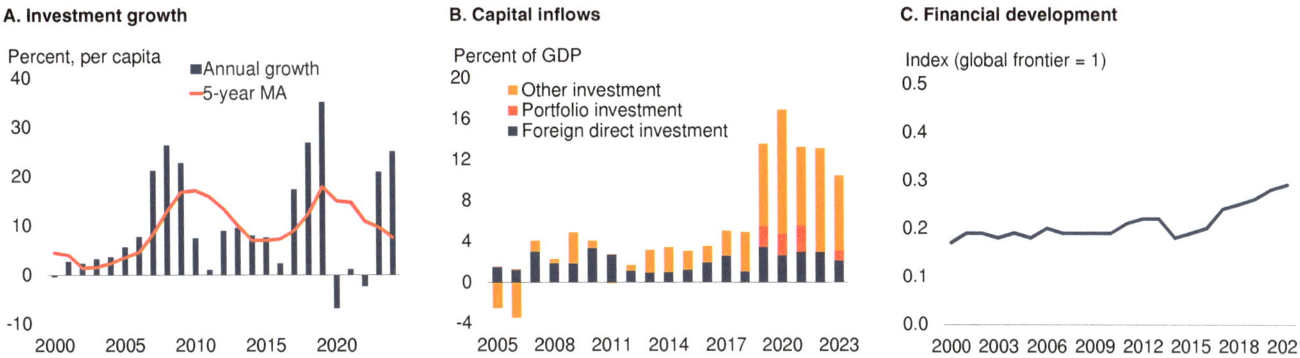

Sources: Haver Analytics; International Monetary Fund; WDI (database); World Bank.
Note: MA = moving average.
A. Bars show annual growth of per capita investment; lines represent the 5-year moving average of the annual growth rate.
B. Bars show annual gross capital inflows from balance of payments data in percent of GDP. Positive values indicate an increase in foreign liabilities, while negative values indicate repatriation of capital.
C. Bars show Financial Development Index, normalized so that 1 = intertemporal frontier and 0 = the lowest intertemporal reading.

Since 2017, the economic policy agenda has featured ambitious reform and transition efforts that have underpinned substantial progress toward a more market-oriented economy, spurring capital inflows (IMF 2025). Combined with buoyant remittances and another period of favorable commodity prices, these reforms have underpinned resilient growth despite regional and global challenges.

Progress toward a more open and competitive economy has continued, but important challenges remain. Growth decomposition exercises show that capital deepening has played a crucial role in driving growth over much of the past quarter century, but this driver is likely to become less potent as the country climbs the income ladder. Sustaining growth is likely to require a greater focus on technical change and productivity-enhancing policies (World Bank 2024d). In this regard, efforts to enhance private sector dynamism and diversify the economy will be important. Conducive reforms could include addressing the still large role of state firms and banks, facilitating the entry and exit of private firms, and improving governance, transparency, and policy implementation capacity (IMF 2025).

Viet Nam

Economic performance

Viet Nam ranks among the 10 fastest-growing economies globally over the twenty-first century so far. Annual GDP per capita growth averaged more than 5 percent over 2000–24, with graduation from low- to lower-middle-income status in 2009. Economic progress over this period coincided with rapid export expansion, industrialization, and growing capital inflows. The sum of exports and imports as a share of GDP increased from 110 percent in 2000 to 166 percent in 2023. This was accompanied by a large shift in employment: the share of workers employed in agriculture fell from 65 percent in 2000 to 33 percent in 2023, while the share in the industrial sector rose from 12 percent to 31 percent. Robust investment growth, albeit with a gradual slowdown over time, saw capital stock per capita increase more than sevenfold between 2000 and 2023 (refer to figure A4.2.5.A). This sustained growth was supported by a generally favorable macroeconomic environment—low unemployment, moderate fiscal and current account deficits, and benign debt levels—albeit with bouts of high inflation in 2008 and 2011 (World Bank 2025a).

Viet Nam has made significant development progress in recent decades. The share of the population living in extreme poverty ($3.00 in 2021 PPP) fell sharply from 29 percent in the 2000s to 1.5 percent in the 2020s.[15] Access to electricity reached 100 percent in 2017, up from

[15] There is a break in welfare aggregates survey comparability for Viet Nam in 2010.

88 percent in 2000. Educational outcomes have improved substantially, while life expectancy has also increased modestly. Overall, Viet Nam ranks in the top quartile of EMDEs on Sustainable Development Goals performance indicators (Baum 2020; World Bank 2024f).

Capital flows, financial development, and index inclusion

Viet Nam was first added to J.P. Morgan's EMBI in 2005, following its debut international sovereign bond issuance. Subsequently, the country was included in all three frontier equity indexes considered in this study—FTSE Russell, MSCI, and S&P—when they were launched. In October 2025, FTSE Russell announced plans to upgrade Viet Nam to secondary emerging market status in September 2026, subject to an interim review in March 2026 (LSEG 2025).

Overall capital inflows as a share of GDP have been relatively stable in recent years, moderating to around 5 percent after peaking at 20 percent in 2007 (refer to figure A4.2.5.B). Foreign direct investment (FDI) has remained a dominant source of financing and investment growth, averaging about 4–5 percent of GDP. Portfolio inflows were kickstarted by capital market integration, reaching 1.5 percent of GDP in 2005 following the inaugural bond issuance and then rising to 8.1 percent of GDP in 2007, coinciding with the country's inclusion in major equity indexes. Since 2010, however, portfolio inflows have been much smaller, averaging less than 1 percent of GDP. Since 2000, Viet Nam has not experienced a severe capital flow reversal.

Viet Nam has also made progress in domestic financial deepening. Domestic credit to the private sector grew rapidly, from 35 percent of GDP in 2000 to 126 percent in 2022. On some measures, however, overall financial development has been more modest, with limitations in capital market efficiency largely offsetting improvements in financial institutions, as reflected in the aggregate Financial Development Index (refer to figure A4.2.5.C).

Policy drivers

Viet Nam's solid economic growth has been underpinned by a sustained focus on economic reform under Doi Moi ("renovation"), which began in 1986. Over this period, reforms have focused on transforming the economy into a more market-oriented system (Nguyen 2024; World Bank 2025a). Manufacturing and exports have been key to sustained growth, with the profile of value-added manufacturing evolving as the economy has developed.

Trade liberalization advanced significantly, including accession to the WTO in 2007 and the

FIGURE A4.2.5 Viet Nam: Economic performance

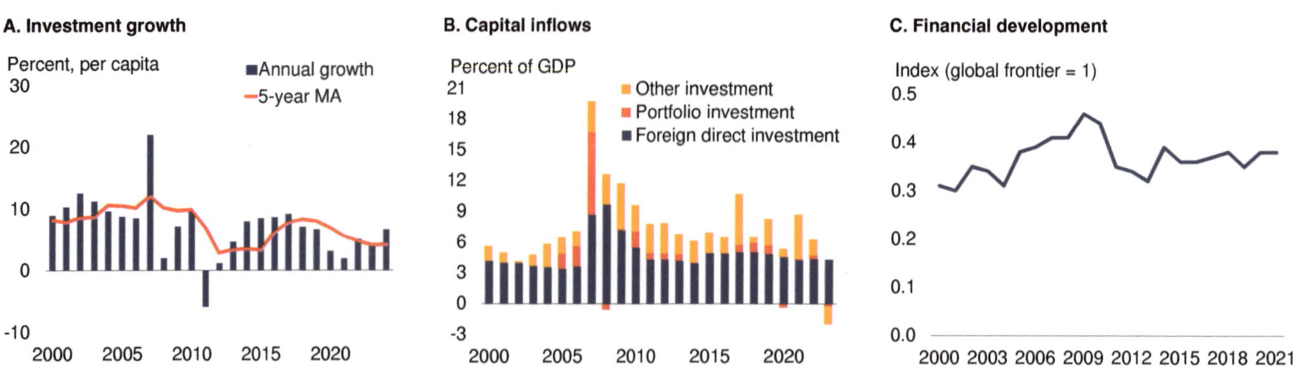

Sources: Haver Analytics; International Monetary Fund; WDI (database); World Bank.

Note: MA = moving average.

A. Bars show annual growth of per capita investment; lines represent the 5-year moving average of the annual growth rate.

B. Bars show annual gross capital inflows from balance of payments data in percent of GDP. Positive values indicate an increase in foreign liabilities, while negative values indicate repatriation of capital.

C. Bars show Financial Development Index, normalized so that 1 = intertemporal frontier and 0 = the lowest intertemporal reading.

conclusion of free trade agreements with major trading partners during the 2000s (World Bank 2024f). A simplified trade licensing regime, lower tariffs, and reduced non-tariff barriers supported rapid export growth (World Bank 2012). Deregulation and reform of state-owned enterprises spurred private sector development, enhancing competition and efficiency (Dang, Nguyen, and Taghizadeh-Hesary 2021). Legal and administrative reforms to strengthen private ownership and investor protection, reduce price controls, and simplify business registration aided both domestic firms and foreign investors, sustaining FDI inflows (Duong and Thanh 2011). Public investment in human capital also increased: spending on education rose from 3.5 percent of GDP in 2000 to 6 percent in 2015, alongside growth in the number of schools and teachers (Baum 2020). Literacy reached 96 percent by 2019. Continued emphasis on education—including targeted investment in foundational learning and vocational skills—has supported manufacturing-led growth and upgrading into higher-value industrial activities, though scope for further improvement remains (OECD 2025).

Sound macroeconomic policies, encompassing both fiscal and monetary policy, have helped safeguard macroeconomic stability (World Bank 2025a). The authorities have demonstrated agility in responding to shocks, weathering the Global Financial Crisis through accommodative fiscal and monetary policies and subsequently tightening conditions to contain inflation while preserving growth momentum (An and Thanh 2024; IMF 2014). Alongside macroeconomic stability, financial market reforms supported Viet Nam's inclusion in major international indexes. From the late 1980s, the authorities took steps to liberalize foreign exchange markets and ease restrictions on foreign ownership and capital and profit repatriation. Capital market deepening in the 1990s and 2000s then led to the launch of exchanges in Ho Chi Minh City and Hanoi, supported by the establishment of a formal stock market regulatory authority (Vuong 2019).

ANNEX 4.3 Data and methodology for empirical exercises

This annex describes the data and methodological framework used for the exercises in boxes 4.2 and 4.3. The former estimates the effect of various factors on the likelihood of an economy being in a capital inflow surge or stop episode, while the latter sheds light on the global financial cycle, using two dynamic factor models to show the relative roles of global, group-specific, and country-specific factors in equity returns and credit growth.

Stops and surges: Data and sample

The analysis is based on quarterly data on capital inflows from IMF Balance of Payments Statistics, obtained from Haver Analytics. Episodes of capital inflow surges and stops are identified using a threshold-based approach that identifies large deviations in gross capital inflows relative to a backward-looking trend, as described in box 4.2. The resulting binary indicators take a value of one in periods classified as a surge or stop and zero otherwise. The relationship between these extreme capital inflow episodes and a set of explanatory variables is examined, with global, domestic, and contagion-related factors—and the variables used to proxy them—informed by the related literature.

Global "push" factors. All variables used to proxy global push factors are constructed from quarterly data. For series originally available at higher frequencies, quarterly averages are taken before applying subsequent transformations. Two variables are used to capture shifts in global sentiment: global risk, measured by the CBOE VIX index, and global economic policy uncertainty, measured using the index developed by Baker, Bloom, and Davis (2016); both are expressed as year-over-year percentage changes.

The aggregate year-over-year global growth rate is calculated using real GDP growth rates, weighted by each economy's share of global GDP in U.S. dollars at average 2010–19 prices and market exchange rates. Oil prices are measured as the year-over-year percentage change in the U.S. dollar average of Brent crude, WTI, and Dubai spot prices. Shifts in long-term interest rates are captured by changes in the 10-year U.S. Treasury yield, obtained from Haver Analytics. U.S. monetary policy shocks are measured using the orthogonalized monetary policy surprise index developed by Bauer and Swanson (2023), which isolates unanticipated changes in policy around FOMC announcements. To mitigate reverse causality and endogeneity concerns, global explanatory variables are lagged by one quarter.

Domestic "pull" factors. Local GDP growth is measured by the year-over-year percentage change in quarterly real GDP in local currency terms. Financial market development is proxied by stock market capitalization, measured as the value of listed domestic companies as a share of GDP and serving as an indicator of equity market size and development; data are sourced from the World Bank's World Development Indicators database. De jure financial openness is measured by the Chinn-Ito Index (Chinn and Ito 2006), based on the IMF's Annual Report on Exchange Arrangements and Exchange Restrictions (AREAER), with higher values indicating fewer restrictions on cross-border capital flows. The exchange rate regime is captured by a dummy equal to one for economies whose de facto exchange rate arrangement is classified as a peg or other tightly managed regime in the AREAER and zero otherwise.

Sovereign ratings are measured by the quarter-over-quarter change in long-term foreign currency ratings from Moody's, S&P, and Fitch, sourced from Bloomberg. Daily ratings from these agencies are converted into numeric values and averaged to obtain quarterly values. Higher values indicate lower credit ratings. Structural variables (annual data) are lagged by four quarters. Other variables (quarterly data) are lagged by one quarter.

Contagion. A group contagion indicator is used to capture potential spillover effects from peers. The indicator is built for each episode type and equals one if an economy in the same classification group—advanced economy, emerging market, frontier market, or other developing economy—has a surge or stop episode. A trade-contagion variable is based on the trade-weighted average of episodes in an economy's trading partners (refer to Forbes and Warnock 2012). Contagion variables are lagged by one quarter.

Stops and surges: Methodology

The factors influencing the probability that an economy experiences a surge or a stop in a given quarter are estimated using a complementary log-log regression, following Forbes and Warnock (2012, 2021). In this setup, $e_{\{it\}}$ is a binary variable that equals one if country i is experiencing a surge (or stop) episode in quarter t, and zero otherwise.

The probability of an episode is modeled as

$$\Pr(e_{\{it\}} = 1) = F(X^{\{G\}}_{\{t\text{-}k\}}\beta^{\{G\}} + X^{\{D\}}_{\{i,t\text{-}k\}}\beta^{\{D\}} + X^{\{C\}}_{\{i,t\text{-}k\}}\beta^{\{C\}}),$$

where $X^{\{G\}}_{\{t-k\}}$ denotes a vector of global "push" factors, $X^{\{D\}}_{\{i,t-k\}}$ denotes a vector of domestic "pull" factors, and $X^{\{C\}}_{\{i,t-k\}}$ denotes a vector of contagion measures, lagged by k quarters, depending on the variable. The complementary log-log regression is appropriate for modeling rare binary events such as capital inflow surges and stops, as it allows for a skewed probability distribution.

This assumes that $F(z) = 1 - exp[-exp(z)]$.

Separate regressions are estimated for surges and stops with country fixed effects. Table A4.3.1 reports baseline results for the full 2000Q1–2024Q4 panel. Table A4.3.2 reports robustness results excluding Global Financial Crisis (2008Q3–2009Q4) and COVID-19 shock (2020Q1–2021Q2) observations. Robust standard errors are clustered at the country level.

Global financial cycle: Methodology

The analysis estimates two separate dynamic factor models (DFMs)—one for monthly equity returns and one for monthly domestic-credit growth—for a panel of 63 advanced economies, emerging markets, and frontier markets over 2000–25.[16] For each financial variable, the DFM decomposes every economy's fluctuations into three orthogonal components: a global factor common to all economies; a group factor common to each country group; and a country-specific factor.

Post-estimation computations show the share of unconditional variance attributable to the global, group, and idiosyncratic components for each economy. Averaging these shares across economies within each group and period allows assessment of how strongly financial variables comove with the global cycle; whether comovement has strengthened or weakened across four subperiods (2001–06, 2007–12, 2013–19, 2020–25); and whether integration is deeper in the equity returns channel than in the credit growth channel.[17]

Tail-risk statistics (skewness, kurtosis, Jarque–Bera) are calculated on the raw monthly factors, while persistence is measured using six-month moving averages to reduce high-frequency noise.[18] The equity factor is heavily left-skewed (–1.98) with fat tails (excess kurtosis = 12.9), so normality is rejected (Jarque–Bera $p < 0.01$). The credit factor is nearly symmetric (skew = –0.16) with fat tails (excess kurtosis = 1.39), and normality is rejected in the monthly raw series (Jarque–Bera $p < 0.01$).

The data set comprises 63 economies (21 advanced economies, 24 emerging markets, and 18 frontier markets).[19] Equity indexes and bank-credit aggregates are taken from CEIC Data and converted to log differences. Economies are classified based on the criteria discussed at the chapter's outset; the full list is presented in annex 4.1.

[16] Implementation follows the Bayesian state-space approach of Kose, Otrok, and Whiteman (2003). A single-factor specification was also estimated, but, consistent with Ha et al. (2025), results indicate that equity and credit cycles need separate global factors to adequately capture their distinct dynamics. Studies typically proxy the global financial cycle by extracting common factors from cross-country data. Two main tools are principal component analysis (PCA) and dynamic factor models (DFMs). PCA provides a static view, identifying linear combinations of contemporaneous data that explain the most cross-sectional variance. DFMs embed these latent factors in a state-space framework, allowing them to change over time and be estimated using Kalman filtering; thereby capturing both cross-sectional links and time-series dynamics.

[17] Sub-periods are defined to match four distinct phases of the global cycle: the pre-Global Financial Crisis period (2001–06), a single crisis period covering the Global Financial Crisis through the euro-area debt crisis (2007–12), the low-rate period (2013–19), and the pandemic-to-tightening phase (2020–25). Combining the highly correlated 2007–12 months avoids splitting the peak stress episode, while the roughly six-year length of each period maintains sample balance. Results are robust to alternative breakpoints.

[18] Monthly AR(1) coefficients are 0.36 for equity and 0.08 for credit; three- and twelve-month smoothing raise them to 0.80 and 0.73, and to 0.96 and 0.94, respectively, with the equity factor consistently more persistent than the credit factor.

[19] The dataset is not fully balanced due to data constraints, notably for frontier markets in the 2000s. The Bayesian state-space approach of Kose, Otrok, and Whiteman (2003) is extended to handle ragged panels and missing observations.

TABLE A4.3.1 Drivers of surges and stops in capital inflows

Period	Full (2000Q1-2024Q4)			
Sample	All economies		Frontier markets	
Type of capital inflows	Total		Portfolio inflows	
Type of episodes	Surges	Stops	Surges	Stops
A. Global "push" factors				
VIX	0.00	0.01***	-0.01*	0.01
Economic policy uncertainty	-0.01***	0.01*	-0.01	-0.00
Oil price	0.00	0.00	0.00	0.01
World GDP growth	0.02	0.04	-0.09	-0.17*
U.S. long term interest rate	-0.30***	-0.14	-0.13	-0.03
U.S. monetary policy surprise	-0.15	2.11*	-3.31	-0.01
B. Domestic "pull" factors				
Stock market capitalization	0.00	0.00	-0.00	0.01*
Financial openness	0.15	1.56**	0.60	0.58
Local GDP growth	0.03*	-0.04	0.03	0.08
Pegged exchange rate	0.07	0.62***	-0.85	0.22
Sovereign ratings	-0.74***	0.18	-0.04	0.48
C. Contagion				
Group contagion	0.88***	0.38*	0.05	0.74
Trade contagion	2.87***	4.64***	4.05**	0.00
Observations	4214	4158	825	836

Source: World Bank.

Note: The table reports estimated coefficients from complementary log-log (cloglog) regressions of capital inflow surge and stop episodes on a set of global "push" factors, domestic "pull" factors, and contagion variables. The dependent variable is binary, taking a value of 1 if a surge or stop episode occurs and 0 otherwise. The pegged exchange rate variable is binary and equals 1 for countries with a de facto peg and 0 otherwise. Statistical significance is based on robust standard errors clustered at the country level. *, **, and *** denote significance at the 10, 5, and 1 percent levels, respectively.

TABLE A4.3.2 Drivers of surges and stops in capital inflows, excluding the Global Financial Crisis and COVID-19 periods

Period	Full Excluding the Global Financial Crisis and COVID-19 Periods			
Sample	All economies		Frontier markets	
Type of capital inflows	Total		Portfolio inflows	
Type of episodes	Surges	Stops	Surges	Stops
A. Global "push" factors				
VIX	0.00	0.01***	-0.01*	0.00
Economic policy uncertainty	-0.01***	0.00	0.00	-0.00
Oil price	0.01	-0.01*	0.00	0.01
World GDP growth	0.01	-0.01	-0.03	-0.17
U.S. long term interest rate	-0.27**	-0.08	-0.12	-0.09
U.S. monetary policy surprise	-2.13	-0.44	2.64	7.46
B. Domestic "pull" factors				
Stock market capitalization	0.00	0.02***	0.01*	0.00
Financial openness	0.10	2.04**	-0.21	1.26
Domestic GDP growth	0.04**	-0.10**	0.02	0.08
Pegged exchange rate	0.10	0.82***	-1.12*	0.03
Sovereign ratings	-0.79***	-0.02	-0.04	0.50
C. Contagion				
Group contagion	0.89***	0.47**	0.66	0.95
Trade contagion	2.92***	3.42***	2.90	-1.19
Observations	3560	2904	694	705

Source: World Bank.

Note: The table reports estimated coefficients from complementary log-log (cloglog) regressions of capital inflow surge and stop episodes on a set of global "push" factors, domestic "pull" factors, and contagion variables. The dependent variable is binary, taking a value of 1 if a surge or stop episode occurs and 0 otherwise. The pegged exchange rate variable is binary and equals 1 for countries with a de facto peg and 0 otherwise. Statistical significance is based on robust standard errors clustered at the country level. *, **, and *** denote significance at the 10, 5, and 1 percent levels, respectively.

References

Acemoglu, D., and J. Robinson. 2012. *Why Nations Fail: The Origins of Power, Prosperity, and Poverty.* New York: Norton.

Adarov, A., ed. 2025. *Promoting Investment Growth.* Washington, DC: World Bank.

Adarov, A., and H. Pallan. 2025. *Foreign Direct Investment in Retreat: Policies to Turn the Tide.* Washington, DC: World Bank.

ADB (Asian Development Bank). 2021. *Kazakhstan: Development Finance Assessment.* Manila: Asian Development Bank.

Ahokpossi, C. 2013. "Determinants of Bank Interest Margins in Sub-Saharan Africa." IMF Working Paper 15/263, International Monetary Fund, Washington, DC.

Al-Sadiq, A., P. Bejar, and I. Otker. 2021. "Commodity Shocks and Exchange Rate Regimes: Implications for the Caribbean Commodity Exporters." IMF Working Paper 21/104, International Monetary Fund, Washington, DC.

Alam, Z., A. Alter, J. Eiseman, H. Kang, M. Narita, E. Nier, and N. Wang. 2019. "Digging Deeper—Evidence on the Effects of Macroprudential Policies from a New Database." IMF Working Paper 19/66, International Monetary Fund, Washington, DC.

An, P., and T. Thanh. 2024. "Economic Growth and Macroeconomic Stability of Viet Nam in the 2001–2023 Period." *Viet Nam's Socio-Economic Development* 29(3).

Anderson, K., E. Ginting, and K. Taniguchi. 2020. "Uzbekistan: Quality Job Creation as a Cornerstone for Sustainable Economic Growth." Asian Development Bank, Manila.

Andreoni, A., and E. Avenyo. 2023. "Critical Minerals and Routes to Diversification in Africa: Linkages, Pulling Dynamics and Opportunities in Medium-High Tech Supply Chains." Background Paper, Economic Development in Africa Report 2023. United Nations Conference on Trade and Development, Geneva.

Aragie, E., X. Diao, D. Spielman, and J. Thurlow. 2024. "The Economywide Recovery Measures in Rwanda during the COVID-19 Pandemic: How Useful a Lesson?" *Journal of Policy Modeling*, 46 (6):1103–24.

Arroyo Marioli, F., and G. Vasishtha. 2025. "Fiscal Policy Procyclicality and Volatility in Commodity-Exporting Emerging and Developing Economies: Determinants and Implications for Growth." World Bank Policy Working Paper 11037, World Bank, Washington, DC.

Arslanalp, S., F. Bornhorst, and M. Poplawski-Ribeiro. 2020. "Portfolio Flows in Emerging Markets: Determinants and Directions." *IMF Economic Review* 68: 274–318.

Arslanalp, S., and T. Tsuda. 2015. "Emerging Market Portfolio Flows: The Role of Benchmark-Driven Investors." IMF Working Paper 15/263, International Monetary Fund, Washington, DC.

Arteta, C., M. A. Kose, F. Ohnsorge, and M. Stocker. 2015. "The Coming U.S. Interest Rate Tightening Cycle: Smooth Sailing or Stormy Waters?" Policy Research Note 100437, World Bank, Washington, DC.

Ashraf, B. 2018. "Do Trade and Financial Openness Matter for Financial Development? Bank-Level Evidence from Emerging Market Economies" *Research in International Business and Finance* 44: 434–58.

Asonuma, T. 2016. "Serial Sovereign Defaults and Debt Restructurings." IMF Working Paper 16/65, International Monetary Fund, Washington, DC.

Asonuma, T., and C. Trebesch. 2016. "Sovereign Restructurings: Pre-Emptive or Post-Default." *Journal of the European Economic Association*, 14(1): 175–214.

Baker, S., N. Bloom, and S. Davis. 2016. "Measuring Economic Policy Uncertainty." *The Quarterly Journal of Economics*, 131(4), 1593–636.

Baldacci, E., S. Gupta, and A. Mati. 2011. "Political and Fiscal Risk Determinants of Sovereign Spreads in Emerging Markets." *Review of Development Economics* 15 (2): 251–63.

Batten, J., and P. Szilagyi. 2007. "Domestic Bond Market Development: The Arirang Bond Experience in Korea." *The World Bank Research Observer* 22 (2): 165–95.

Bauer, M., and E. Swanson. 2023. "A Reassessment of Monetary Policy Surprises and High-Frequency Identification." *NBER Macroeconomic Annual* 37 (1): 87–155.

Baum, A. 2020. "Viet Nam's Development Success Story and the Unfinished SDG Agenda." IMF Working Paper 20/31, International Monetary Fund, Washington, DC.

Bekaert, G., C. Harvey, and C. Lundblad. 2005. "Does Financial Liberalization Spur Growth?" *Journal of Financial Economics*, 77(1): 3–55.

Bekaert, G., C. Harvey, C. Lundblad, and S. Siegel. 2014. "Political Risk Spreads." NBER Working Paper 19786, National Bureau of Economic Research, Cambridge, MA.

Bena, J., M. Ferreira, P. Matos, and P. Peres. 2017. "Are Foreign Investors Locusts? The Long-Term Effects of Foreign Institutional Ownership." *Journal of Financial Economics* 126 (1): 122–46.

Besley, T., I. Bucelli, and R. Velasco, eds. 2025. *The London Consensus: Economic Principles for the 21st Century*. London: LSE Press.

Bhorat, H., B. Coulibaly, R. Newfarmer, and J. Page, eds. 2025. *New Pathways to Job Creation in Africa: The Promise of Industries without Smokestacks.* Washington, DC: Brookings Institution Press.

Blanchard, O., J. Ostry, A. Ghosh, and M. Chamon. 2017. "Are Capital Inflows Expansionary or Contractionary? Theory, Policy Implications, and Some Evidence." *IMF Economic Review* 65 (3): 563–85.

Boyce, T., C. Jiang, D. Padhi, and T. Romano. 2025. *Punching Above Their Weight: Insights from Rwanda and Georgia's B-READY Performance.* Global Indicators Briefs 35. Washington, DC: World Bank Group.

Broner, F., A. Martin, L. Pandolfi, and T. Williams. 2021. "Winners and Losers from Sovereign Debt Inflows." *Journal of International Economics* 130 (May): 103466.

Bruno, V., and H. Shin. 2015. "Cross-Border Banking and Global Liquidity." *The Review of Economic Studies* 82 (2): 535–64.

Calderón, C., and M. Kubota. 2019. "Ride the Wild Surf: An Investigation of the Drivers of Surges in Capital Inflows." *The World Bank Economic Review* 33 (1): 28–52.

Carney, M. 2019. "Pull, Push, Pipes: Sustainable Capital Flows for a New World Order [Speech]. Bank of England, November 11. https://www.bankofengland.co.uk/speech/2014/pull-push-pipes-sustainable-capital-flows-for-a-new-world-order.

Carstens, A. 2019. "Exchange Rates and Monetary Policy Frameworks in Emerging Market Economies." Lecture, London School of Economics, London, May 2, 2019. https://www.bis.org/speeches/sp190502.htm.

Caselli, F., and A. Roitman. 2016. "Non-Linear Exchange Rate Pass-Through in Emerging Markets," IMF Working Papers 16/1, International Monetary Fund, Washington, DC.

Cerutti, E., and S. Claessens. 2024. "The Global Financial Cycle: Quantities versus Prices." IMF Working Paper 24/158, International Monetary Fund, Washington, DC.

CGFS (Committee on the Global Financial System). 2021 "Changing Patterns of Capital Flows." CGFS Paper 66, Bank for International Settlements, Basel.

Chari, A., P. Henry, and P. Mauro. 2025. "Financial Returns on Equity Investments in Infrastructure in Emerging Markets and Developing Economies." IFC Research Note, World Bank Group, Washington, DC.

Chari, A., P. Henry, and H. Reyes. 2021. "The Baker Hypothesis: Stabilization, Structural Reforms, and Economic Growth." *Journal of Economic Perspectives* 35 (3): 83–108.

Chinn, M., and H. Ito. 2006. "What Matters for Financial Development? Capital Controls, Institutions, and Interactions." *Journal of Development Economics* 81 (1): 163–92.

Chowdhury, N., M. Edmonds, and C. Walker. 2015. "Frontier Markets in Asia and Beyond." In *Frontier and Developing Asia: The Next Generation of Emerging Markets,* edited by A. Schipke, 203–23. Washington, DC: International Monetary Fund.

Christie, I., E. Fernandes, H. Messerli, and L. Twining-Ward. 2013. *Tourism in Africa: Harnessing Tourism for Growth and Improved Livelihoods.* Washington, DC: World Bank.

Claessens, S., and M. A. Kose. 2017. "Asset Prices and Macroeconomic Outcomes: A Survey." Policy Research Working Paper 8259, World Bank, Washington, DC.

Claessens, S., M. A. Kose, and M. Terrones. 2011. "Financial Cycles: What, How, When?" IMF Working Paper 11/76, International Monetary Fund, Washington, DC.

Collier, P. 2007. *The Bottom Billion: Why the Poorest Countries are Failing and What Can Be Done About It?* Oxford: Oxford University Press.

Collier, P. 2019. "The Political Barriers to Development in Africa" in Cheeseman, N., *The Oxford Encyclopedia of African Politics*. Oxford: Oxford University Press.

Cortina, J., M. Martinez Peria, S. Schmukler, and J. Xiao. 2023. "The Internationalization of China's Equity Markets." Policy Research Working Paper 10513, World Bank, Washington, DC.

Coulibaly, K., K. Ezemenari, and N. Duffy. 2008. "Productivity Growth and Economic Reform: Evidence from Rwanda." Policy Research Working Paper 4552, World Bank, Washington, DC.

Dang, L., D. Nguyen, and F. Taghizadeh-Hesary. 2021. "State-Owned Enterprise Reform in Viet Nam: Progress and Challenges." Working Paper 1071, Asian Development Bank Institute, Tokyo.

Development Committee. 2025. *Jobs: The Path to Prosperity*. Washington, DC: World Bank.

Djankov, S., C. McLiesh, and A. Shleifer. 2007. "Private Credit in 129 Countries." *The Journal of Financial Economics* 84 (2): 299–329.

Duong, N., and V. Thanh. 2011. "Revisiting Exports and Foreign Direct Investment in Viet Nam." *Asian Economic Policy Review* 6 (1): 112–31.

Emara, N. 2015. "Revisiting Sovereign Ratings, Capital Flows, and Financial Contagion in Emerging Markets." MPRA Paper 68689, University Library of Munich.

Erce, A., E. Mallucci, and M. Picarelli. 2022. "A Journey in the History of Sovereign Defaults on Domestic-Law Public Debt," International Finance Discussion Paper 1338. Washington DC: Board of Governors of the Federal Reserve System.

Erce, A., E. Mallucci, and M. Picarelli. 2024. "Sovereign Defaults at Home and Abroad." European Stability Mechanism Working Paper Series 60.

Farah-Yacoub, J., C. Graf von Luckner, R. Ramalho, and C. Reinhart. 2022. "The Social Costs of Sovereign Default." Policy Research Working Paper 10157, World Bank, Washington, DC.

Fatas, A., B. Gootjes, and J. Mawejje. 2025. "Dynamic Effects of Fiscal Rules: Do Initial Conditions Matter?" Policy Research Working Paper 11066, World Bank, Washington, DC.

Feenstra, R., R. Inklaar and M. Timmer. 2015. "The Next Generation of the Penn World Table." *American Economic Review* 105 (10): 3150–82.

Fitch Ratings. 2025. "Sovereigns 2024 Transition and Default Study." Accessed on November 4, 2025. www.fitchratings.com/research/sovereigns/sovereigns-2024-transition-default-study-27-03-2025.

Forbes, K., and F. Warnock. 2012. "Capital Flow Waves: Surges, Stops, Flight, and Retrenchment." *Journal of International Economics* 88 (2): 235–51.

Forbes, K., and F. Warnock. 2021. "Capital Flow Waves—or Ripples? Extreme Capital Flow Movements since the Crisis." *Journal of International Money and Finance* 116 (September): 102394.

FTSE Russell. 2024. "FTSE Equity Country Classification Process." www.lseg.com/content/dam/ftse-russell/en_us/documents/country-classification/ftse-equity-country-classification-paper.pdf.

Ganson, B., and A. Wennmann. 2016. *Business and Conflict in Fragile States: The Case for Pragmatic Solutions*. London: Routledge.

Gatti, R., C. Özden, J. Torres, L. Baghdadi, E. Sergenti, A. Islam, I. Gaddis, et al. 2025. "Jobs and Women: Untapped Talent, Unrealized Growth." MENAAP Economic Update, October, World Bank, Washington, DC.

Gelos, G., L. Gornicka, R. Koepke, R. Sahay, and S. Sgherri. 2022. "Capital Flows at Risk: Taming the Ebbs and Flows." *Journal of International Economics*, Elselvier, 134.

Ghosh, A., J. Kim, M. Qureshi, and J. Zalduendo. 2014. "Surges." *Journal of International Economics* 92 (2): 266–85.

Ghosh, A., J. Ostry, and M. Qureshi. 2016. "When Do Capital Inflow Surges End in Tears?" *American Economic Review*, 106 (5): 581–85.

Ghosh, A., M. Qureshi, and N. Sugawara. 2014. "Regulating Capital Flows at Both Ends: Does it Work?" IMF Working Paper 14/188, International Monetary Fund, Washington, DC.

Global Solar Atlas. 2025. "SolarGIS World Bank Global." Accessed on November 1, 2025, https://globalsolaratlas.info/map?c=11.609193,8.4375,3.

Ha, J., M. A. Kose, and F. Ohnsorge, eds. 2019. *Inflation in Emerging and Developing Economies: Evolution, Drivers and Policies.* World Bank: Washington, DC.

Ha, J., M. A. Kose, and F. Ohnsorge. 2023. "One-Stop Source: A Global Database of Inflation." Policy Research Working Paper 9737, World Bank, Washington, DC.

Ha, J., M. A. Kose, C. Otrok, and E. S. Prasad. 2025. "Global Macro-Financial Cycles and Spillovers." Federal Reserve Board of Dallas Working Paper No. 2512.

Haselmann, R., K. Pistor, and V. Vig. 2010. "How Law Affects Lending." *The Review of Financial Studies* 23 (2): 549–80.

Hauner, D., A. Prati, and C. Bircan. 2013. "The Interest Group Theory of Financial Development: Evidence from Regulation." *Journal of Banking & Finance* 37 (3): 895–906.

Henry, P. 2003. "Capital Account Liberalization, The Cost of Capital, and Economic Growth." NBER Working Paper 9488, National Bureau of Economic Research, Cambridge, MA.

ICRG (International Country Risk Guide) (database). The PRS Group, INC, Mount Pleasant, SC. Accessed on August 1, 2025. www.prsgroup.com/explore-our-products/icrg/.

IEA (International Energy Agency). 2022. *The Role of Critical Minerals in Clean Energy Transitions: World Economic Outlook Special Report.* Paris: International Energy Agency.

IFC (International Finance Corporation). 2016. *IFC The First Six Decades: A History (Second Edition).* World Bank Group, Washington, DC.

IMF (International Monetary Fund). 2005. "Rwanda: Enhanced Initiative for Heavily Indebted Poor Countries—Completion Point Document." IMF Country Report 05/173, International Monetary Fund, Washington, DC.

IMF (International Monetary Fund). 2014. "Viet Nam: 2014 Article IV Consultation-Press Release and Staff Report." IMF Country Report 14/311, International Monetary Fund, Washington, DC.

IMF (International Monetary Fund). 2019. "Rwanda: Staff Report for the 2019 Article IV Consultation and a Request for a Three-Year Policy Coordination Instrument." IMF Country Report 19/211, International Monetary Fund, Washington, DC.

IMF (International Monetary Fund). 2020. *Global Financial Stability Report: Markets in the Time of COVID-19.* April. Washington, DC, International Monetary Fund.

IMF (International Monetary Fund). 2021. "Issues in Restructuring of Sovereign Domestic Debt." IMF Policy Paper 21/071, International Monetary Fund, Washington, DC.

IMF (International Monetary Fund). 2022. "Review of The Institutional View on The Liberalization and Management of Capital Flows." IMF Policy Paper 2022/08, International Monetary Fund, Washington, DC.

IMF (International Monetary Fund). 2024a. "Republic of Kazakhstan: Financial Sector Assessment Program—Technical Note on Astana International Financial Centre and the Kazakhstan Financial System." IMF Country Report 24/313, International Monetary Fund, Washington, DC.

IMF (International Monetary Fund). 2024b. "Panama: 2024 Article IV Consultation." IMF Country Report 24/188, International Monetary Fund, Washington, DC.

IMF (International Monetary Fund). 2024c. "Republic of Uzbekistan: 2024 Article IV Consultation." IMF Country Report 24/210, International Monetary Fund, Washington, DC.

IMF (International Monetary Fund). 2025. "Republic of Uzbekistan: 2025 Article IV Consultation." IMF Country Report 25/143, International Monetary Fund, Washington, DC.

IMF AREAER (database), International Monetary Fund, Washington, DC. Accessed on November 1, 2025. www.elibrary-areaer.imf.org/Pages/Home.aspx.

IMF Balance of Payments and International Investment Position (database). International Monetary Fund, Washington, DC. Accessed on November 1, 2025. https://data.imf.org/en/datasets/IMF.STA:BOP_AGG.

IMF Coordinated Direct Investment Survey (database), International Monetary Fund, Washington, DC. Accessed November 1, 2025. https://data.imf.org/en/datasets/IMF.STA:DIP.

IMF Coordinated Portfolio Investment Survey (database), International Monetary Fund, Washington, DC. Accessed on November 1, 2025. https://data.imf.org/en/datasets/IMF.STA:PIP.

IMF Financial Development (database), International Monetary Fund, Washington, DC. Accessed on November 1, 2025. https://data.imf.org/en/datasets/IMF.MCM:FDI.

IMF iMaPP Integrated Macroprudential Policy (database), International Monetary Fund, Washington, DC. Accessed on December 23, 2025. https://www.elibrary-areaer.imf.org/Macroprudential/Pages/iMaPPDatabase.aspx.

IMF (International Monetary Fund) and World Bank. 2020. "Staff Note for the G20 International Financial Architecture Working Group: Recent Developments on Local Currency Bond Markets in Emerging Economies." World Bank, Washington, DC.

IMF (International Monetary Fund) and World Bank. 2021. "Guidance Note for Developing Local Currency

Bond Markets." International Monetary Fund, Washington, DC.

IMF (International Monetary Fund) and World Bank. 2024. "Stepping Up Domestic Resource Mobilization: A New Joint Initiative from the IMF and WB." International Monetary Fund, Washington, DC.

Jaramillo, L., and A. Weber. 2013. "Global Spillovers into Domestic Bond Markets in Emerging Market Economies." IMF Working Paper 13/264, International Monetary Fund, Washington, DC.

Jordà, Ò., M. Schularick, and A. Taylor. 2013. "When Credit Bites Back." *Journal of Money, Credit and Banking*, 45 (2): 3–28.

Kacperczyk, M., S. Sundaresan, and T. Wang. 2021. "Do Foreign Institutional Investors Improve Price Efficiency?" *The Review of Financial Studies* 34 (3): 1317–67.

Kose, M. A., S. Kurlat, F. Ohnsorge, and N. Sugawara. 2022. "A Cross-country Database of Fiscal Space." *Journal of International Money and Finance* 128 (November): 102682.

Kose, M. A., and F. Ohnsorge, eds. 2024. *Falling Long-Term Growth Prospects: Trends, Expectations, and Policies.* World Bank: Washington, DC.

Kose, M. A, C. Otrok, and C. Whiteman. 2003. "International Business Cycles: World, Region, and Country-Specific Factors." *American Economic Review* 93 (4): 1216–39.

Kose, M. A., E. Prasad, K. Rogoff, and S. Wei. 2009. "Financial Globalization: A Reappraisal." *IMF Staff Papers* 56 (1): 8–62.

Kose, M. A., E. Prasad, K. Rogoff, and S. Wei. 2010. "Financial Globalization and Economic Policies," In Rodrik, D., and M. Rosenzweig, eds, *Handbook of Development Economics* 5, edited by D. Rodrik and M. Rosenzweig, 4283–359. Amsterdam: Elsevier.

Laeven, L., and F. Valencia. 2020. "Systemic Banking Crises Database II." *IMF Economic Review* 68 (2): 307–61.

Lane, P., and G. M. Milesi-Ferretti. 2018. "The External Wealth of Nations Revisited: International Financial Integration in the Aftermath of the Global Financial Crisis." *IMF Economic Review* 66 (1): 189–222.

LSEG (London Stock Exchange Group). 2025. "FTSE Russell Announces Results of September 2025 Semi-Annual Country Classification Review for Equities and Fixed Income." Press Release, October 7. https://www.lseg.com/en/media-centre/press-releases/ftse-russell/2025/ftse-russell-country-classification-september-2025.

Magnus, G. 2010. *Uprising: Will Emerging Markets Shape or Shake the World Economy?* Hoboken, NJ: Wiley.

Malunda, D., and S. Musana. 2012. "Rwanda Case Study on Economic Transformation." Report for the African Centre for Economic Transformation (ACET). Institute of Policy Analysis and Research, Kigali, Rwanda.

Meh, C., and S. Schmukler, eds. 2025. *Financing Firm Growth: The Role of Capital Markets in Low- and Middle -Income Countries.* International Finance Corporation Research Series. World Bank: Washington, DC.

Miranda-Agrippino, S., and H. Rey. 2020. "U.S. Monetary Policy and the Global Financial Cycle." *Review of Economic Studies* 87 (6): 2754–76.

Miranda Agrippino, S., and H. Rey. 2022. "The Global Financial Cycle." In *Handbook of International Economics* 6, edited by G. Gopinath, E. Helpman, and K. Rogoff, 1–43. Amsterdam: Elsevier.

Moody's Ratings. 2025. "Sovereign Default and Recovery Rates, 1983–2024."

Moreno-Villalaz, J. 2005. "Financial Integration and Dollarization: The Case of Panama." *Cato Journal* 25 (1): 127–40.

MSCI (Morgan Stanley Capital International). 2025. "MSCI Global Market Accessibility Review—June 2025." Morgan Stanley Capital International, New York.

Muir, T. 2017. "Financial Crises and Risk Premia." *Quarterly Journal of Economics* 132 (2): 765–809.

Nguyen, S. 2024. "Industrialization Process in Viet Nam: 40 years of Economic Renovation." *Studies on Russian Economic Development* 35: 928–37.

OECD (Organisation for Economic Co-operation and Development). 2016. *Multi-dimensional Review of Kazakhstan: Volume 1—Initial Assessment.* Paris: OECD Publishing.

OECD (Organisation for Economic Co-operation and Development). 2023. *Insights on the Business Climate in Kazakhstan.* Paris: OECD Publishing.

OECD (Organisation for Economic Co-operation and Development). 2025. *OECD Economic Surveys: Viet Nam 2025.* Paris: OECD Publishing.

Prasad, E., R. Rajan, and A. Subramanian. 2007. "Foreign Capital and Economic Growth." NBER Working Paper 13619, National Bureau of Economic Research, Cambridge, MA.

Prates, D., B. Fritz, and L. F. de Paula. 2023. "Frontier-Market Economies as a New Group of the Financial Periphery: Patterns and Transmission Channels of Global Shocks." *European Journal of Economics and Economic Policies* 20 (2): 282–98.

Puy, D. 2016. "Mutual Fund Flows and the Geography of Contagion." *Journal of International Money and Finance* 60 (February): 73–93.

Quisenberry, C., and B. Griffith. 2010. "Frontier Equity Markets: A Primer on the Next Generation of Emerging Markets." *The Journal of Wealth Management* 13 (3): 50–8.

Raddatz, C., and S. Schmukler. 2012. "On the International Transmission of Shocks: Micro-Evidence from Mutual Fund Portfolios." *Journal of International Economics* 88 (2): 357–74.

Raddatz, C., S. Schmukler, and T. Williams. 2017. "International Asset Allocations and Capital Flows: The Benchmark Effect." *Journal of International Economics* 108 (September): 413–30.

Redifer, L., E. Alper, N. Meads, T. Gursoy, M. Newiak, A. Thomas, and S. Kwalingana. 2020. "The Development Path Less Traveled: The Experience of Rwanda." IMF Departmental Paper 20/10, International Monetary Fund, Washington, DC.

Rey, H. 2015. "Dilemma Not Trilemma: The Global Financial Cycle and Monetary Policy Independence." NBER Working Paper 21162, National Bureau of Economic Research, Cambridge, MA.

Romero, J., H. Vargas, P. Cardozo, and A. Murcia. 2021. "How Foreign Participation in the Colombian Local Public Debt Market Has Influenced Domestic Financial Conditions." *Latin American Journal of Central Banking* 2 (4): 100043.

S&P Dow Jones. 2024. "Country Classification Methodology." https://www.spglobal.com/spdji/en/documents/index-policies/methodology-country-classification.pdf.

S&P Global. 2025. "Default, Transition, and Recovery: 2024 Annual Global Sovereign Default and Rating Transition Study." Accessed November 4, 2025. www.spglobal.com/ratings/en/regulatory/article/-/view/sourceId/13448189.

Salinas, G. 2021. "Proximity and Horizontal Policies: The Backbone of Export Diversification." IMF Working Paper 21/064, International Monetary Fund, Washington, DC.

Sula, O. 2010. "Surges and Sudden Stops of Capital Flows to Emerging Markets." *Open Economies Review* 21 (4): 589–605.

Tang, C., X. Liu, and D. Zhou. 2022. "Financial Market Resilience and Financial Development: A Global Perspective." *Journal of International Financial Markets, Institutions and Money* 80 (September): 101650.

UNDP (United Nations Development Programme). 2021. "Uzbekistan July 2021 SDG Bonds: Allocation and Impact Report." New York, United Nations Development Programme.

USGS (U.S. Geological Survey). 2025. Accessed on November 1, 2025. https://www.usgs.gov/products/data.

Vuong, Q. 2019. "The Financial Economy of Viet Nam in an Age of Reform, 1986-2016." In *Routledge Handbook of Banking and Finance in Asia,* edited by U. Volz, P. Morgan and N. Yoshino, 201–22. New York, NY: Routledge.

WITS (World Integrated Trade Solution). World Bank, Washington, DC. Accessed on November 1, 2025. https://wits.worldbank.org.

World Bank. 2012. *Viet Nam Development Report 2012: Market Economy for a Middle-income Viet Nam.* Washington, DC: World Bank.

World Bank. 2017. *Malaysia Economic Monitor, December 2017: Turmoil to Transformation, 20 Years after the Asian Financial Crisis.* Washington, DC: World Bank.

World Bank. 2022. "Uzbekistan: Country Partnership Framework 2022–26." Washington, DC: World Bank.

World Bank. 2023. *Commodity Markets Outlook: Lower Prices, Little Relief.* April. Washington, DC: World Bank.

World Bank. 2024a. *Global Economic Prospects.* June. Washington, DC: World Bank.

World Bank. 2024b. *Business Ready 2024.* Washington, DC: World Bank.

World Bank. 2024c. *Global Economic Prospects.* January. Washington, DC: World Bank.

World Bank. 2024d. *World Development Report 2024: The Middle Income Trap.* Washington, DC: World Bank.

World Bank. 2024e. *Panama Systematic Country Diagnostic: Locking in Success.* Washington, DC: World Bank Group.

World Bank. 2024f. *Viet Nam 2045: Trading Up in A Changing World. Pathways to a High-Income Future.* Washington, DC: World Bank.

World Bank. 2025a. *Global Economic Prospects.* January. Washington, DC: World Bank.

World Bank. 2025b. *Global Economic Prospects.* June. Washington, DC: World Bank.

World Bank. 2025c. "Kazakhstan Poverty and Equity Assessment 2024." World Bank, Washington DC.

World Bank. 2025d. "Macro Poverty Outlook: April 2025." World Bank, Washington DC.

World Bank International Debt Statistics (IDS) (database). World Bank, Washington, DC. Accessed on November 1, 2025. www.worldbank.org/en/programs/debt-statistics/ids.

World Bank Poverty and Inequality Platform (database). World Bank, Washington, DC. Accessed on November 1, 2025. https://pip.worldbank.org.

World Development Indicators (database). World Bank, Washington, DC. Accessed on November 1, 2025. https://databank.worldbank.org/source/world-development-indicators.

World Economic Outlook (database). International Monetary Fund, Washington, DC. Accessed on November 1, 2025. www.imf.org/en/Publications/SPROLLs/world-economic-outlook-databases.

World Population Prospects (database). United Nations, New York. Accessed on November 1, 2025. https://population.un.org/wpp/.

WTO (World Trade Organization). 2019. *Trade Policy Review: Kazakhstan.* Geneva: World Trade Organization.

Yang, Y., X. Hu, D. Li, and W. Cai. 2025. "Including A-Shares in the MSCI Index and Enterprises' Total Factor Productivity—Impact on China's Micro-Enterprises." *Finance Research Letters* 76 (April): 106925.

STATISTICAL APPENDIX

Real GDP growth

	Annual estimates and forecasts[1] (Percent change)					Quarterly estimates[2] (Percent change, year-on-year)					
	2023	2024	2025e	2026f	2027f	24Q2	24Q3	24Q4	25Q1	25Q2	25Q3e
World	**2.8**	**2.8**	**2.7**	**2.6**	**2.7**	**2.7**	**2.7**	**3.0**	..	..	..
Advanced economies	**1.6**	**1.7**	**1.7**	**1.6**	**1.6**	**1.7**	**1.9**	**1.9**	**1.9**	**1.8**	**1.9**
United States	2.9	2.8	2.1	2.2	1.9	3.1	2.8	2.4	2.0	2.1	2.3
Euro area	0.5	0.9	1.4	0.9	1.2	0.6	1.0	1.4	1.7	1.6	1.4
Japan	0.7	-0.2	1.3	0.8	0.8	-1.2	0.8	0.7	1.6	1.9	0.7
Emerging market and developing economies	**4.4**	**4.3**	**4.2**	**4.0**	**4.1**	**4.1**	**3.9**	**4.6**	..	..	..
East Asia and Pacific	**5.2**	**5.0**	**4.8**	**4.4**	**4.3**	**4.8**	**4.7**	**5.3**	**5.3**	**5.2**	**4.8**
Cambodia	5.0	6.0	4.8	4.3	5.1	..	..	..	..	..	..
China	5.4	5.0	4.9	4.4	4.2	4.7	4.6	5.4	5.4	5.2	4.8
Fiji	9.4	3.5	2.8	3.0	3.1	..	..	..	..	..	..
Indonesia	5.0	5.0	5.0	5.0	5.2	5.0	4.9	5.0	4.9	5.1	5.0
Kiribati	2.7	5.3	3.9	3.2	2.5	..	..	..	..	..	..
Lao PDR	3.7	4.1	4.2	4.0	3.9	4.6	4.2	4.3	4.5	4.9	4.6
Malaysia	3.5	5.1	4.1	4.1	4.0	5.9	5.4	4.9	4.4	4.4	5.2
Marshall Islands [3]	-4.0	3.0	2.5	4.1	2.4	..	..	..	..	..	..
Micronesia, Fed. Sts. [3]	0.8	0.7	1.0	1.5	0.8	..	..	..	..	..	..
Mongolia	7.2	5.1	5.9	5.6	5.5	3.6	3.7	5.5	2.5	8.5	6.3
Myanmar [3,4]	1.0	-1.0	-1.8	3.0	..	..	..	..	..	..	..
Nauru [3]	0.6	1.6	2.1	1.9	1.9	..	..	..	..	..	..
Palau [3]	2.2	12.8	6.7	3.5	2.7	..	..	..	..	..	..
Papua New Guinea	3.8	3.8	4.7	3.5	3.1	..	..	..	..	..	..
Philippines	5.5	5.7	5.1	5.3	5.4	6.5	5.2	5.3	5.4	5.5	4.0
Samoa [3]	15.2	4.8	4.2	4.4	3.3	..	..	..	..	..	..
Solomon Islands	2.7	2.5	2.5	2.6	2.8	..	..	..	..	..	..
Thailand	2.0	2.5	2.0	1.8	2.5	2.3	3.0	3.3	3.2	2.8	1.2
Timor-Leste [5]	2.4	4.1	4.0	3.4	3.8	..	..	..	..	..	..
Tonga [3]	2.8	1.7	2.7	2.3	1.8	..	..	..	..	..	..
Tuvalu	4.0	3.1	3.0	2.6	2.7	..	..	..	..	..	..
Vanuatu	2.1	0.9	1.7	2.8	2.7	..	..	..	..	..	..
Viet Nam	5.1	7.1	7.2	6.3	6.7	7.2	7.4	7.6	7.0	8.2	8.2
Europe and Central Asia	**3.6**	**3.6**	**2.4**	**2.4**	**2.7**	**3.3**	**2.9**	**3.7**	**2.1**	**2.8**	..
Albania	4.0	4.0	3.7	3.5	3.5	3.7	4.4	4.4	3.7	3.5	..
Armenia	8.3	5.9	5.2	4.9	4.7	7.1	6.3	3.8	5.2	6.4	6.2
Azerbaijan	1.4	4.1	1.9	1.8	1.7	..	..	..	..	..	..
Belarus	4.1	4.0	1.9	1.3	0.8	5.6	3.8	2.5	3.2	1.0	..
Bosnia and Herzegovina [5]	2.0	3.0	2.6	3.0	3.2	3.1	3.3	2.6	1.7	1.8	..
Bulgaria	1.7	3.4	3.0	2.9	3.1	3.5	3.5	4.6	2.8	3.5	3.0
Croatia	3.8	3.8	3.1	2.9	2.7	3.8	4.0	3.8	3.3	3.6	2.3
Georgia	7.8	9.7	7.0	5.5	5.0	9.8	10.9	8.5	9.9	7.4	..
Kazakhstan	5.1	5.0	6.0	4.5	3.9	2.6	5.8	7.2	5.6	7.0	..
Kosovo	4.1	4.6	3.8	3.8	3.9	..	..	..	..	..	..
Kyrgyz Republic	9.0	9.0	9.2	6.5	6.8	..	..	..	..	..	..
Moldova	1.2	0.1	2.9	2.7	3.8	2.5	-1.9	-1.3	-1.2	1.1	5.2
Montenegro [2]	6.5	3.2	3.3	3.2	3.2	2.7	2.1	2.5	2.8	3.5	3.1
North Macedonia	2.6	3.0	3.2	3.0	3.0	3.0	2.9	4.3	2.9	3.5	3.8
Poland	0.2	3.0	3.3	3.2	2.9	3.4	2.8	3.5	3.2	3.3	3.8
Romania	2.3	0.9	0.8	1.3	1.9	0.8	0.2	0.8	0.6	2.5	1.2
Russian Federation	4.1	4.3	0.9	0.8	1.0	4.3	3.3	4.5	1.4	1.1	0.6
Serbia	3.7	3.9	2.1	3.0	3.2	4.4	3.5	3.5	1.8	2.0	2.0
Tajikistan	8.3	8.4	8.0	6.2	4.7	..	..	..	..	..	..
Türkiye	5.0	3.3	3.5	3.7	4.4	2.3	2.8	3.2	2.5	4.9	3.7
Ukraine	5.5	2.9	2.0	2.0	4.0	4.0	2.2	-0.1	0.9	0.7	2.1
Uzbekistan	6.3	6.6	6.2	6.0	5.9	..	..	..	..	..	..

Real GDP growth (*continued*)

	Annual estimates and forecasts[1] (Percent change)					Quarterly estimates[2] (Percent change, year-on-year)					
	2023	2024	2025e	2026f	2027f	24Q2	24Q3	24Q4	25Q1	25Q2	25Q3e
Latin America and the Caribbean	**2.4**	**2.4**	**2.2**	**2.3**	**2.6**	**2.6**	**2.5**	**2.7**	**..**	**..**	**..**
Argentina	-1.9	-1.3	4.6	4.0	4.0	-1.1	-1.9	2.6	5.8	6.4	3.3
Bahamas, The	3.0	3.4	2.3	2.1	1.8	4.9	-0.8	7.6	..	..	..
Barbados	4.1	4.0	2.7	2.0	2.0	..	..	..	..	..	..
Belize	0.5	3.5	1.5	2.4	2.2	5.4	0.7	2.1	-2.3	1.4	6.1
Bolivia	3.1	0.7	-0.5	-1.1	-1.5	0.7	-1.4	-3.4	-2.0	-2.8	..
Brazil	3.2	3.4	2.3	2.0	2.3	3.5	4.1	3.6	3.1	2.4	1.8
Chile	0.5	2.6	2.6	2.2	2.1	1.2	2.0	4.0	2.6	3.3	1.6
Colombia	0.7	1.6	2.6	2.6	2.8	1.6	1.8	2.6	2.6	2.1	3.6
Costa Rica	4.9	4.2	4.1	3.6	3.7	5.4	3.8	4.5	4.2	3.7	5.2
Dominica	3.7	2.1	3.1	3.0	2.9	..	..	..	..	..	..
Dominican Republic	2.2	5.0	2.5	4.5	4.5	6.1	5.1	4.1	2.7	2.0	..
Ecuador[2]	2.0	-2.0	3.2	2.0	2.4	-4.1	-1.8	-0.9	3.4	4.3	..
El Salvador	3.5	2.6	3.5	3.0	3.0	2.6	1.0	3.4	2.5	3.9	..
Grenada	4.5	3.7	4.4	3.3	3.0	..	..	..	..	..	..
Guatemala	3.5	3.7	4.0	3.7	3.7	3.7	3.5	4.5	4.0	3.9	..
Guyana	33.8	43.6	14.6	19.6	21.9	49.8	39.5	36.1	..	..	..
Haiti[3]	-1.9	-4.2	-2.0	2.0	2.5	..	..	..	..	..	..
Honduras	3.6	3.6	3.8	3.5	3.7	4.3	3.3	3.0	4.7	3.9	..
Jamaica[2]	2.7	-0.5	-1.3	-2.3	3.7	0.4	-3.2	-0.5	1.1	1.6	..
Mexico	3.4	1.4	0.2	1.3	1.8	2.1	1.4	0.3	0.6	-0.1	-0.1
Nicaragua	4.4	3.6	3.1	3.0	3.0	4.2	0.9	3.4	3.0	4.9	..
Panama	7.4	2.9	3.9	4.1	4.1	2.2	2.0	4.8	5.2	3.4	3.9
Paraguay	5.3	4.7	5.5	3.9	3.9	5.3	3.1	3.6	5.9	5.9	..
Peru	-0.4	3.3	3.0	2.5	2.5	3.8	4.2	4.5	4.0	2.6	3.4
St. Lucia	2.2	3.9	1.8	2.0	2.1	..	..	..	..	..	..
St. Vincent and the Grenadines	5.3	4.1	4.0	2.9	2.7	..	..	..	..	..	..
Suriname	2.4	1.7	1.4	3.5	3.7	..	..	..	..	..	..
Trinidad and Tobago	1.5	2.5	1.4	0.3	2.5	-2.0	2.0	3.4	-2.1	..	..
Uruguay	0.7	3.1	2.3	2.2	2.2	4.5	4.4	3.5	3.6	2.3	1.2
Middle East, North Africa, Afghanistan and Pakistan	**2.1**	**2.6**	**3.1**	**3.6**	**3.9**	**2.2**	**2.6**	**3.8**	**3.2**	**3.0**	**..**
Afghanistan[3]	2.3	2.5	4.3	3.8	3.5	..	..	..	..	..	..
Algeria[2]	4.1	3.7	3.8	3.5	3.3	3.7	2.4	4.2	4.3	3.9	..
Bahrain	3.9	3.1	3.5	3.1	2.9	1.0	2.9	3.4	2.7	2.5	4.3
Djibouti	6.7	6.0	6.0	6.1	6.0	..	..	..	..	..	..
Egypt, Arab Rep.[3]	3.8	2.4	4.4	4.3	4.8	2.4	3.5	4.3	4.8	5.0	5.3
Iran, Islamic Rep.[3]	5.3	3.7	-1.1	-1.5	0.6	3.9	3.5	4.2	3.1	-2.2	0.6
Iraq[2,5]	0.5	-1.5	-0.9	6.5	3.8	0.8	-1.7	-0.6	-3.6	-4.0	..
Jordan	2.9	2.5	2.7	2.8	2.8	2.5	2.5	2.6	2.7	2.8	2.8
Kuwait	-3.6	-2.9	2.7	2.6	2.5	-2.2	-3.9	-0.7	1.0	1.7	..
Lebanon[4]	-0.8	-7.1	3.5	4.0	..	..	..	..	..	..	..
Libya	10.2	1.9	13.3	3.5	3.9	..	..	..	..	..	..
Morocco[2]	3.7	3.8	5.0	4.4	4.4	3.0	5.0	4.2	4.8	5.5	4.0
Oman	1.2	1.7	3.1	3.6	4.0	2.1	1.4	2.0	2.4	2.1	2.0
Pakistan[2,3,5]	-0.2	2.6	3.0	3.0	3.4	3.3	1.6	2.0	2.7	6.2	3.7
Qatar	1.5	2.4	2.8	5.3	6.8	1.5	2.4	6.1	4.9	1.9	2.9
Saudi Arabia	0.5	2.7	3.8	4.3	4.4	1.2	3.9	5.2	3.7	4.5	4.8
Syrian Arab Republic[4]	-1.2	-1.5	1.0	..	..	..	..	..	..	..	..
Tunisia[2]	0.2	1.6	2.6	2.5	2.2	1.4	2.1	2.5	1.6	3.2	2.4
United Arab Emirates	2.9	3.9	4.8	5.0	5.1	3.9	4.3	5.0	3.9	4.5	..
West Bank and Gaza	-4.6	-26.6	3.9	5.1	11.6	-32.3	-30.9	-0.9	9.1	4.7	..
Yemen, Rep.[4]	-2.0	-1.5	-1.5	0.0	..	..	..	..	..	..	..

Real GDP growth (*continued*)

	Annual estimates and forecasts [1] (Percent change)					Quarterly estimates [2] (Percent change, year-on-year)					
	2023	2024	2025e	2026f	2027f	24Q2	24Q3	24Q4	25Q1	25Q2	25Q3e
South Asia	**8.0**	**6.3**	**7.1**	**6.2**	**6.5**	**5.9**	**5.2**	**6.1**	**7.0**	**7.2**	**..**
Bangladesh [3]	5.8	4.2	3.7	4.6	6.1	2.1	2.0	4.5	4.9	3.3	..
Bhutan [3]	4.9	6.1	7.0	7.3	6.1	..	..	..	..	..	..
India [3]	9.2	6.5	7.2	6.5	6.6	6.5	5.6	6.4	7.4	7.8	8.2
Maldives	4.9	3.5	4.2	3.9	4.0	1.6	4.6	2.3	4.8	9.0	8.6
Nepal [2 3]	2.0	3.7	4.6	2.1	4.7	3.3	3.2	3.8	4.2	4.7	..
Sri Lanka	-2.3	5.0	4.6	3.5	3.1	4.1	5.3	5.4	4.8	4.9	5.4
Sub-Saharan Africa	**3.0**	**3.7**	**4.0**	**4.3**	**4.5**	**3.4**	**3.5**	**3.3**	**3.3**	**..**	**..**
Angola	1.3	4.4	2.3	2.6	2.8	6.7	3.9	2.6	3.6	1.1	1.8
Benin	6.4	7.5	7.3	7.0	7.0	6.7	7.3	9.2	7.4	7.6	..
Botswana	3.2	-3.0	-3.0	2.3	3.8	-0.4	-4.2	-2.0	-0.4	-5.3	..
Burkina Faso	3.0	4.8	4.7	4.9	5.1	..	..	..	..	..	..
Burundi	2.7	3.9	4.6	4.9	5.5	4.1	3.1	3.3	1.7	..	..
Cabo Verde	4.8	7.2	5.4	5.2	5.0	..	..	..	..	..	..
Cameroon	3.2	3.5	3.7	3.7	3.9	4.2	3.9	3.3	3.6	3.9	..
Central African Republic	0.7	1.5	2.7	3.0	3.1	..	..	..	..	..	..
Chad	4.1	3.5	3.4	3.7	4.1	..	..	..	..	..	..
Comoros	3.0	3.3	3.4	3.7	3.8	..	..	..	..	..	..
Congo, Dem. Rep.	8.6	6.5	5.1	5.1	5.3	..	..	..	..	..	..
Congo, Rep.	1.9	2.6	2.9	3.2	3.0	..	..	..	..	..	..
Côte d'Ivoire	6.5	6.0	6.3	6.4	6.5	..	..	..	..	..	..
Equatorial Guinea	-5.1	0.9	-1.6	0.4	1.0	..	..	..	..	..	..
Eritrea	2.6	2.9	3.2	3.5	3.6	..	..	..	..	..	..
Eswatini	3.5	3.0	4.2	3.8	2.9	..	..	..	..	..	..
Ethiopia [3]	7.2	8.1	7.2	7.1	7.7	..	..	..	..	..	..
Gabon	2.4	3.4	3.1	3.7	4.1	..	..	..	..	..	..
Gambia, The	5.0	5.3	5.7	5.5	5.3	..	..	..	..	..	..
Ghana	3.1	5.7	4.3	4.6	4.8	5.7	7.0	5.2	6.4	6.5	5.5
Guinea	5.5	5.4	7.5	9.3	11.6	6.9	4.2	7.1	7.4	..	..
Guinea-Bissau	4.5	4.8	5.1	5.2	5.2	..	..	..	..	..	..
Kenya	5.7	4.7	4.9	4.9	5.0	4.6	4.2	5.1	4.9	5.0	..
Lesotho	1.8	2.9	1.3	0.7	1.1	4.2	6.9	5.7	2.6	5.4	..
Liberia	4.7	4.0	4.6	5.4	5.6	..	..	..	..	..	..
Madagascar	4.2	4.2	4.0	4.0	4.4	..	..	..	..	..	..
Malawi	1.9	1.7	1.9	2.6	3.1	..	..	..	..	..	..
Mali	3.5	4.0	4.9	5.0	5.0	5.7	4.1	5.6	0.4	..	..
Mauritania	6.8	6.3	5.3	5.4	5.9	..	..	..	..	..	..
Mauritius	5.0	4.7	3.0	3.4	3.4	4.2	5.2	5.1	4.1	3.6	..
Mozambique	5.5	2.1	1.1	2.8	3.5	4.3	5.6	-5.7	-3.9	-0.9	-0.9
Namibia	4.4	4.0	3.1	3.5	3.8	3.3	2.1	4.0	2.8	1.6	..
Niger	2.0	10.3	6.5	6.7	6.6	..	..	..	..	..	..
Nigeria	3.3	4.1	4.2	4.4	4.4	3.9	4.8	4.2	3.8	4.1	4.2
Rwanda	8.6	7.2	7.0	7.2	7.6	10.3	6.8	4.2	6.6	7.8	11.8
São Tomé and Príncipe	0.4	1.1	2.5	4.0	3.5	..	..	..	..	..	..
Senegal	4.3	6.1	6.4	4.1	4.3	..	..	..	..	..	..
Seychelles	2.3	2.9	3.2	3.2	3.4	3.2	11.3	5.2	3.3	4.6	..
Sierra Leone	5.7	4.3	4.3	4.4	4.6	..	..	..	..	..	..

Real GDP growth (*continued*)

	Annual estimates and forecasts [1] (Percent change)					Quarterly estimates [2] (Percent change, year-on-year)					
	2023	2024	2025e	2026f	2027f	24Q2	24Q3	24Q4	25Q1	25Q2	25Q3e
Sub-Saharan Africa (*continued*)											
Somalia, Fed. Rep.	4.2	4.1	3.0	3.5	3.5	..	..	..	..	..	..
South Africa	0.7	0.6	1.3	1.4	1.5	0.4	0.4	0.8	0.8	0.9	2.1
South Sudan [3]	-1.3	-7.2	-23.8	48.8	0.8	..	..	..	..	..	..
Sudan	-29.4	-14.0	6.1	5.1	3.7	..	..	..	..	..	..
Tanzania	5.1	5.5	6.0	6.2	6.5	..	..	..	..	..	..
Togo	6.4	5.3	5.0	5.4	5.6	..	..	..	..	..	..
Uganda [3]	5.3	6.1	6.3	6.4	9.8	5.7	6.2	5.4	8.4	5.5	4.8
Zambia	5.4	3.8	5.2	5.8	6.0	1.8	2.7	8.3	4.5	5.2	..
Zimbabwe	5.3	1.7	6.6	5.0	5.0	..	..	..	..	..	..

Sources: Haver Analytics; World Bank.

Note: e = estimate; f = forecast. Since joining the euro area—Croatia on January 1, 2023, and Bulgaria on January 1, 2026—both countries have been added to the euro area aggregate and removed from the ECA aggregate in all tables to avoid double counting. The region name "Middle East and North Africa" has been revised to "Middle East, North Africa, Afghanistan and Pakistan," reflecting the inclusion of Afghanistan and Pakistan in the region starting on July 1, 2025.

1. Aggregate growth rates calculated using GDP weights at average 2010-19 prices and market exchange rates.

2. Quarterly estimates are based on non-seasonally-adjusted real GDP, except for advanced economies, as well as Algeria, Ecuador, Morocco, and Tunisia. In some instances, quarterly growth paths may not align to annual growth estimates, owing to the timing of GDP releases. Quarterly data for Iraq, Jamaica, Nepal, and Pakistan are gross value added. Quarterly data for Montenegro are preliminary.

Regional averages are calculated based on data from the following economies.

East Asia and Pacific: China, Indonesia, the Lao People's Democratic Republic, Malaysia, Mongolia, the Philippines, Thailand, and Viet Nam.

Europe and Central Asia: Albania, Armenia, Belarus, Bosnia and Herzegovina, Georgia, Hungary, Kazakhstan, Moldova, Montenegro, North Macedonia, Poland, Romania, the Russian Federation, Serbia, Türkiye, and Ukraine.

Latin America and the Caribbean: Argentina, The Bahamas, Belize, Bolivia, Brazil, Chile, Colombia, Costa Rica, the Dominican Republic, Ecuador, El Salvador, Guatemala, Guyana, Honduras, Jamaica, Mexico, Nicaragua, Panama, Paraguay, Peru, Trinidad and Tobago, and Uruguay.

Middle East, North Africa, Afghanistan and Pakistan: Algeria, Bahrain, the Arab Republic of Egypt, the Islamic Republic of Iran, Iraq, Jordan, Kuwait, Morocco, Oman, Pakistan, Qatar, Saudi Arabia, Tunisia, the United Arab Emirates, and West Bank and Gaza.

South Asia: Bangladesh, India, Maldives, Nepal, and Sri Lanka.

Sub-Saharan Africa: Angola, Benin, Botswana, Burundi, Cameroon, Ghana, Guinea, Kenya, Lesotho, Mali, Mauritius, Mozambique, Namibia, Nigeria, Rwanda, the Seychelles, South Africa, Uganda, and Zambia.

3. Annual GDP is on fiscal year basis, as per reporting practice in the country. For Bangladesh, Bhutan, the Arab Republic of Egypt, Nepal, and Pakistan, the column for 2023 refers to FY2022/23. For Afghanistan, India, and the Islamic Republic of Iran, the column for 2023 refers to FY2023/24.

4. Data for Lebanon (beyond 2026), Myanmar (beyond 2026), the Syrian Arab Republic (beyond 2025), and the Republic of Yemen (beyond 2026) are excluded because of a high degree of uncertainty.

5. Data for Bosnia and Herzegovina are from the production approach. Annual data for Iraq and Pakistan are based on factor cost. Data for Timor-Leste represent non-oil GDP.

Data and Forecast Conventions

The macroeconomic forecasts presented in this report are prepared by staff of the Prospects Group of the Development Economics Vice Presidency, in coordination with staff from the Fiscal Policy and Growth of the Prosperity Vice Presidency and from regional and country offices, and with input from regional Chief Economist offices. They are the result of an iterative process that incorporates data, macroeconometric models, and judgment.

Data. Data used to prepare country forecasts come from a variety of sources. National Income Accounts (NIA), Balance of Payments (BOP), and fiscal data are from Haver Analytics; the World Development Indicators by the World Bank; the *World Economic Outlook*, *Balance of Payments Statistics*, and *International Financial Statistics* by the International Monetary Fund. Population data and forecasts are from the United Nations World Population Prospects. Country- and lending-group classifications are from the World Bank. The Prospects Group's internal databases include high-frequency indicators such as industrial production, consumer price indexes, emerging markets bond index (EMBI), exchange rates, exports, imports, policy rates, and stock market indexes, based on data from Bloomberg, Haver Analytics, IMF *Balance of Payments Stat*istics, IMF *International Financial Statistics*, and J.P. Morgan.

Aggregations. Aggregate growth rates for the world and all subgroups of countries (such as regions and income groups) are weighted averages of country-specific growth rates, calculated using GDP weights at average 2010-19 prices and market exchange rates. Income groups are defined as in the World Bank's classification of country groups.

Output growth forecast process. The process starts with initial assumptions about advanced-economy growth and commodity price forecasts. These are used as conditioning assumptions for the first set of growth forecasts for EMDEs, which are produced using macroeconometric models, accounting frameworks to ensure national account identities and global consistency, estimates of spillovers from major economies, and high-frequency indicators. These forecasts are then evaluated to ensure consistency of treatment across similar EMDEs. This is followed by extensive discussions with World Bank country teams, who conduct continuous macroeconomic monitoring and dialogue with country authorities and finalize growth forecasts for EMDEs. The Prospects Group prepares advanced economy and commodity price forecasts. Throughout the forecasting process, staff use macroeconometric models that allow the combination of judgment and consistency with model-based insights.

Global trade growth forecast process. Global trade growth is calculated as the percentage change in the average of global exports and imports of goods and nonfactor services, both measured in real U.S. dollars. Forecasts for global exports and imports are derived from a bottom-up approach, using country-level forecasts for real exports and imports produced during the forecasting process as described above.

Global Economic Prospects: Selected Topics, 2015-26

Growth and business cycles		
Economics of pandemics		
	Impact of COVID-19 on global income inequality	January 2022, chapter 4
	Regional macroeconomic implications of COVID-19	June 2020, special focus
	Lasting scars of the COVID-19 pandemic	June 2020, chapter 3
	Adding fuel to the fire: Cheap oil during the pandemic	June 2020, chapter 4
	How deep will the COVID-19 recession be?	June 2020, box 1.1
	Scenarios of possible global growth outcomes	June 2020, box 1.3
	How does informality aggravate the impact of COVID-19?	June 2020, box 1.4
	The impact of COVID-19 on global value chains	June 2020, box SF1
	How do deep recessions affect potential output?	June 2020, box 3.1
	How do disasters affect productivity?	June 2020, box 3.2
	Reforms after the 2014-16 oil price plunge	June 2020, box 4.1
	The macroeconomic effects of pandemics and epidemics: A literature review	June 2020, annex 3.1
Informality		
	How does informality aggravate the impact of COVID-19?	June 2020, box 1.4
	Growing in the shadow: Challenges of informality	January 2019, chapter 3
	Linkages between formal and informal sectors	January 2019, box 3.1
	Regional dimensions of informality: An overview	January 2019, box 3.2
	Casting a shadow: Productivity in formal and informal firms	January 2019, box 3.3
	Under the magnifying glass: How do policies affect informality?	January 2019, box 3.4
Inflation		
	Global stagflation	June 2022, special focus 1
	Emerging inflation pressures: Cause for alarm?	June 2021, chapter 4
	Low for how much longer? Inflation in low-income countries	January 2020, special focus 2
	Currency depreciation, inflation, and central bank independence	June 2019, special focus 1.2
	The great disinflation	January 2019, box 1.1
Growth prospects		
	Frontier market economies: Promise, performance, and prospects	January 2026, chapter 4
	From tailwinds to headwinds: Emerging and developing economies in the twenty-first century	January 2025, chapter 3
	Falling graduation prospects: Low-income countries in the twenty-first century	January 2025, chapter 4
	Small states: Overlapping crises, multiple challenges	January 2023, chapter 4
	Global stagflation	June 2022, special focus 1
	Global growth scenarios	January 2021, box 1.4
	The macroeconomic effects of pandemics and epidemics: A literature review	June 2020, annex 3.1
	How deep will the COVID-19 recession be?	June 2020, box 1.1
	Lasting Scars of the COVID-19 Pandemic	June 2020, chapter 3
	Regional macroeconomic implications of COVID-19	June 2020, special focus
	Growth in low-income countries: Evolution, prospects, and policies	June 2019, special focus 2.1
	Long-term growth prospects: Downgraded no more?	June 2018, box 1.1
Global output gap		
	Is the global economy turning the corner?	January 2018, box 1.1
Potential growth		
	Global economy: Heading into a decade of disappointments?	January 2021, chapter 3
	How do deep recessions affect potential output in EMDEs?	June 2020, box 3.1
	Building solid foundations: How to promote potential growth	January 2018, chapter 3
	What is potential growth?	January 2018, box 3.1
	Understanding the recent productivity slowdown: Facts and explanations	January 2018, box 3.2
	Moving together? Investment and potential output	January 2018, box 3.3
	The long shadow of contractions over potential output	January 2018, box 3.4
	Productivity and investment growth during reforms	January 2018, box 3.5
Cross-border spillovers		
	Who catches a cold when emerging markets sneeze?	January 2016, chapter 3
	Sources of the growth slowdown in BRICS	January 2016, box 3.1
	Understanding cross-border growth spillovers	January 2016, box 3.2
	Within-region spillovers	January 2016, box 3.3

Global Economic Prospects: Selected Topics, 2015-26

Growth and business cycles

Productivity		
	How do disasters affect productivity?	June 2020, box 3.2
	Fading promise: How to rekindle productivity growth	January 2020, chapter 3
	EMDE regional productivity trends and bottlenecks	January 2020, box 3.1
	Sectoral sources of productivity growth	January 2020, box 3.2
	Patterns of total factor productivity: A firm perspective	January 2020, box 3.3
	Debt, financial crises, and productivity	January 2020, box 3.4
Investment		
	Foreign direct investment in retreat: Policies to turn the tide	June 2025, chapter 3
	Harnessing the benefits of public investment	June 2024, chapter 3
	Public investment dynamics around adverse events	June 2024, box 3.1
	Macroeconomic impacts of public investment: A literature review	June 2024, box 3.2
	The magic of investment accelerations	January 2024, chapter 3
	Sparking investment accelerations: Lessons from country case studies	January 2024, box 3.1
	Investment growth after the pandemic	January 2023, chapter 3
	Investment: Subdued prospects, strong needs	June 2019, special focus 1.1
	Weak investment in uncertain times: Causes, implications, and policy responses	January 2017, chapter 3
	Investment-less credit booms	January 2017, box 3.1
	Implications of rising uncertainty for investment in EMDEs	January 2017, box 3.2
	Investment slowdown in China	January 2017, box 3.3
	Interactions between public and private investment	January 2017, box 3.4
Forecast uncertainty		
	Scenarios of possible global growth outcomes	June 2020, box 1.3
	Quantifying uncertainties in global growth forecasts	June 2016, special focus 2
Fiscal space		
	Having space and using it: Fiscal policy challenges and developing economies	January 2015, chapter 3
	Fiscal policy in low-income countries	January 2015, box 3.1
	What affects the size of fiscal multipliers?	January 2015, box 3.2
	Chile's fiscal rule—an example of success	January 2015, box 3.3
	Narrow fiscal space and the risk of a debt crisis	January 2015, box 3.4
	Revenue mobilization in South Asia: Policy challenges and recommendations	January 2015, box 2.3
Other topics		
	Fragile and conflict-affected situations: Intertwined crises, multiple vulnerabilities	June 2025, chapter 4
	Education demographics and global inequality	January 2018, special focus 2
	Recent developments in emerging and developing country labor markets	June 2015, box 1.3
	Linkages between China and Sub-Saharan Africa	June 2015, box 2.1
	What does weak growth mean for poverty in the future?	January 2015, box 1.1
	What does a slowdown in China mean for Latin America and the Caribbean?	January 2015, box 2.2

Monetary and exchange rate policies

Financial spillovers of rising U.S. interest rates	June 2023, chapter 3
Asset purchases in emerging markets: Unconventional policies, unconventional times	January 2021, chapter 4
The fourth wave: Rapid debt buildup	January 2020, chapter 4
Price controls: Good intentions, bad outcomes	January 2020, special focus 1
Low for how much longer? Inflation in low-income countries	January 2020, special focus 2
Currency depreciation, inflation, and central bank independence	June 2019, special focus 1.2
The great disinflation	January 2019, box 1.1
Corporate debt: Financial stability and investment implications	June 2018, special focus 2
Recent credit surge in historical context	June 2016, special focus 1
Peg and control? The links between exchange rate regimes and capital account policies	January 2016, chapter 4
Negative interest rates in Europe: A glance at their causes and implications	June 2015, box 1.1
Hoping for the best, preparing for the worst: Risks around U.S. rate liftoff and policy options	June 2015, special focus 1
Countercyclical monetary policy in emerging markets: Review and evidence	January 2015, box 1.2

Global Economic Prospects: Selected Topics, 2015-26

Fiscal policies	
Rebuilding fiscal space: The case for fiscal rules	January 2026, chapter 3
Fiscal challenges in small states: Weathering storms, rebuilding resilience	June 2024, chapter 4
Fiscal policy in commodity exporters: An enduring challenge	January 2024, chapter 4
How does procyclical fiscal policy affect output growth?	January 2024, box 4.1
Do fiscal rules and sovereign wealth funds make a difference? Lessons from country case studies	January 2024, box 4.2
Fiscal policy challenges in low-income countries	June 2023, chapter 4
Resolving high debt after the pandemic: lessons from past episodes of debt relief	January 2022, special focus
How has the pandemic made the fourth wave of debt more dangerous?	January 2021, box 1.1
The fourth wave: Rapid debt buildup	January 2020, chapter 4
Debt: No free lunch	June 2019, box 1.1
Debt in low-income countries: Evolution, implications, and remedies	January 2019, chapter 4
Debt dynamics in emerging market and developing economies: Time to act?	June 2017, special focus 1
Having fiscal space and using it: FiscFal challenges in developing economies	January 2015, chapter 3
Revenue mobilization in South Asia: Policy challenges and recommendations	January 2015, box 2.3
Fiscal policy in low-income countries	January 2015, box 3.1
What affects the size of fiscal multipliers?	January 2015, box 3.2
Chile's fiscal rule—an example of success	January 2015, box 3.3
Narrow fiscal space and the risk of a debt crisis	January 2015, box 3.4

Commodity markets	
Russia's invasion of Ukraine: Implications for energy markets and activity	June 2022, special focus 2
Commodity price cycles: Underlying drivers and policy options	January 2022, chapter 3
Reforms after the 2014-16 oil price plunge	June 2020, box 4.1
Adding fuel to the fire: Cheap oil in the pandemic	June 2020, chapter 4
The role of major emerging markets in global commodity demand	June 2018, special focus 1
The role of the EM7 in commodity production	June 2018, SF1, box SF1.1
Commodity consumption: Implications of government policies	June 2018, SF1, box SF1.2
With the benefit of hindsight: The impact of the 2014–16 oil price collapse	January 2018, special focus 1
From commodity discovery to production: Vulnerabilities and policies in LICs	January 2016, special focus
After the commodities boom: What next for low-income countries?	June 2015, special focus 2
Low oil prices in perspective	June 2015, box 1.2
Understanding the plunge in oil prices: Sources and implications	January 2015, chapter 4
What do we know about the impact of oil prices on output and inflation? A brief survey	January 2015, box 4.1

Globalization of trade and financial flows	
High trade costs: causes and remedies	June 2021, chapter 3
The impact of COVID-19 on global value chains	June 2020, box SF1
Poverty impact of food price shocks and policies	January 2019, chapter 4
Arm's-length trade: A source of post-crisis trade weakness	June 2017, Special Focus 2
The U.S. economy and the world	January 2017, Special Focus
Potential macroeconomic implications of the Trans-Pacific Partnership Agreement	January 2016, chapter 4
Regulatory convergence in mega-regional trade agreements	January 2016, box 4.1.1
China's integration in global supply chains: Review and implications	January 2015, box 2.1
Can remittances help promote consumption stability?	January 2015, chapter 4
What lies behind the global trade slowdown?	January 2015, chapter 4

Prospects Group:
Selected Other Publications on the Global Economy, 2015-26

Commodity Markets Outlook	
New shocks, old tools: Revisiting international commodity agreements in a fragmented world	October 2025
Post-pandemic commodity cycles: A new era?	April 2025
Commodity price synchronization: A new era?	October 2024
Forecasting industrial commodity prices: An assessment	April 2024
Potential near-term implications of the conflict in the Middle East for commodity markets: A preliminary assessment	October 2023
Forecasting industrial commodity prices	April 2023
Pandemic, war, recession: Drivers of aluminum and copper prices	October 2022
The impact of the war in Ukraine on commodity markets	April 2022
Urbanization and commodity demand	October 2021
Causes and consequences of metal price shocks	April 2021
Persistence of commodity shocks	October 2020
Food price shocks: Channels and implications	April 2019
The implications of tariffs for commodity markets	October 2018, box
The changing of the guard: Shifts in industrial commodity demand	October 2018
Oil exporters: Policies and challenges	April 2018
Investment weakness in commodity exporters	January 2017
OPEC in historical context: Commodity agreements and market fundamentals	October 2016
From energy prices to food prices: Moving in tandem?	July 2016
Resource development in an era of cheap commodities	April 2016
Weak growth in emerging market economies: What does it imply for commodity markets?	January 2016
Understanding El Niño: What does it mean for commodity markets?	October 2015
How important are China and India in global commodity consumption?	July 2015
Anatomy of the last four oil price crashes	April 2015
Putting the recent plunge in oil prices in perspective	January 2015

Inflation in Emerging and Developing Economies: Evolution, Drivers, and Policies	
Inflation: Concepts, evolution, and correlates	Chapter 1
Understanding global inflation synchronization	Chapter 2
Sources of inflation: Global and domestic drivers	Chapter 3
Inflation expectations: Review and evidence	Chapter 4
Inflation and exchange rate pass-through	Chapter 5
Inflation in low-income countries	Chapter 6
Poverty impact of food price shocks and policies	Chapter 7

A Decade After the Global Recession: Lessons and Challenges for Emerging and Developing Economies	
A decade after the global recession: Lessons and challenges	Chapter 1
What happens during global recessions?	Chapter 2
Macroeconomic developments	Chapter 3
Financial market developments	Chapter 4
Macroeconomic and financial sector policies	Chapter 5
Prospects, risks, and vulnerabilities	Chapter 6
Policy challenges	Chapter 7
The role of the World Bank Group	Chapter 8

Global Waves of Debt: Causes and Consequences	
Debt: Evolution, causes, and consequences	Chapter 1
Benefits and costs of debt: The dose makes the poison	Chapter 2
Global waves of debt: What goes up must come down?	Chapter 3
The fourth wave: Ripple or tsunami?	Chapter 4
Debt and financial crises: From euphoria to distress	Chapter 5
Policies: Turning mistakes into experience	Chapter 6

Prospects Group: Selected Other Publications on the Global Economy, 2015-26

Global Productivity: Trends, Drivers, and Policies	
Global productivity trends	Chapter 1
What explains productivity growth	Chapter 2
What happens to productivity during major adverse events?	Chapter 3
Productivity convergence: Is anyone catching up?	Chapter 4
Regional dimensions of productivity: Trends, explanations, and policies	Chapter 5
Productivity: Technology, demand, and employment trade-offs	Chapter 6
Sectoral sources of productivity growth	Chapter 7

The Long Shadow of Informality: Challenges and Policies	
Overview	Chapter 1
Understanding the informal economy: Concepts and trends	Chapter 2
Growing apart or moving together? Synchronization of informal- and formal-economy business cycles	Chapter 3
Lagging behind: informality and development	Chapter 4
Informality in emerging market and developing economies: Regional dimensions	Chapter 5
Tackling informality: Policy options	Chapter 6

Commodity Markets: Evolution, Challenges and Policies	
The evolution of commodity markets over the past century	Chapter 1
Commodity demand: Drivers, outlook, and implications	Chapter 2
The nature and drivers of commodity price cycles	Chapter 3
Causes and consequences of industrial commodity price shocks	Chapter 4

Falling Long-Term Growth Prospects	
Potential not realized: An international database of potential growth	Chapter 1
Regional dimensions of potential growth: Hopes and realities	Chapter 2
The global investment slowdown: Challenges and policies	Chapter 3
Regional dimensions of investment: Moving in the right direction?	Chapter 4
Potential growth prospects: Risks, rewards and policies	Chapter 5
Trade as an engine of growth: Sputtering but fixable	Chapter 6
Services-led growth: Better prospects after the pandemic?	Chapter 7

The Great Reversal: Prospects, Risks, and Policies in International Development Association (IDA) Countries	
Introduction	Chapter 1
Characteristics of IDA countries	Chapter 2
Recent developments amid overlapping crises: 2020-23	Chapter 3
Near-term growth prospects: 2024-25	Chapter 4
Output losses, growth, convergence, and poverty	Chapter 5
Risks to the outlook	Chapter 6
Natural resources and demographic dividends	Chapter 7
Investment needs and policies	Chapter 8
Domestic policy priorities	Chapter 9
Global support	Chapter 10
Conclusion	Chapter 11

Fiscal Vulnerabilities in Low-Income Countries	
Introduction	Section 1
Evolution of fiscal positions in LICs	Section 2
Fiscal vulnerability to shocks	Section 3
Fiscal policy options in LICs	Section 4
Conclusion	Section 5

www.ingramcontent.com/pod-product-compliance
Lightning Source LLC
LaVergne TN
LVHW070950210926
848482LV00002B/160
* 9 7 8 1 4 6 4 8 2 2 6 7 4 *